# JOB DESCRIPTIONS

## FOR FILM, VIDEO & CGI

**Responsibilities and Duties
for the CINEMATIC
Craft Categories and
Classifications, 5th Edition**

*including*

## A Career Guide to the Crafts

*in the Appendix*

# MOTION PICTURE PRODUCTION ORGANIZATION

*[see Category sections for classification organization]*

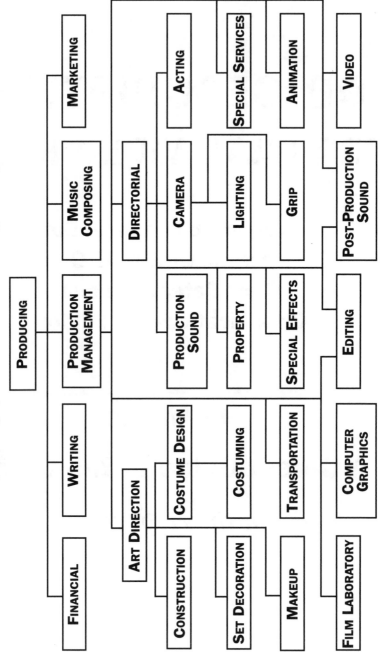

# JOB DESCRIPTIONS

*for*

# FILM, VIDEO & CGI*
*COMPUTER GENERATED IMAGERY

## Responsibilities and Duties for the CINEMATIC Craft Categories and Classifications, 5th Edition

by

## William E. Hines, SOC

## ED-VENTURE FILMS/BOOKS
LOS ANGELES, CA

Published By
ED-VENTURE FILMS/BOOKS
P O Box 23214
Los Angeles, CA 90023

Cataloging Data
Job Descriptions for Film, Video & CGI, 5th Ed. / William E. Hines
342 pp. with 24 flow charts
Includes Appendices, Glossary, Bibliography, Indices
ISBN 0-935873-02-3

791.43'023
I. Title
II. Author
III. Motion Pictures. Job Descriptions
IV. Film. Job Descriptions
V. Video. Job Descriptions
VI. Computer Graphics. Job Descriptions

Library of Congress Catalog Card Number 98-93965

Printed in the United States of America

# TABLE OF CONTENTS

# ACKNOWLEDGMENTS

When a book goes through five editions as this one has, a lot of people deserve to be thanked for their interest and input. No one knows it all. One learns from everyone and from every experience and if not, one has not been paying attention. A veritable legion of teachers, mentors and associates have contributed to the learning process which we call experience. This handbook is the result of a selective compilation of those experiences as they apply to the craft classifications involved in the art and craft of cinematic production.

To begin with, Joe Blaisdell, Video Camera Operator, Lou Favara, Technical Director, Charlie Heard, Key Makeup Artist, Don Henderson, Film Picture Editor and LeRoy Robbins, Production Mixer, offered valuable suggestions for the earlier editions.

The following craftspeople have given valued updated input in areas with which I was relatively unfamiliar:

Jim Claytor, Art Director; Shannon Litten, Costume Supervisor; Tom Baxter, Men's Costumer; Andy Klaiman, Swing Set Dresser; Pat Moudakis, Property Master.

Rusty Meek, Production Manager; Rick Allen, First Assistant Director; Jim Buck, Technical Coordinator; Wally Keske, Propmaker; Polly Businger, Studio Teachers Business Rep; and Tony Cousimano, Studio Drivers Business Rep, checked the text and confirmed the details of their respective craft category responsibilities and duties.

Kent Jorgensen, Key Grip, and Earl Williman, Gaffer, gave valued suggestions and support by carefully examining the text dealing with their areas of expertise.

Bert Leibee, Film Lab Manager, provided much of the information from which the Film Laboratory Category was constructed.

Keith Wester, Production Mixer, and Greg Russell, Re-Recording Mixer, each extended themselves by giving voluminous input in helping to bring the various aspects of the Sound Category to technical accuracy.

David Stump, Motion Control Cinematographer, provided the latest details regarding motion control cinematography.

Allan Lum Li, Video Camera Operator, and Keith McGuire, Video Maintenance Engineer, helped clarify various aspects of the video craft.

The Editing Category benefited from the input of Michael Breddan, Editors Guild Business Rep, and Peter Zinner, Film Picture Editor. Special thanks to David Feldman, Electronic Picture Editor, for his important input detailing the duties involving digital non-linear editing procedures.

The burgeoning field of computer graphics, an essential aspect of computer generated imagery, was brought into focus by the extensive structural detailing provided by Stephen Rosenbaum, Visual Effects Supervisor. Other important details were provided by Jennifer Stump, CG Artist.

Helping to put this handbook together, Lynn Lanning, as designer, formatter and editor, has significantly contributed to the look and reader-friendly organization of the contents. It was her suggestion to include "A Career Guide to the Crafts" which appears in the Appendices.

My wife, Zee, was there to give comfort, support and counsel during the long hours of research, creation and revision.

My ongoing gratitude goes to Professor Bruce Kawin for his concise appraisal of the intent, content and value of this work.

Finally, deep and lasting appreciation goes to Thomas Short, International President of the International Alliance of Theatrical Stage Employees, for taking the time from his busy schedule to review, appraise and recommend in his Foreword the usefulness of this book to his membership and to the industry we all serve.

# FOREWORD

## by Thomas C. Short
## International President, IATSE

The author and publisher are to be congratulated on this major effort at understanding of craft responsibilities and duties of workers in film, video and computer generated imagery to public attention. To my knowledge, this is the first book to handle this particular subject matter in such a detailed, clear, comprehensive and concise way.

*JOB DESCRIPTIONS for FILM, VIDEO & CGI* is an important addition to literature in the field. It contains the essence of what one needs to know to do the work. This book explains in detail the responsibilities and duties of most of the many technical crafts which work in the cinematic media and which are represented by the International Alliance of Theatrical Stage Employees. A chart for each category clearly illustrates its organizational structure.

The author's lengthy association with and understanding of the industry have combined to bring out the salient facts one needs to know about the various crafts in order to perfect the skills necessary to become a professional in the chosen craft.

It used to be that one learned one's craft exclusively in a guild system; that is, one learned on the job from the example or under the guidance of more experienced craftspeople. And this avenue of learning and refining craft skills still exists. As in any profession, practice in the chosen craft leads to technical and artistic mastery. Today, many film schools offer practical and theoretical training in the cinematic arts and crafts. This guide will serve them well.

This handbook should prove to be extremely helpful to those seeking to work in the technical and craft field of the entertainment industry. It will tell them what they need to know to accomplish the job classification which interests them. It will also serve as an aid in understanding what it is that other crafts contribute to the collaborative process of motion picture production.

Because of the thorough way the author has covered this important subject matter, I can recommend this handbook to the members of the Alliance and also to those working in the industry or studying to become competent and professional film, video or CGI craftspeople.

# INTRODUCTION

In 1961, *JOB DESCRIPTIONS* was the first handbook to comprehensively and authoritatively outline the responsibilities and duties of craft personnel in the film and video production crafts. It has gone through four editions since that time and is still the *only* authoritative guide which concisely, yet comprehensively, covers the subject matter. As it did then, this edition details *who* the craftsperson is responsible to, *what* he or she is responsible *for*, and the duties entailed in performing that particular craft.

This, the fifth edition, covers the current responsibilities and duties of more than two hundred fifty craft classifications operating in film, video and in the new field of computer generated imagery. For the first time, the crafts involved in this fast-growing and ever more important and ubiquitous computer graphics field, have been included. An increasing number of film and video productions are utilizing the benefit of computer graphics artistry to modify and enhance the captured imagery. It is now possible to put on film, tape, disc or hard drive whatever can be visualized.

Your attention is called to the preceding organizational graphic titled *The Motion Picture Production Organization,* which includes both above-the-line (creative) and below-the-line (technical) categories involved in the production process. As you can see, the cinematic media are based on a highly collaborative process of technical and creative input involving specialists in a wide variety of crafts contributing to the final result. It is important that not only does everyone know and execute their respective craft responsibilities and duties, but that everyone know and adhere to the hierarchical structure, the chain-of-command and lines-of-communication, of each craft category as well as to how and when the work of each category integrates with contributions from crafts participating in the movie-making process, from pre-production through production and post-production. Without such organization and without the understanding and adherence of each craftsperson contributing to this complex production process, there would be chaos.

Producing, Production Management and Directorial categories and classifications have been included in this edition in order to provide a more complete picture of procedures contributing to the planning, crafting and carrying out of the production process in the cinematic media of film, video and CGI.

To clarify its organizational structure, each craft category section begins with a graphic which illustrates the hierarchical chain-of-command of the craft classifications operating within that category. Twenty-one craft categories are included in this edition. Each category begins with a listing of all the classifications covered by the book within that category and has sequential sections dealing with, and sub-titled: Category Criteria, Category Responsibilities, Category Function, Category Considerations, and Category Requirements, respectively.

Generally, the craft duties have been listed and arranged in approximate chronological order of performance: who does what, and when during Pre-Production, Production and Post-Production and, during each of those phases—the processes of preparation, operation and wrap.

For those seeking to find a place in the collaborative movie-making industry, refer to the useful *A Career Guide to the Crafts* in the Appendix which outlines the skills, knowledge, education, training and experience needed to do the work required in each of the categories covered in this handbook.

The reader will note that the text is gender-neutral throughout. A comprehensive working Glossary, arranged by category, and a helpful Index which locates by page number each time a job classification is referred to in the text, are included for ready reference.

This handbook should be useful for: Producers and Production Managers in planning their technical staffing; inexperienced technical personnel who are in the process of learning and/or refining their craft; teachers and students of the cinematic media; librarians and researchers as a reliable reference tool; and job counselors in advising job-seekers about the essential responsibilities and duties of specific craft positions in the cinematic media.

Remember, each person works *with* others on a production, but **everybody** works *for* the Producer.

—William E Hines, SOC
Los Angeles

# PREFACE

# HOW TO USE THIS HANDBOOK

This handbook has been designed as a working tool to assist the reader in quick-ly and conveniently finding and referring to the responsibilities and duties of the various craft classifications involved in film, video and computer generated imagery.

There are twenty-one craft categories presented, covering more than two hundred fifty craft classifications in film, video, stagecraft and computer graphics which function during the pre-production, production and post-production phases of the cinematic process of making motion pictures. Each category section is marked by **black tabs** positioned in the margins of the outer pages to help the reader conveniently locate, identify and refer to the pages included in each category section.

Each **category section** is preceded by a graphic representation of the hierarchical organizational structure—the chain-of-command and lines-of-communication—of the crafts working within that category.

At the start of each chapter, all **craft classifications** are listed, noting which are category heads and which are sub-heads, followed in order by five important areas of category understanding and structure, consisting of category criteria, responsibilities, function, considerations and requirements.

**Category Criteria** outlines the classifications needed to accomplish the mission of the category work. **Category Responsibilities** is a statement which focuses on the importance of working with and for the Category Head or Sub-Head to whom assigned. **Category Function** is a statement of the principal focus of the work of those craftspeople working in that category. **Category Considerations** deals with the type and number of craft personnel to be considered for a particular production. **Category Requirements** specifies the crafts needed to perform craft functions required for a production.

Each category and each craft classification belonging to that category, with the specific **responsibilities and duties** assigned to each craft, are identified by bold-face letter or numeral for convenient access, notation, referral and review, as necessary. In addition, the duties are listed under the operational phase during which the duties are performed, such as **Pre-Production, Production** and/or **Post-Production**.

To help facilitate a quick find, each time a craft classification appears in the text, that craft is capitalized in bold-face type.

The **table of contents** provides quick page reference to each of more than two hundred fifty craft classifications covered in this manual.

The **appendices** contain a **career guide** for those interested in learning more about a certain craft along with a listing of **guilds and unions** servicing cinematic production and the **professional associations and honorary societies** to which those creative, craft and administrative persons working in the cinematic media are affiliated.

At the beginning of the appendices is a **fast finder** listing of the categories in the career guide with page numbers. Many of the skills and much of the knowledge and experience listed for each category in the career guide can be easily related to the appropriate category. However, the **list of some skills** from the career guide, and which categories they relate to, may offer new pathways for persons with these skills or interests.

The comprehensive **glossary** is also broken down by category and consists of definitions of terms used in the text as well as terms in common use by personnel in each category covered. A quick index to the glossary can be found at the end of it. However, job titles are only in the main index at the end of the book.

The extensive **bibliography** consists of the most important and current titles in print and is broken down by category in alphabetized order so that those categories of interest for follow-up reading can be conveniently referred to.

The **index** provides a convenient reference to each page on which each classification covered is mentioned. It uses bold-face type to indicate on which pages can be found the official outline for each classification, and italic type to signify that an entry is mentioned in the glossary. An entry in bold italic is for the glossary definition of that term.

---

## OTHER BOOKS BY THE AUTHOR:

**Job Descriptions: Responsibilities and Duties for the Film and Video Craft Categories and Classifications**, 1st through 4th ed.

**Operating Cinematography for Film and Video: A Professional and Practical Guide**

# Fast Finder

PRODUCING

PRODUCTION MANAGEMENT

DIRECTORIAL

CAMERA

LIGHTING

GRIP

PRODUCTION SOUND

POST-PRODUC-TION SOUND

ART

CONSTRUCTION

SPECIAL EFFECTS

SET DECORATING

PROPERTY

COSTUMING

WARDROBE

MAKEUP

TRANSPOR-TATION

SPECIAL SERVICES

FILM LAB

EDITING

COMPUTER GRAPHICS

VIDEO

CAREER GUIDE

GLOSSARY

# PRODUCING CATEGORY ORGANIZATIONAL CHART

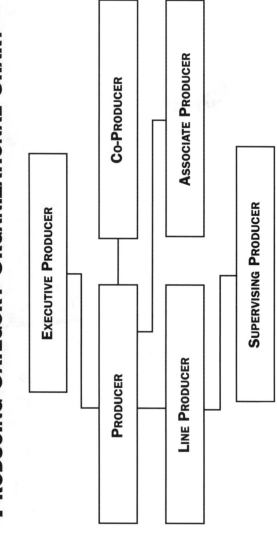

# 1

# PRODUCING CATEGORY

**A. Category Classifications:** There are six (6) classifications in the Producing Category:

1. **Executive Producer (Category Head)**
2. **Producer (Category Head, when no Executive Producer)**
3. **Co-Producer (Category Co-Head, when no Executive Producer)**
4. **Associate Producer**
5. **Line Producer (Category Sub-Head)**
6. **Supervising Producer (Category Sub-Head)**

**B. Category Criteria:**

1. Within the major studio administrative context, the **Executive Producer** has control over, and responsibility for, all production taking place under the aegis of the studio, and assigns **Producers** to the various studio production projects.

2. Within the operational context, the **Producer** has full authority over, and responsibility for, the conduct of the production, and may assign that responsibility to the **Director** for the duration of the image-making phase of the production process.

3. It is the **Producer**'s responsibility to oversee all phases of the picture-making process, from concept through pre-production, production, post-production and marketing, in order to maintain financial and quality control of the property, ever aware of the constraints of the shooting schedule and budget.

4. The **Producer** should have a thorough knowledge and understanding of current Union and Guild working rules and wage rates and of the particular agreement(s) which the Production Company may have with these labor organizations, with individuals employed on the production, and with vendors supplying or servicing the production.

5. The **Producer** provides the **Director** with the necessary production personnel and matériel in order to adequately serve his/her directorial production needs.

6. The **Producer** has the option of allowing the **Director** to take the assigned picture through a first cut and/or a final cut, as specified in the contract agreement between the **Director** and the Production Company.

**7.** On film productions whereon the **Producer** requires assistance in the performance of duties, a **Co-Producer, Associate Producer, Line Producer,** and/or **Supervising Producer** may be hired by the **Executive Producer.**

**8.** Each **Producer** must ensure that production personnel—staff, cast and crew—do not attempt work under any unsafe condition(s), as specified by the Employer, OSHA, Building and Safety Code and fire laws, or in violation of any other safety regulation(s) and practice(s).

**C. Category Responsibilities:** It is the responsibility of each Employee and/or colleague in the Producing Category to work closely and cooperatively with the **Producer** in order to assist him or her in the most efficient use of production elements—personnel and matériel—in order to aid in achieving realization of an optimum finalized product.

**D. Category Function:** The principal function of Producing Category is to produce a finished and financially successful cinematic product from concept to completion and on to marketing and exhibition. This process involves work with the planning and administration of the entire picture-making and promotion process, in each of its various aspects, during each of its phases, from beginning to end.

**E. Category Considerations:**

**1.** Producing Category personnel are used on each production.

**2.** The classification(s) used depends upon the type of motion picture being produced, its budget, production elements and shooting schedule.

**3.** The **Producer, Co-Producer, Associate Producer, Line Producer** and/or **Supervising Producer** should each be given sufficient pre-production time to prepare their respective work for the production process.

**4.** The **Producer** receives and examines the daily production report from the **Production Manager,** checks status of the shooting schedule, and compares money expended with money budgeted for each production department.

**5.** The **Producer** directs the **Production Manager** to allow or withhold permission, therefore funds, requested by category department heads for additional personnel and/or matériel to service the production.

**F. Category Requirements:** Persons in each Producing Category classification must know and follow the chain-of-command and lines-of-communication and must be able to effectively and safely plan, set up and follow through on production schedules and procedures as well as personnel management.

**G. EXECUTIVE PRODUCER**

**1. Responsibilities:** The **Executive Producer** is responsible to the studio CEO, Chairman and/or Board of Directors for the administration, quality and, ultimately, the financial success, of all production output bearing the studio logo.

## 2. Duties:

### ▼ During PRE-PRODUCTION:

**a.** Selecting and overseeing development of a concept and/or story idea into a screenplay;

**b.** Arranging the financing for the production;

**c.** Hiring the **Writer**(s) to write and develop the screenplay;

**d.** Assigning a **Producer** to the project to produce the motion picture;

**e.** Stipulating to the **Producer** that certain individuals be hired to direct, perform in, design the production, photograph and score the production, and that certain production and/or post-production facilities be used;

**f.** Determining the pictures to be produced by the studio, the budget, starting date, shooting schedule, completion date and release date for each;

### ▼ During the PRODUCTION Process:

**g.** Approving any modification in shooting schedule or budget requested by the **Producer**;

**h.** Reading the daily production reports from the **Production Manager**;

**i.** Sitting in on dailies screenings;

**j.** Sitting in on final sound mix sessions;

### ▼ During PRODUCTION and POST-PRODUCTION:

**k.** Seeing that publicity—press books, one-sheets, and other media advertising—is being planned and taken care of by Marketing;

**l.** Seeing that screening dates and venues have been set;

**m.** Otherwise carrying out the duties normally required of this classification.

## 3. Considerations:

**a.** When one (1) or more of the above duties are performed, they are **Executive Producer**'s duties and require an **Executive Producer**.

**b.** An **Executive Producer** is employed when there are a number of motion picture projects being planned and produced under the aegis of a major production company which require supervision and coordination.

# H. PRODUCER

## 1. Responsibilities: The **Producer** is responsible to the **Executive Producer**, if any, otherwise to the financial backers of the production, for producing a quality motion picture project which returns the money invested, plus a profit.

## 2. Duties:

**a. During Phase 1—DEVELOPMENT**—the **Producer** does or oversees the following:

**(1)** Develops a story idea;

**(2)** Hires a **Writer** to write a screenplay;

PRODUCING

**(3)** Approves the screenplay;

**(4)** Develops a package by getting commitments from key principal actors with proven box office appeal, a **Director** with a good track record of successful pictures brought in at or under budget, and a **Production Designer** and **Director of Photography** with similar credentials;

**(5)** Studies and becomes conversant with Union and Guild working rules and wage rates;

**(6)** Prepares a preliminary budget for the proposed project;

**(7)** Prepares a detailed proposal with potential costs, and a release, marketing and distribution plan along with a profit projection;

**(8)** Arranges a completion bond, if necessary;

**(9)** Presents the package—script, actors, **Director**, **Production Designer**, **Cinematographer**, budget and release plan—to prospective and appropriate financial sources for funding consideration.

b. **During Phase 2—PRE-PRODUCTION**—once funding has occurred, the **Producer** begins the following:

**(1)** Sets the starting date for principal photography;

**(2)** Enlarges and augments the administrative production staff;

**(3)** Sees that the production, its financial base and personnel are fully protected by legal advice and insurance coverage;

**(4)** Signs contracts with unions and guilds;

**(5)** Signs up the leading actors and the key supporting cast members— usually through their respective agents;

**(6)** Signs on **Writer**(s) to refine the screenplay, if necessary;

**(7)** Hires the **Director**;

**(8)** Hires a **Production Manager** to refine the budget and prepare a shooting schedule;

**(9)** Signs the **Production Designer** to start planning and begin execution of set design/construction, decoration and overall production design;

**(10)** Signs the **Director of Photography**;

**(11)** Hires a **Costume Designer** to start work on costume design and execution;

**(12)** Hires a **Composer** to start work on the musical score;

**(13)** Arranges studio facilities for shooting;

**(14)** Hires a **Location Manager** to scout for, find and recommend location sites appropriate for the production;

**(15)** Hires a **Casting Director** and completes the casting process;

**(16)** Approves the hiring of technical Category Heads and their personnel;

**(17)** Determines, in consultation with the **Executive Producer, Director, Production Designer** and **Director of Photography**, the type and gauge of film to be used, the aspect ratio in which the film is to be shot and whether the lenses will be spherical or anamorphic;

**(18)** Makes arrangements with a film laboratory for processing, printing and negative cutting, a telecine transfer house, and a sound transfer and re-recording facility;

**(19)** Has numerous meetings with the creative and administrative staffs, requiring decisions that will affect either budget and/or shooting schedule.

**c. During Phase 3—PRODUCTION**—begins the process of principal photography and the following duties:

**(1)** Regularly reviews budget expenditures and shooting schedule status;

**(2)** Views dailies and rough cuts;

**(3)** Coordinates publicity releases;

**(4)** Coordinates the shooting schedule for special visual effects, CGI and/or second unit photography with that of first unit principal photography;

**(5)** Sees that all category departments are on schedule with their work and are keeping within their allotted budget;

**(6)** Approves or denies any category departmental requests for additional personnel and/or matériel;

**(7)** Hires or fires staff, cast or crew personnel, as necessary;

**(8)** Makes decisions as to change of schedule or location, due to weather, cast illness or replacement, or other reason;

**(9)** Has more meetings with creative staff, Production Management and key technical personnel requiring decisions which affect budget and/or shooting schedule.

**d. During Phase 4—POST-PRODUCTION**—the following duties apply:

**(1)** Continues the publicity and begins an advertising campaign and marketing plans;

**(2)** Sees that the editing procf3s is keeping pace with the scheduled release date;

**(3)** Approves the final cut;

**(4)** Coordinates the completion and delivery of all elements—special visual effects, animation, second unit, inserts, stock footage, opticals, dióital graphics and title art—to Editing for inclusion in the finished product;

**(5)** Arranges facilities for recording the music score, ADR, Foley, and final dubbing mix;

**(6)** Approves the final re-recording mix of sound elements;

**(7)** Arranges test screenings and sneak previews, as needed, evaluating audience and focus-group response to the product and authorizing modifications prior to striking release prints;

**(8)** Authorizes and approves any re-editing and re-mixing;

**(9)** Orders and approves trailer preparation;

**(10)** Acquires additional funding, as necessary;

**(11)** Sets or approves exhibition schedule;

**(12)** Approves the answer print;

**(13)** Orders release prints and press kits.

**(14)** Sees that the negative and printing elements are stored properly and safely;

e. **During Phase 5—MARKETING (Publicity, Release, Distribution, Exhibition)**—the following duties apply:

**(1)** Continues careful coordination of the publicity and advertising campaign with the marketing plans;

**(2)** Makes deals for ancillary markets income—exhibition and merchandising—domestic and foreign;

**(3)** Sees that all rental and lease items are returned and that all bills and financial obligations are paid;

**(4)** Checks final status of budget expenditures;

**(5)** Checks box office reports and distribution income figures;

**(6)** Makes provision for residual, participation and deferred payments;

**(7)** Prepares regular status reports for, and sees that disbursements from exhibition profits are remitted to, the financial sources during the economic life of the picture.

**3. Considerations:**

a. When one (1) or more of the above duties are performed, they are **Producer**'s duties and require a **Producer**.

b. A **Producer** is employed for a sufficient period to satisfactorily carry out pre-production, production shooting, and post-production responsibilities. Because of the varying nature and duration of film productions, the employment tenure of the **Producer** is negotiable.

**I. CO-PRODUCER**

**1. Responsibilities: Co-Producers** are mutually responsible to the **Executive Producer**, if any, otherwise to the financial backers of the production, for performing shared duties in helping produce a financially successful motion picture project.

**2. Duties:** [See **Producer**'s duties, above.]

## J. ASSOCIATE PRODUCER

**1. Responsibilities:** The **Associate Producer** is responsible to the **Producer** for performing assigned duties, often arranging financing, supervising stage insert or second unit or concurrent digital and other graphics effects work, or post-production processes, in helping produce a financially successful motion picture project.

**2. Duties:** [Specified **Producer**'s duties above, as assigned by the **Producer**.]

## K. LINE PRODUCER

**1. Responsibilities:** The **Line Producer** is directly responsible to the **Producer** for overseeing the myriad daily details of the actual production process, and seeing that the production proceeds on schedule and within budget constraints.

**2. Duties:** [See **Producer**'s production duties, above.]

## L. SUPERVISING PRODUCER

**1. Responsibilities:** The **Supervising Producer**, a title used mainly for television episodic, specials, or sitcom programming production, often called a **Post-Production Supervisor** on feature film production, is responsible to the **Producer** for overseeing a post-production phase, such as, ADR, Foley, second unit, stage inserts, digital/computer graphics effects, editing and/or final mix.

**2. Duties:** [Specified **Producer**'s duties above, as assigned by the **Producer**.]

▼ When acting as a **Post-Production Supervisor**, the following duties apply:

    **a.** Directing the **Assistant Editor** to prepare voice track cue sheets for dubbing or ADR purposes, if there is no **Dialogue/ADR Editor;**

    **b.** Planning, scheduling and supervising dubbing, ADR and Foley sessions;

    **c.** Preparing and/or approving orders prepared by the **Assistant Editor** for sound transfers, opticals and other laboratory services, editing supplies and rentals, stock footage and titles.

**3. Considerations:** The **Post-Production Supervisor** is normally responsible for coordinating all work done by the **Picture Editor, Supervising Sound Editor, Music Editor, Sound Effects Editor, ADR Editor, Foley Editor, Assistant Editor**s and a **Negative Cutter** who have been hired to work on the production.

# Production Management Category Organizational Chart

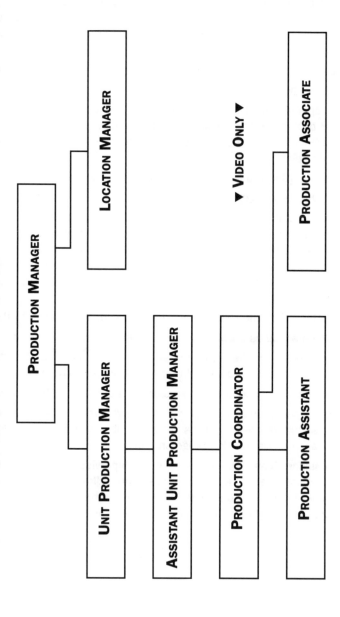

# 2

# PRODUCTION MANAGEMENT CATEGORY

**A. Category Classifications:** There are seven (7) classifications in the Production Management Category:

▼ **For FILM and VIDEO:** ▼

1. **Production Manager (Category Head)**

2. **Unit Production Manager (Category Sub-Head)**

3. **Assistant Unit Production Manager**

4. **Location Manager**

5. **Production Coordinator**

6. **Production Assistant**

▼ **Only Video Production uses this classification:**

7. **Production Associate**

**B. Category Criteria:**

1. The management of the production is the prime responsibility of personnel in the Production Management Category.

2. On productions on which the **Producer** does not actively perform **Production Manager** duties, a **Production Manager** is employed.

3. As the **Producer**'s representative, the **Production Manager** allocates and spends Company funds on behalf of the Company.

4. A **Production Manager** needs to have and apply: A thorough knowledge of the essentials comprising cinematic production and the management skills required to plan, schedule, budget, staff, supply and operate a cinematic production.

5. On a feature film with more than one (1) unit shooting concurrently, each additional unit has a **Unit Production Manager**.

6. On productions whereon the **Production Manager** requires assistance in the performance of duties, a **Unit Production Manager** is hired before an **Assistant Unit Production Manager** is hired.

7. During pre-production, a **Unit Production Manager** may be employed to assist the **Production Manager**.

8. On television programming series such as episodics and sitcoms, there is a **Unit Production Manager** for each series.

9. A **Location Manager** is employed to locate, recommend, acquire and manage location sites for production purposes.

10. A **Production Coordinator** is hired to coordinate certain specified aspects of the production process and handles communications with the staff, cast and crew to those ends.

11. **Production Assistants** are assigned to specific Category Heads to assist in a general way.

12. The **Production Assistant** may be assigned by the **Production Manager** to the **Director, Assistant Director, Unit Production Manager** or **Stylist**, to whom the **Production Assistant** is then responsible to assist in the respective duties, as directed.

13. A **Production Associate** is used in television production and is assigned to assist the Directorial team and to be a liaison between Directorial and Production Management.

14. The **Production Manager** and **Unit Production Manager** must ensure that production and Production Management personnel—staff, cast and crew—do not attempt work under any unsafe condition(s), as specified by the Employer, OSHA, Building and Safety Code and fire laws, or in violation of any other safety regulation(s) and practice(s).

C. **Category Responsibilities:** It is the responsibility of each Employee in the Production Management Category to work cooperatively with the **Production Manager,** or with the Sub-Head to whom assigned, in order to assist in achieving a safe, optimum and most efficient operation of the production process.

D. **Category Function:** The principal function of Production Management personnel involves planning, executing and maintaining a realistic budget and production schedule compatible with the production in process, and to actively and responsibly manage money, time and personnel in as efficient and safe a manner as possible within the budgetary and scheduling parameters.

E. **Category Considerations**:

1. Production Management personnel are used on each production or project which requires extensive budgeting, scheduling and logistical planning and management.

2. The classifications used depend upon the type of motion picture produced, upon the type and quantity of personnel and matériel used, and upon the extent of logistical coordination required.

3. The **Production Manager** and **Unit Production Manager** should each be given sufficient pre-production time to prepare their respective work for the production process and enough time to wrap their work.

F. **Category Requirements:** Employees in each Production Management Category classification must know and follow the chain-of-command and lines-of-communication and must be able to effectively and safely set up and manage budgets, shooting schedules and production personnel.

▼ **Classifications Used for Both FILM & VIDEO** ▼

**G. PRODUCTION MANAGER**

**1. Responsibilities:** The **Production Manager (PM)** is directly responsible to the **Producer**, is the **Producer**'s representative, and works in close cooperation with the **First Assistant Director** during shooting. The **PM** is the behind-the-scenes expediter and, with direct input from the **Producer, Director, Production Designer** and Department Category Heads, is responsible for budgeting, arranging and scheduling all production elements—staff, cast, crew and matériel—in the most efficient manner possible and arranging payment therefor.

**2. Duties:**

▼ **During PRE-PRODUCTION:**

**a.** Reading and annotating the script within the context of production management—budgeting and scheduling;

**b.** Budgeting productions—estimating the total budget based on itemized or departmental estimates of required matériel and personnel, plus a duration- of-shooting estimate;

**c.** Preparing a sequential scene-by-scene script breakdown, listing all cast, atmosphere players, sets, location sites, set dressing, props, costumes, makeup, camera, lighting and grip equipment, specialized equipment and special effects, etc;

**d.** Getting a list of specific items—personnel and matériel—required by and from each Category Head—i.e., Art, Construction, Set Dressing, Property, Wardrobe, Camera, Lighting, Grip, Sound, Special Effects, Transportation, etc;

**e.** Preparing a shooting schedule for budgetary purposes;

**f.** Scheduling the production;

**g.** Hiring technical personnel required for the production;

**h.** Having a thorough knowledge and understanding of current Union and Guild working rules and wage rates and of the particular agreement(s) which the **Producer**, or Production Company, may have with these labor organizations, with individuals employed on the production, and with vendors supplying or servicing the production;

**i.** If the Company is signatory to a Union agreement, determining that each technical employee is a Union member in good standing, operating in the classification granted by the Union, and available for work during the period set for employment and negotiating deal memos with technical personnel;

**j.** Selecting, arranging for clearances, permits, etc, and overseeing the preparation of location sites;

**k.** Selecting, arranging for and overseeing the preparation of studio settings;

**l.** Seeing that necessary contracts, deal memos, permits, releases and clearances are prepared, signed and adhered to;

**m.** Ordering sets and props built and costumes fabricated;

▼ **During the PRODUCTION Process:**

**n.** Expediting and coordinating the work of all production departments at all times;

**o.** Arranging sequences to be shot in the most expeditious, efficient, safe and economical order practicable;

**p.** Giving daily and timely advance notification to the cast and crew for next-day work calls—time and place; order of scenes to be shot; sets to be used; equipment, personnel and job requirements, etc;

**q.** Procuring and returning supplies and equipment;

**r.** Arranging transportation for staff, cast, crews and matériel;

**s.** Arranging for quarters and subsistence for staff, cast and crew(s);

**t.** Keeping time sheets for staff, cast and crews;

**u.** Authorizing all purchase/lease/rental orders and expenditures;

**v.** Disbursing Company funds for the production;

**w.** Seeing that the paperwork for all payroll and approved expenditures are regularly sent to Production Accounting for recording and payment;

**x.** Seeing that payroll checks and receipted reimbursements are distributed to staff, cast and crew on a timely basis;

▼ **During POST-PRODUCTION:**

**y.** Seeing that all Company property is accounted for, that all billing has been sent to Production Accounting for payment;

**z.** Otherwise carrying out the duties normally required of this classification;

**aa.** Providing the hand tools normally employed in this craft.

**3. Considerations:**

**a.** When one (1) or more of the above duties are performed, they are **Production Manager**'s duties and require a **Production Manager**.

**b.** A **Production Manager** is employed for a sufficient period to satisfactorily carry out pre-production, production shooting, and post-production responsibilities. Because of the varying nature of film production, the employment tenure of the **Production Manager** is negotiable.

**H. UNIT PRODUCTION MANAGER**

**1. Responsibilities:** The **Unit Production Manager (UPM)** is directly responsible to the **Production Manager** and is responsible for carrying out the production plan, as set forth by the **Production Manager**, in the most efficient and effective manner possible.

**PRODUCTION MANAGEMENT** (side tab)

**2. Duties—during PRE-PRODUCTION and PRODUCTION:**

  **a.** Reading and annotating the script within the context of budget and shooting schedule concerns;

  **b.** Having a thorough knowledge and understanding of current Union and Guild working rules and wage rates and of the particular agreement(s) which the **Producer,** or Production Company, may have with these labor organizations, with individuals employed on the production, and with vendors supplying or servicing the production;

  **c.** The duties are those of the **Production Manager** while the **Unit Production Manager** is on location, or otherwise managing first or second units, in the personal absence of the **PM**, when charged with the responsibility;

  **d.** Assisting the **Production Manager** in the performance of duties;

  **e.** Otherwise carrying out the duties normally required of this classification;

  **f.** Providing the hand tools normally employed in this craft.

**3. Limitations:** A **Unit Production Manager** does not do production management work unless there is a functioning **Production Manager** to report to.

**4. Considerations:** A **Unit Production Manager** is employed on those productions requiring unit management under a **Production Manager**, such as most studio television programming—episodic and sitcom series—and second unit production, especially that of a second unit production which takes place concurrently with first unit production, as well as that of first unit (principal photography) production with sufficient scope to require the services of a **Unit Production Manager**.

## I. ASSISTANT UNIT PRODUCTION MANAGER

**1. Responsibilities and Duties—all during the PRODUCTION Process:** The **Assistant Unit Production Manager** is directly responsible to the **Unit Production Manager** and assists the **UPM** in the performance of those duties.

**2. Considerations:**

  **a.** **Assistant Unit Production Managers** work under the supervision of the **Unit Production Manager**.

  **b.** An **Assistant UPM** is employed when the **Unit Production Manager** requires assistance in the performance of duties. No person is employed as such unless there is a functioning **UPM** employed for the production period.

## J. LOCATION MANAGER

**1. Responsibilities:** The **Location Manager** is directly responsible to, and reports to, the **Production Manager** and is responsible for locating and making arrangements for appropriate location sites, both interior and exterior, serving as liaison between the site owners and Production Management, in order to help facilitate pre-production scouting and the ensuing production process.

**2. Duties:**

▼ **During PRE-PRODUCTION:**

**a.** Reading the script, noting therein geographical locations which are cited along with the time of year and day during which the action takes place;

**b.** Consulting with the *decision group*—the **Producer, Art Director/Production Designer, Director, Director of Photography** and **Production Manager**—as to any parameters of choice they might have in mind regarding the geographical location, the polar orientation, the architectural style and the physical dimensions and configuration of the desired shooting site(s);

**c.** Preparing for preliminary location scouting by researching appropriate publications and pictorial files for potentially usable shooting sites;

**d.** Planning preliminary scouting trips for the purpose of selecting several possible shooting sites which most closely satisfy the parameters set by the decision group during preliminary conferences;

**e.** Arranging the itinerary, transportation, food and lodging for all personnel involved in all scouting trips;

**f.** Personally inspecting each proposed or potential shooting site, shooting polaroids and/or stills thereof—showing north, south, east, west views of the exterior and surroundings and of each side of each structure and of each wall of each interior room to be utilized;

**g.** Preparing a planned lay-out drawing of the property and a floor plan of the structures to be utilized, indicating the location of doors, windows and skylights, practical electrical fixtures and outlets and the main power supply terminal, noting the voltage and amperage available;

**h.** Noting all dimensions of the exterior and interior (those areas to be utilized and/or photographed), the polar orientation of the property and structures thereon, the path the sun tracks across the property, approximate time of sunrise and sunset at the time of year planned for production at each site, the area and seasonal weather and wind patterns, the distance to transportation terminals, medical facilities, and food and lodging accommodations, and the designation, condition and traffic flow of the roads connecting the location sites thereto;

**i.** Listing all conditions placed on the use of the property by the owner(s)/manager(s)/tenant(s) as well as any and all federal, state and/or local regulations concerning the use of public property, streets and walkways in the area;

**j.** Arranging all location data in appropriate order for presentation to the decision group for its collective consideration and selection of specific locations for the principal scouting group to inspect and affirm;

**k.** Leading the principal scouting group, which often consists of the **Director**, the **Art Director/Production Designer**, **Director of Photography** and the **Production Manager**;

**l.** Once location sites have been selected, firming up the arrangements made with owner(s), manager(s), tenant(s) and/or officials for utilizing the shooting sites and their environs by obtaining contractual commitments and permits—among which are fees and/or a rental/lease arrangement, duration of use, access to the property and its structures for photographic use, care and accountability for the condition of surfaces, furnishings and accouterments, and liability insurance therefor;

▼ **During the PRODUCTION Process:**

**m.** Promptly forwarding receipts for all authorized expenditures to the **Production Manager**;

**n.** Negotiating extensions for location rights when production shooting will not be completed within the agreed-to time period or when additional shooting will be required at a later date;

▼ **During POST-PRODUCTION:**

**o.** Upon completion of shooting, seeing that each location site has been returned to agreed-upon order and condition and, when refurbishing is completed, having each owner sign an acknowledgment thereof;

**p.** Passing all executed documents to, and informing, the **Production Manager** that all locations have been closed and the owners settled with;

**q.** Otherwise performing the duties normally required of this classification;

**r.** Providing the hand tools normally employed in this craft.

**3. Consideration:** A **Location Manager** generally works through pre-production and during production until shooting at each location site has been completed and the location sites have been put back in agreed-to order and condition.

## K. PRODUCTION COORDINATOR

**1. Responsibilities:** The **Production Coordinator (PC)** is directly responsible to the **Unit Production Manager** for assisting the **UPM** in coordinating the working elements of the production process.

**2. Duties—all during the PRODUCTION Process:**

**a.** Preparing, and revising as necessary, a Staff & Crew List;

**b.** Seeing that each day's Call Sheet from the **UPM** is duplicated and available and/or distributed to staff, cast and crew;

**c.** Phoning each on-call performer, atmosphere person and day-hired crew member to give a work call for the following work day;

**d.** Arranging meal accommodations for staff, cast and crew;

**e.** Arranging travel itinerary and lodging for staff personnel on company business;

**f.** Seeing that sufficient copies of the script and its revisions are distributed to the cast and to key crew personnel;

**g.** Otherwise carrying out the duties normally required of this classification;

**h.** Providing the hand tools normally employed in this craft.

3. **Consideration:** The **Production Coordinator** is given specified duties by the **Unit Production Manager** and may in turn utilize the assistance of one or more **Production Assistants**.

## L. PRODUCTION ASSISTANT

1. **Responsibilities:** The **Production Assistant (PA)**is directly responsible to, and assists, the **Unit Production Manager**, and may assist the **Director**, **Assistant Director**, **Production Coordinator** and/or **Stylist** when so assigned by the **UPM**.

2. **Duties—during PRE-PRODUCTION and PRODUCTION:**

### a. In assisting the Director and/or Assistant Director:

**(1)** Taking notes during casting sessions;

**(2)** Taking production notes and timings from television commercial storyboards and conferences and transcribing them;

**(3)** Typing, duplicating and distributing Call Sheets to staff, cast, crew;

**(4)** Keeping clients informed and making arrangements for meetings, luncheons, dinners and hotel, travel and transportation reservations;

**(5)** Bringing refreshments, as requested;

**(6)** Running errands.

### b. In assisting the Production Manager:

**(1)** Keeping and transcribing production notes and reports;

**(2)** Arranging reservations for meals, lodging and travel for staff, cast and crew;

**(3)** Informing **Crafts Service** daily of the number of people to be served during the following production day;

**(4)** Attending/answering the stage and/or location telephones and taking and delivering messages for the staff, cast and crew;

**(5)** Collating/integrating revised script pages into current script copies;

**(6)** Running errands.

### c. In assisting the Production Coordinator:

**(1)** Phoning each on-call performer, atmosphere person and day-hired crew member to give a work call for the following work day;

**(2)** Running errands.

**d. In assisting the Stylist:**

**(1)** Taking notes during production meetings and transcribing them;

**(2)** Checking the availability and cost of, picking up and returning, items of wardrobe, props and/or set dressing, if minimal;

**(3)** Running errands.

**e.** Assisting the **Producer, Director, Assistant Director, Production Manager, Production Coordinator** and/or **Stylist,** to whom assigned, in the performance of their duties;

**f.** Otherwise carrying out the duties normally required of this classification;

**g.** Providing the hand tools normally employed in this craft.

**3. Considerations:**

**a.** A **Production Assistant** is used to assist the **Unit Production Manager** or the person or department to whom assigned.

**b.** The purpose of the **Production Assistant** is to assist in the coordination and efficient operation of the administrative production process, but not to function in duty areas covered by any individual production classification.

▼ **Classification Used Only for VIDEO**▼

**M. PRODUCTION ASSOCIATE**

**1. Responsibilities:** The **Production Associate (PA)** is used in TV and video production only, is directly responsible to the **Producer** or **Production Manager**, and as the liaison between the **Director** and Production Management, is responsible for maintaining an efficient flow of communications between these entities and of handling scheduling matters, as requested.

**2. Duties—all during the PRODUCTION Process:**

**a. In assisting the Director and/or Associate Director:**

**(1)** Taking assigned production notes during casting sessions, blocking, run-throughs and rehearsals;

**(2)** Taking production notes and timings from television commercial storyboards and conferences, and transcribing them;

**(3)** Transcribing all assigned production notes for convenience of Directorial and Production Management;

**(4)** Informing Production Management of any changes in scheduling—cast, special equipment, scene changes, etc—requested by Directorial;

**(5)** Keeping clients informed and making arrangements for meetings, luncheons, dinners and hotel, travel and transportation reservations, as necessary;

**(6)** Bringing refreshments, as needed;

**(7)** Running errands.

PRODUCTION MANAGEMENT

**b. In assisting the Production Manager:**

**(1)** Keeping and transcribing production notes and reports;

**(2)** Typing, duplicating and distributing Call Sheets to staff, cast, crew;

**(3)** Phoning each on-call performer, atmosphere person and day-hired crew member to give a work call for the following work day;

**(4)** Arranging staff, cast and crew reservations for meals, lodging and travel;

**(5)** Attending/answering the stage and/or location telephones and taking messages for the staff, cast and crew;

**(6)** Collating/integrating revised script pages into current script copies;

**(7)** Running errands.

**c. Assisting the Producer, Director, Associate Director and/or Unit Production Manager** to whom assigned, in the performance of their duties;

**(1)** Otherwise performing the duties normally required of this classification;

**(2)** Providing the hand tools normally employed in this craft.

**3. Considerations:**

**a.** A **Production Associate** is used to assist the Directorial unit during television pre-production and production phases and to provide liaison with Production Management.

**b.** The purpose of the **Production Associate** is to assist in the coordination and efficient operation of the Directorial and administrative production processes, but not to function in duty areas covered by any individual production classification.

**NOTES**

# DIRECTORIAL CATEGORY ORGANIZATIONAL CHART

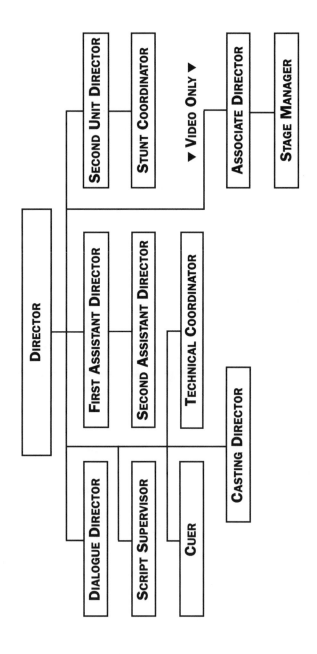

DIRECTOR

FIRST ASSISTANT DIRECTOR

SECOND ASSISTANT DIRECTOR

TECHNICAL COORDINATOR

DIALOGUE DIRECTOR

SCRIPT SUPERVISOR

CUER

CASTING DIRECTOR

SECOND UNIT DIRECTOR

STUNT COORDINATOR

▼ VIDEO ONLY ▼

ASSOCIATE DIRECTOR

STAGE MANAGER

# 3

# DIRECTORIAL CATEGORY

**A. Category Classifications:** There are twelve (12) classifications in the Directorial Category:

▼ **Film & Video Production** use five (5) **Directorial** classifications in common:

1. **Director (Category Head)**
2. **Casting Director (Category Sub-Head)**
3. **Dialogue Director**
4. **Script Supervisor**
5. **Cuer/Prompter Operator**

▼ **Only Film Production** uses these five (5) Directorial classifications:

6. **Second Unit Director (Category Sub Head)**
7. **First Assistant Director (Category Sub-Head)**
8. **Second Assistant Director**
9. **Stunt Coordinator**
10. **Technical Coordinator**

▼ **Only Video Production** uses these two (2) Directorial classifications:

11. **Associate Director (Category Sub-Head)**
12. **Stage Manager**

**B. Category Criteria:**

1. The **Director** is given by the **Producer** full authority over, and responsibility for, the conduct of the production.

2. It is the **Director**'s responsibility for properly orchestrating the performance by actors and for effective and efficient dramatic use of the production elements in order to bring the project in on schedule and within budgetary limits.

3. A **Director** needs to know and effectively apply: Cinematic production planning; cinematic structure and the process of editing; principles of dramaturgy; performing skills; writing skills; management techniques.

4. The **Director** is provided the necessary production personnel and matériel by the **Producer** to adequately serve his/her directorial production needs.

5. The **Director**, leader of the on-stage image-making process, sets the mood and pace of production by his/her actions, demeanor and intent.

6. On film productions, the **Director** has the option, depending upon the agreement with the Production Company, of taking the picture through a first and/or final cut, for which he/she is compensated.

7. A **Director** generally is not required during the photography of stock shots, process plates or inserts.

8. On productions whereon the **Director** requires assistance in the performance of duties, a **First Assistant Director** is hired before **Second Assistant Directors** are hired.

9. Large crowd or battle scenes which use many extras or atmosphere players and which utilize extensive multiple camera coverage, may require several **Second Assistant Directors** in order to safely and properly plan, stage and coordinate the atmospheric action and camera coverage.

10. **Second Unit Director** and **Stunt Coordinator** work closely to safely and effectively plan, rehearse and shoot stunt sequences.

11. On video productions, whereon the **Director** requires assistance in the performance of duties, an **Associate Director** is hired.

12. In film production, a sufficient number of **Second Assistant Directors** are employed to adequately assist the **Director** and **First Assistant Director** in managing and directing large numbers of extras, atmosphere people or mobs, or where distances requiring two-way radio transmission are involved.

13. The **Model Builder, Propmaker, Special Effects Technician, Special Effects Assistant, Animal Specialist, Wrangler, First Aid Technician, Studio Teacher, Crafts Service** and **Utility** personnel are directly responsible to the **First Assistant Director** when functioning on the set during production shooting.

14. The **Dialogue Director** gives any dialogue changes, which are made by the **Director** during off-camera rehearsals, to the **Script Supervisor** prior to the on-camera rehearsal.

15. The **Dialogue Director** does not perform **Script Supervisor** duties.

16. The **Cuer** or **Prompter Operator** receives from the **Script Supervisor** a copy of the lines of dialogue which are to be imprinted on cue cards, or on scrolls used on mechanized or digital prompting equipment.

17. The **Cuer/Prompter Operator** works cooperatively with the **First Assistant Camera Operator** or the **Video Utility** and/or **Video Camera Operator**, respectively, when attaching electronic cueing apparatus to cine or electronic camera(s).

18. The **Technical Coordinator** is used on multi-camera audience film sitcoms during blocking, rehearsals and on through show time with the audience in attendance, in order to help facilitate and coordinate camera dolly movement.

19. The **Technical Coordinator** may be called upon by the **Director** to assist in setting camera positions during camera blocking.

20. The **Associate Director** and **Stage Manager** are classifications used for video productions.

21. The **Casting Director** directs the casting process for the production.

22. All Directorial personnel operating underwater with breathing apparatus must be SCUBA certified.

**DIRECTORIAL**

**23.** The **Director** and each Directorial Category Sub-Head must ensure that directorial and production personnel under their supervision—staff, cast and crew—do not attempt work under any unsafe condition(s), as specified by the Employer, OSHA, Building and Safety Code and fire laws, or in violation of any other safety regulation(s) and practice(s).

**C. Category Responsibilities:** It is the responsibility of each Employee in the Directorial Category to work closely and cooperatively with the **Director** in order to assist in the optimum and most efficient visual realization of the **Director**'s conceptualization of the story elements on film or video tape.

**D. Category Function:** The principal function of Directorial Category personnel involves work with the shooting script in its various aspects; with directing actors and camera crew in the planning and blocking of shots; with the dialogue and/or with the conformance of the recorded takes to the script, and vice versa; and with maintaining an efficiency and pace during the production process which assures fulfilling the shooting schedule within the allotted time and budget.

**E. Category Considerations:**

**1.** Directorial Category personnel are used on each production which utilizes dialogue and/or matching action.

**2.** The classification(s) used depends upon the type of motion picture being produced, its budget, production elements and shooting schedule.

**3.** The **Director, First Assistant Director, Associate Director, Script Supervisor, Dialogue Director, Technical Coordinator** and **Cuer** should each be given sufficient pre-production time to prepare their respective work for the production process.

**4.** The **First Assistant Director** is allowed sufficient post-production time to complete production reports and present them to the **Unit Production Manager** or **Producer**. The **Script Supervisor** is normally given sufficient post-production time to finalize and deliver the shooting script and production notes to the **UPM** or **Producer**.

**F. Category Requirements:** Employees in each Directorial Category classification must know and follow the chain-of-command and lines-of-communication and must know and be able to effectively apply the techniques associated with their respective craft classification.

▼ **Classifications Used for Both FILM & VIDEO** ▼

**G. DIRECTOR**

**1. Responsibilities:** The **Director** is directly responsible to the **Producer**, and is responsible for directing the production activities of the staff, cast and crew as creatively, efficiently and effectively as possible in order to obtain optimum (dramatic) interpretation of the script, outline and/or storyboard, within the constraints of time and budget, while obtaining optimum photographic coverage thereof so that each shot, scene and sequence will cut together, flow and give life to the finally realized production, whether dramatic, comedic, promotional or documentary in nature.

**DIRECTORIAL**

**DIRECTORIAL**

### 2. Duties:

#### ▼ During PRE-PRODUCTION:

a. Reading and annotating the script for meaning, emotion, action, continuity, plot and character development, as necessary;

b. Breaking down the scenes in the script into shot setups and numbering or renumbering shots, as necessary;

c. Working closely with the **Producer** in the casting of all performers and other personnel who appear in the camera frame;

d. Consulting with the **Production Designer** regarding set design and the overall creative conceptual visualization for the production;

e. Surveying the locations and having a voice in selecting them;

f. Determining the requirements of the set, set dressing, costumes, makeup, props, etc, for their proper dramatic perspective and functioning;

g. Breaking down the shooting script into sequences, scenes, and individual shots in preparation of shooting;

h. Plotting the camera angles and movement for such scenes and shots;

#### ▼ During the PRODUCTION Process:

i. Planning and executing the work in such a way as to most efficiently utilize the talents of staff, cast and crew;

j. Translating and transferring the written word to cinematic images—telling the written story cinematically;

k. Working with and rehearsing the performers in understanding and interpreting character development and the emotional levels to be maintained during each shot, scene and sequence;

l. Rehearsing cast, extras, special effects and stunt personnel, as well as camera and sound, prior to the take;

m. Preparing, and carrying, a shot list of individual shots planned to be covered during each shooting day, and checking off each shot when it is satisfactorily done;

n. Working closely with the **Director of Photography** in communicating the desired "**look**" of the production, scene-by-scene and in its totality, and in setting angles and camera movement;

o. Blocking and directing the action of all actors, extras, vehicles, livestock, and the camera(s);

p. Requesting and using video assist to monitor the framed action;

q. Lining up or checking the action through the camera viewfinder at any time during rehearsals or before and/or following each take;

r. Giving cues to actors and crew through Assistant Directors, during rehearsals and takes;

s. Directing the dialogue;

**t.** Making script changes as deemed necessary in order to achieve appropriate transferral of the story—its action line and dialogue—to the recording medium—film, video or digital;

**u.** Deciding on the use and placement of cueing equipment;

**v.** Permitting no last-minute post-rehearsal changes in blocking or timing when shooting sequences involving stunts and/or special effects;

▼ **During PRODUCTION and POST-PRODUCTION:**

**w.** Supervising the first cut and, if authorized, the final cut;

**x.** Supervising ADR sessions;

**y.** Checking temp-dubs and sitting in on the final mix and print master mix with the **Producer** and **Picture Editor** and signing off if approving the result;

**z.** Otherwise carrying out the duties normally required of this classification;

**aa.** Providing the hand tools normally employed in this craft.

**3. Considerations:**

**a.** When one (1) or more of the above duties are required, a **Director** is called for.

**b.** The **Director** is employed for a sufficient period to satisfactorily carry out pre-production, production shooting (including conferences and viewing rushes) and post-production (through the first or final cut) responsibilities, as granted by agreement with the **Producer** or Production Company.

## H. CASTING DIRECTOR

**1. Responsibilities:** The **Casting Director** is directly responsible to the **Producer** until a **Director** is hired, after which the **Casting Director** is responsible to the **Director** for interviewing, recommending and scheduling appropriately screened principal players, supporting cast and bit players for interview and consideration by the **Director** and/or the *decision group*—the **Executive Producer**, the **Producer**, the **Director** and, sometimes, the starring actor(s).

**2. Duties—all during PRE-PRODUCTION:**

**a.** Reading and annotating the script and understanding the theme and character motivations presented therein;

**b.** Being made aware of any preferences which the **Producer**(s) and/or **Director** might have regarding the casting of certain roles;

**c.** Noting the number of principal players required, the sex, age, emotional and physical characteristics of each character to be cast, the physical requirements for each role;

**d.** Noting the number of supporting players called for, their gender, age, and emotional and physical characteristics, and the physical and ethnic requirements, if any, for each role;

**e.** Noting the number of bit players called for, their gender, age, and emotional and physical characteristics, and the physical and ethnic requirements, if any, for each bit;

    **f.** Developing a list of talent from résumé, photo and video files, performance notes, and previous interviews, thought to be appropriate to be considered for filling each principal, supporting and bit role;

    **g.** Contacting each performer through his/her agent to check for availability and interest in the project;

    **h.** Requesting updated résumés, photos, films and video tapes for performers under consideration;

    **i.** Sending scripts to the agents or performers;

    **j.** Scheduling performers for an interview or audition with the decision group;

    **k.** Briefing the decision group on the background and credits of each performer who is to be interviewed;

    **l.** Seeing that each candidate is interviewed and/or auditioned to the satisfaction of members of the decision group;

    **m.** Keeping a memorandum of the interview/audition proceedings and the comments and decision of the decision group regarding each candidate;

    **n.** Casting bit and atmosphere players in the absence of decision group interest in this process;

    **o.** Otherwise carrying out the duties normally required of this classification;

    **p.** Providing the hand tools normally employed in this craft.

**3. Considerations:** A **Casting Director** is used when the **Producer, Director** or the decision group requires assistance in casting a production.

## I. DIALOGUE DIRECTOR

**1. Responsibilities:** The **Dialogue Director** is directly responsible to the **Director** for matters pertaining to delivery of dialogue by performers in order to maintain an accurate and consistent delivery thereof.

**2. Duties—all during PRODUCTION:**

    **a.** Reading and annotating the script within the context of dialogue direction, as necessary;

    **b.** Going over and running lines of dialogue with the actor(s) off-camera during rehearsals and prior to the take to assure that the lines are memorized and facilely delivered;

    **c.** Following the script dialogue during each take, making sure no lines have been deleted, changed or added and, if so, advising the **Director** and **Script Supervisor** at the end of each take;

    **d.** Making note of any deletions, changes, or ad-libs and calling these to the attention of the **Director** and **Script Supervisor** immediately following the take;

    **e.** Coaching actors in the proper delivery of the lines—interpretation, phrasing and the like—if so qualified and if given the responsibility by the **Director**;

    **f.** Coaching actors in the proper delivery (rhythm and pronunciation) of dialects and/or accents and/or foreign languages, if so qualified;

**g.** Otherwise carrying out the duties normally required of this classification;

**h.** Providing the hand tools normally employed in this craft.

**3. Considerations:** A **Dialogue Director** is used when the **Director** requires assistance in working with the performer(s) in the delivery of dialogue.

## J. SCRIPT SUPERVISOR

**1. Responsibilities:** The **Script Supervisor** is directly responsible to the **Director** for maintaining all details of the shooting script in a form and style which clearly reflect the production filming process—making detailed notation as to directorial decisions and modifications made, printed takes, pickup shots, etc; and indicates any and every modification of the script both to the **Director** and to the **Picture Editor**.

**2. Duties:**

▼ **During PRE-PRODUCTION:**

**a.** Reading the script;

**b.** Preparing script pages to facilitate annotations and production notes;

▼ **During the PRODUCTION Process:**

**c.** Keeping the shooting script detailed, accurate and current for the benefit of the **Director** during pre-production modifications and shooting, and to facilitate editing thereafter;

**d.** Accurately recording all changes in dialogue and action during pre-production and production;

**e.** Recording camera placement and movement, the taking lens, the T-stop and any filtering, frame rate or shutter angle variation from normal used for each take;

**f.** Recording actor condition, position(s), and distance(s) from the camera(s);

**g.** Recording prop and set dressing condition and locations;

**h.** Recording hand prop use and any variation in condition because of use thereof during a take;

**i.** Recording costume items, conditions and arrangement preceding and following each take;

**j.** Keeping accurate and detailed records of everything that occurs in frame during each take so that planned juxtaposed shots may be successfully matched in all respects at any time;

**k.** Operating a Polaroid camera, when deemed necessary, for the one and only purpose of recording prop, wardrobe and actor positions and condition thereof at the beginning and/or end of a take;

**l.** Keeping record of scene numbers and takes, noting which takes are accepted by the **Director** for printing and which are not;

**m.** Giving the scene number to the **First Assistant Camera Operator** and/or to the **Second Assistant Camera Operator** and to the **Production Mixer** for slating and notation in the camera and sound report records;

**n.** Making note of any comments by the **Director** regarding action blocking, interpretation and/or editing; also making note of special situations such as "Under Protest" request(s) by the **Director of Photography** or **Production Mixer**;

**o.** Prompting, and running lines with, actors in the absence of a **Dialogue Director**, and otherwise assisting the **Director** at rehearsals;

**p.** Timing all rehearsals and takes by stop watch, and recording all timings;

**q.** At the close of each shooting day, apprising the **Director** of any scheduled scenes on the shot list left unphotographed, omitted or incomplete and getting the list of scenes planned for the following day's shooting schedule from the **Director** or **First Assistant Director**;

**r.** Apprising the **Director** of any planned or required wild sound takes not recorded;

**s.** Apprising the **Director** of any camera or actor or object positioning or movement which may violate the action line and thereby result in a possible mismatch or disorientation, which may cause editing problems later;

▼ **During PRODUCTION and POST-PRODUCTION:**

**t.** Organizing, cleaning up and delivering to the **Director, Picture Editor** or **Producer** at the close of production, or within a few days thereafter, the shooting script with all script notes, take records, scene changes, sketches and photos plus all comments, additions, deletions or omissions which have occurred during production;

**u.** Otherwise carrying out the duties normally required of this classification;

**v.** Providing a stop watch and other hand tools normally employed in this craft.

**3. Considerations:**

**a.** There is a **Script Supervisor** on each production, and shooting unit thereof, requiring dialogue and/or matching action.

**b.** In addition to the duration of production, the **Script Supervisor** is generally used for at least two (2) days prior to the start of production to prepare, and at least one (1) day following production in order to finalize production script notes, but in any event, is given adequate pre- and post-production time to plan, prepare and finalize the shooting script for use by the **Director** and **Picture Editor** during the editing process.

**K. CUER/PROMPTER OPERATOR**

**1. Responsibilities:** The **Cuer/Prompter Operator** is directly responsible to the **Director** for the accuracy and legibility of the cue copy and for the placement and pacing of the cue copy in order to facilitate its reading by the performer(s).

2. **Duties—all during PRODUCTION:**

   **a.** Placing the selected text of an approved script or story board on cue cards, sheets, rolls or electronic/digital readouts;

   **b.** Setting up, operating, and disassembling whatever cueing apparatus, whether manual, mechanical or electronic, is obtained for the production to enable the actors to read or refer to their lines while performing before the camera(s);

   **c.** Attaching such equipment to the film or video camera(s) with the approval of the **Director of Photography** or **Technical Director**, respectively, and with the assistance of the **First Assistant Camera Operator** (for film) or **Video Utility** (for video) personnel, respectively;

   **d.** Placing such floor equipment to afford optimum convenience and visibility for the performer(s) and, with the approval of the **Director of Photography**, so as not to interfere with camera, sound, lighting or grip equipment or procedures;

   **e.** Keeping the cue cards, or cue scroll line synchronized to the pacing of each performer's delivery;

   **f.** Making any changes in the text on the cue cards, cue sheet or cue scroll, according to the **Director**;

   **g.** Assuring the correct content, legibility and placement of blackboard, cards, cue sheets, or electronic or digital roll-up;

   **h.** Wearing an intercom headset when required—particularly during video production;

   **i.** Otherwise carrying out the duties normally required of this classification;

   **j.** Providing the hand tools normally employed in this craft.

3. **Considerations:** A **Cuer** or **Prompter Operator** is employed when cueing duties or equipment are utilized on the production.

▼ **Classifications Used Only for FILM** ▼

## L. SECOND UNIT DIRECTOR

1. **Responsibilities:** The **Second Unit Director** is directly responsible to the **Director** of the first unit—the unit shooting principal photography—and is responsible for maintaining the look and style of the action established by the principal **Director** in order that the footage shot by the second unit—whether action or chase sequences, mob scenes, battles, stampedes, stunts and/or special effects—integrates seamlessly with that of the first unit.

2. **Duties—all during PRODUCTION:**

   **a.** Reading and annotating the script for meaning, emotion, action, continuity, plot and character development, as necessary;

   **b.** Consulting with the principal **Director** regarding the portions of the production to be covered by the second unit and how he or she wishes that coverage to be planned and captured;

c. Breaking down the scenes in the script to be covered by the second unit into shot setups and numbering or renumbering shots, as necessary;

d. Looking at scenes and sequences already photographed by the first unit to get a sense of how the second unit work should fit in and match;

e. Preparing a shot list for the material to be covered;

f. Supervising the production of a storyboard to cover action sequences involving chases, stunts, and/or special effects;

g. Translating and transferring the written word to cinematic images—telling the written story cinematically;

h. Planning and executing the work in such a way as to most efficiently utilize the talents of staff, cast and crew;

i. Consulting with the **Production Designer** regarding the overall creative conceptual visualization for the production;

j. Consulting with the **Costume Supervisor** regarding the proper and matching wardrobe for doubles and atmosphere personnel to wear;

k. Consulting with the **Key Makeup Artist** regarding matching makeup and hairdressing for doubles and atmosphere personnel;

l. Surveying the locations and having a voice in selecting them;

m. Breaking down the shooting script into sequences, scenes, and individual shots in preparation of shooting;

n. Plotting the camera angles and movement for such scenes and shots;

o. Preparing, and carrying, a shot list of individual shots planned to be covered during each shooting day and checking off each shot when it is satisfactorily done;

p. Working closely with the **Unit Production Manager** in the planning of each shooting day;

q. Working closely with the **Director of Photography** in communicating the desired "**look**" of the production, scene-by-scene and in its totality, and in setting angles and camera movement in order to match and or seamlessly cut with first unit footage;

r. Blocking and directing the action of all stunt personnel, extras, vehicles, livestock, and the camera(s);

s. Rehearsing doubles, extras, special effects, stunt personnel, and camera and sound prior to each take;

t. Lining up or checking the action through the camera viewfinder at any time during rehearsals or before and/or following each take;

u. Giving cues to atmosphere personnel and crew through **Assistant Directors** during rehearsals and takes;

**v.** Making script changes as deemed necessary in order to achieve appropriate transferral of the story—its action line and dialogue—to the recording medium;

**w.** Deciding on the use and placement of special effects matériel;

**x.** Permitting no last-minute, post-rehearsal changes in blocking or timing when shooting sequences involving stunts and/or special effects;

**y.** Otherwise carrying out the duties normally required of this classification;

**z.** Providing the hand tools normally employed in this craft.

**3. Considerations:**

**a.** When one (1) or more of the above duties are required, a **2nd Unit Director** is called for.

**b.** The **2nd Unit Director** is employed for a sufficient period to satisfactorily carry out the planning and shooting of second unit coverage of large-scale action, stunts and special effects, either separate or combinations thereof.

## M. FIRST ASSISTANT DIRECTOR

**1. Responsibilities:** The **First Assistant Director (1st AD)** is directly responsible to the **Director** and assists the **Director** in the performance of directorial duties—administrative and production—and may perform the function of **Producer**'s representative. The **1st AD** works in close cooperation with the **Unit Production Manager**. The **1st AD** is the on-the-set expediter, and is responsible for maintaining optimum coordination among crew categories and actors in order to sustain the production pace required by the shooting schedule as set by the **Director**.

**2. Duties:**

▼ **During PRE-PRODUCTION:**

**a.** Reading and annotating the script within the context of determining the most efficient and effective means of planning the production schedule;

**b.** Timing out the shooting script scene-by-scene;

**c.** Estimating final footage;

**d.** Preparing a script breakdown, listing probable requirements of bit players and extras in each scene;

▼ **During the PRODUCTION Process:**

**e.** Conforming to the day-to-day shooting schedule, as prepared and approved by the **Production Manager**, as closely as the production pace, the weather, and cast availability permit;

**f.** Roughing out the action of the actors preparatory to shooting the scene, if the **Director** so requests;

**g.** Arranging and overseeing background and atmospheric action;

**h.** Assisting the **Director** in the handling and direction of groups of extras, **Animal Handler**s, **Special Effects Technician**s and stunt people in mob scenes, special effects events, stunts, battles and stampedes;

**i.** Coordinating the activities of **Second Assistant Director**s, if any;

**j.** Limiting the number of people riding in or on insert cars or towed camera platforms during rehearsals and shooting;

**k.** Overseeing special effects—pyrotechnics, working props and special wire-gag rigging—in liaison with the **Director**;

**l.** Cueing cast and crew, when authorized by the **Director**;

**m.** Handling organizational matters and expediting shooting for the **Director**;

**n.** After consultation with the **Director**, presenting the proposed shooting schedule for the following day to the **Unit Production Manager** for approval, reproduction and timely dissemination to staff, cast and crew;

**o.** Prior to each day's shoot, preparing with the **Director**, from the following day's shooting schedule a personal sequential shot list;

**p.** Checking off each shot on the shot list when finalized;

**q.** Obtaining photographic releases from people and property owners, whose likeness or property may appear in frame during production;

**r.** Signing Employees', performers', extras' and Steward's Time Records, Start Slips and reimbursement authorizations;

**s.** Authorizing overtime and hazard pay for cast and crew, and notifying the **Unit Production Manager** so that special insurance coverage can be put in place;

**t.** Making sure that everything and everybody needed during the production will be on hand in the right place at the right time and in the proper condition for production purposes;

**u.** Having a thorough knowledge and understanding of current Union and Guild working rules and wage rates and of the particular agreement(s) which the **Producer**, or Production Company, may have with these labor organizations and with cast members and individuals employed on the production;

**v.** Seeing that only authorized people are on the stage or in the shooting area during production;

**w.** Seeing that doors and vents and air conditioning equipment on stage are secured prior to the take, and then opened or reactivated during setup time;

**x.** Checking with camera and sound personnel immediately preceding each take to make sure they are ready to function;

**y.** Requesting quiet on the set prior to giving the order to roll sound;

**z.** Ensuring that production personnel do not attempt work under any unsafe condition(s), as specified by the Building and Safety Code and fire laws, or in violation of any other safety regulation(s) and practice(s);

**aa.** Ensuring that only essential personnel are aboard moving camera vehicles, and that all such personnel are safetied, and informed and have clear understanding about vehicular speed, speed changes, and maneuvering;

**ab.** Assisting the **Director** in the performance of directorial duties;

▼ **During PRODUCTION and POST-PRODUCTION:**

**ac.** Completing all forms which need to be sent to Production Management for final disposition and filing:

**ad.** Otherwise carrying out the duties normally required of this classification;

**ae.** Providing the hand tools normally employed in this craft.

3. **Optional Duties:** The **First Assistant Director**, in addition to other duties, may assist the **Unit Production Manager** in the performance of certain production duties.

4. **Considerations:**

    **a.** A **First Assistant Director** is employed on all feature productions and on those productions where the **Director** requires the services of a **1st AD**.

    **b.** The **First Assistant Director** is employed for a sufficient period in order to satisfactorily carry out pre-production, production shooting, and post-production responsibilities.

**N. SECOND ASSISTANT DIRECTOR**

1. **Responsibilities:** The **Second Assistant Director (2nd AD)** is directly responsible to the **First Assistant Director** and assists the **1st AD** in the performance of assistant directorial production duties, particularly when large numbers of atmosphere people and/or stunt people are being used and when multiple camera units are being employed to cover stunt and/or special effects action.

2. **Duties—all during PRODUCTION:**

    **a.** Reading and annotating the script and production plan within the context of determining the most efficient means of planning and/or supervising assigned action;

    **b.** Arranging, positioning and blocking movement and business of atmosphere people, as specified by the **Director** or **First AD**;

    **c.** Assisting the **First AD** in the performance of assistant directorial duties;

    **d.** Otherwise carrying out the duties normally required of this classification;

    **e.** Providing the hand tools normally employed in this craft.

3. **Considerations:** A **Second Assistant Director** is employed on those productions requiring the services of a **2nd AD**.

**O. STUNT COORDINATOR**

1. **Responsibilities:** The **Stunt Coordinator** is directly responsible to the **Director** and assists the **Director** in the planning, staging and execution of stunts involving stunt personnel, vehicles, rolling stock, aircraft, marine craft, and

animals, marking and/or recommending to the director camera positions and taking steps to insure the safety of personnel manning the camera positions during stunts, and coordinating all aspects of the stunt process in order to optimize the visual aspect of the stunts.

**2. Duties—all during PRODUCTION:**

    **a.** Reading and annotating the script within the context of movement, camera placement, stunt choreography, safety and logistics;

    **b.** Making certain that the elements of the stunt are thoroughly understood by all personnel involved with the stunt—stunt, camera and support personnel;

    **c.** Planning and choreographing of all stunt elements—position and movement of personnel and vehicles;

    **d.** Making a dry run at reduced speed in order to allow all personnel involved to confirm the planned path, to check surface conditions and/or weather conditions, to affirm camera placement and to refine the choreography of other stunt vehicles and stunt performers involved;

    **e.** Observing proper and adequate safety and protective procedures for personnel and equipment along the planned stunt route under the prevailing weather conditions;

    **f.** Checking to make sure that each stunt vehicle is mechanically sound, operational and safe;

    **g.** Making certain that each **Stunt Driver** is clear-headed and alert and understands the position, movement and timing of his vehicle in relation to others in the stunt;

    **h.** Making sure that all attached equipment and systems are operational, secure and safe for personnel to be around, ride, and to operate;

    **i.** Supervising all coupling of towed platforms or vehicles;

    **j.** Limiting the number of people riding in or on the stunt vehicle during rehearsals and shooting;

    **k.** Making certain that personnel riding in the stunt vehicles are properly safetied in place;

    **l.** Working with the **Key Special Effects Technician** on the use and placement of special effects matériel;

    **m.** Making and/or permitting no change in blocking or timing after locking in the choreography for sequences involving stunts and/or special effects prior to shooting the scene;

    **n.** Otherwise carrying out the duties normally required of this classification;

    **o.** Providing the hand tools normally employed in this craft.

**3. Considerations:** A **Stunt Coordinator** shall see that a **Stunt Associate** is positioned by each camera on the action side of that camera.

**P. TECHNICAL COORDINATOR**

  **1. Responsibilities:** The **Technical Coordinator** is directly responsible to the **Director**, notating in his or her copy of the script the movement and assigned coverage of the cameras for each sequence based on the **Director**'s actor/camera blocking and shot assignment, and is responsible for coordinating all camera dolly movement during rehearsals and show time filming.

  **2. Duties—all during PRODUCTION:**

    **a.** Reading and annotating the script within the context of coordinating camera movement with actor movement in conformity with the **Director**'s blocking;

    **b.** Making careful and complete notation in his or her shooting script exactly when each camera dolly moves, the sequential number of each move, the direction in which each move is to be made, what or whom each camera is framing, and whenever a camera is "**on-the-air**" during a move;

    **c.** Checking, prior to each rehearsal and the show time filming, to insure that each **Dolly Grip** and **Camera Operator** is wearing an intercom headset and that the headset is on and tuned to the correct channel (if RF type);

    **d.** Giving each **Dolly Grip** advance notification via headset communication when each dolly move is to be made and to which numbered position it is to be made;

    **e.** Giving assistance to each **Camera Operator** who requests it, such as a reminder to alter subject framing, dumping off or swish-panning from one actor to another, racking focus from one depth plane to another, or giving the **Camera Operator** a line cue on which to make the move or modification;

    **f.** Making notation of each change in camera blocking and/or coverage in the shooting script and making each operative camera crew affected aware of those changes;

    **g.** Otherwise carrying out the duties normally required of this classification;

    **h.** Providing the tools normally employed in this craft.

  **3. Considerations:**

    **a.** A **Technical Coordinator** is used to coordinate camera dolly movement on multiple camera film sitcoms filmed before a live audience.

    **b.** It may not be necessary to use a **Technical Coordinator** on a multiple camera sitcom employing a block-and-shoot technique.

▼ **Classifications Used Only for VIDEO** ▼

**[See the Video Category for Responsibilities & Duties]**

**Q. ASSOCIATE DIRECTOR**

**R. STAGE MANAGER**

# CAMERA CATEGORY ORGANIZATIONAL CHART

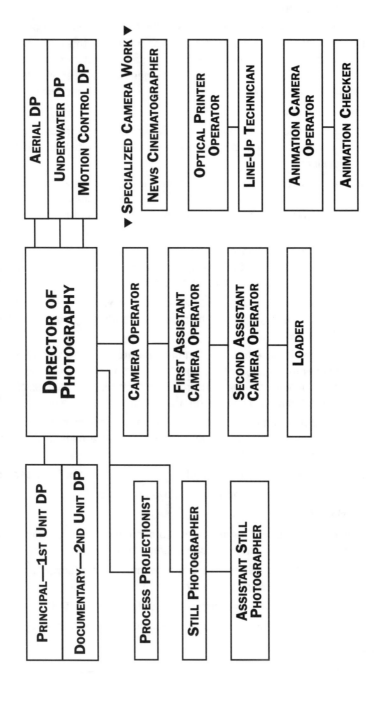

**PRINCIPAL—1ST UNIT DP**

**DOCUMENTARY—2ND UNIT DP**

**DIRECTOR OF PHOTOGRAPHY**

**AERIAL DP**

**UNDERWATER DP**

**MOTION CONTROL DP**

▼ **SPECIALIZED CAMERA WORK** ▼

**NEWS CINEMATOGRAPHER**

**OPTICAL PRINTER OPERATOR**

**LINE-UP TECHNICIAN**

**ANIMATION CAMERA OPERATOR**

**ANIMATION CHECKER**

**CAMERA OPERATOR**

**FIRST ASSISTANT CAMERA OPERATOR**

**SECOND ASSISTANT CAMERA OPERATOR**

**LOADER**

**PROCESS PROJECTIONIST**

**STILL PHOTOGRAPHER**

**ASSISTANT STILL PHOTOGRAPHER**

# 4

# CAMERA CATEGORY

**A. Category Classifications:** There are seventeen (17) classifications in the Camera Category, including five (5) sub-specialties of **Director of Photography**:

  **1. Director of Photography:**

    **a. Director of Photography—First Unit Cinematographer** [Principal Photography, using continuity lighting for interiors and exteriors; also includes studio process and other specialties] **(Category Head)**

    **b. Documentary** or **Second Unit Cinematographer (Category Head)**

    **c. Aerial Cinematographer (Category Head)**

    **d. Underwater Cinematographer (Category Head)**

    **e. Motion Control Cinematographer (Category Head)**

  **2. Camera Operator**

  **3. First Assistant Camera Operator [Focus-Puller—Follow-Focus Person]**

  **4. Second Assistant Camera Operator [Slater—Clapper Person]**

  **5. Loader**

  **6. Process Projectionist**

  **7. Still Photographer (Category Sub-Head)**

  **8. Assistant Still Photographer**

  ▼ **For SPECIALIZED Camera Work:**

  **9. News Cinematographer (Category Head)**

  **10. Optical Printer Operator (Category Head)**

  **11. Line-up Technician**

  **12. Animation Camera Operator (Category Head)**

  **13. Animation Checker**

**B. Category Criteria:**

  **1.** Employees holding classification within the Camera Category perform all job procedures which are utilized on interior or exterior production, on the ground, airborne, in or underwater, on location and/or on a sound stage.

  **2.** A **Director of Photography** of the appropriate cinematographic specialty is used during all production shooting, other than the news-gathering type, and is in charge of all technical procedures directly pertaining to cinematography during the production process.

3. A **Director of Photography** needs to know and apply: In addition to film and tape stocks and lighting design, the capability of every camera currently used in production and its lenses, filters, control heads—manual and remote, mounts and mobile platforms; as head of the technical team effort during the production process, the interpersonal managerial skills used to work with performers and heads of other collaborating crafts.

4. **Directors of Photography—First Unit Cinematographers:** Do principal cinematography on features, featurettes, shorts, and on television programming series, specials, MOWs and commercials; and do special effects cinematography. (See Glossary for definitions of these cited types of production and techniques.)

5. **Documentary** and **Second Unit Cinematographers** photograph, respectively, documentary-type productions, as defined in the Glossary, or second unit sequences, as defined in the Glossary.

6. **Aerial Cinematographers** photograph aerial sequences while airborne, as defined in the Glossary.

7. **Underwater Cinematographers** photograph underwater sequences while submerged, as defined in the Glossary.

8. All camera personnel operating underwater with breathing apparatus must be SCUBA certified.

9. **Motion Control Cinematographers** photograph complex shots which require the camera to precisely repeat complex moves on multiple axes during multiple passes with complete and accurate computer-programmed motion control replication, as defined in the Glossary.

10. **News Cinematographers** photograph news-gathering-type productions, as defined in the Glossary.

11. **Animation Camera Operators** photograph animation-type productions, as defined in the Glossary.

12. **Optical Printer Operators** photograph optical effects. This procedure is defined in the Glossary.

13. The **Director of Photography** has the option of operating a camera at any time he or she deems necessary or advisable, but only for purposes of precision or artistic interpretation and not to exclude or replace a **Camera Operator**.

14. A **Camera Operator** is used to operate—physically manipulating each assigned and functioning camera requiring such operation.

15. When the **Camera Operator** requires assistance in setting up, moving and breaking down camera equipment and/or in following focus or in the operation of other variable camera controls, a **First Assistant Camera Operator** is used on each such camera on which such assistance is needed.

16. When the **First Assistant Camera Operator** requires assistance in the operation of variable camera controls, loading and unloading film magazines,

slating, making camera reports, moving, setting up and wrapping camera equipment and the like, a **Second Assistant Camera Operator** is used.

17. When multiple cameras are used concurrently, or when the **Second Assistant Camera Operator** requires assistance in loading film, a **Loader** is used.

18. For photographic purposes, the **Director of Photography** may request the use, or modification, of makeup or costuming on any or all actors being photographed.

19. A **Director of Photography** qualified in aerial, underwater, time-lapse, stop-motion, rear or front process, matte, blue/green/red screen, registration, miniature and models, or other photographic specialty, may be called in to take charge of cinematography of such sequences in a production, under the supervision of the **Director of Photography** assigned to the production.

20. When process cinematography is planned, a **Process Projectionist** is used.

21. When still photographs are to be made during production procedures or for publicity purposes, a **Still Photographer** is used.

22. It is recommended that the **Director of Photography** or **Cinematographer** be employed for at least one (1) preliminary conference and/or survey in order to become familiar with the script, **Director,** actors, sets, wardrobe, locations, etc.

23. The **Director of Photography** has the option of having "**U.P.**" [Under Protest] recorded on the slate board and Camera Report should the **DP** be directed to photograph a shot against his or her objection; however, it may be more prudent to advise the **Script Supervisor** and note the details in the Camera Report; the responsible person—**Director, Producer** or **Production Manager**—directing the **Director of Photography** to photograph such shot then assumes all respon-sibility for the technical quality thereof, without recourse.

24. The **Director of Photography** and each Camera Category Sub-Head must ensure that camera personnel and production personnel under their supervision, do not attempt work under any unsafe condition(s), as specified by the Employer, OSHA, Building and Safety Code and fire laws, or in violation of any other safety regulation(s) and practice(s).

C. **Category Responsibilities:** It is the responsibility of each Employee in the Camera Category to work cooperatively with the **Director of Photography**, or with the Sub-Head to whom assigned, in order to assist in achieving the optimum and most efficient realization of the photographed elements on film.

D. **Category Function:** Since nearly everything that is done during pre-production and production, either directly or indirectly, is done for one purpose only—and that is for presentation to the camera, the camera is both the focus and locus of activity on the set. The principal function of Camera Category personnel is to be prepared to capture the imagery presented by designing appropriate lighting for that subject matter, selecting the taking lens and filters, placing and moving the camera in order to best frame and capture the desired imagery and action on film.

**E. Category Considerations:**

**1.** Camera Category personnel are used on each production or project on which motion picture and/or still cameras are used.

**2.** The classification(s) used depends upon the type of motion picture produced and upon the type and quantity of camera equipment used.

**3.** The **Director of Photography** and **First Assistant Camera Operator** should each be given sufficient pre-production time to prepare their respective work and/or equipment for the production process.

**F. Category Requirements:** Employees in each Camera Category classification must know and follow the chain-of-command and lines-of-communication and must be able to effectively and safely set up and operate the camera matériel selected for each job and associated with their respective craft classification.

**G. DIRECTOR OF PHOTOGRAPHY**

**1. Sub-Specialties:** There are five (5) sub-specialties of **Director of Photography**:

    **a. First Unit Principal Cinematography: The First Unit DP** is directly responsible to the **Director. Responsibilities** include, but are not limited to, principal photography, using continuity lighting; working in crew strength on studio and/or location production; matching camera direction and lighting values from scene to scene; supervising studio process or other specialized shooting; in charge of, and responsible for, all production cinematography. See **G-2** and **G-3** below, for further listing of responsibilities and duties.

    **b. Documentary** and **Second Unit Cinematography:** When working in crew strength, both the **Documentary and 2nd Unit DP** are directly responsible to the **Director**; or to the **Producer** when working alone. In addition to the **Director of Photography** responsibilities and duties noted under **G-3** below, **specialized responsibilities** and **requirements** include working alone, with light-weight camera equipment, in the following photographic situations:

        **(1)** Where the safety of additional personnel would be jeopardized (hazardous locations or camera positions);

        **(2)** Where photographing the subject matter could be jeopardized by additional personnel in the area (wild life or limited space);

        **(3)** Inserts shooting—run-bys, table-top, environmental cutaways, etc;

        **(4)** Stock footage shooting;

        **(5)** Shooting process plates;

        **(6)** Shooting establishing shots (location).

        ▼ **Responsibilities while shooting in crew strength** include:

        **(7)** Establishing shots with performing doubles (2nd unit location);

        **(8)** Battle, mob and stampede sequences (2nd unit location);

**(9)** Background action for process plates;

**(10)** Documentary productions, as defined in the Glossary.

**c. Aerial Cinematography:** The **Aerial DP** is directly responsible to the **Director. Responsibilities** include working alone or in crew strength while airborne; in immediate charge of all air-to-air and air-to-ground photography, lighting procedures and matériel; and, where space is limited, operating the camera during the mission(s). In addition to the **Director of Photography** responsibilities and duties noted under **G-2** and **G-3** below, **specialized duties** and **requirements** include:

**(1)** Selecting, installing and operating various stabilized camera mounting rigs, whether remotely controlled or manually operated;

**(2)** Wearing a restraining harness while airborne and operating a camera, especially when positioned in an open doorway or hatchway;

**(3)** Safetying, before take-off, all loose matériel to be carried aloft;

**(4)** Thoroughly planning every aspect of each aerial mission with the pilot(s), performers and technicians participating, and then carefully carrying out that plan, exactly;

**(5)** Utilizing voice communication and predetermined hand signals with pilots of subject and object aircraft and talking them through planned maneuvers.

**d. Underwater Cinematography:** The **Underwater DP** is directly responsible to the **Director. Responsibilities** include working alone or in crew strength while under water; in immediate charge of all underwater photography, lighting procedures and matériel; operating the camera during shooting procedures. In addition to the **Director of Photography** responsibilities and duties noted under **G-2** and **G-3** below, **specialized duties** and **requirements** include:

**(1)** Being SCUBA certified;

**(2)** Understanding oceanic surface and underwater conditions, such as weather, current and visibility variations which might occur at the shooting location at any time of day or night during the season;

**(3)** Selecting and thoroughly and carefully preparing and testing the diving gear to be used;

**(4)** Determining the balance, buoyancy and stability of the camera housing for each setup;

**(5)** Selecting, preparing and testing the underwater camera, lighting and sound systems and the effects equipment to be used;

**(6)** Thoroughly planning each dive with those performers and technicians participating, and then carefully and precisely carrying out that plan;

**(7)** Being aware of the refractive effect of light under water and applying that knowledge to the selection of the shooting lens and to a flat or domed lens port, while taking special care with focus;

**(8)** Understanding how reflection, refraction, color absorption and scattering change the nature of light under water and applying that knowledge to camera positioning relative to the subject matter in order to achieve optimum imagery.

e. **Motion Control Cinematography:** The **Motion Control DP** is directly responsible to the **Director** for delivering the visualized shot(s) and to the **Visual Effects Supervisor** for keeping the shot(s) within acceptable visual parameters for CG compositing. **Responsibilities** include working alone or in crew strength while planning, setting up and shooting motion control shots, scenes and sequences. **Specialized duties** and **requirements** include:

**(1)** Ensuring the visual quality of motion-controlled cinematography which is the gathering of multiple elements from exactly the same position in space for different layers of photography;

**(2)** Checking with the **Visual Effects Supervisor** for any pre-viz (pre-visualized) data which should be incorporated into the multiple-pass design;

**(3)** Determining the movement of the principal element in relation to that of the camera, taking into consideration the visual elements and their movement, if any, that must be added to the principal element in the shot for the finished composite;

**(4)** Programming all movement and sweetening and modifying a pass based on imported CG data, suggestions and feedback while determining the type and number of matte passes which are needed by motion control to properly composite the event in order to achieve the desired effect;

**(5)** Breaking the passes down into garbage mattes and matte passes for each of such elements as backgrounds, beauty, lighting, shadows, smoke, haze, star field, clouds, vapor trails, precipitation, weapons firing, missile trajectory, hits and explosions and the like;

**(6)** Determining in what order each matte pass will be shot, what visual elements will be included in the pass and what elements will be matted out;

**(7)** Selecting the appropriate motion control program for the effect;

**(8)** Encoding and inputting the data for computer control and programming the motion and positioning of the elements in the shot using a motion control program;

**(9)** Ensuring that each axis of movement and position of each element in frame as well as that of the camera and camera platform is precisely repeated and tracked for each pass, taking great care that for any given frame of a move during a shot: camera—pan, tilt, roll, focus, zoom; boom—up, down, left, right; track—in, out, left, right; and the model—pan, tilt, roll, track—toward, away, left, right; that every axis will be in exactly the same place on every pass on each frame;

**(10)** Determining the correct exposure for each pass;

**(11)** Executing the individual matte passes in the most effective and expedient order;

**(12)** Exporting the composited shot along with the programmed control data to the Computer Graphics Department for inspection, input and execution of CG work;

2. **Responsibilities:** The **Director of Photography (DP)** is the **First Camera Person**, supervises the technical production personnel, and is directly responsible to the **Director** for the efficient functioning of those categories and classifications under his or her technical direction and for assisting the **Director** in translating the screenplay into visual images, within the creative and budgetary latitude afforded, for optimum aesthetic visual effect.

3. **Duties:**

▼ **During PRE-PRODUCTION:**

**a.** Reading the script and annotating it regarding visual ideas, mood, lighting, special mechanical and/or optical/digital add-on effects and camera moves;

**b.** Scouting all locations and shooting sites;

**c.** Consulting with the **Director, Art Director/Production Designer** and **Producer** regarding production values, matériel and time requirements;

**d.** Conferring with the **Visual Effects Supervisor** regarding CG requirements when scenes involving CGI compositing are planned;

**e.** Maintaining optimum photographic quality of the production;

**f.** Selecting the camera(s), camera accessories and associated equipment to be used;

**g.** Selecting and testing the lenses to be used;

**h.** Selecting and testing the film stock(s) to be used;

**i.** Determining and/or approving the type, quality and quantity of lighting and grip equipment to be used;

**j.** Preparing comparative equipment and materials budgets in support of the type, quality and quantity of camera, lighting and grip equipment requested, if necessary;

**k.** Visually checking, and/or film-testing, sets, settings, scenic art, set dressing, costumes, actors, hair, makeup, props, special effects and process components for photographic purposes;

▼ **During the PRODUCTION Process:**

l. Supervising (directly or indirectly) the crews on each of the cameras in use on the production (first and second units);

m. Working with the **Director** in the general lining up and matching of both action and screen direction, etc, of the shots;

n. Setting the camera positions, angles and moves with the **Director**;

o. Planning and supervising all production lighting—developing the light plot, determining the position of key, fill, back and background lighting units, the lighting ratios, the color and/or degree of diffused quality, if any, of the light, etc;

p. Determining all exposures;

q. Selecting the lens for each shot;

r. Selecting lenticular filtering and diffusion, if any, for each shot;

s. Setting the composition for the **Camera Operator** prior to each take, as necessary;

t. Viewing all dailies and/or cinexes for quality control;

▼ **During PRODUCTION and POST-PRODUCTION:**

u. Supervising the timing of the work and answer prints, and/or of the colorizing and timing of the film transfer to video tape;

v. Otherwise carrying out the duties normally required of this classification;

w. Providing the exposure meters and hand tools normally employed in this craft.

4. **Considerations:**

a. When one (1) or more of the above duties are required, use of a **Director of Photography** is indicated.

b. The **Director of Photography** is normally given adequate pre-production time to plan and prepare for the production work.

c. The **Director of Photography** directs the technical work of the entire crew (first and second units) during the production process.

d. It is highly recommended that the **Director of Photography** be included in pre-production consultation and in any location scouting trips in order to better insure optimum and efficient photographic utilization of the location site(s) and the set(s).

e. It is also highly recommended that the **Director of Photography** be present at the film-to-tape transfer sessions and at film timing sessions for the CRI, prior to release printing.

**H. CAMERA OPERATOR**

1. **Responsibilities:** The **Camera Operator** is the **Second Camera Person** and is directly responsible to the **Director of Photography** for maintaining the

composition, focus and camera movement desired by **Director of Photography** and may reject any take during which the composition, focus (if reflex), or camera moves are deemed to be faulty, or during which any undesired person, object or effect encroaches in the camera frame.

2. **Duties—during PRE-PRODUCTION Film Tests and the PRODUCTION Process:**

   a. Reading the script;

   b. Lining up and insuring proper functioning of the assigned camera, the friction, fluid, geared, or remotely controlled head, and related equipment;

   c. Positioning the dolly seat for optimum position and maximum comfort prior to each static or moving shot;

   d. Adjusting the ocular diopter setting to optimum personal visual focus;

   e. Making sure that a ground glass with appropriately scribed aspect ratio is in place and that the ground glass illuminator, if any, functions properly;

   f. Checking that each fresh load of film has been properly threaded in the camera;

   g. Checking that the buckle switch has been reset and the footage counter has been zeroed with each fresh film load;

   h. Checking that the shutter angle position, T-Stop and frame rate are correctly set prior to each take;

   i. Checking that the proper lens, cam, matte box, matte and view finder, if any, are mounted and correctly positioned prior to each take;

   j. Determining that the front element of the taking lens, including optical flats and filter(s), is properly flagged against any encroaching light which might cause flare;

   k. Checking the lens shade and having the **First Assistant** adjust the lid and/or matte box to clear the widest lens position prior to making the shot;

   l. Operating the camera at all times required, within non-hazardous limits, whether from a static, mobile or remote position, in the studio or on location, above or under either ground or sea, on a moving vehicle or in an airborne or marine craft, on cranes, lifts, hoists, or cable rigs under adverse operational or climatic conditions;

   m. Operating a camera hand-held, or mounted on a Steadicam™ or other stabilizing body mount, in a Pogo-Cam™ or DoggiCam™ configuration, or a camera remotely controlled;

   n. Making sure that the camera is properly racked-over (if of that type) and positioned, ready to expose film prior to each rehearsal and take;

   o. Properly composing, framing and following the subject matter of the shot, as indicated by the **Director** and/or **Director of Photography**;

   p. Discussing and perfecting focus, zoom, frame rate and any T-stop changes with the **First Assistant Camera Operator** during rehearsal(s);

**q.** Discussing and perfecting dolly, crane or boom moves with the **Dolly, Crane** or **Boom Grip**(s) during rehearsal(s);

**r.** Giving the **Boom Operator** safe limits on microphone and/or boom positioning in order to avoid encroachment in frame of this equipment or its shadow(s);

**s.** Giving the **Camera Assistant**, who is ready to slate a sound take, the cue to mark the take when the camera has achieved proper sound speed;

**t.** Advising the **Director** and the **Director of Photography**, immediately following a take, whether or not the take has been satisfactory and, if not, prepared to cite specifically any and all reasons why the take was not satisfactory;

**u.** Wearing an intercom headset and/or protective gear when required to do so on the particular production;

**v.** Otherwise carrying out the duties normally required of this classification;

**w.** Providing the hand tools normally employed in this craft.

**3. Considerations:**

**a.** When one (1) or more of the above duties are required, use of a **Camera Operator** is indicated.

**b.** There is a **Camera Operator** assigned to, and operating, each camera utilized, except for: a locked-off camera; a camera mounted in a fixed housing, on or in a vehicle or other conveyance; or a placed and dedicated stunt camera which is activated remotely.

**I. FIRST ASSISTANT CAMERA OPERATOR [FOCUS-PULLER—FOLLOW-FOCUS PERSON]**

**1. Responsibilities:** The **First Assistant Camera Operator (1st AC) [aka: Focus-Puller—Follow-Focus Person]** is the **Third Camera Person** and is directly responsible to the **Camera Operator** for the appropriate assigned camera and its related equipment being promptly and properly set up and operationally checked for functional reliability; for assisting in any technical operation of the camera; for determining focus distance; for setting the lens stop and adjusting zoom lens sizing for and/or during all takes; for placing designated filtration in the lenticular system; for the designated film stock being promptly and properly labeled and threaded in the camera; for keeping accurate records of the scene takes and expended footage; for coordinating the equipment needs of additional **Camera Assistant**s when additional cameras are required for coverage; and for the camera equipment and film inventory at the start and end of each shooting day, in order to help keep the production process flowing in a smooth and efficient manner.

## 2. Duties:

▼ **During PRE-PRODUCTION:**

**a.** Keeping current with every camera, lens, filter, support and accessory being used in the business;

**b.** Reading and annotating the script from a camera equipment perspective;

**c.** Checking the camera equipment list as prepared by the **Director of Photography**;

**d.** Prepping all camera equipment prior to pick-up from the supplier, insuring that all ordered equipment is operational and accounted for;

▼ **During the PRODUCTION Process:**

**e.** Sending camera equipment back to the supplier when no longer needed, or for replacement when faulty or damaged;

**f.** Checking the Call Sheet each afternoon for the list of scenes to be shot the following day and, with the concurrence of the **DP** and **UPM**, ordering any camera equipment needed;

**g.** Unpacking, assembling, inventorying (before and after use), adjusting, dis-assembling and packing the assigned camera and its associated equipment;

**h.** Checking the dust mattes, if any, for open position and the ground glass for proper aspect ratio scribe lines and positioning in the ocular system;

**i.** Checking all variable controls and settings on the camera to insure the proper operation and setting of each;

**j.** Checking each lens and optical accessory for damage and cleanliness, and each lens for proper seating, focus and operational functioning;

**k.** Seeing that the friction, geared or remotely controlled head is firmly installed on the camera mount and is fully and freely operative; that the camera is properly mounted, balanced, clean, oiled and operative; that the proper motors (camera, zoom lens, iris and/or focus), and controls therefor, are in place and connected to the proper electrical current, warmed up and ready to function;

**l.** Field maintaining of the camera and its associated equipment;

**m.** Placing a barney on the camera when needed;

**n.** Installing the camera and/or lens in a blimp when required;

**o.** Placing a loaded film magazine on the camera, threading film carefully in the transport mechanism, checking film loops and perforations for proper flow movement, and adjusting the pitch control to reduce internal camera noise; thereafter, unthreading the film and removing the exposed magazine from the camera;

**p.** Resetting the buckle switch;

**q.** Setting the footage counter to zero with each fresh film load;

**r.** Keeping the camera lenses (both ends) and filters (both sides) clean and properly positioned in or on the camera;

**s.** Seeing that the proper follow-focus cams, if any, are in place to conform the parallax viewfinder, if any, to the taking lens;

**t.** Seeing that the viewfinder is properly positioned and the mattes and viewfinder lens, if any, are set to conform to the taking lens;

**u.** Cleaning, placing and replacing filters, gauzes, diopters, lenticular and ocular extension tubes, mattes and registration frames in the lenticular system, as required;

**v.** Checking the front element of the taking lens, including front filter(s), in order to insure that no back or "kicker" lights, or light reflections, are causing flare;

**w.** Setting and/or checking the T-stop (which is received only from the **Director of Photography**) prior to each take;

**x.** Taping distances to subject matter from the camera film plane and setting lens focus marks and zoom lens position marks;

**y.** Marking floor positions of actors with chalk or tape, and exterior ground positions with "T"s during blocking and for rehearsals, removing marks for takes, as necessary;

**z.** Utilizing a small video receiver, mounted on the left side of the lens and feeding it directly off the video tap in the camera, in order to monitor frame composition and sizing;

**aa.** Sizing the zoom lens so that the slate is large and legible in the frame during the slating process;

**ab.** After setting the proper frame rate, checking the frame rate readout at the beginning, during, and near the end of each take to ensure that the camera is running, and running at speed;

**ac.** Following focus and making zoom lens sizing moves during rehearsals and takes;

**ad.** Referring to a depth of field chart when questions arise concerning splitting and maintaining focus between a foreground and background subject;

**ae.** When not required to follow focus during a take, and a wild (variable speed) camera motor is being used, riding the adjustable control on the camera motor to keep it at the desired frame rate on the tachometer, or riding the control on the variable shutter, or changing T-stops, or sliding the graduated color-correction, diffusion or neutral density filter when such operations are required during a take;

CAMERA

**af.** Periodically (particularly following each print take) pulling and checking the film gate for emulsion buildup or dust, sand or hair particles;

**ag.** Keeping Camera Reports, logging each take and its expended footage, and all technical notations which the **Director of Photography** may require;

**ah.** Physically carrying the camera and tripod to another nearby setup, making sure that the tripod legs are securely positioned and locked off, and that the camera is level;

**ai.** Supervising the transportation of the camera and its associated equipment;

**aj.** Seeing that all camera batteries are properly charged and operative;

**ak.** Carrying out the duties of the **Second Assistant Camera Operator** when employment of a **Second Assistant** is not required;

**al.** Assisting in any technical operation of the camera(s) during the process of synchonizing the camera to 24 fps, to video monitors, or to a process projector, or when installing cueing apparatus on the camera;

**am.** Upon wrapping, assembling all camera equipment, checking to be sure all rented elements are present and accounted for against the check out list from the vendor, and seeing that the equipment is returned to the vendor;

**an.** Otherwise carrying out the duties normally required of this classification;

**ao.** Providing the hand tools normally employed in this craft.

▼ **For Aerial Camera Work**:

**ap.** Setting up beside the aircraft, and balancing the camera support rig, with a loaded film camera attached, on all axes;

**aq.** Removing door(s) and/or hatch cover(s) and seats from the aircraft, with the permission, and under the supervision, of the **Pilot** of the aircraft;

**ar.** Incrementally breaking down and installing the interior camera mount in the aircraft, checking and adjusting the balance and tension modes, as necessary;

**as.** Seeing that the camera is connected to a power source and is fully functional in all control systems and that the gyro group, if any, is activated;

**at.** Seeing that the **Aerial Cinematographer** or **Camera Operator** is comfortable and securely safetied in position on the mount, and that light meters and loaded film magazines will be secure and readily accessible during the flight;

**au.** Installing an exterior mount for a remotely controlled rig, under the supervision, and with the approval, of a licensed aeronautic mechanic;

**av.** Operating the focus, sizing or ramping controls when the **Camera Operator** requires such assistance;

**aw.** At the completion of each job assignment, removing interior and/or exterior mounts and camera gear and restoring the aircraft doors, hatches and seats under the supervision of the pilot and/or licensed aeronautical mechanic.

▼ **For Underwater Camera Work:**

**ax.** Setting up, on land or deck, underwater camera rigs, installing a loaded camera in the housing, and checking that all control systems are fully functional;

**ay.** Assisting the **Underwater Cinematographer** in getting into SCUBA gear and into the water;

**az.** Handing the fully prepped underwater camera housing to the **Underwater Cinematographer;**

**ba.** Upon completion of a dive, receiving the underwater camera housing from the **Underwater Cinematographer;**

**bb.** Carefully opening the housing, removing exposed film from the camera, loading fresh film for the next dive and closing the housing;

**bc.** Having a backup rig ready to go;

**bd.** After each day's work, washing and removing all salt water and residue from equipment surfaces and thoroughly drying and cleaning the equipment and accessories, as needed.

**3. Considerations:**

**a.** When one (1) or more of the above duties are required, use of a **First Assistant Camera Operator** is indicated.

**b.** A **First Assistant Camera Operator** is employed on all productions which are shooting synchronous sound using clap-sticks, whereon the **Camera Operator** is using geared or remote head camera control, or body stabilizing devices, and following focus is required.

**c.** A **First Assistant Camera Operator** is employed for each camera used, except that when more than one (1) fixed, housed, or tied-off camera is used, fewer than this number of **1st AC**s may be used.

**J. SECOND ASSISTANT CAMERA OPERATOR [SLATER—CLAPPER PERSON]**

**1. Responsibilities:** The **Second Assistant Camera Operator (2nd AC)** [aka: Slater—Clapper Person] is the **Fourth Camera Person,** is directly responsible to the **First Assistant Camera Operator** and is responsible for seeing that a sufficient number of film magazines are loaded and ready before helping the **First Assistant** set up and check out camera equipment, thereafter slating—insuring proper visual and audial identification of—each take.

**2. Duties—all during the PRODUCTION Process:**

**a.** Checking with the **Loader** and insuring that sufficient film magazines, loaded with the appropriate emulsion(s), are ready and appropriately labeled—film type and footage—and with a Camera Report form attached thereto;

**b.** Helping the **First Assistant Camera Operator** set up and check out camera equipment—lenses; camera motors; optical accessories; variable adjustments; friction, geared and remote heads, etc;

**c.** Preparing the camera slate, noting thereon: The **Production Company; Production Title** and/or **number; Director; Cinematographer; date**; and **take number** for each take: Whether day, night or day-for-night type shot; interior or exterior; sound or MOS; special filtration or lighting notes; frame rate or shutter variations; information for the laboratory, **Picture Editor** and Production Company or for purposes of other specific documentation;

**d.** Receiving the upcoming scene number from the **Script Supervisor** and entering the number on the camera slate and on the Camera Report;

**e.** Slating all scenes for the camera(s), whether sound or MOS takes;

**f.** Presenting the slate to the camera(s) in a timely manner and place which is in line with the shot angle(s) and does not require the **Camera Operator**(s) to search for it;

**g.** When the **First Assistant** is following focus during a take and a wild motor is being used, riding the adjustable control on the camera motor to keep it at the desired frame rate on the tachometer, and/or riding the shutter angle control, or the T-stop, or the zoom control, when required;

**h.** Assisting the **First Assistant Camera Operator** in setting up, checking and wrapping camera equipment;

**i.** Handling cable when a hard-wired video assist tap is used on a camera;

**j.** Making film end-tests, as necessary;

**k.** Placing all exposed film magazines in their cases and seeing that exposed film mags are delivered to the **Loader** for down-loading and delivery to the lab;

**l.** Preparing orders for film stock, equipment and supplies;

**m.** Receiving all film stock, equipment and supplies and directing them to the appropriate camera craft person;

**n.** Getting refreshments or tools, taking or making needed phone calls, for the **Director of Photography, Camera Operator** and/or **First Assistant** when the persons holding these classifications are too involved to do this for themselves;

**o.** Otherwise carrying out the duties normally required of this classification;

**p.** Providing the hand tools normally employed in this craft.

**3. Optional Duties:** The **Second Assistant** may be given the duty of keeping Camera Reports, provided it does not interfere with the prime duties above outlined.

**4. Considerations:**

    **a.** A **Second Assistant Camera Operator** is employed on all multiple-camera productions.

    **b.** A **Second Assistant Camera Operator** is employed on all productions not requiring a **Loader**.

    **c.** A **Second Assistant Camera Operator** is employed on all productions employing synchronous sound.

## K. LOADER

**1. Responsibilities:** The **Loader** is the **Fifth Camera Person**, is directly responsible to the **Second Assistant Camera Operator** and is responsible for promptly and properly loading and downloading film magazines with the appropriate film stock, properly labeling all loaded magazines and cans of exposed and unexposed film stock, and keeping accurate records of exposed and unexposed film.

**2. Duties—all during the PRODUCTION Process:**

    **a.** Receiving raw film stock and camera supplies from the **Producer, Unit Production Manager**, or from the designated Company Representative;

    **b.** Keeping up-to-date inventory on all film raw stock and exposed camera original film;

    **c.** Loading and downloading the film magazines;

    **d.** Placing identifying tapes on the film magazines and cans of exposed film (company, production title or number, roll number, magazine number, emulsion number and amount of footage on each roll);

    **e.** Preparing the exposed film for shipment and/or delivery to the film lab;

    **f.** Repackaging and properly labeling all film short-ends;

    **g.** Delivering the exposed film and short-ends, along with appropriate copies of the Camera Reports, to the **Producer** or the designated Company Representative;

    **h.** Preparing orders for film raw stock and loading supplies;

    **i.** Otherwise carrying out the duties normally required of this classification;

    **j.** Providing the hand tools normally employed in this craft.

**3. Considerations:** A **Loader** is used on each multi-camera production and on those productions where excessive loading, slating, camera equipment and/or multiple camera adjustments during a take are necessary, during which the **Second Assistant Camera Operator** requires assistance.

## L. PROCESS PROJECTIONIST

**1. Responsibilities:** The **Process Projectionist** is directly responsible to the **Director of Photography** for the proper axial alignment and synchronization of the front or rear process projector with the camera and for maintaining

**CAMERA**

the desired framing, focus, stability and illumination level of the projected image on the process screen in order to help assure optimum photographic results therefrom.

**2. Duties—all during the PRODUCTION Process:**

   **a.** Setting up, properly positioning (as specified) and assuring proper functioning of the process projector, screen and related equipment;

   **b.** Assisting the **First Assistant Camera Operator** in interlocking the process projector with the camera to insure proper synchronization and alignment;

   **c.** Setting the projector at the proper frame rate and making any other adjustments thereto as may be necessary or required;

   **d.** Setting the projector shutter angle at the proper position and making fades as may be required;

   **e.** Maintaining the projector arc or lamp at the proper overall brilliance on the process screen, adjusting the power supplied and/or placing filters in the projector to eliminate a hot center, as necessary, or as directed by the **Director of Photography**;

   **f.** Assuring uniform quality and desired color temperature of the film image on the process screen;

   **g.** Standing by and operating the process projector at all times, as required;

   **h.** Rewinding the process film plate and threading or unthreading film in the projector, as required;

   **i.** Striking the process projector, the screen and related gear;

   **j.** Otherwise carrying out the duties normally required of this classification;

   **k.** Providing the hand tools normally employed in this craft.

**3. Considerations:** A **Process Projectionist** is used when any front or rear projection of slides or motion picture film is required in conjunction with the photography of live action.

## M. STILL PHOTOGRAPHER

**1. Responsibilities:** The **Still Photographer** is directly responsible to the **Director of Photography** when working as a member of the production crew, otherwise, to the Employer, or the **Film Publicist**, and is responsible for obtaining adequate still photographic coverage of the production, personnel or events associated with the production or Company, desired by the **Producer** or the authorized agent.

**2. Duties—during PRE-PRODUCTION, PRODUCTION and POST-PRODUCTION:**

   **a.** Reading the script, if applicable;

   **b.** Shooting all production, publicity or record stills required by the production (i.e., those requested by the **Producer**, **Director**, **Script Supervisor**,

**Art Director/Production Designer**, **Set Decorator**, **Prop Master**, **Key Wardrobe**, **Key Makeup Artist**, **Key Hairdresser** or **Publicist**);

**c.** Determining the type of film, still camera(s) and related equipment to be utilized, and being duly compensated for use of personal matériel;

**d.** Working in cooperation with camera, electrical and grip personnel while shooting film on the active set or production site;

**e.** Using blimped still cameras when working during sound takes;

**f.** Supervising all lighting for still filming purposes off the set or location site and in the still studio or elsewhere;

**g.** Determining and setting exposure, focus, shutter speed and composition;

**h.** Keeping Camera Reports, captions, personal releases, etc;

**i.** Processing and printing exposed film or delivering film to the still lab for processing and printing;

**j.** Otherwise carrying out the duties normally required of this classification;

**k.** Providing exposure meters and hand tools normally employed in this craft.

**3. Considerations:**

**a.** A **Still Photographer** is used to shoot any production, publicity or record stills of whatever nature required during pre-production, production and/or post-production.

**b.** A **Still Photographer** is duly compensated for providing personal camera gear, lighting equipment and film for an assignment.

**N. ASSISTANT STILL PHOTOGRAPHER**

**1. Responsibilities and Duties—during PRE-PRODUCTION, PRODUCTION and POST-PRODUCTION:** The **Assistant Still Photographer** is directly responsible to the **Still Photographer** and assists in the setting up and wrapping process where and when the amount and type of still camera equipment, or the nature of the job, requires additional personnel to safely, properly and efficiently handle and staff such equipment and assignment.

**2. Considerations:** An **Assistant Still Photographer** does not operate still cameras.

▼ **Classifications Used for SPECIALIZED Camera Work**▼

**O. NEWS CINEMATOGRAPHER**

**1. Responsibilities:** The **News Cinematographer** is directly responsible to the Employer, or to the news **Director**, if one is assigned, for providing efficient and adequate photographic coverage of an event and for the technical quality of the image on film.

**2. Duties—during ASSIGNMENTS:**

**a.** The selection, positioning and proper functioning of the camera and related equipment;

**b.** Selection of the film stock;

**c.** Loading and downloading film magazines and labeling them;

**d.** Threading and unthreading film in the camera;

**e.** Applying filters to the camera, as needed;

**f.** Using cameras designed for hand-held or light tripod use;

**g.** Operating cameras designed for single system sound, handling the photographic operation only;

**h.** Determining and setting proper composition, exposure and focus;

**i.** Lighting the shot(s) only with portable battery-powered lighting equipment;

**j.** Keeping Camera Reports and Caption Records;

**k.** Preparing film for shipment;

**l.** Otherwise carrying out the duties normally required of this classification;

**m.** Providing the hand tools normally employed in this craft.

**3. Limitations:** The **News Cinematographer** may not:

**a.** Operate sound equipment of either single or double system type;

**b.** Set multiple stand lights requiring AC or DC power tie-in;

**c.** Operate cameras not designed for hand-held or light tripod use;

**d.** Handle any other function specifically or normally assigned to other categories or classifications.

**4. Considerations:**

**a.** A **News Cinematographer** does not function as a production **Cinematographer**.

**b.** **News Cinematographer**s may be employed on news-gathering type assignments when the above responsibilities and duties are applicable, otherwise other classifications of Camera Category and appropriate personnel of other categories will be used.

## P. OPTICAL PRINTER OPERATOR

**1. Responsibilities:** The **Optical Printer Operator** is directly responsible to the Employer (unless the **Director** or **Director of Photography** or **Picture Editor** is supervising the work, in which event the responsibility is placed with such individual) for efficiently preparing the optical units and rephotographing these units, combined with the original photography, in accordance with the Exposure (or Count) Sheet in a manner best suited for optimum visual realization of this material.

**2. Duties—as a STAFF Job:**

**a.** Setting up, operating and wrapping the optical printer—camera and projector—and related accessories and associated equipment;

**b.** Loading, identifying and downloading all film magazines utilized;

**c.** Changing the lens(es), film movement, gate(s) and drive mechanism(s) in the optical printer in conformance with the film stock and procedure to be used;

**d.** Threading film print elements in the projector and/or in the camera, as required, along with the raw stock, bipacking, as necessary, and unthreading the exposed film;

**e.** Positioning all art work and other elements to be photographed;

**f.** Setting lighting units and placing controls thereon, as necessary;

**g.** Placing selected filters in the projector lamp house and/or in the optical system of the printer;

**h.** Determining and setting exposure, focus, shutter angle and frame rate;

**i.** Installing lenses, aspect mattes, filters, diopters and diffusion in the optical system of the printer, as appropriate;

**j.** Following the instructions in the Exposure (or Count) Sheet for the optical effects specified;

**k.** Setting and controlling all camera and projector—aerial and/or main—movements;

**l.** Preparing all pre-ops (preparatory) material—high contrast matte work, etc—in the building of film units for compositing with camera original material;

**m.** Setting the automatic follow-focus cam on moving shots;

**n.** Setting the footage-frame counters;

**o.** Accomplishing all specified fades, dissolves, wipes, zooms, camera moves, oil dissolves, soft or out-of-focus effects, reverse action, flips, spins, flow-ups, reductions, turn-over dupes, optical cuts, hold frame(s), supers, matted and double-matted supers, title burn-ins, shot repositions, shot pushes, skip frame(s), split screens, registrations, film wedges, unsqueezing and scanning anamorphic material, rotoscoping, traveling mattes, streaks/smears, slit-scans, etc;

**p.** Periodically checking for and trouble-shooting mechanical malfunctions in the optical printer;

**q.** Insuring the cleanliness of the optical system in the optical printer at all times, checking the system after each run or after a maximum of 1,000 feet of film has run through the optical printer;

**r.** Installing and adjusting the liquid gate, setting the pressure dial and maintaining constant pressure and flow through the liquid gate during its use;

**s.** Preparing—canning and labeling—all exposed film stock for shipment to the film laboratory;

**t.** Canning and labeling all short ends;

**u.** Viewing all dailies;

CAMERA

**v.** Otherwise carrying out the duties normally required of this classification;

**w.** Providing the hand tools normally employed in this craft.

**3. Considerations:** An **Optical Printer Operator** is used on all jobs utilizing optical printing procedures and equipment.

## Q. LINE-UP TECHNICIAN

**1. Responsibilities:** The **Line-up Technician** is directly responsible to the **Optical Printer Operator** for the preparation of the Exposure or Count Sheet and for the clarity and logic thereof.

**2. Duties—as a STAFF Job:**

**a.** Preparation of the Exposure, or Count, Sheet from information and specifications supplied by the **Picture Editor**, for the use of the **Optical Printer Operator** in the compositing of dupe negative picture elements and/or the rephotographing of original picture elements;

**b.** Checking the exposure sheet before giving it to the **Optical Printer Operator**;

**c.** Noting all optical effects, the duration of each effect in footage and frames, and the roll and edge numbers involved in the length of each effect;

**d.** Viewing all dailies for quality control and conformance to the exposure sheet;

**e.** Otherwise carrying out the duties normally required of this classification;

**f.** Providing the hand tools normally employed in this craft.

**3. Considerations:** A **Line-up Technician** is the customer contact person and is used when optical printer effects are to be utilized in a production.

## R. ANIMATION CAMERA OPERATOR

**1. Responsibilities:** The **Animation Camera Operator** is directly responsible to the Employer for the proper functioning and alignment of the animation camera and related equipment, the proper placement and sequencing of images and the movement thereof, and the photographic quality of the subject material.

**2. Duties—as a STAFF Job:**

**a.** The preparation and maintenance of the animation camera and its accessories, the camera crane, animation stand and table, and all associated material;

**b.** Testing and aligning the camera, crane, stand and table;

**c.** Selecting, loading, downloading and canning film, marking proper identification on magazines and film cans and sending the exposed film to the film lab for processing;

**d.** Threading and unthreading film in the animation camera;

**e.** Setting and adjusting the footage-frame counter;

**f.** Selecting and installing lenses on the camera and filters, diopters, extension tubes and diffusion in the optical system;

**g.** Setting, trimming and adjusting the lights and lighting-control accessories;

**h.** Placing and aligning the art work;

**i.** Setting the focus and/or tying in the automatic follow-focus cam on moving shots;

**j.** Setting and/or operating the variable shutter angle for fades and dissolves;

**k.** Determining exposure and setting the T-stop;

**l.** Computing and/or setting the frame rate and/or the movement of the camera and/or the subject material;

**m.** Slating or otherwise identifying each run or take;

**n.** Following the Bar or Exposure Sheet instructions (as prepared by the **Animation Editor**) during all filming;

**o.** Placing and aligning and otherwise properly registering the cels, objects or projected aerial images in the field of view on the animation table, shadow board and/or at the camera film plane;

**p.** Determining and adjusting the position and movement of the camera, zoom lens and subject material with each exposure, as specified;

**q.** Accomplishing all required fades, dissolves, wipes, zooms, reverses and scratch-offs, flips, spins, multiple exposures, split screens, title burnins, etc, with the camera in forward or reverse mode, a frame at a time;

**r.** Keeping the Camera Log;

**s.** Insuring the cleanliness of the camera, lenses and optical accessories, platen and cels at all times, and checking the system after each run;

**t.** Periodically checking for and trouble-shooting mechanical malfunctions in the animation camera and stand;

**u.** Otherwise carrying out the duties normally required of this classification;

**v.** Providing exposure meters and hand tools normally employed in this craft.

**3. Considerations:** An **Animation Camera Operator** is used on those jobs utilizing animation camera procedures and equipment.

### S. ANIMATION CHECKER

**1. Responsibilities and Duties—as a STAFF Job:** The **Animation Checker** is directly responsible to, and assists, the **Animation Camera Operator**, when the shooting schedule or complexity of the animation filming require this assistance, particularly the checking of cel, camera, stand and table positions against the Bar or Exposure Sheet and the keeping of a Camera Log during the filming procedures.

2. **Considerations:** An **Animation Checker**, used when the **Animation Camera Operator** requires assistance, does not operate the animation camera, table, stand, or the lighting units.

# Lighting Category Organizational Chart

▼ Production ▼

▼ Rigging ▼

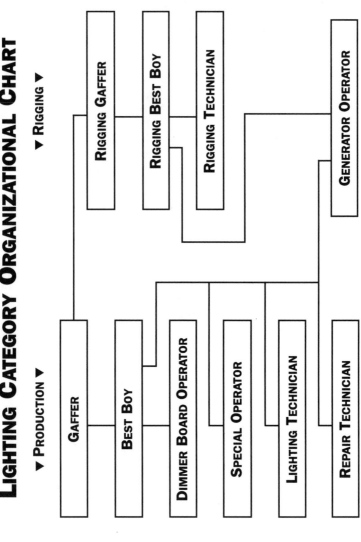

# 5

# LIGHTING CATEGORY

**A. Category Classifications:** There are ten (10) classifications in the Lighting Category:

▼ **For Production Procedures:**

1. **Chief Lighting Technician [Gaffer] (Category Head)**
2. **Assistant Chief Lighting Technician [Best Boy] (Category Sub-Head)**
3. **Dimmer Board Operator**
4. **Special Operator**
5. **Lighting Technician**
6. **Repair Technician**

▼ **for Rigging Procedures:**

7. **Rigging Gaffer (Category Sub-Head)**
8. **Rigging Best Boy**
9. **Rigging Technician**

▼ **For Production and Rigging Procedures:**

10. **Generator Operator**

**B. Category Criteria:**

1. Employees holding classification within the Lighting Category perform all job functions pertaining to cinematographic electrical lighting procedures which are utilized on interior or exterior production, airborne or underwater, on location and/or on the sound stage.

2. All lighting personnel need to know knot-tying techniques as well as electrical circuitry and the laws that govern electricity, its behavior and all safety factors involved in its use.

3. A **Gaffer** is used on a set or location where cinematographic electrical lighting procedures are utilized, and is in charge of the technical procedures pertaining thereto, as directed by the **Director of Photography**.

4. A **Gaffer** needs to know and apply: Electrical circuitry and balancing the power demand on each leg of the tie-in; the output, lighting quality and coverage pattern of every lighting unit made, their power requirements, their size and weight; how to efficiently, effectively and safely plan and tie in lighting units to a dimmer board.

**LIGHTING**

5. The number of **Lighting Technicians** to be used is determined by the **Producer**, within the parameters of the collective bargaining agreement under which the aforementioned classifications are covered, taking into consideration the requirements needed to safely, effectively and efficiently complete their tasks, such as:

   a. The quantity, weight and type of lighting and electrical equipment and material to be used;

   b. The number, complexity and location(s) of lighting set-ups;

   c. The duration and pace of the shooting schedule.

6. In figuring lighting crew size, it is recommended that on each day of shooting, when studio-type lamps of more than two thousand (2,000) watts capacity each are used, a **Gaffer** and **Best Boy** be employed. One (1) **Technician** should operate (elevate, pan, tilt, set, focus, install diffusion and trim) each arc light. A **Gaffer** and **Best Boy** should be employed in the event a set is lighted by units placed both on the floor and off the floor—on sets, perms, catwalks, greenbeds or grids. When lighting units are attached to and accessible from perms, catwalks, greenbeds or parallels, at least one (1) **Technician** should remain on the floor with the **Gaffer** and as many other **Technicians** above and/or on the floor as may be effectively used. These considerations are in recognition of the physical task of safely, effectively and efficiently handling such equipment.

7. When the **Gaffer** requires assistance in setting up, placing, safetying, numbering, moving, operating or breaking down and wrapping lighting equipment, a **Best Boy** is used.

8. When the **Gaffer** and **Best Boy** require assistance in their duties, one (1) or more **Lighting Technicians** are used, as needed.

9. When arc lights, follow-spot lights or handheld lights are used on a production, a **Special Operator** is assigned to each such unit.

10. When extensive lighting circuitry and/or lighting changes are required, as for sitcoms, the designated circuitry with numbered lamps, on a separate dimmer, is run through a dimmer board; a **Dimmer Board Operator** then activates the appropriate circuitry and controls the intensity of the lighting.

11. When mobile electrical generating equipment is utilized, a **Generator Operator** is used to operate such equipment.

12. All Lighting Category personnel will endeavor to use hand signals and/or communicate via RF headsets whenever possible during lighting procedures in order to help maintain a quiet and efficient operation.

13. A lighting rigging crew consists of a **Rigging Gaffer**, **Rigging Best Boy** and sufficient **Rigging Technician**s in order to safely and efficiently install lamps and cable runs on scaffolding, perms, greenbeds, sets and/or grids.

LIGHTING

**14.** During rigging procedures, and anytime a lamp is installed overhead on the set, on greenbeds, or on pipe grids, each lamp and the barn door or snoot assembly attached thereto must be securely safetied at that time and at all times while mounted.

**15.** It is recommended that for all location and studio productions requiring artificial lighting, the **Gaffer** be employed for one (1) preliminary conference and/or survey, with the **Director of Photography**, to enable the **Gaffer** to scout and become familiar with the location(s), the electrical supply and outlets, sets and set sketches, etc, in order to determine, with agreement of the **Director of Photography**, the amount and type of electrical and associated grip equipment required to handle and facilitate the job.

**16.** All Lighting personnel operating underwater with breathing apparatus must be SCUBA certified.

**17.** The **Gaffer** and each Lighting Category Sub-Head must ensure that lighting personnel do not attempt work under any unsafe condition(s), as specified by the Employer, OSHA, Building and Safety Code and fire laws, or in violation of any other safety regulation(s) and practice(s).

**C. Category Responsibilities:** It is the responsibility of each Employee in the Lighting Category to work cooperatively with the **Gaffer** in order to assist in achieving a safe, optimum and efficient operation during all lighting procedures.

**D. Category Function:** The principal function of Lighting Category personnel involves procedures with production lighting equipment and its various applications pertaining to the placement, safetying, control and operation thereof.

**E. Category Considerations:**

**1.** Lighting Category personnel are used on each production on which production lighting equipment, methods and techniques are used.

**2.** The classification(s) used depends upon the type and quantity of electrical and lighting equipment used.

**3. Set Lighting Technician**s used on rigging procedures, during production, may at times function on production procedures as well, when such procedures are minimal and take place as part of production procedures and duties.

**F. Category Requirements:** Employees in each Lighting Category classification must know and follow the chain-of-command and lines-of-communication and must be able to effectively and safely set up and operate the electrical and lighting equipment selected for each job and associated with their respective craft classification.

▼ **Classification Used During PRODUCTION PROCEDURES** ▼

**G. CHIEF LIGHTING TECHNICIAN [GAFFER]**

**1. Responsibilities:** The **Chief Lighting Technician (CLT)**, the **Gaffer**, is directly responsible to the **Director of Photography** for supervising an efficient operation of the electrical lighting crew in order to expedite lighting the set in a manner directed, and for the balance desired, by the **Director of Photography**.

**2. Duties:**

▼ **During PRE-PRODUCTION:**

a. Reading and annotating the script within the context of lighting and electrical requirements—luminaries and globes, stands and mounting devices, cable, connectors, power sources, scrims, diffusion, gels;

b. Scouting and/or reviewing scouting reports of location sites and stage sets in order to determine, with the consent and accord of the **Director of Photography**, the type and amount of electrical and lighting equipment required to service the production;

c. Answering to the **Unit Production Manager** with regard to the set lighting budget and staffing requirements;

d. Preparing and submitting instrument schedules and lighting plots for rigging purposes;

e. Ordering lighting and electrical support equipment and expendables;

▼ **During the PRODUCTION Process:**

f. Supervising the loading, transportation and unloading of all lighting equipment;

g. Supervising the bulbing, assembling, repair (as necessary), rigging, numbering lamps for dimmer board circuitry, operating and striking of all lighting equipment;

h. Supervising all hot main-line electrical connections;

i. Supervising the balancing of load on the respective feed legs of the power source;

j. Consulting with the **Director of Photography** prior to each lighting set-up in order to determine the selection and placement of lighting units; the quality, color, intensity at the light-beam interruption points and spread of the light from each unit; and the appropriate light level and balance on the background, midground, foreground and on the actors, as specified by the **Director of Photography**;

k. Instructing **Lighting Technician**s to place light modifying materials— scrims, diffusion, patterns and/or gels—in specified lamps, along with adjusting the degree, or spread, of light coverage—flood or spot—in order to control the color, scatter, intensity and spread of the light emitted from each instrument;

l. Supervising set lighting personnel during all lighting procedures, using RF communications and/or hand signals as much as possible in order to help maintain a quiet operation;

m. Making certain that each area of the set or setting is receiving the proper amount and quality of light and with the appropriate balance which the **Director of Photography** has specified;

**n.** During each take, carefully observing the lighting set-up for burn-outs, lamps not turned on or properly focused on the action, lamps turned on which should not be on, slippage in lamp setting, and boom shadows;

**o.** Standing by the **Director of Photography** for light-modifying instructions during rehearsals and takes;

**p.** Seeing that lamps are turned off when not required for photographic purposes and that all incandescent bulbs are periodically rotated to mini- mize color changes and burn-outs;

**q.** Periodically checking operating lamps for proper color temperature output;

**r.** Maintaining, repairing and modifying all cable and lighting equipment during production, as necessary;

**s.** Otherwise carrying out the duties normally required of this classification;

**t.** Providing the gloves and hand tools normally employed in this craft, including a volt/ohm/ammeter and exposure meter.

**3. Considerations:** A **Gaffer** is used when a production utilizes augmentative lighting.

## H. ASSISTANT CHIEF LIGHTING TECHNICIAN [BEST BOY]

**1. Responsibilities:** The **Assistant Chief Lighting Technician (ACLT)**, or **Best Boy**, is directly responsible to the **Gaffer** and expedites procedures per- formed by the lighting crew.

**2. Duties—all during the PRODUCTION Process:**

**a.** Reading the script;

**b.** Supervising rigging and striking procedures for the **Gaffer**;

**c.** Making all hot main-line electrical connections during production procedures;

**d.** Balancing the load on the respective feed legs of the power source dur- ing production procedures;

**e.** Coding and tying off all cable runs;

**f.** Making connections to all spiders during production procedures;

**g.** Insuring that each lamp, its barndoor and/or snoot assembly are safetied as it is installed overhead on pipe grids, green beds or set headers;

**h.** Supervising the installation of lighting units on mobile platforms and the power cable runs thereto;

**i.** Operating mobile lamps;

**j.** Seeing that all unemployed cable is coiled and stored clear of the set along with all non-employed lamps;

**k.** Assisting the **Gaffer** in the performance of electrical procedures;

**l.** Otherwise carrying out the duties normally required of this classification;

**m.** Providing the gloves and hand tools normally employed in this craft, carrying these items on one's person while working.

**3. Considerations:** A **Best Boy** is the first **Lighting Technician** employed to assist the **Gaffer**.

## I. DIMMER BOARD OPERATOR

**1. Responsibilities:** The **Dimmer Board Operator** is directly responsible to the **Gaffer** for bringing the intensity of stage lights up or down, or remotely controlling color gel wheels, or pivoting light sources upon command of the **Gaffer** or on cue, during rehearsals and takes.

**2. Duties—all during the PRODUCTION Process:**

**a.** Reading the script;

**b.** Making notation in the script where light changes requested by the **Director of Photography** occur;

**c.** Making and checking connections of the set lighting circuits to the appropriate channels in the dimmer control board, under the supervision of the **Gaffer** or **Best Boy**;

**d.** Placing a number, corresponding to the number appearing on each mounted lamp, on the respective control board circuit dimmer channel, or switch, for each lamp on that circuit;

**e.** Placing a scene number for each lighting setup;

**f.** Marking the script for exact timing of light changes along with the intensity levels of particular instruments;

**g.** Preparing a lighting cue sheet designating the particular set, time of day, light change(s), and circuits involved;

**h.** Bringing the lights up on cue on the specific set, at the appropriate intensity, for the time of day or night, or effect, required;

**i.** Otherwise carrying out the duties normally required of this classification;

**j.** Providing the hand tools normally employed in this craft.

**3. Considerations:** The **Dimmer Board Operator** handles all dimmer board console control procedures.

## J. SPECIAL OPERATOR

**1. Responsibilities:** The **Special Operator** is directly responsible to the **Gaffer** and **Best Boy** for operating an arc light, follow-spot light or handheld light in an accurate, safe, and efficient manner at all times.

**2. Duties—all during the PRODUCTION Process:**

**a.** Setting up, operating and striking the assigned special lighting instruments, such as arcs, follow spots or handheld lighting units required for each set-up;

**b.** Placing the proper gel, scrim, pattern and/or diffusion on the lighting unit, as specified by the **Director of Photography** or **Gaffer**;

**c.** In operating an arc light unit—positioning, elevating, panning, tilting, focusing, installing and adjusting carbons, trimming and installing gels, scrims, shutters and diffusion, as directed by the **Director of Photography** or **Gaffer**;

**d.** In operating a follow-spot unit—positioning, elevating, panning, tilting, focusing, installing bulbs, gels, scrims, shutters, color gel wheels and diffusion, as directed by the **Director of Photography** or **Gaffer** and keeping the light beam at the proper spread and trained upon the assigned subject matter at all times, whether static or moving;

**e.** In operating a handheld unit—installing in the lighting unit the gels, scrims and diffusion required by the **Director of Photography** or **Gaffer** and moving with the assigned subject matter, keeping the light trained upon the assigned subject matter at all required times;

**f.** Otherwise carrying out the duties normally required of this classification;

**g.** Providing the hand tools normally employed in this craft.

**3.** **Considerations: Special Operator**s operate all lighting units which are assigned to follow specific subject matter or action, or are moved or adjusted during a shot.

## K. LIGHTING TECHNICIAN

**1. Responsibilities:** The **Lighting Technician** is directly responsible to the **Gaffer**, or to the **Best Boy** when the **Gaffer** has given the **Best Boy** such authority, and assists the **Gaffer** and **Best Boy** in the performance of their duties, and in so doing will remain ever alert for hand signals from the **Gaffer** and **Best Boy** for lighting modifications, in order to maintain a quiet, efficient and safe operation during production.

**2. Duties—all during the PRODUCTION Process:**

**a.** Setting up, safetying, operating and wrapping all production lamps—incandescents, fluorescents, vapors, halogens, arcs—and associated equipment during production procedures;

**b.** Making electrical connections to spiders, boxes, lamps, fans and practicals;

**c.** Operation of such equipment as is normally associated with lighting control on the lamp itself;

**d.** Rigging, dressing, safetying, numbering, applying diffusion and light controlling devices and material to the lamps, and striking lamps, cables and associated equipment, as required;

**e.** Assisting the **Gaffer** and **Best Boy** in the performance of duties;

**f.** Otherwise carrying out the duties normally required of this classification;

**g.** Providing the gloves and hand tools normally employed in this craft, carrying these items on one's person while working.

**3. Considerations: Lighting Technicians** rig, place, safety, operate, repair and strike all electrical lighting equipment and accessories.

## L. REPAIR TECHNICIAN

**1. Responsibilities:** The **Repair Technician** is directly responsible to the **Gaffer** and is responsible for keeping all lighting equipment used on a production—control consoles, luminaires, cable, scrims, etc—in good repair and operating order.

**2. Duties—all during the PRODUCTION Process:**

    **a.** Standing by at all times during production shooting, ready to repair or replace set lighting equipment;

    **b.** Repairing or replacing malfunctioning set lighting equipment, as requested;

    **c.** Having access to a supply of parts and tools used to repair lighting instruments and their accessories;

    **d.** Otherwise carrying out the duties normally required of this classification;

    **e.** Providing the gloves and hand tools normally employed in this craft, carrying these items on one's person while working.

**3. Considerations:** A **Repair Technician** repairs and replaces lighting equipment and support matériel and also operates such equipment, as necessary.

▼ **Classification Used During RIGGING PROCEDURES** ▼

## M. RIGGING GAFFER

**1. Responsibilities:** The **Rigging Gaffer** is directly responsible to the production **Gaffer** during electrical rigging and derigging procedures on sets and/or settings where lighting units must be installed on scaffolding, perms, greenbeds, pipe grids and/or set headers in order to light cycloramas, translights, backings and the like in order to prepare and be ready for principal photography.

**2. Duties—during PRE-PRODUCTION and PRODUCTION:**

    **a.** Checking with the production **Gaffer** and **Director of Photography** regarding the type, number and positioning of lighting units to be mounted on sets, scaffolding, perms, greenbeds and/or pipe grids;

    **b.** Ordering all matériel needed to accomplish the electrical rigging needed at the shooting site with the approval of the **Unit Production Manager**;

    **c.** Before allowing any personnel or electrical lighting matériel thereon, checking to insure that all scaffolding, greenbeds and pipe grids are structurally sound and securely and accurately positioned, stabilized and safetied;

    **d.** Supervising the placement, connection, ID'ing, tying off and securing of all power cable runs;

    **e.** Supervising the installation, connection to cable runs, and securing and safetying of all lighting units;

**f.** Making sure that each light is operational and that the lights are placed to provide adequate lighting for the sets and action areas;

**g.** Making sure that all installed lighting units and attached accessories are properly safetied;

**h.** With the approval of the production **Gaffer** and **Director of Photography**, pre-lighting the sets, backings and action areas;

**i.** Supervising the striking of electrical and lighting matériel following principal photography, and with permission of the **Unit Production Manager**;

**j.** Otherwise carrying out the duties normally required of this classification;

**k.** Providing the gloves and hand tools normally employed in this craft, carrying these items on one's person while working.

**3. Considerations:** A **Rigging Gaffer** is used when a production requires the rigging of sets or production sites preparatory to principal photography on those sites.

## N. RIGGING BEST BOY

**1. Responsibilities:** The **Rigging Best Boy** is directly responsible to the **Rigging Gaffer** for assisting in and expediting all electrical rigging and derigging procedures.

**2. Duties—during PRE-PRODUCTION and PRODUCTION:**

**a.** Assisting the **Rigging Gaffer** in the performance of the electrical rigging, pre-lighting and derigging procedures;

**b.** Supervising rigging, safetying and striking procedures for the **Rigging Gaffer**;

**c.** Seeing that all unused rigging matériel is returned to storage when rigging has been completed;

**d.** Otherwise carrying out the duties normally required of this classification;

**e.** Providing the gloves and hand tools normally employed in this craft, carrying these items on one's person while working.

**3. Considerations:** A **Rigging Best Boy** is the first **Technician** employed to assist the **Rigging Gaffer**.

## O. RIGGING TECHNICIAN

**1. Responsibilities:** The **Rigging Technician** is directly responsible to the **Rigging Gaffer**, or **Rigging Best Boy** when the **Rigging Gaffer** has given the **Rigging Best Boy** such authority, and assists the **Rigging Gaffer** and **Rigging Best Boy** in the performance of their duties. The **Rigging Technician** is responsible for functioning efficiently to help expedite set lighting preparation rigging procedures.

**2. Duties—during PRE-PRODUCTION and PRODUCTION:**

**a.** Placing, connecting and securing all power cable runs on greenbeds, grids, scaffolding, platforms, mobile mounts, sets and settings;

**b.** Installing, safetying and connecting lighting units on greenbeds, grids, scaffolding and set headers;

**c.** Otherwise carrying out the duties normally required of this classification;

**d.** Providing the gloves and hand tools normally employed in this craft, carrying these items on one's person while working.

**3. Considerations: Rigging Technicians** rig, place, secure, safety, operate, move, lift, carry and strike all electrical lighting matériel during the rigging and derigging processes.

▼ **Classification Used During Both PRODUCTION and RIGGING** ▼

**P. GENERATOR OPERATOR**

**1. Responsibilities:** The **Generator Operator** is directly responsible to the **Gaffer** for maintaining the generator at a consistent desired electrical output (voltage, amperage—and cycles, if AC) during cinematography.

**2. Duties—all during the PRODUCTION Process:**

**a.** Placing, securing, baffling the motor noise, maintaining, fueling and refueling, operating and servicing portable electrical generating equipment;

**b.** Making the main power connection at the generator;

**c.** Standing by and monitoring the operation of the generating equipment at all times during operation of that equipment;

**d.** Observing proper safety precautions at all times;

**e.** Otherwise carrying out the duties normally required of this classification;

**f.** Providing the gloves and hand tools normally employed in this craft.

**3. Considerations**: A **Generator Operator** is used for each generator employed on the production.

**NOTES**

# GRIP CATEGORY ORGANIZATIONAL CHART

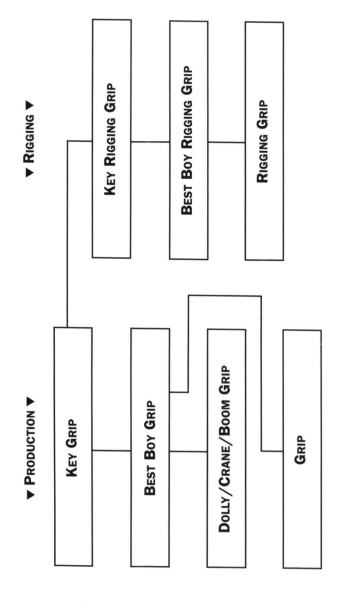

▼ PRODUCTION ▼

▼ RIGGING ▼

KEY GRIP

BEST BOY GRIP

DOLLY/CRANE/BOOM GRIP

GRIP

KEY RIGGING GRIP

BEST BOY RIGGING GRIP

RIGGING GRIP

# 6

# GRIP CATEGORY

**A. Category Classifications:** There are seven (7) classifications in the Grip Category:

▼ **For Production Procedures:**

1. **Key Grip (Category Head)**

2. **First Assistant Grip [Best Boy] (Category Sub-Head)**

3. **Dolly/Crane/Boom Grip**

4. **Grip**

▼ **For Rigging Procedures:**

5. **Key Rigging Grip (Category Sub-Head)**

6. **Best Boy Rigging Grip**

7. **Rigging Grip**

**B. Category Criteria:**

1. Employees holding classification within the Grip Category perform all job functions pertaining to cinematographic grip procedures which are utilized on interior or exterior production, airborne or under water, on location and/or on the sound stage.

2. Grip personnel need to know knot-tying techniques as well as construction techniques and how to use the tools of the construction trade in a safe and efficient manner.

3. A **Key Grip** is used on a set or location where cinematographic grip procedures are utilized, and is in charge of the technical procedures pertaining thereto, as directed by the **Director of Photography**.

4. The number of **Grip**s to be used is determined by the **Producer**, within the parameters of the collective bargaining agreement under which the aforementioned classifications are covered, taking into consideration the requirements needed to safely, effectively and efficiently complete their tasks, such as:

    **a.** The quantity, weight and type of grip equipment and material to be used;

    **b.** The number, complexity and location(s) of camera set-ups;

    **c.** The duration and pace of the shooting schedule.

5. For example, for safety when human cargo is aboard, it is recommended that on each day of shooting, when the camera is mounted on a:

    **a.** Camera dolly, at least one (1) **Dolly Grip** is used to operate the dolly;

b. Camera crane, at least two (2) **Crane Grip**s are used to operate the crane arm—one (1) **Grip** to control elevation movement and one (1) **Grip** to control horizontal swing movement and/or, on a large crane, that there is a **Grip** at each end of the boom—and two (2) **Crane Grip**s to drive the crane—one (1) **Grip** for forward drive and one (1) **Grip** for reverse drive—when such equipment is utilized;

c. In any event, there should be an adequate number of **Crane Grips** to operate the equipment in a safe manner to get the shot; the division should be made considering such elements as whether the camera is manned or remotely controlled, the size of the crane, the complexity of the shot, the velocity of camera, chassis and/or arm movement, the environment where the shot is being made, the weather and time of day, and any other elements which may require additional personnel to safely, effectively and accurately control the crane arm and chassis;

d. Camera boom or jib arm, at least one (1) **Boom Grip** is used to operate the boom arm and at least one (1) **Boom Grip** to drive the carriage.

6. When mobile camera mounts are utilized, one (1) or more **Dolly**, **Crane** or **Boom Grip**s, as appropriate, are used to operate such equipment, as specified in **5c** above.

7. All Grip Category personnel will endeavor to use RF headset communication and/or hand signals whenever possible during grip procedures in order to help maintain a quiet and efficient operation.

8. When the **Key Grip** requires assistance in setting up, moving, operating or breaking down grip equipment, a **Best Boy Grip** is used.

9. When the **Key Grip** and **Best Boy Grip** require assistance in their duties, one (1) or more **Grip**s are used, as needed.

10. A grip rigging crew, consists of a **Key Rigging Grip**, **Best Boy Rigging Grip** and sufficient **Rigging Grips** to safely and efficiently install, maintain and wrap rigging—scaffolding, greenbeds, pipe grids, trusses, block-and-falls, chain motors and dolly and crane track.

11. During rigging procedures, and anytime a light control device is installed on the set, on greenbeds, or on pipe grids, each device attached thereto must be securely safetied at that time and at all times thereafter while mounted.

12. All Grip personnel operating underwater with breathing apparatus must be SCUBA certified.

13. The **Key Grip** and each Grip Category Sub-Head must ensure that grip personnel do not attempt work under any unsafe condition(s), as specified by the Employer, OSHA, Building and Safety Code and fire laws, or in violation of any other safety regulation(s) and practice(s).

C. **Category Responsibilities:** It is the responsibility of each Employee in the Grip Category to work cooperatively with the **Key Grip** in order to assist in achieving the optimum and most efficient operation of the various production procedures in which **Grip**s are involved—principally lighting control, camera movement, set rearrangement, structural construction and support, and rigging.

D. **Category Function:** The principal function of Grip Category personnel involves procedures to facilitate and/or actuate camera movement and placement, placing and operating reflectors, placing light-modifying controls—cutters, scrims, diffusion, gels, patterns—to control, shape and modify the production illumination, as well as moving and hzndling sets, and erecting scaffolding, trusses, chain motors, settings, backings, cycs, translights and company matériel.

E. **Category Considerations:**

1. Grip Category personnel are used on each production on which there is camera movement, settings to be erected or moved, greenbeds, catwalks, grids, or cycloramas or scenic backdrops to be hung, reflectors and overhead scrims to be utilized and/or company material to be moved, loaded or unloaded.

2. The classification(s) used depends upon the type and quantity of grip material and services required.

3. Grip Category personnel used on rigging procedures, during production, should not function on production procedures as well.

F. **Category Requirements:** Employees in each Grip Category classification must know and follow the chain-of-command and lines-of-communication and must be able to effectively and safely set up and operate the grip equipment and related material selected for each job and associated with their respective craft classification.

▼ **Classification Used During PRODUCTION PROCEDURES** ▼

G. **KEY GRIP**

1. **Responsibilities:** The **Key Grip**, the **First Company Grip**, works with the **Gaffer**, and is directly responsible to the **Director of Photography**, and to the **Gaffer** during lighting procedures when a **Gaffer** is employed on a production. The **Key Grip** is responsible for setting all reflectors and light-modifying control devices and for supervising and coordinating the operation of the Grip crew as efficiently, effectively and safely as practicable in order to prepare the set and expedite lighting, camera placement and camera movement procedures involving Grip personnel.

2. **Duties:**

▼ **During PRE-PRODUCTION:**

a. Reading, analyzing and annotating the script within the context of grip procedures and matériel—grip stands, lighting control matériel, construction matériel and expendables;

b. Reviewing the scouting report and consulting with the **Director of Photography**, the **Gaffer** and other Category Heads regarding the type and amount of grip equipment which will be required to service the production;

▼ **During the PRODUCTION Process:**

**c.** Overseeing and coordinating all responsibilities of the Grip Category—seeing that things get taken care of by grip personnel promptly, efficiently and safely;

**d.** Supervising the loading, unloading, placement and adjustment of all grip equipment and material (century stands, flags, gobos, scrims, screens, cukes, cutters, cycloramas, backings, backdrops, lumber, duvetyn, rope, wire, nails, screws, clamps, etc);

**e.** Supervising the loading, unloading and positioning of scenery, settings and scenic matériel;

**f.** Assisting personnel of other categories in loading, unloading and moving their equipment and material;

**g.** Supervising rigging, altering, safetying, handling and moving floor and overhead scaffolding, greenbeds, parallels, sets, ceilings, scenery, backings, drops, cycloramas, translights, process screens, overhead lighting grids, and striking them;

**h.** Erecting dressing tents and positioning and securing portable dressing rooms and comfort stations;

**i.** Positioning, manning, focusing and stabilizing reflectors;

**j.** Cutting to fit, installing and/or positioning diffusion sheeting and window gels;

**k.** Assisting the personnel of the Camera, Lighting, Set Dressing, Property, Wardrobe, Production Sound and Special Services Categories in the handling and moving, but not in the installation or operation, of their equipment and materials;

**l.** Consulting with the **Director of Photography** and **Gaffer** prior to each lighting set-up in order to determine the selection and placement of lighting control material—cutters, scrims, diffusion, gels, patterns—and the placement, replacement or removal of ceiling pieces;

**m.** Consulting with the **Director of Photography** prior to each set-up regarding placement, replacement or removal of ceiling pieces, wild walls, and backings and the positioning of dolly track, reflectors and overhead diffusion, scrims and solids;

**n.** Operating the ventilators and stage doors;

**o.** Supervising the laying, leveling, cleaning and striking of all dolly/crane/boom track or platforms;

**p.** Operating all hoists, block-and-tackle, scissor-lifts, fork-lifts, etc;

**q.** Minor repairing of scenery, sets, backings, drops, cycloramas, etc, during production;

**r.** Giving hand signals to Grip personnel during production procedures whenever practicable, in order to help minimize ambient noise level;

**s.** Responsibility for the Grip Box and its contents;

**t.** Otherwise carrying out the duties normally required of this classification;

**u.** Providing the gloves and hand tools normally employed in this craft, carrying these items on one's person while working.

3. **Considerations:**

**a.** A **Key Grip** is used when a production utilizes grip equipment and procedures.

**b.** A **Key Grip** may supply a Grip Box if properly compensated for the use thereof.

## H. FIRST ASSISTANT GRIP [BEST BOY GRIP]

1. **Responsibilities:** The **First Assistant Grip** or **Best Boy Grip**, the **Second Company Grip**, is directly responsible to the **Key Grip** for safely and effectively expediting procedures performed by the Grip crew and for the ordering, maintaining and scheduling of equipment, materials and personnel required to service the needs of the Grip Category.

2. **Duties—all during the PRODUCTION Process:**

**a.** Reading the script;

**b.** Assisting the **Key Grip** in the performance of the grip procedures;

**c.** Supervising for the **Key Grip** all immediate rigging, safetying and striking procedures on the set, in the studio or on the location site;

**d.** Inventorying all grip matériel, as necessary;

**e.** Seeing that all grip matériel is properly stored when not in use;

**f.** Supervising maintenance of all grip matériel, as necessary;

**g.** Insuring that all grip equipment used overhead is properly safetied;

**h.** Otherwise carrying out the duties normally required of this classification;

**i.** Providing the gloves and hand tools normally employed in this craft, carrying these items on one's person while working.

3. **Considerations:** A **Best Boy Grip** is the first Grip employed to assist the **Key Grip**

## I. DOLLY/CRANE/BOOM GRIP

1. **Responsibilities:** The **Dolly/Crane/Boom Grip** is directly responsible to the **Key Grip** and works closely with the **Camera Operator** in coordinating moving shots during blocking, rehearsals and takes, operating the mobile camera platform smoothly, synchronizing mobile camera platform movement with the movement of the subject matter, accurately hitting position marks, in order to help make each take as technically and aesthetically perfect as possible.

2. **Duties—all during the PRODUCTION Process:**

**a.** Reading the script, if on a multiple-camera film sitcom;

**b.** Setting up and checking all mobile camera platforms for proper operation, and wrapping such equipment after use;

**c.** Affixing the geared, friction, fluid or remotely controlled head to the mobile camera platform and adjusting the head for level;

**d.** Placing, adjusting and removing all accessories such as side boards, platforms and risers on dollies or cranes;

**e.** Maintaining appropriate air pressure in a mobile camera platform hydraulic system and tires;

**f.** Operating all functions of the dolly, crane, boom and/or jib arm;

**g.** Laying, leveling, cleaning, and striking dolly tracks, dance floors, crane and boom beds;

**h.** Marking start and stop positions for the dolly, crane or boom arm and chassis;

**i.** Marking elevation and/or swing positions for the boom arm or crane;

**j.** Marking the direction of, distance to, and configuration of the move to, each stop position;

**k.** Precutting tapes for floor marking of dolly stop positions to conserve time, during camera blocking of multi-camera film sitcoms;

**l.** Finessing dolly moves to coordinate perfectly with the movement of the subject matter;

**m.** Making dolly movies of varying configurations, such as tracking, crabbing, "chinese-ing," banana-ing, fish-tailing, or combination moves thereof;

**n.** Wearing an intercom headset when required to do so by the production technique being used, such as multi-camera film sitcoms and during coordinated crane moves and while working high on scaffolding, parallels, greenbeds or perms;

**o.** Weight-checking the lift capability of cherry-pickers, aerial work platforms and similar lift mechanisms prior to allowing human loads aboard in order to assure the safety of personnel;

**p.** Maintaining proper counterbalance weight on the boom, crane or jib arm;

**q.** Locking, or otherwise securing, the dolly, boom, jib or crane arm when not in use, when static, or when changing the personnel or equipment load, and until proper counterbalancing weight can be applied to the boom, jib or crane arm;

**r.** Standing by the boom or crane arm at all times when personnel are aboard in order to ensure their safety;

**s.** Moving the microphone boom perambulator during moving shots when a **Utility Sound Technician** (film) or **Audio Utility** (video) person is not present;

**t.** Otherwise carrying out the duties normally required of this classification;

**u.** Providing the gloves and hand tools normally employed in this craft, carrying these items on one's person while working.

3. **Considerations:** The prime responsibility for operating dollies, cranes, booms and jib arms falls to a sufficient number of **Dolly**, **Crane** or **Boom Grip**s to fully staff such apparatus, thereby assuring optimal functional safety and operation of such equipment.

## J. GRIP

1. **Responsibilities:** The **Grip** is directly responsible to the **Key Grip**, or **Best Boy Grip** when the **Key Grip** has given the **Best Boy Grip** such authority, and assists the **Key Grip** and **Best Boy Grip** in the performance of their duties. The **Grip** is responsible for functioning efficiently to help expedite safe and effective set preparation and lighting procedures, and in so doing will remain ever alert for hand signals from the **Key Grip** for procedural modifications in order to help maintain a quiet, efficient operation during production.

2. **Duties—during the PRODUCTION Process:**

   **a.** Operation of all grip equipment and associated gear;

   **b.** Pulling cable, if any, during moving camera shots;

   **c.** Moving the microphone boom perambulator during takes when such moves are required and a **Utility Sound Technician** (film) or **Audio Utility** (video) person is not available;

   **d.** Rigging and striking greenbeds, grids, trusses, scaffolding, cycloramas, drops, backings, wild set walls, ceiling and/or crane track bed and platforms;

   **e.** Safetying each scrim, cutter or cuckaloris as each such lighting control device is installed overhead, placing sandbags on the base of lamp stands and/or grip stands which are at extended height and/or which are positioned on uneven terrain and/or when there are strong windy conditions prevailing;

   **f.** Installing safety bars on camera cars, and installing safety posts, rails and/or cable retainers on flatbed mobile camera trailer platforms;

   **g.** Assisting the **Key Grip**, the **Best Boy Grip** and the **Dolly**, **Crane** and **Boom Grip**s in the performance of their duties;

   **h.** Otherwise carrying out the duties normally required of this classification;

   **i.** Providing the gloves and hand tools normally employed in this craft, carrying these items on one's person while working.

3. **Considerations: Grip**s rig, place, secure, safety, operate, move, lift, carry and strike all grip equipment and accessories and set pieces.

▼ **Classification Used During RIGGING PROCEDURES** ▼

## K. KEY RIGGING GRIP

1. **Responsibilities:** The **Key Rigging Grip** is directly responsible to the **Unit Production Manager** during grip rigging and derigging procedures on sets and/or settings where scaffolding, greenbeds and/or pipe grids, cycloramas, translights, backings and the like must be installed in order to prepare and be ready for electrical and lighting rigging procedures followed by principal photography.

**2. Duties—during PRE-PRODUCTION and PRODUCTION:**

a. Checking with the **Director of Photography** regarding the number, positioning and height of scaffolding, greenbeds and/or pipe grids required for lighting procedures;

b. Consulting with the **Art Director** regarding placement of backings, cycloramas, translights and/or ceiling pieces;

c. Ordering all matériel needed to accomplish the grip rigging needed at the shooting site with the approval of the **Unit Production Manager**;

d. Coordinating the construction and placement of all scaffolding;

e. Coordinating the installation of all greenbeds and pipe grids to conform to the layout plan of the sets and action areas;

f. Checking to insure that all scaffolding, greenbeds, trusses and pipe grids are structurally sound and securely and accurately positioned, stabilized and safetied;

g. Installing side hand rails on all greenbeds for safety purposes;

h. Supervising the striking of grip rigging matériel following principal photography, with permission of the **Unit Production Manager**;

i. Otherwise carrying out the duties normally required of this classification;

j. Providing the gloves and hand tools normally employed in this craft, carrying these items on one's person while working.

**3. Considerations:** A **Key Rigging Grip** is used when a production requires the rigging of sets or production sites preparatory to principal photography.

## L. BEST BOY RIGGING GRIP

**1. Responsibilities:** The **Best Boy Rigging Grip** is directly responsible to the **Key Rigging Grip** for assisting in and expediting all grip rigging and derigging procedures.

**2. Duties—during PRE-PRODUCTION and PRODUCTION:**

a. Assisting the **Key Rigging Grip** in the performance of the grip rigging and derigging procedures;

b. Supervising rigging, safetying and striking procedures for the **Key Rigging Grip**;

c. Seeing that all unused rigging matériel is returned to storage when rigging has been completed—and after rigging has been struck and wrapped;

d. Otherwise carrying out the duties normally required of this classification;

e. Providing the gloves and hand tools normally employed in this craft, carrying these items on one's person while working.

**3. Considerations:** A **Best Boy Rigging Grip** is the first Grip employed to assist the **Key Rigging Grip**.

## M. RIGGING GRIP

1. **Responsibilities:** The **Rigging Grip** is directly responsible to the **Key Rigging Grip**, or **Best Boy Rigging Grip** when the **Key Rigging Grip** has given the **Best Boy Rigging Grip** such authority, and assists the **Key Rigging Grip** and **Best Boy Rigging Grip** in the performance of their duties. The **Rigging Grip** is responsible for functioning safely and efficiently to help expedite set preparation rigging procedures.

2. **Duties—during PRE-PRODUCTION and PRODUCTION:**

   a. Rigging, maintaining and striking of rigging matériel—greenbeds, grids, scaffolding, cycloramas, drops, backings, wild set walls, ceiling and/or crane track bed, platforms and mobile mounts on sets and settings;

   b. Otherwise carrying out the duties normally required of this classification;

   c. Providing the gloves and hand tools normally employed in this craft, carrying these items on one's person while working.

3. **Considerations: Rigging Grip**s rig, place, secure, safety, operate, move, lift, carry, strike and wrap all grip equipment and accessories and set pieces during the rigging and derigging process.

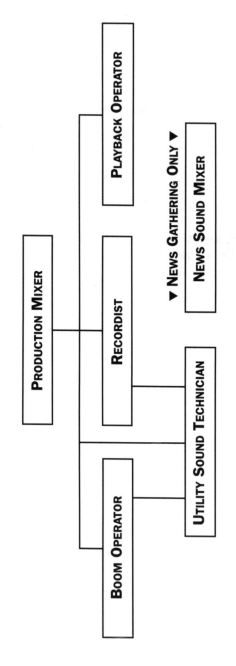

# Sound Category Organizational Chart

## ▼ Production Sound Section ▼

- Production Mixer
  - Boom Operator
    - Utility Sound Technician
  - Recordist
  - Playback Operator

## ▼ News Gathering Only ▼

- News Sound Mixer

# 7

# SOUND CATEGORY

**A. Category Classifications:** There are nineteen (19) classifications in the Sound Category, of which there are six (6) classifications in the **PRODUCTION SOUND** Section:

▼ For RECORDING Production Dialogue:

1. Production Mixer (Category Head)

2. Recordist

3. Boom Operator

4. Playback Operator (Category Sub-Head)

5. News Sound Mixer (Category Head)

6. Utility Sound Technician

and thirteen (13) classifications in the **POST-PRODUCTION SOUND Section**:

▼ For RE-RECORDING Sound:

7. Lead Re-Recording Mixer (Category Head)

8. Music Re-Recording Mixer (Category Sub-Head)

9. Sound Effects Re-Recording Mixer (Category Sub-Head)

10. Lead Recordist [Dummy Room Supervisor] (Category Sub-Head)

11. Dummy Loader

▼ For RECORDING Music and Dialogue Replacement:

12. Scoring Mixer (Category Sub-Head)

13. Scoring Recordist

14. ADR Mixer (Category Sub-Head)

▼ For RECORDING and MAKING Sound Effects:

15. Foley Mixer (Category Sub-Head)

16. Sound Effects Specialist [Foley Artist]

▼ For TRANSFERRING Original Sound:

17. Transfer Recordist

▼ For RE-RECORDING and MIXING & MAKING Sound Tracks:

18. Projectionist

▼ For MAINTENANCE of Sound Equipment:

19. Maintenance Engineer (Category Sub-Head)

**B. Category Responsibilities:** It is the responsibility of each Employee in the Sound Category to work cooperatively with the Category Head, or with the Sub-Head to whom assigned, in order to assist in achieving the optimum and most efficient realization of the recorded and/or re-recorded elements on magnetic tape or optical film.

**C. Category Function:** The principal function of Sound Category personnel involves work with magnetic recording equipment and its various applications pertaining to recording or re-recording superior quality audible sound—dialogue, sound effects and music—on magnetic tape or disc.

**D. Category Considerations:**

**1.** Sound Category personnel are used on each production on which sound recording and/or re-recording equipment and procedures are used.

**2.** The classification(s) and personnel used depend upon the type and quantity of sound equipment utilized.

### ▼ PRODUCTION SOUND SECTION ▼

**E. Production Sound Criteria:**

**1.** Employees holding classification within the Production Sound Section of the Sound Category perform all job functions within their respective classification pertaining to production sound procedures which are utilized on interior or exterior production, on location and/or on the sound stage.

**2.** A **Production Mixer** is used on a set or location where sound—dialogue and incidental effects—other than for newsreel purposes, is recorded, and is in charge of all technical procedures directly pertaining to sound recording during the production process.

**3.** A **Production Mixer** needs to know and apply: The tools, techniques and methods best suited to achieve optimum production sound quality; the collaborative skills used to work with the **Director, Director of Photography**, others on the crew, and actors.

**4.** A **News Sound Mixer** is used where and when double system sound is being recorded of a news event. (See the Glossary for the definition of news production.)

**5.** A **Playback Operator** is used when a performance is being photographed to pre-recorded sound playback.

**6.** During production, a **Production Mixer** will be used when sound effects or a sound effects cue track is required for television commercials or industrial or educational films and the like.

**7.** The boom perambulator is moved by the **Utility Sound Technician**.

**8.** When the **Production Mixer** requires assistance:

    **a.** In the operation of the sound recorder, a **Recordist** is used;

    **b.** In the operation of a microphone boom, fishpole, shotgun or parabolic mic, a **Boom Operator** is used;

    **c.** In the placement of RF transmitters and antennae, and lavaliere and RF microphones, a **Boom Operator** is used, assisted by a **Utility Sound Technician**, when necessary.

**9.** When the **Production Mixer** and/or the **Boom Operator** require assistance in setting up, moving, and breaking down sound equipment, a **Utility Sound Technician** is used.

**10.** When the **Playback Operator** requires assistance in setting up, moving or breaking down playback equipment, a **Utility Sound Technician** is used.

**11.** When the **News Sound Mixer** requires assistance in setting up, moving or breaking down newsreel sound equipment, a **Utility Sound Technician** is used.

**12.** The **Production Mixer** has the option to voice slate "Under Protest" and to note this ("**U.P.**") on the camera slate and Sound Report should the **Mixer** be directed to record a take against his or her objection; however, it may be more prudent to advise the **Script Supervisor** and note the details in the Sound Report. The responsible person—**Director**, **Producer** or **Production Manager**—who has directed the **Production Mixer** to record or print such take, then assumes all responsibility for the technical sound quality thereof, without recourse. [It should be noted that ambient noise may be adversely affecting the quality of the sound track and, to correct the problem when possible, either terminating the intruding noise, or planning on replacing the dialogue and/or sound in post production.]

**13.** All Production Sound personnel operating underwater with breathing apparatus must be SCUBA certified.

**14.** The **Production Mixer** and each Production Sound Section Sub-Head must ensure that production sound personnel do not attempt work under any unsafe condition(s), as specified by the Employer, OSHA, Building and Safety Code and fire laws, or in violation of any other safety regulation(s) and practice(s).

**F. Category Requirements:** Employees in each classification of the Production Sound Section of the Sound Category must know and follow the chain-of-command and lines-of-communication and must be able to effectively and safely set up and operate the production sound equipment selected for each job and associated with their respective craft classification.

    ▼ **Classifications Used for RECORDING Production Dialogue** ▼

**G. PRODUCTION MIXER**

    **1. Responsibilities:** The **Production Mixer** is directly responsible to the **Director** for the recording, and the quality of, all on-set or on-location production sound—dialogue and incidental sound effects—synchronous and "wild," and is responsible to the **Director of Photography** for the proper placement of the boom or other microphones, so as not to encroach on lighting patterns in camera frame, and strives to maintain optimum sound quality under all production conditions.

**2. Duties:**

▼ **During PRE-PRODUCTION:**

**a.** Reading and annotating the script within the context of sound recording dialogue and ambient sound;

**b.** Noting, from the shooting sites indicated, the type and quantity of sound equipment likely to be required to properly service the production;

**c.** Selecting the sound equipment and raw stock and arranging rental, lease or purchase of it/them, as applicable;

▼ **During the PRODUCTION Process:**

**d.** Supervising the loading, transportation and unloading of all sound equipment;

**e.** Supervising and/or setting up, breaking down and wrapping the sound equipment;

**f.** Operation and field maintenance of the mixing console, recording and associated equipment;

**g.** Selecting the positions for the recording equipment and the microphones (the latter with the agreement of the **Director of Photography**);

**h.** Analyzing the camera coverage—single or multiple cameras, angle, tight or wide coverage, taking lens and perspective—then selecting the particular microphones to be used on or for performers for each setup;

**i.** Supervising the **Boom Operator** in the mounting or attaching of microphones to stands, sound booms, fishpoles, and performers, etc, and/or the placing of such equipment on the set or for audience response during sitcoms;

**j.** Placing, or directing the placement of, battens by the **Utility Sound Technician**(s);

**k.** Operating the warning lights and audio sound signals on sets preparatory to, and following, sound takes where these devices are provided;

**l.** Checking that all encroaching ambient sound is terminated or sufficiently suppressed prior to rolling the tape;

**m.** Notifying the **First Assistant Director** of the source of any extraneous noise; **1st AD** will then see that the noise is terminated or controlled by assuring that stage doors and vents are closed, air conditioning, refrigerators and phones are turned off during the take, and turned back on after the take;

**n.** Recording sound alignment head tones at the beginning of every tape reel to be recorded upon—one, to establish playback level of the material to be recorded, another to establish the decode phase of noise reduction, noting on the sound slate and Sound Report the type of noise reduction employed, another to set proper phase alignment and high frequency playback alignment, and yet another to set low frequency playback adjustment to a "0" level—generally, a minus 8 dbm on a Nagra will be set to zero level on the particular playback VU meter;

**o.** Recording dialogue and incidental sound effects during production takes;

**p.** Recording concurrent sound from the boom mic and RF mics on separate tracks;

**q.** Playing back the head tones immediately after recording to insure compatible and correct output;

**r.** Loading and unloading the recorder;

**s.** Keeping Sound Reports, logging each take and its expended time, and all other technical notations which will help optimize the transfer process;

**t.** Recording a presence track at each studio and location where synchronous sound is recorded;

**u.** Notifying the **Director** of any sound anomaly immediately following each sound take;

**v.** Voice slating wild sound takes from the console mic when a **Boom Operator** or **Utility Sound Technician** is not required;

**w.** Preparing the recorded tape for shipment and/or delivery to the Sound Transfer Studio;

**x.** Otherwise carrying out the duties normally required of this classification;

**y.** Providing the hand tools normally employed in this craft.

**3. Considerations**:

**a.** A **Production Mixer** is used when production sound is recorded.

**b.** It is recommended that the **Production Mixer** be included in pre-production consultation and on any location scouting trips in order to better insure optimum recorded sound on locations during production.

## H. RECORDIST

**1. Responsibilities:** The **Production Recordist** is directly responsible to the **Production Mixer** for operating tape recorders which are separate from the mixing console and seeing that such recorders are properly set up, threaded, adjusted, connected to the mixing console, and operative.

**2. Duties—all during the PRODUCTION Process:**

**a.** Reading and annotating the script within the context of sound recording;

**b.** Setting up, connecting to the mixing console, and operating tape recorders;

**c.** Checking that the recording heads are clean and that the recorders are recording and fully operative in all modes;

**d.** Seeing that each tape recorder is properly loaded and threaded with appropriate raw stock, at its proper start position;

**e.** Keeping all necessary reports pertinent to recording production sound;

**f.** Writing identifying numbers and titles on all recorded tape reels;

g. Preparing recorded material for delivery to the transfer house;

h. Wrapping the recorders and their associated equipment;

i. Assisting the **Production Mixer** in the performance of duties;

j. Otherwise carrying out the duties normally required of this classification;

k. Providing the hand tools normally employed in this craft.

3. **Considerations:** A **Production Recordist** is used when recording equipment which is separate from the mixing console is used to capture production sound, such as for film sitcoms with a live audience.

## I. BOOM OPERATOR

1. **Responsibilities:** The **Boom Operator** is directly responsible to the **Production Mixer** for operating the microphone boom or fishpole, shotgun or parabolic microphone, in order to pick up the desired voice, sound effects and/or music at the perspective desired by the **Mixer**, giving special attention to the frame line limits given by the **Camera Operator**, thereby causing no microphone, boom or their shadows to appear on personnel, objects or surfaces within the camera frame.

2. **Duties—all during the PRODUCTION Process:**

a. Reading and annotating the script within the context of boom operating;

b. Noting on the script the performer(s) who will be covered by each microphone in each shot/scene, the dialogue to be delivered and the position(s) from which each performer delivers dialogue;

c. Setting up, breaking down and wrapping the microphones, microphone boom, fishpole and stand, RF mics and transmitters, and associated equipment;

d. Testing and adjusting the controls on, and movement limits of, the mic boom and, if on a perambulator, setting the height of the boom post and the **Boom Operator**'s seat, and adjusting the television monitor mounted on the boom post for optimum viewing position;

e. Memorizing the dialogue which will be delivered during each shot in order to facilitate the timing of boom movement and mic facings and to maximize the quality of the dialogue picked up from each performer;

f. Placing the script pages containing the dialogue to be recorded in a secure and visible position during rehearsals and takes;

g. Attaching the proper microphone to the mic boom, fishpole, hand guidance system and to the person of performers;

h. While operating the boom or fishpole, keeping the microphone placed and faced in the proper position at all times to achieve the acoustic results—perspective and presence—required for each sound take, and wearing earphones to monitor and facilitate this;

i. Working closely with the camera, lighting and grip crews to assure that the microphone will not appear in the scene or cast mic or boom shadows on personnel, objects or surfaces which will be photographed;

**j.** Moving the mic and boom or fishpole around the set and through the lighting pattern to determine potential problem areas which will create boom shadows in frame;

**k.** Checking with the **Camera Operator**(s) to determine camera-safe vertical swing and extension limits for the mic and its boom or fishpole;

**l.** Assisting the **Production Mixer** in testing microphone pickup and positioning;

**m.** Voice slating wild sound takes;

**n.** Assisting the **Production Mixer** in the performance of duties;

**o.** Otherwise carrying out the duties normally required of this classification;

**p.** Providing the hand tools normally employed in this craft.

**3. Considerations:** A **Boom Operator** is used on any set or location where a fishpole, microphone boom, shotgun or parabolic microphone is used or when the **Production Mixer** requires assistance in setting up, installing or affixing audio recording equipment to performers or mounts.

## J. PLAYBACK OPERATOR

**1. Responsibilities:** The **Playback (PB) Operator** is directly responsible to the **Production Mixer**, or to the **Director** when a **Production Mixer** is not required (for pre-production rehearsals), and is responsible for setting and maintaining the playback material at the proper playback speed and sound level.

**2. Duties—all during the PRODUCTION Process:**

**a.** Reading and annotating those portions of the script where playback technique will be employed;

**b.** Setting up all equipment relating to the playback equipment;

**c.** Placing the playback speakers and equipment on the set so as not to be in the scene or interfere with production procedures of other personnel;

**d.** Connecting power to the playback equipment;

**e.** Properly marking start and stop cues with splicing tape on a playback tape or corresponding reference numbers on a CD disc player so that the playback is at the proper place;

**f.** Ensuring that sync is maintained under time code constraints;

**g.** Maintaining playback volume at the most effective level;

**h.** Cutting off the speaker(s) when completing the playback so that if synchronous sound is being recorded, noise will not emit from the speaker(s);

**i.** Remaining at the PB equipment at all times between PB takes;

**j.** Operating the PB equipment during rehearsal periods and shot takes;

**k.** Taking cue from the **Director** or **Assistant Director** for playback;

    **l.** Otherwise carrying out the duties normally required of this classification;

    **m.** Providing the hand tools normally employed in this craft.

**3. Considerations:** A **Playback Operator** is used when pre-recorded music, dialogue and/or click tracks are employed for cueing the actors in synchronizing their lip movements to the particular audio cue.

## K. NEWS SOUND MIXER

**1. Responsibilities:** The **News Sound Mixer** is directly responsible to the **News Cinematographer** or to the **News Director**, if one is assigned, and is responsible for the quality of the sound which he/she mixes and records, and strives to maintain optimum sound quality under even the most adverse conditions.

**2. Duties—all during each Assignment:**

    **a.** Setting up, positioning and wrapping the sound equipment and its related accessories;

    **b.** Positioning the microphone(s), attaching them to the persons of performers, as necessary;

    **c.** Operating the mixing console, single or double system;

    **d.** Keeping Sound and Camera Reports;

    **e.** Turning double system sound tape(s) in for transfer;

    **f.** Otherwise carrying out the duties normally required of this classification;

    **g.** Providing the hand tools normally employed in this craft.

**3. Considerations:**

    **a.** A **News Sound Mixer** functions, when required, on news productions only. (See the Glossary, news production defined.)

    **b.** A **News Sound Mixer** is employed on news-type assignments when the above responsibilities and duties are applicable, otherwise other classifications of Sound personnel are used.

## L. UTILITY SOUND TECHNICIAN

**1. Responsibilities:** The **Utility Sound Technician** is directly responsible to the **Production Mixer** for promptly supplying, connecting, pulling, dressing, disconnecting and storing all power and microphone cable residing within the province of the Sound Category.

**2. Duties—all during the PRODUCTION Process:**

    **a.** Loading and unloading all sound equipment and related transported gear;

    **b.** Setting up, cabling, installing batteries in Comtek transmitter and receivers, distributing Comtek headset and receiver to the **Director** and **Script Supervisor** so they can clearly hear the production dialogue;

    **c.** Checking and organizing radio mic batteries, receivers and transmitters;

    **d.** "Jamming the slate"— checking and setting electronic slates every four (4) hours;

e. Ensuring that all rechargeable batteries are fully charged and that on-cart chargers have power and are fully functional;

f. Attaching the selected microphone to a stand or assisting the Boom Operator in placing a mic on the person of performers;

g. Assisting the **Costumer** in the placement of the RF microphone and its transmitter on the person of each performer using such equipment—and retrieving the mic and transmitter when the performer is changing costumes or is finished for the day;

h. Assisting the **Production Mixer** in checking out microphones and in setting up and testing RF transmitter equipment, placing the transmitting and/or receiving antenna as close to the action as practicable and adjusting them as frequently as necessary;

i. Voice slating wild sound takes;

j. Stringing microphone cable from the mixing console to the boom, static mic positions, or lavaliere mics, properly separating such cables from, and/or positioning relative to, AC power lines, coiling the cables and placing them clear of the set when not in use;

k. Supplying a line tap from the camera to the **Video Assist Operator**;

l. Locating and eliminating all extraneous noise with the help of the **First AD** or, if on location, the **Location Manager**;

m. Seeing that all phones are blocked and all refrigerators and air conditioning units are turned off prior to each sound take, and then activated thereafter;

n. Handling all microphone and other associated sound equipment cables, pulling such cable during moving shots, as necessary;

o. Moving the boom perambulator about the set, from position to position, and during static takes or moving shots, as necessary;

p. Placing battens and/or rubber-back floor mats, as directed by the **Production Mixer**;

q. Distributing RF headsets to **Camera Operator**s, **Dolly Grip**s and the **Technical Coordinator**; and collecting these sets at the close of each shooting day on which such communication is required;

r. Prerigging a scheduled mobile camera platform and/or towing rig for sound;

s. Assisting the **Production Mixer, Recordist** (if required), **Boom Operator**, and **Playback Operator** in the performance of their duties;

t. Otherwise carrying out the duties normally required of this classification;

u. Providing the hand tools normally employed in this craft.

3. **Considerations:** A **Utility Sound Technician,** unless bumped up in classification by the **Production Mixer**, does not operate any sound equipment and is used when the **Production Mixer, Recordist, Boom Operator** or **Playback Operator** requires assistance in the performance of duties.

# Sound Category Organizational Chart

## ▼ Post-Production Sound Section ▼

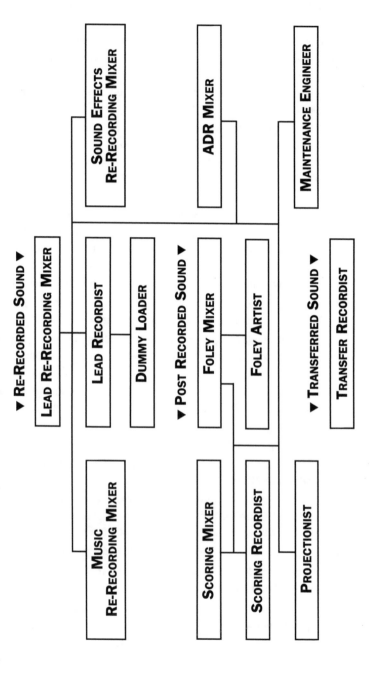

### ▼ Re-Recorded Sound ▼

- Lead Re-Recording Mixer
  - Music Re-Recording Mixer
  - Sound Effects Re-Recording Mixer
  - Lead Recordist
  - Dummy Loader

### ▼ Post Recorded Sound ▼

- Foley Mixer
  - Scoring Mixer
  - ADR Mixer
  - Foley Artist
  - Scoring Recordist
  - Projectionist

### ▼ Transferred Sound ▼

- Transfer Recordist
- Maintenance Engineer

**▼ POST PRODUCTION SOUND SECTION ▼**

## M. Post-Production Sound Criteria:

**1.** Employees holding classifications within the Post Production Sound Section of the Sound Category perform all job functions pertaining to recording, re-recording and sound transfer procedures performed in the recording studio.

**2.** All the sounds, all the ambiances, all the Foley, and all the hard effects are assembled and provided by Sound Effects Editing and mixed by **Re-Recording Mixer**s.

**3.** The **Lead Re-Recording Mixer** is in technical charge of all sound procedures during studio recording and re-recording.

**4.** A **Lead Re-Recording Mixer** needs to have and apply: A thorough knowledge of sound recording and re-recording techniques and parameters—microphones, filters, recording devices and materials, recording consoles, patching, acoustics; managerial skills.

**5.** On a three-person re-recording team, the **Lead Re-Recording Mixer** will handle the dialogue tracks; on a two-person re-recording team, the **Lead Re-Recording Mixer** will mix the dialogue and music tracks.

**6.** When the **Lead Re-Recording Mixer** requires assistance in setting up, patching and operating the mixing console and other on-line equipment, during pre-dub, sub-dub and final mixing phases:

    **a.** For dialogue, music, and/or sound effects tracks, one (1) or more **Re-Recording Mixer**s are used, as needed—a **Music Re-Recording Mixer** for music tracks and a **Sound Effects Re-Recording Mixer** for sound effects tracks;

    **b.** For operating the sound dummies, a **Lead Recordist** is used;

    **c.** For operating the projector, a **Projectionist** is used.

**7.** For recording original music, a **Scoring Mixer** is used.

**8.** For assisting in placing and patching microphones for orchestral scoring sessions, a Maintenance Engineer is used.

**9.** For recording original, ambient sound effects, a **Production Mixer** is used.

**10.** For recording original created sound effects, a **Foley Mixer** is used.

**11.** For creating live sound effects, **Foley Artist**s are used.

**12.** For recording automatic dialogue replacement, an **ADR Mixer** is used.

**13.** For transferring original production dialogue, recorded Foley effects or ADR, a **Transfer Recordist** is used.

**14.** The **Lead Recordist** is responsible for supervising the dummy room.

**15.** When the **Lead Recordist** requires assistance in setting up, patching, loading, threading, unthreading, unloading and labeling recorded rolls of magnetic tape, one (1) or more **Dummy Loader**s are used, as needed.

16. When the **Projectionist** requires assistance in setting up portable projection equipment, a **Utility** person may be used.

17. The **Lead Re-Recording Mixer** and each Post-Production Section Sub-Head must ensure that Post-Production Sound personnel do not attempt work under any unsafe condition(s), as specified by the Employer, OSHA, Building and Safety Code and fire laws, or in violation of any other safety regulation(s) and practice(s).

18. Although the trend is toward 100% digital processing, the recording, transfer and re-recording systems should have the capability of accommodating analog-to-analog, analog-to-digital, digital-to-analog, and digital-to-digital procedures with data inputted and outputted from and/or to a variety of modalities.

N. **Category Requirements:** Employees in each classification in the Post-Production Sound Section of the Sound Category must know and follow the chain-of-command and lines-of-communication and must be able to effectively and safely set up and operate the sound re-recording equipment selected for each job and associated with their respective craft classification.

▼ Classifications Used for RE-RECORDING Sound ▼

O. **LEAD RE-RECORDING MIXER**

1. **Responsibilities:** The **Lead Re-Recording Mixer** is directly responsible to the **Supervising Sound Editor**, the Employer or the Appointed Representative for maintaining optimum sound quality and perspective in the mixing of the sound tracks of the picture or project, consistent with the material being re-recorded.

2. **Duties:**

▼ **During the Preliminary Phase:**

a. Scheduling and/or assigning all Re-Recording Sound Employees if so charged by the Re-Recording Studio Employer;

b. Supervising all personnel and conditions relating to the re-recording process;

c. Informing the **Lead Recordist** of the sequence of tracks or units, i.e., which track shall go on which dummy, which dummy patches to which re-recording console;

d. Advising the **Projectionist** of the reel sequence required in projection of the picture material;

e. Supervising the patching of input from the dummy room to the dialogue elements control console, setting equalization, attenuation, modulation and other sound filtering controls;

f. Selection of microphones and placement thereof, if used;

g. Looking at the initial **Director**'s cut on a video tape of the picture to be dubbed along with its dialogue work track in order to get a feel for the movie; and/or

**h.** Making a temp or test dub with the **Music** and **Sound Effects Re-Recording Mixers**, with the **Director** and **Supervising Sound Editor** in attendance, before ADR, scoring or sound effects have been recorded, using the uncorrected production dialogue tracks, adding canned music and sound effects, to get an idea of how the elements of the movie will come together and what will be needed for the final dub;

▼ **During the Pre-dub Phase:**

**i.** Checking the cue sheets for the dialogue elements for each reel to be pre-dubbed;

**j.** Previewing the first reel with the synchronized production dialogue elements to be pre-dubbed;

**k.** Supervising the patching of the dialogue elements to the dialogue control console, setting equalization, attenuation, modulation parameters and other sound filtering controls;

**l.** Informing the **Lead Recordist** of the sequence of tracks or units, i.e., which track shall go on which dummy, which dummy patches to which re-recording console;

**m.** Advising the **Projectionist** of the reel sequence required in projection of the picture material;

**n.** Selecting and pre-dubbing a couple of the production dialogue tracks at a time to 6-track digital tape;

**o.** Selecting and pre-dubbing a couple of the ADR tracks at a time to 6-track digital tape;

**p.** Pre-dubbing the ADR loop group voice tracks, a few at a time, to 6-track digital tape;

**q.** Balancing the differing levels on each production dialogue track, taking out or reducing any undesirable ambient noise;

**r.** Completing pre-dubbing of all dialogue/voice tracks to three 6-track digital tape tracks for a total of eighteen dialogue tracks for the final mix phase;

**s.** Mixing and making the combination of all dialogue tracks and/or units to the satisfaction of the **Producer, Director** and the **Picture Editor** and/or **Supervising Sound Editor**;

▼ **During the Dubbing, or Final Mix Phase:**

**t.** Preparing to make the final mix with the **Music** and **Sound Effects Re-Recording Mixers** at their respective consoles and the **Producer, Director** and/or **Picture Editor** in attendance;

**u.** Reviewing for proper form, distributing appropriate cue sheets to the various **Re-Recording Mixers**, and following the cue sheets during runthroughs and takes, and modifying the cue counts, as necessary;

**v.** Checking the cue sheets for the dialogue elements for each reel to be pre-dubbed;

**w.** Taking tone from the pre-dub in order to establish a zero-level so the dialogue tracks will sound exactly the same as when they were laid down in pre-dub;

**x.** Building the mix, because the mixing consoles are fully automated and will play back each fader move that is made, by going through the reel and making the dialogue elements sound as good as possible in preparation for the dubbing and later addition of music and sound effects;

**y.** Informing the **Lead Recordist** of the sequence of tracks or units, i.e., which track shall go on which dummy, which dummy patches to which re-recording console;

**z.** Advising the **Projectionist** of the reel sequence required in projection of the picture material;

**aa.** Riding gain on three (3) or more pre-dubbed 6-track dialogue track(s) during the final mix;

**ab.** Riding gain on and mixing the dialogue tracks while panning and placing the dialogue on the 6-track digital mag at left, center, right, left surround, right surround and/or on the boom (sub-woofer) channel, as appropriate;

**ac.** Recording all dialogue elements for each reel to one (1) 6-track digital mag track, or other multi-track digital medium;

**ad.** Directing other **Re-Recording Mixer**s regarding changes in track level and cues;

**ae.** Completing the session, resulting in one (1) 6-track digital tape recording of the panned, placed and mixed dialogue tracks per reel;

**af.** Making the combination of all tracks and/or units to the satisfaction of the **Producer**, **Director** and **Picture Editor**, having them sign off on each reel for which the total sound is acceptable;

▼ **During the Print Master Phase:**

**ag.** Preparing to make the print master with the **Music** and **Sound Effects Re-Recording Mixer**s at their respective mixing consoles and the **Producer**, **Director** and/or **Picture Editor** in attendance;

**ah.** Setting the master level for the composite track;

**ai.** Setting visual time/footage counter(s) at 0000 read-out;

**aj.** Informing the **Lead Recordist** of the sequence of tracks or units, i.e., which track shall go on which dummy, which dummy patches to which re-recording console;

**ak.** Advising the **Projectionist** of the reel sequence required in projection of the picture material;

**al.** Re-setting the time/footage counter(s) to 0000 after each run;

**am.** Print mastering for releases three (3) times, one (1) in each of three (3) digital formats—Dolby, Digital Theater System (DTS) and Sony Dynamic Digital System (SDDS)—plus a two-track optical backup;

**an.** Checking the finished prints against the print master for sound quality;

**ao.** Preparing an M&E (music and effects only—minus dialogue) track for foreign release;

**ap.** Otherwise carrying out the duties normally required of this classification;

**aq.** Providing the hand tools normally employed in this craft.

**3. Considerations:** A **Lead Re-Recording Mixer** is used whenever the combining of two (2) or more recorded tracks is required.

## P. MUSIC RE-RECORDING MIXER

**1. Responsibilities:** The **Music Re-Recording Mixer** is directly responsible to the **Lead Re-Recording Mixer** under re-recording conditions. The **Music Re-recording Mixer** is responsible for maintaining optimum re-recorded sound quality while augmenting the story and its imagery with a complementary level of musical background.

**2. Duties:**

▼ **During the Preliminary Phase:**

**a.** Looking at the **Director**'s cut on a video tape of the picture to be dubbed;

**b.** Checking to ensure that all patching from the dummy room to the music mixing console—sound dummies and the multi-track digital magnetic recorder, whether mag, digital DA88, DAT tape, random access digital hard drive from a Pro Tools TDM system—has been properly done;

**c.** Participating in a temp or test dub with representative canned music to get a feel for the movie with the **Director** and **Supervising Sound Editor** in attendance;

▼ **During the Pre-dub Phase:** The **Music Re-Recording Mixer** does not participate in pre-dub procedures.

▼ **During the Dubbing, or Final Mix Phase:**

**d.** Checking the cue sheets for the music elements for each reel to be dubbed;

**e.** Previewing the first reel with the synchronized production dialogue elements to be pre-dubbed;

**f.** Taking tone from the ProTools system drive so that the music score tracks will sound exactly the same as when they were recorded by the **Scoring Mixer**;

**g.** Supervising the patching of the music elements control panel, setting equalization, attenuation, modulation parameters and other sound filtering controls;

**h.** Informing the **Lead Recordist** of the sequence of tracks or units, i.e., which track shall go on which dummy, which dummy patches to the music re-recording console;

i. Advising the **Projectionist** of the reel sequence required in projection of the picture material;

j. With the all-important dialogue run completed by the **Lead Re-Recording Mixer**, going through the reel and balancing the music elements against the dialogue elements as naturally as possible, keeping the music score at complementary levels to the dialogue levels;

k. Selecting and pre-dubbing a couple of the music scoring tracks at a time to 6-track digital tape;

l. Following the music cue sheets during run-throughs and takes, and modifying the cue counts, as necessary;

m. Riding gain on and mixing the music tracks while panning and placing the music on the 6-track digital mag at left, center, right, left surround, right surround and/or on the boom (sub-woofer) channel, as appropriate;

▼ **During the Print Mastering Phase:**

n. Assisting the **Lead Re-Recording Mixer** in attaining the correct balance during the process of combining all the music and sound effects tracks with the dialogue tracks;

o. Riding gain on and mixing the assigned music tracks used in the re-recording of the edited material;

p. Otherwise carrying out the duties normally required of these classifications;

q. Providing the hand tools normally employed in these crafts.

3. **Considerations:** A **Scoring/Sound Effects Mixer** is used when conditions require music and/or sound effects to be combined, whether being originally recorded or re-recorded in the studio.

## Q. SOUND EFFECTS RE-RECORDING MIXER

1. **Responsibilities:** The **Sound Effects Re-Recording Mixer** is directly responsible to the **Lead Re-Recording Mixer** during final dubbing and to the **Supervising Sound Editor** during pre-dub for maintaining optimum sound quality and perspective in the mixing of the sound tracks of the picture or project, consistent with the material being re-recorded while augmenting the story and its imagery with a complementary level of accompanying sound effects.

2. **Duties:**

▼ **During the Preliminary Phase:**

a. Looking at the **Director**'s cut on a video tape of the picture to be dubbed;

b. Checking to ensure that all patching from the dummy room to the sound effects mixing console—sound dummies and the multi-track magnetic recorder—has been properly done;

c. Participating in a temp or test dub with representative canned sound effects to get a feel for the movie with the **Director** and **Supervising Sound Editor** in attendance;

▼ **During the Pre-dub Phase:**

**d.** Checking the cue sheets for the sound effects elements for each reel to be pre-dubbed;

**e.** Previewing the first reel with the sound effects elements to be pre-dubbed;

**f.** Setting equalization, attenuation, modulation and other sound filtering controls in order to balance, pan, equalize and treat the elements to be mixed;

**g.** Categorizing, selecting and pre-dubbing recorded natural background or ambient sounds—traffic, air, wind, rain, thunder, birds, crickets, etc—one category of tracks at a time, to 6-track digital mag, until completed;

**h.** Categorizing, selecting and pre-dubbing recorded hard effects—explosions, gunshots, ricochets, crashes, door slams, sirens—any sound other than ambient or Foley effects;

**i.** Selecting and pre-dubbing Foley sound effects—a category of sounds at a time—to 6-track digital mag, keeping the footsteps separate from the prop sounds, and the footsteps of the principal character on a separate track from those of the background character, until completed;

**j.** Panning and placing the sounds on the 6-track digital mag at left, center, right, left surround, right surround and/or on the boom (sub-woofer) channel, as appropriate;

**k.** Completing the pre-dubbing of all sound effects tracks, usually totaling up to eighty or 120 channels;

▼ **During the Dubbing, or Final Mix Phase:**

**l.** Checking the cue sheets for the sound effects elements for each reel to be dubbed;

**m.** Taking tone from the pre-dub tracks in order to establish a zero-level so the background, Foley and hard effects tracks will sound exactly the same as when they were laid down in pre-dub;

**n.** With the all-important dialogue run completed by the **Lead Re-Recording Mixer**, and the music run completed by the **Music Re-Recording Mixer**, going through the reel and balancing the sound effects elements against the dialogue and music elements as naturally as possible, keeping sound effects at complementary levels to the dialogue and music levels;

**o.** Mixing up to twenty (20) or more 6-track digital sound effects tracks from the pre-dub;

**p.** Supervising the patching of the sound effects control panel, setting equalization, attenuation, modulation parameters and other sound filtering controls;

**q.** Following the sound effects cue sheets during run-throughs and takes, and modifying the cue counts, as necessary;

**r.** Informing the **Lead Recordist** of the sequence of tracks or units, i.e., which track shall go on which dummy;

   **s.** Advising the **Projectionist** of the reel sequence required in projection of the picture material;

   **t.** Riding gain on and mixing the sound effects track(s) while panning and placing the sound effects on the 6-track digital mag at left, center, right, left surround, right surround and/or on the boom (sub-woofer) channel, as appropriate;

   **u.** Directing other **Re-Recording Mixer**s regarding changes in track level and cues;

   **v.** Setting the master level for the composite track;

   **w.** Setting visual time/footage counter(s) at 0000;

   ▼ **During the Print Mastering Phase:**

   **x.** Making the combination of all tracks and/or units to the satisfaction of the **Producer, Director** and/or **Editorial Sound Supervisor**;

   **y.** Re-setting the time/footage counter(s) to 0000 after each run;

   **z.** Otherwise carrying out the duties normally required of this classification;

   **aa.** Providing the hand tools normally employed in this craft.

  **3. Considerations:** A **Sound Effects Re-Recording Mixer** is used whenever the mixing of sound effects tracks is required.

## R. LEAD RECORDIST [DUMMY ROOM SUPERVISOR]

  **1. Responsibilities:** The **Lead Recordist** is directly responsible to the **Lead Re-recording Mixer**, or to the **Scoring** or **Foley Mixer** when recording live music or sound effects in the studio, or to the Employer when transferring sound from mode to mode, for insuring that the recording head is in the proper position to record on the appropriate sound stock, that there is sufficient sound stock in each recorder to record each take, that the recorders are fully operational and are set at the proper recording level and that each dummy has been properly patched to its appropriate mixing console, and is correctly loaded with the correct recorded material, ready to roll and feed their contents to the individual **Re-Recording Mixer**s in perfect synchronization.

  **2. Duties:**

   **a.** Supervising the dummy room, which contains the playback and recording equipment;

   **b.** Patching all input lines from the dummy room to the dialogue, music and sound effects control consoles;

   **c.** Patching from each mixing control console to its recorder;

   **d.** Checking all incoming pre-recorded material for the dub, whether 24-track digital DA88 tape, 33 to 48-track digital tape, DA88 8-track DAT tapes, 2-, 4-, 6-track magnetic tape, Pro Tools disk, or other standard recording media;

   **e.** Seeing that each dummy and recorder is properly loaded—each dummy with proper prerecorded material, at its proper start mark, the recorder(s) loaded with appropriate raw stock, footage counters set at zero read-out—and that the system—sound dummies and projector—is interlocked and ready to roll in synchronization;

**f.** Operating, checking and cleaning all recording equipment;

**g.** Keeping all necessary reports pertinent to sound transfer, re-recording, or voice/music/sound effects recording;

**h.** Writing identifying numbers and titles on head leaders and containers for all rolls of recorded magnetic film, tape or disk;

**i.** Preparing recorded material for shipment, delivery or storage;

**j.** If recording equipment is of a portable nature, setting up and checking out such portable equipment;

**k.** Informing the **Lead Re-Recording Mixer**, or if operating separately, the **Music** or **Sound Effects Re-Recording Mixer**, when the dummies and recorder(s) are ready to roll;

**l.** Degaussing all tape or magnetic film stock to be used in recording the material, labeling it "ERASED" for easy identification, and cleaning the tracks and the recording and playback heads, as necessary;

**m.** When operating in a transfer room:

**(1)** Keeping all sound logs;

**(2)** Using appropriate 1/4″ or 16mm, 17-1/2mm, or 35mm transfer playback machine, with matching pulse lead and resolver, and appropriate magnetic raw stock;

**(3)** Marking transfer stock with appropriate "take and scene" number(s), if required;

**(4)** Transferring only those takes indicated on production logs;

**(5)** Setting the recording level to coincide with the head tone reference level set at the head of every roll of the original production recording(s).

**n.** If required to pick up over telephone lines, operating production recording equipment;

**o.** Operating the interlock system under all conditions;

**p.** Otherwise carrying out the duties normally required of this classification;

**q.** Providing the hand tools normally used in this craft.

**3. Considerations:** A **Lead Recordist** is used at any studio transfer room or re-recording service which records or re-records voice, music and sound effects, or which transfers any original or reprint recording to a like or different medium.

## S. DUMMY LOADER

**1. Responsibilities:** The **Dummy Loader** is a **Recordist** directly responsible to the **Lead Recordist [Dummy Room Supervisor]** for assuring proper line up, interlock and track feed of all dummies to which assigned during each run.

**POST-PRODUC-
TION SOUND**

### 2. Duties:

a. Loading all reproducing film and/or tape in the proper playback start mark position on the designated equipment;

b. Setting time/footage counters to 0000 prior to each run;

c. Placing each dummy under his or her responsibility "**on the line**" in interlock position as directed by the **Lead Recordist** when the **Lead Re-Recording Mixer** is ready to roll a take;

d. When each run is concluded, rewinding film and/or tape to head, placing each tape element on its start mark and locking the machines to insure precise interlock synchronization;

e. Informing the **Lead Recordist** and/or **Lead Re-Recording Mixer** when all elements are in place and the machines are ready to roll;

f. Repairing tracks, as necessary, under the supervision of the **Lead Recordist** and/or the **Picture Editor** or **Supervising Sound Editor**;

g. Cleaning the tape track, guide rollers and playback head of each assigned machine, as necessary;

h. Otherwise carrying out the duties normally required of this classification;

i. Providing the hand tools normally employed in this craft.

### 3. Considerations: A **Dummy Loader** is used when the **Lead Recordist** requires assistance in the preparation and operation of sound dummies.

▼ **Classifications Used for RECORDING MUSIC and DIALOGUE** ▼

## T. SCORING MIXER

### 1. Responsibilities: A **Scoring Mixer**, when used to record original music for a specific motion picture or purpose, is directly responsible to the **Scoring Conductor** and is responsible for recording a high fidelity music track which carries the mood of the story in synchronization with the picture.

### 2. Duties:

a. When mixing live scoring for motion pictures of any kind, the **Scoring Mixer** is chief of recording, and the first **Scoring Mixer** hired is in charge of such music recording and of any additional **Scoring Mixer**s who are hired subsequently to assist in such recording;

b. When **Scoring Mixer**s are making recordings of music at locations under other than recording studio conditions, making sure to achieve correct perspective of such music or musical effects in order to facilitate the job of re-recording;

c. Obtaining correct balance of original music for later re-recording;

d. Knowing how to read a simple piano lead sheet and playing one (1) musical instrument to facilitate optimum rapport with the **Scoring Conductor**;

e. Selecting the microphones to be used for the recording session;

f. Setting up a click track for the use of the **Scoring Conductor**;

**g.** Placing of microphones in the various orchestral sections by the **Scoring Mixer**, assisted by the **Maintenance Engineer**, so as to capture the finest reproduction obtainable of the instrumental music;

**h.** Recording each instrumental section on a separate track;

**i.** Recording on a digital medium, with the option of recording to a hard drive by use of ProTool, or similar proprietary software for direct transfer to the re-recording facility;

**j.** Otherwise carrying out the duties normally required of these classifications;

**k.** Providing the hand tools normally employed in these crafts.

**3. Considerations:** When recording an original music score, a **Scoring Mixer** is used.

## U. SCORING RECORDIST

**1. Responsibilities:** The **Scoring Recordist** is directly responsible to the **Scoring Mixer** for operating tape recorders which are separate from the mixing console and seeing that such recorders are properly set up, threaded, adjusted, connected to the mixing console, and operative during the musical scoring session(s).

**2. Duties:**

**a.** Setting up, connecting to the mixing console, and operating tape recorders;

**b.** Checking that the recording heads are clean and that the recorders are recording and fully operative in all modes;

**c.** Seeing that each tape recorder is properly loaded and threaded with appropriate raw stock, at its proper start position;

**d.** Assisting the **Scoring Mixer** by helping set up microphones in the various instrumental sections of the music recording group;

**e.** Keeping all necessary reports pertinent to recording scoring sound;

**f.** Writing identifying numbers and titles on all recorded tape reels;

**g.** Preparing recorded material for delivery to the transfer house;

**h.** Wrapping the recorders and their associated equipment;

**i.** Assisting the **Scoring Mixer** in the performance of duties;

**j.** Otherwise carrying out the duties normally required of this classification;

**k.** Providing the hand tools normally employed in this craft.

**3. Considerations:** A **Scoring Recordist** is used when recording equipment which is separate from the mixing console is used to capture performed music scoring sessions.

## V. ADR MIXER

**1. Responsibilities:** The **ADR Mixer** is directly responsible to the **Director** of the automatic dialogue replacement session and works with the **Dialogue/ADR**

**Editor** of the ADR material for maintaining optimum sound quality and per-spective in the mixing of the ADR takes for the picture or project in order to ensure optimum sound quality of the replacement dialogue.

2. **Duties:**

  a. Recording all actors reciting lines for dialogue replacement;

  b. Recording all group loop performers adding ambient voice sounds of group babble, exclamations, etc, to scenes with groups of people on camera in a scene or to scenes which require adding multiple voices to various individual players on- or off-screen in a scene;

  c. Supervising all personnel and conditions relating to the ADR recording process;

  d. Patching and supervising the patching of the control panel, setting equal-ization, attenuation, modulation parameters and other sound filtering controls;

  e. Selection of microphones and placement thereof;

  f. Advising the **Projectionist** of the reel, loop and/or segment sequence required in projection of the segments of the picture requiring voice replacement;

  g. Providing each actor doing voice replacement with a headset for an audio feed from each segment during the voice dubbing process;

  h. Running each ADR segment, in which existing dialogue is to be replaced, repeatedly for each actor during rehearsals and takes until the **Director** has chosen a take which he or she feels delivers the feeling of the scene and is in precise synchronization with the picture;

  i. Going on to each ADR segment in turn, for rehearsals and takes, until the session has been completed;

  j. Preparing the recorded tape for shipment and/or delivery to the Sound Transfer Studio;

  k. Otherwise carrying out the duties normally required of this classification;

  l. Providing the hand tools normally employed in this craft.

3. **Considerations:** An **ADR Mixer** is used whenever automatic dialogue re-placement is required for a production.

▼ **Classifications Used for RECORDING and MAKING SOUND EFFECTS** ▼

W. **FOLEY MIXER**

  1. **Responsibilities:** The **Foley Mixer** is directly responsible to the **Director** or the **Foley Editor** for maintaining optimum sound quality and perspective in the recording of the Foley specialized sound for the picture or project, con-sistent with the material being re-recorded.

**2. Duties:**

   **a.** Recording all sound effects created by **Foley Artist**s;

   **b.** Supervising all personnel and conditions relating to the sound effects recording process;

   **c.** Patching and supervising the patching of the control panel, setting equalization, attenuation, modulation parameters and other sound filtering controls;

   **d.** Selecting microphones and placing them in order to pick up the best sound for each effect being created in the Foley pits on the Foley stage;

   **e.** Recording each effect on a separate track for re-recording control;

   **f.** Recording each character's footsteps on a separate track for re-recording control;

   **g.** Working from a sound effects cue sheet prepared by the **Foley Artist**(s);

   **h.** Advising the **Projectionist** of the reel sequence required in projection of the picture material;

   **i.** Re-setting the time/footage counter(s) to 0000 after each run;

   **j.** Preparing the recorded tape for shipment and/or delivery to the Sound Transfer Studio;

   **k.** Otherwise carrying out the duties normally required of this classification;

   **l.** Providing the hand tools normally employed in this craft.

**3. Considerations:** A **Lead Re-Recording Mixer** is used whenever the combining of two (2) or more recorded tracks is required.

## X. SOUND EFFECTS SPECIALIST [FOLEY ARTIST]

**1. Responsibilities:** The **Sound Effects Specialist** or **Foley Artist** is directly responsible to the **Foley Mixer** during the recording on a digital audio workstation of live sound effects, and is responsible for selecting sound effects cues from tape or disc recordings and purchasing, renting, constructing (when necessary) and creatively operating sound effects devices during live, in real time, recording sessions, either to specified clock time and/or in synchronization with picture in order to create and generate appropriate sound effects for the picture.

**2. Duties:**

   **a.** Reading and annotating the script within the context of the production of supplementary sound effects—live and canned;

   **b.** Preparing a list of sound effects required by the film or tape production;

   **c.** Selecting appropriate sound effects cues from tape or disc recordings and from digital storage;

   **d.** Preparing a sound effects cue sheet for the **Foley Mixer** to use during the recording session;

e. Ordering, designing, developing, constructing, maintaining and operating implements, props and other equipment used in creating live sound effects;

f. Ordering materials for the construction and repair of such equipment;

g. Operating all sound-creating matériel used in the Foley arena, during testing, rehearsals and takes, whether on the floor or in the specially designed surface pits;

h. Placing microphones and checking sound quality and levels to assure optimum effect and pickup of the created sounds;

i. Layering sound effects to create a full, rich audio reality;

j. Otherwise carrying out the duties normally required of this classification;

k. Providing the hand tools normally employed in this craft.

3. **Considerations:**

a. A **Sound Effects Specialist** works with matériel which produces, or can be used to produce, sound effects and does not operate recording equipment.

b. A **Foley Artist** is a **Sound Effects Specialist** who creates sound effects—such as footsteps, clothes rustling, body blows, falls, minor collisions, etc—in synchronization with projected picture images.

c. Sound effects are defined as all those sounds—exclusive of live voice, or live music, or those sounds picked up on the production track—which are used to create, or recreate, the appropriate illusion of audio-visual reality in a film or tape production.

▼ **Classification Used for TRANSFERRING ORIGINAL SOUND** ▼

## Y. TRANSFER RECORDIST

1. **Responsibilities:** The **Transfer Recordist** is directly responsible to the Employer for maintaining the transfer recorder at the proper audio level(s) at all times during the transfer process.

2. **Duties:**

a. Transferring original sound tracks to tape or disc as per directions noted on the Sound Report;

b. Aligning the transfer machine(s) properly prior to each transfer;

c. Checking the head tone and setting the zero level at an appropriate level for the transfer—generally, a minus 8 dbm on a Nagra on the particular playback VU meter;

d. Keeping all sound logs;

e. Using appropriate 1/4″ or 16mm, 17 1/2mm, or 35mm transfer playback machine, with matching pulse lead and resolver, and appropriate magnetic raw stock;

**f.** Marking transfer stock with appropriate "take and scene" number(s), if required;

**g.** Transferring only those takes indicated on production sound report logs;

**h.** Setting the recording level to coincide with the reference level set on the head of every roll of the original production recording(s);

**i.** If required to pick up over telephone lines, operating appropriate recording equipment;

**j.** Returning all original material and transferred sound to the Production Company;

**k.** Degaussing all tape or magnetic film stock to be used in recording the material, labeling it "ERASED" for easy identification, and cleaning the tracks and the recording and playback heads, as necessary;

**l.** Otherwise carrying out the duties normally required of this classification;

**m.** Providing the hand tools normally employed in this craft.

**3. Considerations:** A **Transfer Recordist** is used when sound transfer equipment is utilized.

▼ Classification Used for RE-RECORDING and RECORDING PROCEDURES ▼

## Z. PROJECTIONIST

**1. Responsibilities:** The **Projectionist** is directly responsible to the **Lead Re-Recording Mixer** when working in a recording or re-recording studio context, or to the Employer when on a straight projection assignment, for maintaining the picture at optimum viewing standard while screening the film.

**2. Duties:**

**a. Under studio recording or re-recording conditions:**

**(1)** Threading film into the projector, maintaining proper emulsion position;

**(2)** Setting and maintaining the arc, or bulb, at proper brilliance;

**(3)** Placing the correct lens and aspect matte in the projector(s) used;

**(4)** Positioning the aspect cut-off mattes of the screen, if any, to conform to the projected aspect ratio;

**(5)** Maintaining optimal focus of the image on the screen;

**(6)** Positioning the "start mark" on the film in the gate behind the lens prior to each recording or re-recording run;

**(7)** Informing the **Lead Recordist** and/or **Lead Re-Recording Mixer** when the projector is loaded, on the start mark, ready to run and "on the line";

**(8)** Putting the projector on or off interlock when directed to do so by the **Lead Re-Recording Mixer**;

**(9)** Splicing and/or repairing film damaged in projection, making certain the film length is not affected by such repair (under supervision of the **Sound Supervisor** or **Film Editor**, if available);

**(10)** Cleaning the film gate and lens, and lubricating the mechanism, as necessary.

b. **When on a straight projection assignment with portable or installed equipment:**

**(1)** Setting up the projector(s), screen(s), and sound speaker(s), as necessary;

**(2)** Selecting and installing the appropriate projection lens and aspect ratio matte;

**(3)** Cleaning the lens and film gate, as necessary;

**(4)** Threading film through the projector transport system;

**(5)** Making a test run of a few feet in order to set image size, screen-to-projector distance, focus and sound level;

**(6)** Projecting the film for the purposes of the assignment, at the time specified, for the time required, and making change-overs smoothly;

**(7)** Maintaining optimal arc/lamp brilliance, focus and sound level during the screening;

**(8)** Activating the house lights, screen curtains and aspect ratio mattes, and the house recorded music, during intermissions;

**(9)** Rewinding and repairing the film, as necessary;

**(10)** Wrapping the projection equipment, if portable.

c. Otherwise carrying out the duties normally required of this classification;

d. Providing the hand tools normally employed in this craft.

**3. Considerations:**

a. A **Projectionist** is used when projection equipment is utilized.

b. The **Projectionist** is required to stand by the projector(s) at all times during projection. The **Projectionist** normally operates not more than two (2) projectors concurrently.

▼ **Classification Used for MAINTENANCE of SOUND EQUIPMENT** ▼

**AA. MAINTENANCE ENGINEER**

**1. Responsibilities:** The **Maintenance Engineer** is directly responsible to the Employer for maintaining all electronic and mechanical equipment associated with the recording and re-recording processes at optimum operational standards.

**2. Duties:**

a. Repairing and maintaining all electronic recording and re-recording equipment, projectors and associated equipment;

**b.** Checking and replacing tubes, resistors, relays, transistors, transformers, condensers, wiring, and other components, as necessary;

**c.** Preparing, repairing and replacing all microphone cables, power cords and wiring used;

**d.** Making periodic frequency checks of the electronics equipment;

**e.** Aligning all reproduction and recording heads on all recording equipment, including the photoelectric cell and its mattes;

**f.** Assisting **Scoring**, **ADR** or **Foley Mixer** in placing microphones, patching procedures, running cable, setting up and wrapping sound gear;

**g.** Otherwise carrying out the duties normally required of this classification;

**h.** Providing the hand tools normally employed in this craft.

**3. Considerations:** The **Maintenance Engineer** provides a distortion meter and a volt/ohm/ammeter plus the hand tools normally employed in this craft, unless on staff, in which case the Company provides such test equipment and tools.

# Art Category Organizational Chart

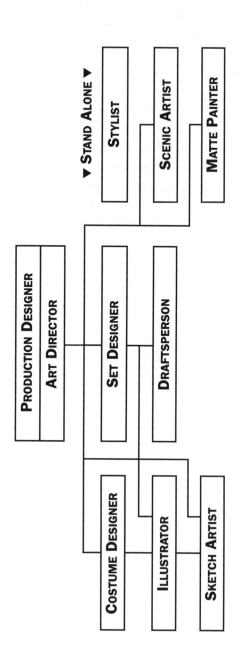

**Production Designer**

**Art Director**

**Set Designer**

**Draftsperson**

**Costume Designer**

**Illustrator**

**Sketch Artist**

▼ **Stand Alone** ▼

**Stylist**

**Scenic Artist**

**Matte Painter**

# 8

# ART CATEGORY

**A. Category Classifications:** There are nine (9) classifications in the Art Category:

1. **Art Director or Production Designer (Category Head)**
2. **Set Designer**
3. **Costume Designer (Category Sub-Head)**
4. **Stylist (Category Sub-Head)**
5. **Scenic Artist (Category Sub-Head)**
6. **Illustrator**
7. **Matte Painter**
8. **Sketch Artist**
9. **Draftsperson**

**B. Category Criteria:**

1. Employees holding classification within the Art Category perform all job functions pertaining to the production design, planning and execution of cinematographic settings, scenery, costumes and set dressing which are utilized on interior or exterior production, airborne or underwater, on location and/or on the sound stage.

2. On all productions requiring overall production design and/or original design of sets, scenery, costumes and/or furniture and props, an **Art Director** or **Production Designer** is used to plan and supervise such work.

3. An **Art Director/Production Designer** needs to know and apply: The principles of cinematic design and construction and a thorough knowledge of the most effective use of matériel involved; costume design and execution; the aesthetic effect of color, texture and form.

4. On those productions using an **Art Director**, the **Art Director** supervises all sets, furniture, model and prop construction and finishing, scenic art work, and set dressing, and coordinates costuming, makeup and hair styling.

5. The **Set Designer** renders all set drawings and oversees the drafting of all elevation and floor construction plans;

6. A **Scenic Artist** may be used to execute scenic art work without an **Art Director** being employed, provided no other **Art Director** duties are required, in which event the **Scenic Artist** is directly responsible to the **Producer**.

7. Only on television commercial productions and still photographic assignments which do not require set design or construction, a **Stylist** may be

**113**

used, if desired, so long as the **Stylist**'s function is consultative and advisory only, and on the set, the **Stylist** does not physically handle props, wardrobe, set dressing, makeup, hair, script or other matériel which is normally handled by other categories and classifications of work.

8. When the **Art Director** requires assistance in:

   a. Executing perspective renderings of sets, set dressing, props and/or the storyboard for production design, a **Sketch Artist** is used;

   b. Executing plan or elevation drawings for set construction, a **Draftsperson** is used;

   c. Researching, selecting and planning the placement of items of set dressing, a **Set Decorator** is used;

   d. Researching and designing costumes and selecting accessories therefor, a **Costume Designer** is used;

   e. Designing and executing scenic displays, a **Scenic Artist** is used.

9. When the **Set Designer** requires assistance in executing set illustrations and design elements, a **Sketch Artist** and/or **Draftsperson** is used.

10. When the **Costume Designer** requires assistance in executing set illustrations and design elements, a **Sketch Artist** is used.

11. When the **Stylist** requires assistance in researching, planning, selecting and/or picking up set dressing, props and/or items of wardrobe for television commercials, a **Production Assistant** is used.

12. When the **Scenic Artist** requires assistance in researching, planning and executing scenic renderings, a **Sketch Artist** is used.

13. When the **Illustrator** requires assistance in preparing illustrations for storyboards, a **Sketch Artist** is used.

14. When a **Matte Painter** requires assistance in preparing mattes, a **Sketch Artist** is used.

15. All Art personnel operating underwater with breathing apparatus must be SCUBA certified.

16. The **Art Director** and each Art Category Sub-Head must ensure that art personnel do not attempt work under any unsafe condition(s), as specified by the Employer, OSHA, Building and Safety Code and fire laws, or in violation of any other safety regulation(s) and practice(s).

C. **Category Responsibilities:** It is the responsibility of each Employee in the Art Category to work cooperatively with the **Art Director,** or with the Sub-Head to whom assigned, in order to assist in achieving the optimum and most efficient operation of the various procedures within this category.

D. **Category Function:** The principal function of Art Category personnel involves work developing a design concept for the production and then designing the settings, selecting and/or designing the set dressings and/or costumes for the production and supervising the execution thereof consistent with the period, style and mood of the production project.

**E. Category Considerations:**

**1.** Art Category personnel are used on each production on which there is design for construction of settings and/or creation of costumes and/or coordination of set dressings.

**2.** The classification(s) used depends upon the type of cinematic production being produced and also upon the type and number of art functions required on that project.

**F. Category Requirements:** Employees in each Art Category classification must know and follow the chain-of-command and lines-of-communication and must know and be able to effectively apply the techniques associated with their respective craft classification.

**G. ART DIRECTOR/PRODUCTION DESIGNER**

**1. Responsibilities:** The **Art Director/Production Designer** is directly responsible to the **Producer**, or the **Producer**'s designee; works in close cooperation with the **Director**; and is responsible for developing a design concept and maintaining consistency and accuracy in the renderings of the art elements and their execution in order to ensure pictorial perfection of the settings.

**2. Duties:**

▼ **During PRE-PRODUCTION:**

**a.** Reading and annotating the script, analyzing it visually and dramaturgically within the context of art direction and/or overall production design;

**b.** Visualizing, researching, designing and supervising all art work associated with the production—production design and/or the storyboard; set design and construction; set decoration and set dressing; furniture, prop and costume design, and the execution thereof; and picture titles—based on the script and on the **Producer**'s, **Director**'s and **Director of Photography**'s input, requirements and approval;

**c.** Planning and executing the complete production design of the picture if called upon to do so, receiving credit as **Production Designer**;

**d.** Determining from the script, the number and type of sets and set dressing required;

**e.** Preparing a schedule breakdown, from the script, of set construction requirements—building and finishing materials, furniture, properties, drapes, fixtures and other set dressing in consultation with the **Construction Coordinator**, **Set Decorator** and **Property Master**;

**f.** Preparing and presenting a budget breakdown of estimated set costs to the **Production Manager** for approval;

g. Selecting and/or designing furniture, properties, backdrops, scenic cycloramas and other set dressings;

h. Directing the **Set Designer** to provide color sketches, construction diagrams, floor plans and elevation drafts, and/or **Sketch Artist** detail drawings for Set Construction personnel;

i. Participating in the selection of location sites;

j. Ordering scale models made by a **Model Builder** of designed settings for the use of the **Director** in planning his action blocking, the **Director of Photography**, the **Set Decorator**, and others;

k. Ordering and overseeing the fabrication of mechanical units and working props from schematic drawings;

l. Selecting paint, wall and floor covering materials for color, texture and pattern coordination;

m. Directing style, size and placement of signs, logos and lettering;

n. Overseeing fabrication of ornamental plaster and plastic work along with sculptured units;

o. Overseeing backdrop painting by **Scenic Artists** and the placement on-set thereof;

p. Selecting trees and shrubbery for landscape dressing;

q. Selecting plumbing fixtures, hardware and lighting fixtures of appropriate period and directs installation thereof;

r. Selecting fabrics and special drapery and upholstery materials;

s. Selectsing and/or approving interior and exterior decorative furnishings;

t. Overseeing the design and construction of rolling, floating, flying and other property stock;

u. Consulting with the **Director** concerning sequences involving montage and/or CGI elements;

▼ **During the PRODUCTION Process:**

v. Conferring with the **Director** and **Director of Photography** regarding process and trick shots;

w. Conferring and cooperating with the **Director of Photography** with respect to illumination accommodation on the settings;

x. Seeing that each set and setting is properly set up, complete and functional in all respects and modifying the design, construction and dressing, as necessary, to accommodate the **Director** and **Director of Photography**;

y. Otherwise carrying out the duties normally required of this classification;

z. Providing the hand tools normally employed in this craft.

3. **Considerations:**

a. An **Art Director** is used when set design and/or the coordination of set dressing and wardrobe is required.

**b.** The **Art Director** is given adequate preparation time to plan, assign and execute applicable work and duties.

**c.** It is highly recommended that the **Art Director/Production Designer** be included on any location scouting trips in order to help insure optimum preparation and utilization of the location(s).

## H. SET DESIGNER

**1. Responsibilities:** The **Set Designer** is directly responsible to the **Art Director/Production Designer** and is responsible for designing the set according to sketches, notes and specifications made or approved by the **Art Director/Production Designer**.

**2. Duties—during PRE-PRODUCTION:**

**a.** Reading and analyzing the script from a set design perspective;

**b.** Consulting with the **Art Director/Production Designer** to review sketches, renderings, notes and specifications;

**c.** Researching the architectural style and construction of interiors and exteriors for the period;

**d.** Overseeing the work of **Sketch Artist**s and **Draftsperson**s assigned to work on set design elements;

**e.** Consulting with the **Construction Coordinator** regarding specific design elements required and the feasibility of substitution thereof;

**f.** Otherwise carrying out the duties normally required of this classification;

**g.** Providing the hand tools normally employed in this craft.

**3. Considerations:** The **Set Designer** does not construct the set or any element thereof, but may arrange to acquire certain construction elements and make them available to the **Construction Coordinator**, as necessary.

## I. COSTUME DESIGNER

**1. Responsibilities:** The **Costume Designer** is directly responsible to the **Art Director/Production Designer** for designing the costumes and accessories in a manner accurately reflecting the period, and/or the **Art Director/Production Designer**'s overall production design requirements, and best suited to give optimum aesthetic and photographic realization of the costumes.

**2. Duties—during PRE-PRODUCTION:**

**a.** Reading and analyzing the script in the context of costume design;

**b.** Planning, designing and supervising execution of costumes and accessories at the direction and subject to the approval of the **Art Director/Production Designer**;

**c.** Preparing line drawings and color sketches for approval by the **Art Director/Production Designer**;

**d.** Selecting materials and preparing patterns for costume fabrication;

**e.** Preparing orders for materials necessary to execute this work;

**f.** Otherwise carrying out the duties normally required of this classification;

**g.** Providing the hand tools normally employed in this craft.

### 3. Considerations:

**a.** A **Costume Designer** is used when the **Art Director/Production Designer** requires assistance in the design and execution of costumes.

**b.** The **Costume Designer** is given adequate preparation time to plan and design the costuming, and supervises the execution of all costumes.

## J. STYLIST

**1. Responsibilities:** The **Stylist** is used only on TV commercials and is directly responsible to the **Producer** of the TV commercial. The **Stylist** is responsible for maintaining consistency and accuracy in selection and placement of props, set dressing and wardrobe and of the color and style coordination of these items and of makeup and hair styling throughout the TV commercial production, in order to help ensure the optimum aesthetic and photographic effect of those elements.

### 2. Duties:

▼ **During PRE-PRODUCTION:**

**a.** Reading and annotating the script and/or reviewing and annotating the storyboard;

**b.** Determining from the script and/or story board, the number and type of prop, set dressing and wardrobe items required;

**c.** Preparing a schedule breakdown for the use of the **Prop Master**, **Key Wardrobe** person and **Set Decorator** in order to facilitate the physical handling of these elements on the set;

▼ **During PRODUCTION and POST-PRODUCTION:**

**d.** Visualizing, researching, selecting, coordinating and supervising the placement of props and set dressing, the type, design and color of the wardrobe, the style of both makeup and hairdressing;

**e.** Following the shoot, collecting and accounting for all prop and set dressing items and wardrobe items, and returning them to the vendors;

**f.** Otherwise carrying out the duties normally required of this classification;

**g.** Providing the hand tools normally employed in this craft.

### 3. Considerations:

**a.** The **Stylist** may be used on TV commercial production and still photographic assignments only.

**b.** The **Stylist** does not physically place props, handle wardrobe, or apply makeup or hairdressing to the performer(s).

**c.** The **Stylist** is given adequate preparation time to plan and execute duties.

**d.** The **Stylist** prepares a schedule breakdown for the use of the **Prop Master**,

**Key Wardrobe** person and **Set Decorator** in order to facilitate the physical handling of these elements on the set.

e. It is recommended that the **Stylist** be included on any location scouting trips in order to help insure optimum preparation and utilization of the location setting(s).

## K. SCENIC ARTIST

**1. Responsibilities:** The **Scenic Artist** is directly responsible to the **Art Director/Production Designer**, or as specified in Category Criteria, above, for the proper technical and aesthetic expression of the work of executing scenic backings, drops, cycloramas and glass shots in order to meet the highest aesthetic photographic standards thereof.

**2. Duties—during PRE-PRODUCTION:**

a. When executing artwork for a specific production, reading the script for an understanding of the scenic requirements;

b. Preparing orders for painting materials and any special equipment needed in the preparation and application of the materials to the backings, drops, flats, cycloramas and/or glass mattes;

c. Preparing and/or working from approved sketches of the planned scenic rendering(s);

d. Supervising all **Artist**s assigned to assist in preparing scenic art work;

e. Supervising film tests of scenic art work;

f. Otherwise carrying out the duties normally required of this classification;

g. Providing the hand tools normally employed in this craft.

**3. Considerations:**

a. A **Scenic Artist** is used when the design and execution of scenic art is necessary.

b. The **Scenic Artist** may be assisted by one (1) or more **Sketch Artist**s when necessary.

## L. ILLUSTRATOR

**1. Responsibilities:** The **Illustrator** is directly responsible to the **Art Director/Production Designer**, or as specified in Category Criteria, above, for preparing illustrated storyboards of scenes or sequences specified by the **Art Director/Production Designer** or **Director** in order to present the proposed action and scenic elements in the clearest way possible to facilitate production planning and shooting.

**2. Duties—during PRE-PRODUCTION and PRODUCTION:**

a. Reading and annotating the script sequences to be storyboarded in order to determine the most effective way to prepare and present the storyboarded sequences;

**b.** Conferring with the **Production Designer** and/or **Director** for their input, as necessary;

**c.** Determining whether to employ photographs of the settings and proposed setups, and/or sketches thereof, to illustrate the storyboard(s);

**d.** Adding descriptive text to each illustration, or as provided by Directorial;

**e.** Otherwise carrying out the duties normally required of this classification;

**f.** Providing the hand tools normally employed in this craft.

**3. Considerations:** An **Illustrator** is used when a need for storyboarding a production sequence is required.

## M. MATTE PAINTER

**1. Responsibilities:** The **Matte Painter** is directly responsible to the **Art Director/Production Designer** for preparing mattes which, when applied to optical camera work, will effectively bar imagery in specific portions of the frame from being transmitted, thereby permitting the compositing of other imagery in its place during the optical compositing process.

**2. Duties—during PRE-PRODUCTION, PRODUCTION and POST-PRODUCTION:**

**a.** When executing artwork for a specific production, reading the script for an understanding of the scenic requirements;

**b.** Preparing orders for painting materials and any special equipment needed in the preparation and application of the materials during the matte painting process;

**c.** Preparing and/or working from approved sketches of the planned scenic rendering(s) and the areas to be matted out;

**d.** Viewing film tests of the executed matte painting work;

**e.** Otherwise carrying out the duties normally required of this classification;

**f.** Providing the hand tools normally employed in this craft.

**3. Considerations:** A **Matte Painter** is used when the design and painting of mattes are necessary.

## N. SKETCH ARTIST

**1. Responsibilities:** The **Sketch Artist** is directly responsible as specified in Category Criteria, above, and is responsible for accurately executing sketches and/or detailed plan and elevation drawings of sets and set dressing, in order to facilitate construction thereof.

**2. Duties—during PRE-PRODUCTION and PRODUCTION:**

**a.** Assisting the person in the Art Category to whom assigned;

**b.** Detailing and/or coloring storyboard, costume and proposed setting sketches;

**c.** Accurately and clearly executing all assigned work in the proper form and on appropriate materials;

    **d.** Otherwise carrying out the duties normally required of these classifications;

    **e.** Providing the hand tools normally employed in these crafts.

**3. Considerations: Sketch Artist**s are used to assist other Art Category personnel in the performance of specified duties.

## O. DRAFTSPERSON

**1. Responsibilities:** The **Draftsperson** is directly responsible as specified in Category Criteria, above, and is responsible for accurately executing detailed plan and elevation drawings of sets, in order to facilitate their accurate construction.

**2. Duties—during PRE-PRODUCTION and PRODUCTION:**

    **a.** Assisting the person in the Art Category to whom assigned;

    **b.** Executing plan and elevation drawings for the construction of sets, scenery, furniture and/or specialized props;

    **c.** Accurately and clearly executing all assigned work in the proper form and on appropriate materials;

    **d.** Otherwise carrying out the duties normally required of these classifications;

    **e.** Providing the hand tools normally employed in these crafts.

**3. Considerations: Draftsperson**s are used to assist other Art Category personnel in the performance of specified duties.

# Construction Category Organizational Chart

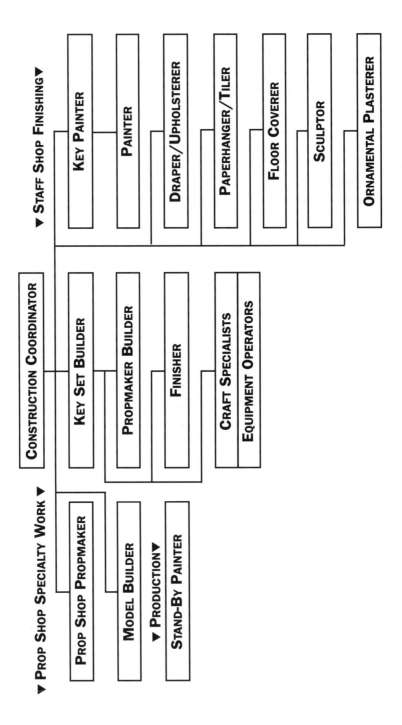

▼ Prop Shop Specialty Work ▼

Construction Coordinator

▼ Staff Shop Finishing▼

Prop Shop Propmaker

Model Builder

▼ Production▼

Stand-By Painter

Key Set Builder

Propmaker Builder

Finisher

Craft Specialists

Equipment Operators

Key Painter

Painter

Draper/Upholsterer

Paperhanger/Tiler

Floor Coverer

Sculptor

Ornamental Plasterer

# 9

# CONSTRUCTION CATEGORY

A. **Category Classifications:** There are eighteen (18) classifications in the propmaking Construction Category, including two (2) divisions of **Construction Specialist**s:

▼ **For the CONSTRUCTION Process:**

1. **Construction Coordinator (Category Head)**

2. **Key Set Builder (Foreman—Category Co-Head)**

3. **Propmaker Builder**

4. **Finisher**

5. **Construction Specialists:**

   a. **Craft Specialists: Cabinet Maker; Wood Carver; Stone, Metal, Clay or Plastics Sculptor; Stone, Brick, Plaster, Foam, Cement or Concrete Mason; Glazier; Welder; Mechanic; Metal Worker; Plumber; Pipe Fitter; Electrician, and other craft specialties; and**

   b. **Equipment Operators of: Crane, Bulldozer, Power Roller, Power Shovel, Earth Mover, Earth Compactor, Pile-Driver, Trencher, Skip-Loader, Cherry-Picker, Fork-Lift, Air Hammer, and other heavy equipment.**

▼ **For the FINISHING Process from the Staff Shop:**

6. **KEY PAINTER (Foreman—Category Sub-Head)**

7. **Painter**

8. **Draper**

9. **Upholsterer**

10. **Paperhanger**

11. **Tiler**

12. **Floor Coverer**

13. **Sculptor**

14. **Ornamental Plasterer**

▼ **For SPECIALTY Work from the Prop Shop:**

15. **Prop Shop Propmaker (Category Sub-Head)**

16. **Model Builder (Category Sub-Head)**

▼ **For the Production Process:**

17. **Stand-by Painter**

**B. Category Criteria:**

**1.** Employees holding classification within the Construction Category perform all job functions pertaining to set construction and to location site preparation procedures which are utilized on interior or exterior production, on location and/or on the sound stage.

**2.** A **Construction Coordinator** is used on each production whereon set construction or alteration is required for use on a sound stage or on location, interior or exterior, and is in technical charge of all production construction work, but does not design sets, set dressing or props.

**3.** The **Construction Coordinator** is directly responsible to the **Art Director/ Production Designer** for the look of the sets and to the **Production Manager** for the work and timely completion of all sets and settings.

**4.** A **Key Set Builder** needs to know and apply: Cinematic set construction tools and techniques; appropriate matériel to each set construction project; managerial skills.

**5.** The **Key Painter** is in charge of all decorative and standard painting.

**6.** The **Key Set Builder** is directly responsible to the **Construction Coordinator** for completing the work on schedule.

**7.** On those productions not employing a **Construction Coordinator**, the **Key Set Builder** is directly responsible to the **Art Director/Production Designer** for the look of the construction.

**8.** Should an **Art Director/Production Designer** not be employed on a production, the **Construction Coordinator** is directly responsible to the **Production Manager**.

**9.** **Construction Specialists**, when working on set construction or location preparation, are directly responsible to the **Art Director/Production Designer**, or to the **Construction Coordinator**, as assigned.

**10.** **Utility** personnel may be used to assist **Construction Specialist**s in the performance of the non-skilled aspects of the particular specialty.

**11.** When the **Model Builder** and/or **Prop Shop Propmaker** are required to function on the set during production shooting—physically setting up, modifying, dressing models or miniatures, operating, disassembling or removing models or mechanized operative props, as the case may be—they each function within the Property Category and are directly responsible to the **Property Master** during the production process.

**12.** When the **Key Set Builder** requires assistance in:

    **a.** Set Construction, one (1) or more **Propmaker Builders** are used, as needed;

    **b.** Set painting, a **Key Painter** is used;

    **c.** Set draping, a **Draper** is used;

    **d.** Set or set prop upholstery, an **Upholsterer** is used;

    **e.** Set paper hanging or tiling, a **Paperhanger** and/or **Tiler** is used;

CONSTRUCTION

**f.** Carpeting or floor covering, a **Carpeter** and/or **Floor Coverer** is used;

**g.** Sculpting, a **Sculptor** is used;

**h.** Ornamental set plastering, an **Ornamental Plasterer** is used;

**i.** Model or miniature construction, a **Model Builder** is used;

**j.** Hand prop or set prop construction, a **Prop Shop Propmaker** is used;

**k.** Such craft specialties as: Cabinet making and wood carving; stone, brick, plaster, cement or concrete masonry; glass, metal or plastic work; welding; plumbing, pipe fitting; electrical work, etc, **Craft Specialist**s of appropriate specialty are used;

**l.** Set construction or location preparation on which such heavy equipment as: A crane, bulldozer, power shovel, earth mover, earth compactor, pile driver, skip loader, cherry-picker, fork-lift, air hammer, etc, **Equipment Operator**s of appropriate specialty are used.

**13.** sistance, one (1) or more **Propmaker Builder**s are added, as needed.

**14.** When a **Key Painter** requires assistance, one (1) or more **Painter**s are added, as needed.

**15.** When a **Draper, Upholsterer, Paperhanger, Tiler, Ornamental Plasterer, Model Builder, Propmaker Builder** or **Craft** or **Construction Specialist** requires general and unspecialized assistance, **Utility** personnel may be used.

**16.** The Employer provides all power tools required to accomplish the fabrication process.

**17.** All Construction personnel operating underwater with breathing apparatus must be SCUBA certified.

**18.** The **Construction Coordinator** and each Construction Category Sub-Head must ensure that construction personnel do not attempt work under any unsafe condition(s), as specified by the Employer, OSHA, Building and Safety Code and fire laws, or in violation of any other safety regulation(s) and practice(s).

**C. Category Responsibilities:** It is the responsibility of each Employee in the Construction Category to work cooperatively with the **Construction Coordinator**, or with the Sub-Head to whom assigned, in order to assist in achieving the optimum and most efficient operation of the various procedures within this category.

**D. Category Function:** The principal function of Construction personnel involves company property-making work—constructing, assembling and finishing cinematic settings, set dressing, miniatures, models and working props to the exacting specifications of the **Art Director/Production Designer**.

**E. Category Considerations:**

**1.** Construction Category personnel are used on each production on which there is set construction and finishing.

**2.** The classification(s) used depends upon the type of motion picture being produced and upon the number of settings, props and models to be constructed and dressed.

CONSTRUCTION

**F. Category Requirements:** Employees in each Construction Category classification must know and follow the chain-of-command and lines-of-communication and must be able to effectively and safely set up and operate the set and for site construction equipment and related material selected for each job and associated with their respective craft classification.

### ▼ Classifications Used for the CONSTRUCTION Process ▼

## G. CONSTRUCTION COORDINATOR

**1. Responsibilities:** The **Construction Coordinator** is directly responsible as specified in Category Criteria above, and is responsible for coordinating the construction and detailing of settings, furniture, set dressing, working props, models and miniatures on a schedule to be finished, painted and ready for dressing and principal photography.

**2. Duties—during PRE-PRODUCTION and PRODUCTION:**

   **a.** Reading and annotating the script within the contextual requirements of all production construction—matériel, personnel and scheduling;

   **b.** Preparing a budget breakdown of estimated costs for personnel and matériel and the time schedule involved in the construction process for the **Producer** or **Production Manager**;

   **c.** Approving purchase orders and invoices;

   **d.** Seeing that all plans, drawings and specifications for construction of sets, set dressing, working props, breakaways, models and miniatures are received from the **Art Director** and distributed to the appropriate construction crafts people;

   **e.** Meeting with Set Decoration, Special Effects and any other category which will interface with construction to determine that they have everything they need from the Construction Category;

   **f.** Visiting construction sites and sets, seeing that all construction is proceeding at a pace which will assure that all construction production elements are ready, delivered to the set or location site, properly detailed and finished, set up and ready for dressing and principal photography;

   **g.** Otherwise carrying out the duties normally required of this classification;

   **h.** Providing the hand tools normally employed in this craft.

**3. Considerations:** A **Construction Coordinator** is used when production construction work is extensive and intensive and requires coordination with other categories and departments or aspects of the production process.

## H. KEY SET BUILDER

**1. Responsibilities:** The **Key Set Builder** is directly responsible as specified in Category Criteria above, and is responsible for constructing the sets, furniture and set dressing required by the production as efficiently, accurately and economically as possible in order to achieve the desired functional result.

**2. Duties—during PRE-PRODUCTION and PRODUCTION:**

**a.** Reading and annotating the script within the context of set construction—matériel, personnel and scheduling;

**b.** Preparing a budget breakdown of costs for personnel and matériel and the time schedule involved in the construction process for the **Construction Coordinator**;

**c.** Constructing the required sets and dressings from approved plans, drawings and specifications for studio or location use;

**d.** Laying out the floor or surface, marking or taping where the set walls will be set up;

**e.** Preparing orders for the construction materials and equipment required;

**f.** Supervising all construction of sets and settings;

**g.** Supervising the installation of the completed set pieces at the shooting site on stage or location;

**h.** Constructing all necessary set and site scaffolding for the production;

**i.** Making certain all set construction is structurally sound;

**j.** Otherwise carrying out the duties normally required of this classification;

**k.** Providing the hand tools normally employed in this craft.

**3. Considerations:**

**a.** A **Key Set Builder** is used when construction for production purposes takes place.

**b.** A **Key Set Builder** works with material and major tools provided by the **Producer**.

**I. PROPMAKER BUILDER**

**1. Responsibilities:** The **Propmaker Builder** is a construction specialist directly responsible to the **Key Set Builder** and assists in the performance of that person's duties.

**2. Duties—during PRE-PRODUCTION and PRODUCTION:**

**a.** The setting up and operation of any shop or mill equipment for wood, metal, or plastics;

**b.** Assisting in inventorying and ordering construction matériel, and picking it up;

**c.** Constructing sets and settings from plans and specifications;

**d.** Having a working knowledge of carpentry skills as well as welding, cutting, stamping, forming and trimming of metal structures, as necessary;

**e.** Preparing, loading and making local delivery of finished set pieces;

**f.** Positioning and erecting all set pieces at the shooting site;

**g.** Striking set pieces when photography using those pieces has been completed and the **Production Manager** has given the go-ahead to strike;

**h.** Assisting the **Key Set Builder** in the performance of set construction duties;

**i.** Otherwise carrying out the duties normally required of this classification;

**j.** Providing the hand tools normally employed in this craft.

**3. Considerations:**

**a.** A **Propmaker Builder** is a construction specialist who receives work assignments from the **Key Set Builder**.

**b.** Among the working skills a **Propmaker Builder** must have are: carpentry, milling, machine shop, welding, and work in wood, metal, leather, plastics, glass and foam.

## J. FINISHER

**1. Responsibilities:** The **Finisher** is directly responsible to the **Key Set Builder** and is responsible for putting finishing and decorative touches on the set, such as fabricating and installing special trim molding, dado, fascia and/or valance work or applying plastic, papier mâché or foam to structural surfaces.

**2. Duties—during PRE-PRODUCTION and PRODUCTION:**

**a.** Reading construction plans and referring to sketches of the setting;

**b.** Fabricating and installing special trim molding, dado, beading, fascia and/or valance work;

**c.** Applying wood, metal, plastic, papier mâché, fiberglas or foam to structural surfaces;

**d.** Operating power and hand tools of the trade;

**e.** Otherwise carrying out the duties normally required of this classification;

**f.** Providing the hand tools normally employed in this craft.

**3. Considerations: Finisher**s are employed on those jobs requiring special carpentry finishing skills.

## K. CONSTRUCTION SPECIALISTS:

CRAFT SPECIALISTS—CABINET MAKER; WOOD CARVER; STONE, METAL, CLAY or PLASTICS SCULPTOR; STONE, BRICK, PLASTER, FOAM, CEMENT or CONCRETE MASON; GLAZIER; WELDER; METAL WORKER; MECHANIC; PLUMBER; PIPE FITTER; ELECTRICIAN, and other craft specialties; and

EQUIPMENT OPERATORS of—CRANE, BULLDOZER, POWER ROLLER, POWER SHOVEL, EARTH MOVER, EARTH COMPACTOR, PILE-DRIVER, TRENCHER, SKIP-LOADER, CHERRY-PICKER, FORK-LIFT, AIR HAMMER, and other heavy equipment.

**1. Responsibilities:** The **Construction Specialist** is directly responsible to the **Construction Coordinator** for executing the specialty as efficiently, accurately and economically as possible in order to achieve the desired functional result.

**2. Duties—during PRE-PRODUCTION and PRODUCTION:**

**a.** Performing the particular specialty from approved drawings and/or specifications;

**b.** Preparing orders for materials and equipment required, as authorized;

**c.** Operating any special tools and equipment used in the particular specialty;

**d.** Otherwise carrying out the duties normally required of these classifications;

**e.** Providing the hand tools normally employed in the particular specialty.

**3. Considerations:** A **Construction Specialist** with the appropriate specialty is employed to execute that specialty which is required on a particular stage set or on a location production construction project.

▼ **Staff Shop Classifications Used for the FINISHING Process** ▼

## L. KEY PAINTER

**1. Responsibilities:** The **Key Painter** is directly responsible to the **Construction Coordinator** for achieving the proper artistic execution of set painting in order to meet the highest aesthetic and photographic standards thereof.

**2. Duties—during PRE-PRODUCTION and PRODUCTION:**

**a.** Preparing orders for set painting materials and any special equipment needed in the preparation and application of the materials to the sets, studio and props;

**b.** Making a paint list of the type, color and mix used on each set, for later matching and touch-up as necessary;

**c.** Mixing and applying all paint to studio and/or location settings—floors, walls and ceilings—and props and set dressing, as specified;

**d.** Executing all special painting such as airbrush or fine line work (i.e., gilt, aging, scrolls, special designs, art paintings, etc) as applied to sets, cycloramas, backings, drops, costumes and costume items, set dressing, props, animals, vegetation and objects, as directed;

**e.** Tinting water or other components of the natural environment as required for production purposes;

**f.** Removing paint applied to components of the natural environment after production purposes have been satisfied;

**g.** Otherwise carrying out the duties normally required of this classification;

**h.** Providing the hand tools normally employed in this craft.

**3. Considerations:** A **Key Painter** is used when paint is applied to settings, dressings, props, etc, but does not create scenic design on cycles, backings, etc.

## M. PAINTER

**1. Responsibilities:** The **Painter** is directly responsible to the **Key Painter** for mixing and applying paint in such fashion as to help achieve optimum photographic results.

**2. Duties—during PRE-PRODUCTION and PRODUCTION:**

**a.** Mixing, matching and applying paint base and finishing agents to the surfaces of the set, studio floor, walls, backings and props, as required;

**b.** Picking up paint and painting matériel, as required;

    **c.** Assisting the **Key Painter** in the performance of set painting duties;

    **d.** Otherwise carrying out the duties normally required of this classification;

    **e.** Providing the hand tools normally employed in this craft.

**3. Considerations: Painter**s are used to assist the **Key Painter** in the performance of painting duties.

## N. DRAPER and UPHOLSTERER

**1. Responsibilities:** The **Draper** and **Upholsterer** are directly responsible to the **Set Decorator** for appropriate creative arrangement and application of draping and upholstery material to the set and set pieces in a style best suited to help achieve optimum photographic realization thereof and to the **Construction Coordinator** for completing their work on schedule.

**2. Duties—during PRE-PRODUCTION and PRODUCTION:**

    **a.** For the **Draper**: The execution, arranging, hanging and necessary modifications of all curtains, draperies, cascades, festoons, bunting, netting and swags required for a given production;

    **b.** For the **Upholsterer**: Installing any necessary upholstery—suspension, stuffing and covering—on furniture, sets and props;

    **c.** For **both**: Ordering draping and/or upholstery material, as authorized;

    **d.** Otherwise carrying out the duties normally required of this classification;

    **e.** Providing the hand tools normally employed in these crafts.

**3. Considerations**: A **Draper** and/or an **Upholsterer** is employed on those productions on which the **Key Set Builder** requires drapery and/or upholstery assistance.

## O. PAPERHANGER and TILER

**1. Responsibilities:** The **Paperhanger** and **Tiler** are directly responsible to the **Set Decorator** for applying wallpaper and other coverings to the surfaces of the set in a style best suited to help achieve optimum photographic realization thereof and to the **Construction Coordinator** for completing their work on schedule.

**2. Duties—during PRE-PRODUCTION and PRODUCTION:**

    **a.** Applying paper, tile and other adhesive materials to the surfaces of the sets, studio floor, walls and ceiling, and to props, as specified in the construction plans and sketches;

    **b.** Ordering such surface-covering materials, as authorized;

    **c.** Removing all such applied materials when photography has been completed and the **Production Manager** has given authorization to do so;

    **d.** Otherwise carrying out the duties normally required of these classifications;

    **e.** Providing the hand tools normally employed in these crafts.

**3. Considerations:** A **Paperhanger** and/or **Tiler** is employed on those productions on which the **Construction Coordinator** requires this specialized assistance.

## P. FLOOR COVERER

**1. Responsibilities:** The **Floor Coverer** is directly responsible to the **Set Decorator** for applying carpetry and coverings to the floor surfaces of the set in a style best suited to help achieve optimum photographic realization thereof and to the **Construction Coordinator** for completing their work on schedule.

**2. Duties—during PRE-PRODUCTION and PRODUCTION:**

**a.** Applying carpetry or other covering material to the floor surfaces of the sets and settings, as specified in the construction plans and sketches;

**b.** Ordering such surface-covering materials, as authorized;

**c.** Removing all such applied materials when photography has been completed and the **Production Manager** has given authorization to do so;

**d.** Otherwise carrying out the duties normally required of these classifications;

**e.** Providing the hand tools normally employed in these crafts.

**3. Considerations:** A **Floor Coverer** is employed on those productions on which the **Construction Coordinator** requires this specialized assistance.

## Q. SCULPTOR

**1. Responsibilities:** The **Sculptor** is directly responsible to the **Set Decorator** for the appropriate execution of assigned sculpture work in order to help achieve optimum photographic realization thereof and to the **Construction Coordinator** for completing work on schedule.

**2. Duties—during PRE-PRODUCTION and PRODUCTION:**

**a.** Designing and planning items of sculpture from production sketches by the Art Department;

**b.** Ordering such sculpture materials, as authorized;

**c.** Executing such sculptured items, as authorized;

**d.** Removing all such applied materials when photography has been completed and the **Production Manager** has given authorization to do so;

**e.** Otherwise carrying out the duties normally required of these classifications;

**f.** Providing the hand tools normally employed in these crafts.

**3. Considerations:** A **Sculptor** is employed when sculptured pieces are required.

## R. ORNAMENTAL PLASTERER

**1. Responsibilities:** The **Ornamental Plasterer** is directly responsible to the **Set Decorator** for the appropriate execution of ornamental plastering in order to help achieve optimum photographic realization thereof and to the **Construction Coordinator** for completing work on schedule.

**2. Duties—during PRE-PRODUCTION and PRODUCTION:**

**a.** Planning, preparing materials, executing, altering and setting up such ornamental plastering, whether decorative facing or sculpture, as may be required by the production;

**b.** Physically assembling, installing, modifying, disassembling and/or removing such ornamental plastering work, as required;

**c.** Ordering material required to construct and complete such ornamental work, as authorized by the **Production Manager**;

**d.** Otherwise carrying out the duties normally required of this classification;

**e.** Providing the hand tools normally employed in this craft.

**3. Considerations:** An **Ornamental Plasterer** is used when decorative plaster work is necessary.

▼ **Prop Shop Classifications Used for SPECIALTY Work** ▼

## S. PROP SHOP PROPMAKER

**1. Responsibilities:** The **Prop Shop Propmaker** is directly responsible to the **Construction Coordinator**, and as specified in Category Criteria above, and is responsible for a creative and functional design of special props in order to help achieve optimum photographic realization thereof.

**2. Duties—during PRE-PRODUCTION and PRODUCTION:**

**a.** Reading and annotating the script within the context of the construction project and use of special props;

**b.** Referring to sketches, renderings and blueprints of the proposed props received from the **Art Director** or **Production Designer**;

**c.** Ordering needed matériel, as authorized;

**d.** Planning, designing, executing, altering and setting up such special hand or set props as may be required by the production;

**e.** Using all tools and materials necessary to achieve the desired result;

**f.** Physically setting up, modifying, dressing, operating, disassembling, removing and storing such special props, as required;

**g.** Otherwise carrying out the duties normally required of this classification;

**h.** Providing the hand tools normally employed in this craft.

**3. Considerations:** A **Prop Shop Propmaker** is used on those productions requiring construction of props.

## T. MODEL BUILDER

**1. Responsibilities:** The **Model Builder** is directly responsible to the **Construction Coordinator**, and as specified in Category Criteria above, and is responsible for a creative, appropriate and functional design of model or miniature construction in order to help achieve optimum photographic realization thereof.

**2. Duties—during PRE-PRODUCTION and PRODUCTION:**

**a.** Reading and annotating the script within the context of planning and executing the construction of models and miniatures for photographic use;

**b.** Referring to sketches, renderings and blueprints of the proposed models and/or miniatures received from the **Art Director** or **Production Designer**;

CONSTRUCTION

**c.** Researching, preparing plans, constructing, painting and otherwise fabricating, finishing, furnishing and dressing models and miniatures of all types for motion picture production;

**d.** Physically setting up, modifying, dressing, operating, disassembling, removing and storing such models and miniatures as required;

**e.** Ordering needed materials, as authorized;

**f.** Otherwise carrying out the duties normally required of this classification;

**g.** Providing the hand tools normally employed in this craft.

**3. Considerations:**

**a.** A **Model Builder** is used on those productions or jobs requiring construction of models and/or miniatures.

**b.** The **Model Builder** is directly responsible to the **Construction Coordinator**.

▼ **Classification Used for the PRODUCTION Process** ▼

**U. STAND-BY PAINTER**

**1. Responsibilities:** The **Stand-By Painter** is directly responsible to the **Key Painter** for mixing, matching and applying paint to unpainted, discolored, mismatched or damaged surfaces which require paint, and to the **Director of Photography** for the photographic acceptance of the application, in order to realize optimum photographic results.

**2. Duties—all during the PRODUCTION Process:**

**a.** Being available on short notice to attend to the immediate painting needs of a production in progress;

**b.** Checking the surfaces to be painted and noting the colors needed;

**c.** Checking the set construction paint list for the type and colors of paint used on the particular sets or settings, in order to have the correct paints to mix and match for the required on-site painting, repainting or touchup work;

**d.** Preparing the surface(s) and applying the paint in a manner which matches the paint of the area being repaired or added to;

**e.** When finished, getting approval from the **Director of Photography**;

**f.** Otherwise carrying out the duties normally required of this classification;

**g.** Providing the hand tools normally employed in this craft.

**3. Considerations:** The **Stand-By Painter** is used to prepare or repair the paint cover on any set item surfaces, on short notice, and therefore must be readily available to maintain all set surfaces ready for photographic purposes.

# Special Effects Category Organizational Chart

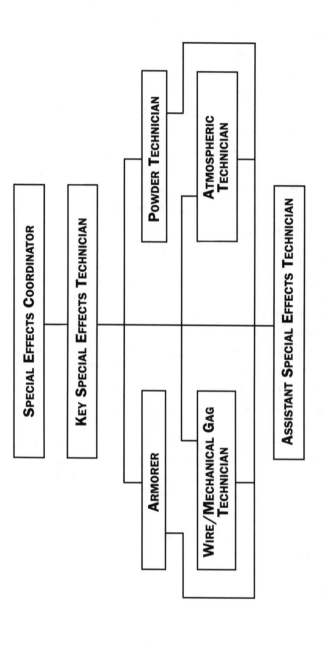

# 10

# SPECIAL EFFECTS CATEGORY

**A. Category Classifications:** There are seven (7) classifications in the Special Effects Category:

1. **Special Effects Coordinator (Category Head)**

2. **Key Special Effects Technician (Category Sub-Head)**

3. **Armorer**

4. **Powder Technician**

5. **Wire and Mechanical Gag Technician**

6. **Atmospheric Technician**

7. **Assistant Special Effects Technician**

**B. Category Criteria:**

1. Employees holding classification within the Special Effects Category perform specialized job functions which are outside the purview of other job craft categories, but which are utilized in the Prop Shop, on interior or exterior production, on location and/or on the sound stage.

2. **Special Effects Technician**s must be experienced in working with: chemicals, wood, plastics, glass, metals, leather, rubber and urethane materials; mill work—lathe, router, cutting and welding; preparing breakaways in sets and props; miniatures; models; electrical and electronic applications; hydraulics—pumps, motors, gimbals, air cannon, air mortars and counterbalancing; vehicle roll cages, ramps, tow and release connections; rigging—flying people and objects; gas, diesel and electric power systems; wind, air, water, rain, snow, fire, smoke, fog and haze effects.

3. When the **Key Special Effects Technician** requires assistance in the preparation, setup and breakdown of special effects, an **Assistant Special Effects Technician** is used. In the handling of explosives and pyrotechnics, only personnel properly trained and licensed in the State where the work takes place may function in this capacity. Licensing required, usually granted by the State Fire Marshall, includes:

   a. A **Class 3 License**, the applicant for which must have a clean criminal record and pass a qualification test—experience is not required;

   b. A **Class 2 License**, which may be provided to an applicant who has had at least two (2) years of hands-on experience, has five (5) letters of recommendation from licensed **Key Special Effects Technician**s with whom worked, and has passed a comprehensive test;

c. A **Class 1 License**, which may be granted to an applicant who has demonstrated at least five (5) years of hands-on experience with an unblemished safety record, has at least five (5) letters of recommendation from licensed **Key Special Effects Technician**s with whom worked, and has passed comprehensive written and practical tests;

d. A **Key Special Effects Technician** or **Powder Technician** specialist who supervises or handles explosives or pyrotechnics must hold a Class 1 License. **Assistant Special Effects Technician**s who handle explosives or pyrotechnics under moderate supervision must hold a Class 2 License; **Special Effects Technician**s with a Class 3 License must only work with explosives and pyrotechnics under constant supervision of those holding a Class 1 or Class 2 card.

4. When weaponry is utilized on a production, an **Armorer** is used.

5. When pyrotechnics — fire and/or explosives — are employed on a production, a **Powder Technician** is used.

6. When wire or mechanical special effects are planned, a **Wire and Mechanical Gag Technician** is used.

7. When a production requires special atmospheric preparations for visual effect, an **Atmospheric Technician** is used.

8. All Special Effects personnel operating underwater with breathing apparatus must be SCUBA certified.

9. The **Special Effects Coordinator** and each Special Effects Category Sub-Head must ensure that special effects personnel and production personnel under their supervision, do not attempt work under any unsafe condition(s), as specified by the Employer, OSHA, Building and Safety Code and fire laws, or in violation of any other safety regulation(s) and practice(s).

**C. Category Responsibilities:**

1. During all prep time (preparation for shooting), it is the responsibility of each Employee in the Special Effects Category to work cooperatively with the **Special Effects Coordinator**, or with the Sub-Head to whom assigned, in order to assist in achieving the optimum and most efficient operation of the various procedures within this category.

2. During all actual shooting takes, the **Special Effects Coordinator** and the **Key Special Effects Technician** are directly responsible to the **Property Master**.

**D. Category Function:** The principal function of Special Effects personnel involves work designing, constructing, assembling, preparing, handling, rigging and use of firearms, explosives, incendiaries, man-made rain, floods, wind, dust, smoke, fog or snowfall, wire and mechanical gags, breakaways, etc, for presentation to the camera of the specially conceived and designed visual effects resulting therefrom.

SPECIAL EFFECTS

**E. Category Considerations:**

**1.** Special Effects Category personnel are used on each production on which there are special effects.

**2.** The classification(s) used depends upon the type of motion picture being produced and upon the number and type of special effects to be prepared and executed.

**F. Category Requirements:** Employees in each Special Effects Category classification must know and follow the chain-of-command and lines-of-communication and must be able to effectively and safely set up, operate and use the special effects equipment and related material selected for each job and associated with their respective craft classification.

**G. SPECIAL EFFECTS COORDINATOR**

**1. Responsibilities:** The **Special Effects Coordinator** is directly responsible to the **Director** for the look and to the **Production Manager** for the cost and is responsible for safely, efficiently and effectively coordinating the planning, preparation, rigging and operation of all special effects in a manner designed to help achieve efficient and optimum photographic realization thereof.

**2. Duties—during PRE-PRODUCTION and PRODUCTION:**

**a.** Reading and annotating the script, and analyzing the action sequences in which special effects take place;

**b.** Determining how best to prepare each special effects gag—how long it will take, whether it can be done first or second unit, whether added visual effects will be necessary, and the number of cuts necessary to give to the **Editor**;

**c.** Checking with visual effects specialists to determine that mechanical effects and CGI will coalesce;

**d.** Preparing a list of special effects and the time and cost of producing those effects;

**e.** Presenting the time/cost breakdown to the **Production Manager** for approval;

**f.** Giving the go-ahead to various special effects technicians to begin work on their specialties;

**g.** Checking regularly with Prop Shop personnel, to see that special effects gags are coming along on schedule;

**h.** Seeing that all gags are properly and successfully tested and refined, as necessary, to assure their safe and effective function during production shooting;

**i.** Seeing that all gags and operating personnel are present on the shooting site and ready to deliver the special effects required;

**j.** Otherwise carrying out the duties normally required of this classification;

**k.** Providing the hand tools normally employed in this craft.

**SPECIAL EFFECTS**

3. **Considerations:** The **Special Effects Coordinator** must be knowledgeable about all aspects of special effects work—how it is accomplished, the time it will take to prepare and execute—and must have the managerial skills to see that it is done effectively, efficiently and safely.

## H. KEY SPECIAL EFFECTS TECHNICIAN

1. **Responsibilities:** The **Key Special Effects Technician** is directly responsible to the **Special Effects Coordinator** and as specified in Category Criteria, above, and is responsible for safely, efficiently and effectively planning and rigging all special effects in a manner designed to help achieve optimum photographic realization thereof.

2. **Duties—during PRE-PRODUCTION and PRODUCTION:**

   a. Reading and annotating the script and analyzing the action sequences in which special effects take place;

   b. Designing the special effects as requested;

   c. Working with the **Key Makeup Artist** in preparing and applying special effects makeup and then activating the devices in the makeup;

   d. Supervising the preparation, handling, rigging and use of firearms, explosives, incendiaries, man-made rain, floods, wind, dust, smoke, fog or snowfall, wire and mechanical gags, etc;

   e. Taking adequate precautions to insure the safety of all personnel and livestock coming in close proximity to any potentially hazardous setup(s);

   f. Insuring that special effects personnel do not attempt work under any unsafe condition(s), as specified by the Building and Safety Code and fire laws, or in violation of any other safety regulation(s) and practice(s);

   g. Protecting adjacent property from fallout or damage resulting from explosions, pyrotechnic, windblown or other special effects;

   h. Dressing the set to simulate weather conditions (rain, snow, mud, etc) or mood effects (cobwebs, dust, mildew, coloring pools of water, wetting surfaces, etc), as required;

   i. Operating wind machines;

   j. Responsibility for ordering, caring for, handling and inventorying all Special Effects matériel;

   k. Seeing that all **Assistant Special Effects Technician**s are properly licensed when working with live ammunition, explosives, or pyrotechnics;

   l. Otherwise carrying out the duties normally required of this classification;

   m. Providing the hand tools normally employed in this craft.

3. **Considerations:**

   a. When any explosives are used in a production, a **Key Special Effects Technician**, licensed by the State of residence as a **Powder Expert**, must be used.

SPECIAL EFFECTS

    **b.** A qualified **Key Special Effects Technician** is used to handle, rig and operate any special rigging of a hazardous nature to cast, crew or livestock.

    **c.** The **Key Special Effects Technician** is compensated and/or reimbursed for any material used from the personal Special Effects Box.

    **d.** A take, or rehearsal, involving special effects, is not started until the **Key Special Effects Technician** has given the **Director** a clearly acknowledged clearance to proceed; the positioning and timing of the on-camera action and effects must not vary from that of the final rehearsal.

## I. ARMORER

    **1. Responsibilities:** The **Armorer** is a **Special Effects Technician** directly responsible to the **Key Special Effects Technician** for selecting and preparing any and all weaponry to be used in the production, distributing weapons to appointed performers and then collecting the weapons when the scene has been shot.

    **2. Duties—during PRE-PRODUCTION and PRODUCTION:**

        **a.** Reading and annotating the script and analyzing the action sequences in which armament—firearms and weaponry—of specific kind and amount is used;

        **b.** Figuring the type and amount of weaponry required for the production and the estimated time of its use and the cost, and presenting this information to the **Key Special Effects Technician** and **Special Effects Coordinator** for approval;

        **c.** Upon authorization: selecting, ordering and procuring approved weaponry;

        **d.** Reproducing and fabricating such weaponry in breakaway or dummy mode, as required;

        **e.** Marking each piece of weaponry as to which player will have the piece or pieces during each scene in which such weaponry is used;

        **f.** Distributing each piece of weaponry—real or fake—to assigned players;

        **g.** Demonstrating to each player the proper use of such weaponry;

        **h.** After each scene, collecting all items of weaponry from the players and storing them;

        **i.** Shooting chalk projectiles to simulate bullet hits, as directed;

        **j.** Otherwise carrying out the duties normally required of this classification;

        **k.** Providing the hand tools normally employed in this craft.

    **3. Considerations:** When weapons of any kind are used in a production, an **Armorer** must be employed and is in charge of handling, handing out, issuing handling precautions, collecting and caring for such weaponry while it is being used in the production.

### J. POWDER TECHNICIAN

**1. Responsibilities:** The **Powder Technician** is a **Special Effects Technician** directly responsible to the **Key Special Effects Technician** for safely, efficiently and effectively planning and executing pyrotechnic events—powder, heavy fire, explosives, squibs, and the like—for optimum photographic realization thereof.

**2. Duties—during PRE-PRODUCTION and PRODUCTION:**

    **a.** Reading and annotating the script and analyzing the action sequences in which pyrotechnic effects are to take place;

    **b.** Figuring the type and amount of powder, explosives and flammable components required for the production, the estimated time of its use and the cost, and presenting this information to the **Key Special Effects Technician** and **Special Effects Coordinator** for approval;

    **c.** Upon authorization, selecting, ordering and procuring approved pyrotechnic matériel;

    **d.** Planning the deployment, charge and use of each pyrotechnic item—powder, explosives, squibs, mortars, flammable materials;

    **e.** Supervising the connection of each pyrotechnic device to the master control console;

    **f.** Marking the position of each explosive and pyrotechnic device to be used in a scene and marking safe pathways through the pyrotechnic field for the safe passage of cast, extras, and production personnel;

    **g.** Testing certain explosive and pyrotechnic devices, as necessary;

    **h.** Manning the control console and activating the pyrotechnic items on cue;

    **i.** Checking to see that all inactivated pyrotechnic items are recovered, deactivated and removed from the playing field, along with expended matériel;

    **j.** Otherwise carrying out the duties normally required of this classification;

    **k.** Providing the hand tools normally employed in this craft.

**3. Considerations:**

    **a.** When any explosives are used in a production, a **Powder Technician**, licensed by the State of residence as a **Powder Expert**, must be used.

    **b.** The **Powder Technician** is compensated and/or reimbursed for any material used from the personal Special Effects Box.

### K. WIRE and MECHANICAL GAG TECHNICIAN

**1. Responsibilities:** The **Wire and Mechanical Gag Technician** is a **Special Effects Technician** directly responsible to the **Key Special Effects Technician** for safely, efficiently and effectively preparing and executing assigned wire and/or mechanical rigging for special effects in order to achieve optimum photographic realization thereof.

SPECIAL EFFECTS

**2. Duties—during PRE-PRODUCTION and PRODUCTION:**

  **a.** Reading and annotating the script and analyzing the action sequences in which wire and/or mechanical gags are to take place;

  **b.** Figuring the type and amount of wire and/or mechanical rigging required for the production, the estimated time of its construction in the Prop Shop, its use and the cost, and presenting this information to the **Key Special Effects Technician** and **Special Effects Coordinator** for approval;

  **c.** Upon authorization, selecting, ordering and procuring approved special rigging matériel;

  **d.** Fabricating the special rigging required for the special effects scenes;

  **e.** Testing the special rigging and adjusting the rigging, as necessary;

  **f.** Operating any such rigging involving performers supported in harness;

  **g.** Operating, or instructing players in the operation of, any special effects gags which a player must operate on-camera;

  **h.** Lining up any wire gags involving flying knives, axes, arrows, spears, projectiles and the like, and adjusting the rigging, as necessary;

  **i.** Otherwise carrying out the duties normally required of this classification;

  **j.** Providing the hand tools normally employed in this craft.

**3. Considerations:** When wire or mechanical gags are used on a production to fly performers or objects or to execute a mechanical special effect, a **Wire and Mechanical Gag Technician** must be used.

## L. ATMOSPHERIC TECHNICIAN

**1. Responsibilities:** The **Atmospheric Technician** is a **Special Effects Technician** directly responsible to the **Key Special Effects Technician** for safely, efficiently and effectively preparing and executing assigned atmospheric special effects—wind, water, rain, snow, fog, smoke and fire—in order to achieve optimum photographic realization thereof.

**2. Duties—during PRE-PRODUCTION and PRODUCTION:**

  **a.** Reading and annotating the script and analyzing the action sequences in which atmospheric effects are to take place;

  **b.** Figuring the type and amount of atmospheric matériel required for the production, the estimated time of its use and the cost, and presenting this information to the **Key Special Effects Technician** and **Special Effects Coordinator** for approval;

  **c.** Upon authorization, selecting, ordering and procuring approved special atmospheric matériel;

  **d.** Preparing and testing the atmospheric special effect to assure a correct and consistent result, as necessary;

  **e.** Operating any applicator(s) to dispense the atmospheric agent—Ritter fans, fog machines, dye applicators, faux snow dispensers, hoses, rain rigs, and the like;

**f.** Getting approval of the **Director of Photography** as to the area to be treated, and the quantity and density of the atmospheric material;

**g.** Maintaining the atmospheric look throughout the shot, scene and sequence;

**h.** Cleaning up the residue, if any, following each shot and after the scene is wrapped;

**i.** Otherwise carrying out the duties normally required of this classification;

**j.** Providing the hand tools normally employed in this craft.

**3. Considerations:** When visual atmospheric conditions, such as wind, water, rain, snow, fog, smoke, or fire, must be created for a production, **Atmospheric Technician**s are used.

## M. ASSISTANT SPECIAL EFFECTS TECHNICIAN

**1. Responsibilities:** The **Assistant Special Effects Technician** is directly responsible to the **Key Special Effects Technician** and to the specific **Special Effects Technician** to whom assigned and assists in the performance of special effects duties.

**2. Duties—during PRE-PRODUCTION and PRODUCTION:**

**a.** Reading and annotating the script and analyzing the action sequences in which special effects take place;

**b.** Rigging of all special effects under the supervision of the **Key Special Effects Technician**;

**c.** Picking up, inventorying and preparing special effects material for transportation;

**d.** Clearly identifying all hazardous areas and installations for the protection of production personnel—cast, crew, staff and visitors;

**e.** Promptly and completely removing all special effects rigging and inactivated explosives and incendiary devices following the final take of the setup during which such matériel has been utilized;

**f.** Carrying out the duties normally required in assisting the **Key Special Effects Technician** and any other **Special Effects Technician** to whom assigned;

**g.** Otherwise carrying out the duties normally required for this classification;

**h.** Providing the hand tools normally employed in this craft.

**3. Considerations:** An **Assistant Special Effects Technician** does not rig or remove special effects unsupervised by the **Key Special Effects Technician**.

<u>**NOTES**</u>

# SET DECORATING CATEGORY ORGANIZATIONAL CHART

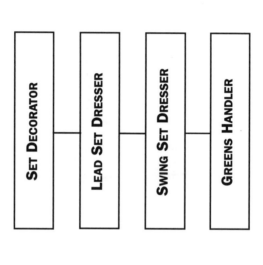

# 11

# SET DECORATING CATEGORY

**A. Category Classifications:** There are four (4) classifications in the Set Decorating Category:

1. **Set Decorator (Category Head)**
2. **Lead Set Dresser (Category Sub-Head)**
3. **Swing Set Dresser**
4. **Greens Handler**

**B. Category Criteria:**

1. Employees holding classification within the Set Decorating Category perform all job functions pertaining to production decorating procedures which are utilized on interior or exterior production, on location and/or on the sound stage.

2. When the **Set Decorator** requires assistance in the procurement, placement, handling, hauling, maintenance and return of set dressing matériel, **Set Dressers** are used.

3. When the **Set Decorator** requires assistance in the procurement, placement, handling, hauling, maintenance and return of set dressing greenery, a **Greens Handler** is used.

4. During production shooting, the **Lead Set Dresser** and the **Swing Set Dressers** are on hand to move, remove, place or replace items of set dressing as requested by the **Director**, the **Director of Photography**, the **Art Director/ Production Designer**, the **Set Decorator** or the **Camera Operator**.

5. Set decorating personnel need to know and apply strict accountability procedures to the acquiring, use, placing, maintaining, inventorying and storage of items of set dressing.

6. All Set Decorating personnel operating underwater with breathing apparatus must be SCUBA certified.

7. The **Set Decorator** and **Lead Set Dresser** must ensure that set decorating personnel do not attempt work under any unsafe condition(s), as specified by the Employer, OSHA, Building and Safety Code and fire laws, or in violation of any other safety regulation(s) and practice(s).

8. **Set dressing** is defined as those objects, fixtures and furnishings attached to, or hung on or from, the walls and ceilings of settings and/or placed on the floor or about the production site for cinematographic purposes.

a. For **interiors**: furniture, drapes, curtains, blinds and shutters; lighting fixtures; major standing appliances; all hardware and household appliances; potted plants; pictures, cabinets and other appurtenances affixed to the set walls, ceiling or floor, or made an integral part thereof.

b. For **exteriors**: houses, shacks, out-buildings and other structures; fences; trees, shrubs, flowers and grass; rocks, stones, gravel, bricks, soil and boards; non-moving rolling, floating, submerged and airborne stock of all types; animals and insects of all kinds; other appurtenances affixed to the ground or positioned in or under water, or made an integral part thereof.

C. **Category Responsibilities:** It is the responsibility of each Employee in the Set Decorating Category to work cooperatively with the **Set Decorator** in order to assist in achieving the optimum and most efficient operation of the various procedures within this category.

D. **Category Function:** The principal function of Set Decorating Category personnel involves supporting and contributing to the vision of the **Director** and the creative concept of the **Production Designer** by carefully selecting, caring for and supervising the placing of set dressing items on and about sets and settings in order to help create a multi-dimensional ambient reality for the story.

E. **Category Considerations;**

1. Set Decorating Category personnel are used on each production on which there are items of set dressing used.

2. The classification(s) used depend upon the type and quantity of such set dressing.

F. **Category Requirements:** Employees in each Set Decorating Category classification must know and follow the chain-of-command and lines-of-communication and must be able to effectively and safely set up and account for all items of set dressing selected, utilized and entrusted to their care for each job associated with their respective craft classification.

G. **SET DECORATOR**

1. **Responsibilities:** The **Set Decorator** is directly responsible to, and assists, the **Art Director/Production Designer** when an **Art Director/Production Designer** is required on a production, otherwise to the **Producer**; works in close cooperation with the **Director**; and is responsible for the visualization, selection and placement of set dressing and decoration in a manner best suited to give optimum aesthetic and photographic realization of the settings.

2. **Duties:**

▼ **During PRE-PRODUCTION:**

a. Reading, analyzing and annotating the script and/or storyboard from a set decoration perspective;

**b.** Examines and analyzes the **Art Director/Production Designer**'s set decoration list, sketches, renderings, floor plans, elevation drawings, and blueprints of the settings, or photos and dimensions of the location sites;

**c.** Making a scene-by-scene breakdown of set decoration items;

**d.** Researching the period for appropriate items to acquire or have fabricated;

**e.** Preparing a list of set decoration items which conform to the period, style, size, shape, pattern, color and perspective of the setting (specially sized and positioned if forced) required by the setting, by each scene of the setting, and for the overall production;

**f.** Checking with the various supply sources for availability of the required set decoration items;

**g.** Supervising the **Lead Set Dresser** in selecting furniture and dressing for all settings—studio and location sites—based on the **Art Director/Production Designer**'s floor plans, elevation drawings, sketches, renderings and set dressing list;

**h.** Ordering from prop and supply houses all set dressing needed for production;

**i.** Ordering any set dressing items which are not available for rent or purchase made to order by the Prop Shop;

**j.** Supervising the work of **Drapers**, **Floor Coverers**, **Upholsterers**, **Tilers**, **Greens Handlers** and **Set Dressers**;

**k.** Checking all items delivered by set and prop supply houses for quality control;

▼ **During the PRODUCTION Process:**

**l.** Supervising the placement of set dressing by **Set Dressers**;

**m.** Consulting with the **Art Director/Production Designer**, **Producer** and/or **Director**, as specified above, regarding changes, revision and/or modification of set decoration;

**n.** Otherwise carrying out the duties normally required of this classification;

**o.** Providing the hand tools normally employed in this craft.

**3. Considerations:**

**a.** A **Set Decorator** is used on each production requiring items of set decoration.

**b.** A **Set Decorator** is used for a sufficient length of time to plan, procure and supervise placement of set dressing items.

**c.** The **Set Decorator** does not physically place set dressing or set props, but may direct the **Set Dressers** or **Prop Master**, respectively, to place such items.

## H. LEAD SET DRESSER

**1. Responsibilities:** The **Lead Set Dresser** is directly responsible to the **Set Decorator** for dressing the set efficiently, appropriately and in conformity with the set decoration plan of the **Set Decorator** in order to help achieve optimum photographic realization thereof.

**2. Duties:**

▼ **During PRE-PRODUCTION:**

a. Reading and annotating the script and/or storyboard within the context of cinematic set dressing requirements;

b. Examining the list of set decoration items prepared by the **Set Decorator**;

c. Helping determine where each set decoration item can be obtained;

d. Calling vendors and other supply sources to determine availability and cost of each item;

e. Accompanying the **Set Decorator** in shopping, selecting and ordering set decoration items;

▼ **During the PRODUCTION Process:**

f. Personally picking up, or causing to pick up and transport, all set decoration items from the various supply sources;

g. Seeing that all set decoration items are brought to the set or location site;

h. Inventorying and/or photographing by Polaroid or videotape each item to establish its condition;

i. Listing, numbering and colorcode tagging each item as to its precise placement on the set for each scene and sequence in which it belongs;

j. Placing corresponding numbered and colorcoded tapes on the set to indicate each item and its precise placement on the set or setting;

k. Giving a copy of the set decoration list to the **Swing Set Dresser** for the physical placement of set decoration items;

l. Maintaining all set dressing and related items in good condition while retained, or in use, by the production;

m. Operating a Polaroid camera for the purpose of recording the position and condition of set dressing items at the beginning and/or end of a take;

n. Picking up and delivering replacement and/or additional items, as required;

o. Inventorying and checking each item against its earlier photographed status for present condition before returning items to the originating supply source;

p. Submitting all such records to the **Production Manager** for proper dispensation;

q. Making minor repairs and modifications to set dressing items, as directed;

▼ **During POST-PRODUCTION:**

**r.** Seeing that all set dressing items are returned to vendors, owners or to Company storage facilities;

**s.** Otherwise carrying out the duties normally required of this classification;

**t.** Providing the hand tools normally employed in this craft.

**3. Considerations:**

**a.** Each shooting unit of the production—first and second units—requiring set dressing uses a **Set Dresser**.

**b.** The **Set Dresser** is used for a sufficient length of time to procure and return all set dressing.

## I. SWING SET DRESSER

**1. Responsibilities:** The **Swing Set Dresser** is directly responsible to the **Lead Set Dresser** for dressing the set efficiently, appropriately and in conformity with the set decoration plan of the **Set Decorator** in order to help achieve optimum photographic realization thereof.

**2. Duties—all during the PRODUCTION Process:**

**a.** Reading the script and/or storyboard within the context of set dressing;

**b.** Examining the list of numbered/color coded set decoration items, noting the setting and scenes in which each item appears, and the position where each is placed;

**c.** Physically placing each item in its specified position;

**d.** Moving and re-marking set decoration items, as necessary, in order to accommodate actor, camera or special effects positioning, or to help achieve better lighting or composition, or to help facilitate moving camera shots;

**e.** Making note of each change in position of any set decoration item, whether made at the request of the **Director**, an actor, the **Director of Photography**, a **Camera Operator**, or the **Key Special Effects Technician**;

**f.** When the scene is finished and the setup is wrapped, removing each set decoration item and returning it to the care of the **Lead Set Dresser**;

**g.** Otherwise carrying out the duties normally required of this classification;

**h.** Providing the hand tools normally employed in this craft.

**3. Considerations:**

**a.** A **Swing Set Dresser** is used on each shooting unit of a production which uses extensive items of set dressing.

**b.** A **Swing Set Dresser** does not handle set or hand props.

## J. GREENS HANDLER

**1. Responsibilities:** The **Greens Handler** is directly responsible to the **Set Decorator** for maintaining all greens in the desired condition and quantity, in order to help achieve optimum photographic realization thereof.

**2. Duties—during the PRODUCTION Process:**

▼ **During PRE-PRODUCTION and PRODUCTION:**

**a.** Checking the list of greenery for each scene, set and setting as specified by the **Set Decorator**;

**b.** Ordering, selecting, renting and/or buying the plants, foliage and/or trees which constitute set dressing, as authorized;

**c.** Maintaining all such greenery in good condition while in custodial care;

**d.** Cutting, trimming, pruning and placing such greenery, as required;

**e.** Assisting the **Set Dresser** in placing, positioning, coloring, striking, etc, all such greenery items;

**f.** Inventorying all greenery items and the matériel required for their keeping, shaping, coloring, etc;

**g.** Loading, supervising transportation, unloading and arranging storage of all greenery items;

▼ **During PRODUCTION and POST-PRODUCTION:**

**h.** Seeing that all greens are returned to the vendors or to Company storage or nursery facilities;

**i.** Otherwise carrying out the duties normally required of this classification;

**j.** Providing the hand tools normally employed in this craft.

**3. Considerations:** A **Greens Handler** handles only greens and associated matériel.

**NOTES**

# Property Category Organizational Chart

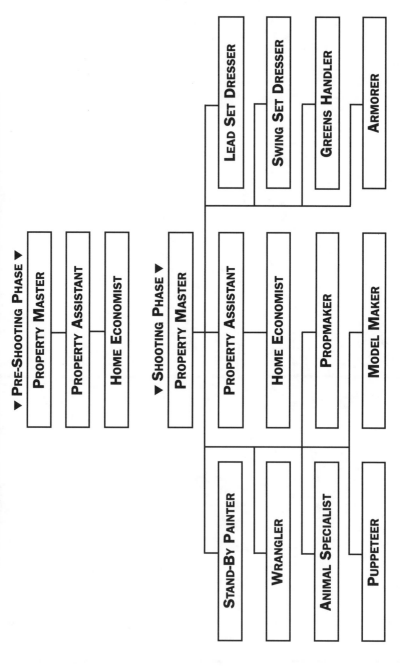

**▼ Pre-Shooting Phase ▼**

- Property Master
- Property Assistant
- Home Economist

**▼ Shooting Phase ▼**

- Property Master
  - Property Assistant
  - Home Economist
  - Propmaker
  - Model Maker
  - Stand-By Painter
  - Wrangler
  - Animal Specialist
  - Puppeteer
  - Lead Set Dresser
  - Swing Set Dresser
  - Greens Handler
  - Armorer

# 12

# PROPERTY CATEGORY

**A. Category Classifications:** There are three (3) classifications in the Property Category:

   **1. Property Master (Category Head)**

   **2. Property Assistant**

   **3. Home Economist**

**B. Category Criteria:**

   **1.** Employees holding classification within the Property Category perform all job functions pertaining to production property procedures which are utilized on interior or exterior production, on location and/or on the sound stage.

   **2.** A **Property Master** is used on each set and location where set props, hand props and/or action props are utilized, is in charge of all technical procedures pertaining to the procurement, placement and maintenance of such items, and is the custodian of all hand and set props, special effects material, firearms, blank ammunition and any Company and personnel property and money charged to his or her care; and physically positions, or causes to be positioned, all such property items.

   **3.** A **Property Master** needs to know and apply strict accountability procedures to the acquiring, use, placing, maintaining, inventorying and storage of company property entrusted to his or her care.

   **4.** During actual production shooting, the **Property Master** maintains the integrity of the dressed sets or setting and is in charge of all set dressing, **Set Dressers** and **Special Effects Technicians** and is physically present at the set at all times for each take during such shooting.

   **5.** On those productions employing an **Art Director** and **Set Decorator**, the **Property Master** is directly responsible to the **Art Director/Production Designer** and consults with the **Set Decorator** on set prop placement.

   **6.** The **Property Master** receives advance moneys from the **Producer** or **Production Manager** for procuring needed property items prior to and during production. The **Property Master** is fully responsible for such moneys, gets receipts for all expenditures and returns the receipts and all unexpended funds to the **Producer** or **Production Manager** at the close of production.

   **7.** Although an Armorer may be used to handle and disburse working firearms and blank ammunition, all blank ammunition and firearms remain in the sole care and custody of the **Property Master** at all times when not in use, and the **Property Master** shall have or acquire proper permits and/or license for purchase, handling and use of such arms and ammunition.

8. When the **Property Master** requires assistance in the procurement, placement, handling, maintenance and return of set props and hand props, a **Property Assistant** is used.

9. When the procurement and preparation of foodstuffs is required for photographic purposes, a **Home Economist** is used.

10. When the **Model Builder** and/or **Propmaker** are required to function on the set during production shooting—physically setting up, modifying, dressing models or miniatures, operating, disassembling or removing models or mechanized operative props, as the case may be—they each function within the Property Category and are directly responsible to the **Property Master** during the production process.

11. All Property personnel operating underwater with breathing apparatus must be SCUBA certified.

12. The **Property Master** must ensure that Property Category personnel do not attempt work under any unsafe condition(s), as specified by the Employer, OSHA, Building and Safety Code and fire laws, or in violation of any other safety regulation(s) and practice(s).

13. **Set props** are defined as those items placed about the set or shooting site which may be affixed to the set walls and ceiling and/or placed on its floor, or are of such size or type as generally to be considered fixed—such as: Pictures, mirrors and lighting fixtures; floor lamps, furniture, stands and statuary; large appliances; large greenery (trees, shrubs, potted plants); rolling, floating, submerged and flying stock; large television commercial product(s); etc—which are used or manipulated by performers during rehearsals and takes.

14. **Hand props** are defined as those items of property carried on or by the person and used, carried, handled or manipulated by the performer(s), such as: Portable appliances; containers of all types; weapons and their ammunition and holsters; tools; utensils; portable devices; money; toys; games; sporting equipment; food and drink; smoking materials; writing implements; portable mechanized props; TV commercial product(s); office and household supplies; etc.

C. **Category Responsibilities:** It is the responsibility of each Employee in the Property Category to work cooperatively with the **Property Master** in order to assist in achieving the optimum and most efficient operation of the various procedures within this category.

D. **Category Function:** The principal function of Property Category personnel involves the care and handling of company property, work with hand props and set dressing props—the care and placing thereof—and maintaining the integrity of the set or setting once the set has been decorated.

E. **Category Considerations:**

1. Property Category personnel are used on each production on which there are hand and/or set action props used.

**2.** The classification(s) used depends upon the type and quantity of such hand and/or set action props.

**F. Category Requirements:** Employees in each Property Category classification must know and follow the chain-of-command and lines-of-communication and must be able to effectively and safely set up and account for all items of company property that have been selected, utilized and entrusted to their custody for each job associated with their respective craft classification.

**G. PROPERTY MASTER**

**1. Responsibilities:** The **Property Master** is directly responsible as specified in Category Criteria, above, and is responsible for maintaining the count, condition, placement and use of all items of property in order to help achieve efficient and optimum dramatic and photographic realization thereof.

**2. Duties:**

▼ **During PRE-PRODUCTION:**

**a.** Reading and annotating the script, within the context of cinematic property—hand, set and action props—requirements;

**b.** Preparing from script breakdown, a list of all hand props, by character name and scene numbers, and set props, by scene and set numbers;

**c.** Selecting and procuring through rental, purchase or manufacture of necessary hand and set props—straight, special and breakaway—and such other related items as may be requested by the **Director, Art Director/ Production Designer**, **Set Decorator** or **Costume Designer**;

**d.** Taking a Polaroid photo or video tape of each prop to establish condition in which it was received;

▼ **During the PRODUCTION Process:**

**e.** Scheduling training time for players who must use power tools, computers, wheel chairs, motorboats, and the like;

**f.** Distributing to, and collecting from, each performer all hand props used each production day;

**g.** Physically placing prop items on the set, whether extensive or tabletop in size;

**h.** Maintaining all props and related items in good condition while retained, or in use, by the production;

**i.** Operating a Polaroid camera for the purpose of recording position and condition of hand and action props at the beginning and/or end of a take;

**j.** Checking with the **Script Supervisor** with regard to details like maintaining consistency by matching the hand prop used from one scene to the next, i.e., its liquid level or length of ash, which hand it was in, and like concerns;

**k.** Operating, or supervising the operation of, all moving or mechanized props;

**l.** Purchasing and preparing all food and liquid props and placing these props for photographic purposes;

**m.** For TV commercials, being custodian of and physically handling all product items to be used and/or photographed, pouring beer and other liquids, as necessary;

**n.** Returning, or arranging for the return of, all prop items as their usefulness to the production ends;

**o.** Inventorying the type, quantity and condition of all property items after use and prior to return;

**p.** Submitting all such records to the **Production Manager** for proper dispensation;

**q.** Acting as custodian of the Company chairs, umbrellas, water and watercoolers, coffee and thermos containers (and preparing or procuring the contents thereof), as well as all and any other items whatsoever which are provided by the Employer for the general comfort and accommodation of the staff, cast and crew;

**r.** Making minor repairs and modifications to property items, as directed;

**s.** Maintaining the Prop Wagon and/or Prop Box;

**t.** Insuring that property personnel do not attempt work under any unsafe condition(s), as specified by the Building and Safety Code and fire laws, or in violation of any other safety regulation(s) and practice(s);

**During POST-PRODUCTION:**

**u.** Seeing that all items of Company property are accounted for and returned to vendors, owners or Company storage facilities;

**v.** Otherwise carrying out the duties normally required of this classification;

**w.** Providing the hand tools normally employed in this craft.

**3. Considerations:**

**a.** Each shooting unit of the production—first and second units—requiring props uses a **Property Master**, except that one (1) **Property Master** may service both units if the units are not shooting concurrently.

**b.** A **Property Master** is used on those productions requiring hand or set props. The **Property Master** is used for a sufficient length of time to procure, care for and return all props, in addition to duties during the regular shooting schedule.

**H. PROPERTY ASSISTANT**

**1. Responsibilities:** The **Property Assistant** is directly responsible to the **Property Master** for helping facilitate the work of the Property Category.

**2. Duties—all during the PRODUCTION Process:**

**a.** Securing from the **Property Master** all property items needed for the day's shooting;

**b.** Helping dress the set with these prop items, placing and positioning them;

**c.** Marking the floor, wall, ceiling and/or ground position of each set prop in order to facilitate resetting of such items, as required;

**d.** Moving and placing such items as noted in Category Criteria, above;

**e.** Vacuuming, dusting, cleaning and polishing props, as necessary, prior to the take in which such items are employed;

**f.** Striking all prop items from the set after their use and returning said prop items to the **Property Master**;

**g.** Picking up and returning required property items to the supply source during production;

**h.** Assisting the **Property Master** in the performance of category duties;

**i.** Otherwise carrying out the duties normally required of this classification;

**j.** Providing the hand tools normally employed in this craft.

**3. Considerations:** A **Property Assistant** is used to assist the **Property Master** and does not function unsupervised by a **Property Master.**

## I. HOME ECONOMIST

**1. Responsibilities:** The **Home Economist** is directly responsible to the **Property Master** for having all required food items ordered, prepared and arranged sufficiently in advance of photography, in the manner desired by the **Director**, so that production time is not wasted and the desired photographic result is obtained.

**2. Duties:**

▼ **During PRE-PRODUCTION:**

**a.** Ordering, purchasing, preparing, placing and arranging food items to be consumed, displayed and/or otherwise utilized for photographic purposes;

▼ **During the PRODUCTION Process:**

**b.** Maintaining a ready reserve of such prepared food items for subsequent use and/or takes;

**c.** Maintaining proper sanitary conditions in the preparation and handling of any and all food items to be consumed;

**d.** Cleaning the utensils and food preparation area before and after use thereof, disposing of leftovers;

**e.** Otherwise carrying out the duties normally required of this classification;

**f.** Providing the hand tools normally employed in this craft.

**3. Considerations:**

**a.** A **Home Economist** is used on productions when prepared food is required for photographic purposes.

**b.** A **Home Economist** shall be properly licensed to handle and prepare food.

# Costuming Category Organizational Chart

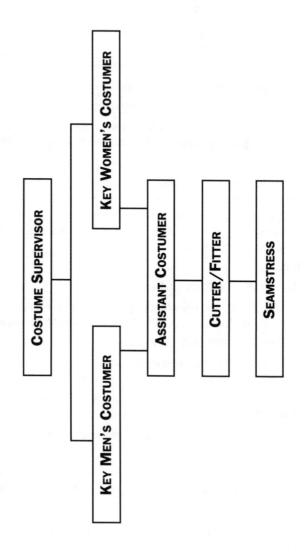

# 13

## COSTUMING CATEGORY

**A. Category Classifications:** There are six (6) classifications in the Costuming Category:

1. **Costume Supervisor (Category Head)**
2. **Key Men's Costumer**
3. **Key Women's Costumer**
4. **Assistant Costumer**
5. **Cutter/Fitter**
6. **Seamstress**

**B. Category Criteria:**

1. Employees holding classification within the Costuming Category perform all job functions pertaining to production costuming procedures which are utilized on interior or exterior production, on location and/or on the sound stage.

2. For original costuming, the **Costume Supervisor** is the liaison and coordinator between the **Costume Designer** and the fabricators—the **Cutter**s and **Seamstress**es.

3. For acquired costuming, either purchased, rented or loaned, the **Costume Supervisor** is the liaison and coordinator between the **Art Director** and the **Key Costumers**

4. During production shooting, the **Key Costumer**s are physically present on the set at all times.

5. The **Costume Supervisor** is directly responsible to the **Director of Photography** for the photographic acceptability (color and pattern) of the costumes and accessories.

6. When the **Costume Supervisor** requires assistance in the procurement, handling, teching, aging, maintenance and return of items of wardrobe, an **Assistant Costumer** is used.

7. When the **Costume Supervisor** requires assistance in fitting performers into items of wardrobe and in making needed alternations in such wardrobe, a **Cutter/Fitter** is used.

8. The **Costume Supervisor** must ensure that costuming personnel do not attempt work under any unsafe condition(s), as specified by the Employer, OSHA, Building and Safety Code and fire laws, or in violation of any other safety regulation(s) and practice(s).

**C. Category Responsibilities:** It is the responsibility of each Employee in the Costuming Category to work cooperatively with the **Costume Supervisor** in order to assist in achieving the optimum and most efficient operation of the various procedures within this category.

**D. Category Function:** The principal function of Costuming Category personnel involves the planning and preparation of costuming required for a cinematic production, and ensures that each performer and atmosphere player is costumed appropriately for each scene in the production.

**E. Category Considerations:**

**1.** Costuming Category personnel are used on each production on which items of costuming are to be coordinated, whether by design and execution, purchase, rental or on loan.

**2.** The classification(s) used depends upon the type and quantity of such costuming items and whether such items are designed and created, purchased, borrowed or rented.

**F. Category Requirements:** Employees in each Costuming Category classification must know and follow the chain-of-command and lines-of-communication and must be able to effectively and safely organize and manage all items of costuming selected for each job and associated with their respective craft classification.

**G. COSTUME SUPERVISOR**

**1. Responsibilities:** The **Costume Supervisor** is directly responsible to the **Costume Designer** for gathering complete and accurate body measurements from cast members and atmosphere personnel who will be dressed in costumes, either fabricated, purchased or rented for the production and then seeing that such costume wear is complete, and properly fitted to the persons wearing them.

**2. Duties:**

▼ **During PRE-PRODUCTION:**

**a.** Reading and annotating the script and analyzing it within the context of costuming considerations—type and number of costumes and accessories for each scene;

**b.** Preparing a costume schedule (wardrobe plot) which includes, by scene number and character, the costume items and changes to be effected during the production by each performer;

**c.** Getting from each performer the physical measurements and clothes sizes in order to assure proper fit of all costume items whether purchased, rented or specially fabricated;

**d.** Supervising measuring, manufacture and fittings of fabricated costumes;

**e.** Selecting, renting or buying any clothing, costumes, accessories or items thereof, necessary to the production;

**f.** Seeing that every item of costuming apparel fits, and is appropriate;

▼ **During the PRODUCTION Process:**

**g.** Supervising modifications in the condition of wardrobe items—aging, teching, staining, soiling, tearing, shredding, soaking, etc;

**h.** Otherwise carrying out the duties normally required of this classification;

**i.** Providing the hand tools normally employed in this craft.

**3. Considerations:**

**a.** A **Costume Supervisor** functions on any production requiring any sort of "character" or period costuming worn by cast or atmosphere personnel.

**b.** The **Costume Supervisor** is given a sufficient length of time to carry out pre-production, production and post-production duties.

## H. KEY MEN'S COSTUMER

**1. Responsibilities:** The **Key Men's Costumer** is directly responsible to the **Costume Supervisor** for supervising the measuring of male cast members and for the fitting of costume items on their persons.

**2. Duties:**

▼ **During PRE-PRODUCTION:**

**a.** Reading and annotating the script within the context of male costuming requirements;

**b.** Receiving a complete costuming list for each male cast member, and for atmosphere personnel, when applicable, from the **Costume Supervisor**;

**c.** Acquiring the physical measurements of each male cast member to accurately determine his pants, shirt, coat, jacket, sweater, shoes, glove, ring and hat size;

**d.** If for a fabricated costume, sending the measurements to the fabricating department;

**e.** If for purchased or rented costume, acquiring the correct sizes from the vending or costume company;

**f.** As the costume(s) is (are) ready, calling each male performer in for a preliminary fitting, pinning and marking each costume item for necessary alteration(s);

**g.** Sending the costume(s) to the **Cutter/Fitter**(s) for alterations;

**h.** Calling each male performer in for a final fitting;

**i.** If no further alterations are required, cataloguing each costume, along with the costume accessories, by actor and/or character name and the scene number in which the costume is worn;

▼ **During the PRODUCTION Process:**

**j.** Seeing that all costume items are given into the custody of the **Key Wardrobe** person as soon as possible prior to the scheduled shooting of the scenes requiring those costume items;

**k.** Being present at all times during shooting to assure that costumes worn by male performers are correct, complete and not in need of repair or alteration;

**l.** Otherwise carrying out the duties normally required of this classification;

**m.** Providing the hand tools normally employed in this craft.

### 3. Considerations:

**a.** A **Key Men's Costumer** functions on any production requiring any sort of "character" or period costuming whether fabricated, purchased or rented.

**b.** The **Key Men's Costumer** is given a sufficient length of time to carry out pre-production, production and post-production duties.

## I. KEY WOMEN'S COSTUMER

**1. Responsibilities:** The **Key Women's Costumer** is directly responsible to the **Costume Supervisor** for supervising the measuring of female cast members and for the fitting of costume items on their persons.

### 2. Duties:

▼ **During PRE-PRODUCTION:**

**a.** Reading and annotating the script within the context of female costuming requirements;

**b.** Receiving a complete costuming list for each female cast member, and for atmosphere personnel, when applicable, from the **Costume Supervisor**;

**c.** Acquiring the physical measurements of each female cast member to accurately determine her dress, blouse, coat, jacket, sweater, shoes, glove, ring and hat size;

**d.** If for a fabricated costume, sending the measurements to the fabricating department;

**e.** If for purchased or rented costume, acquiring the correct sizes from the vending or costume company;

**f.** As the costume(s) is (are) ready, calling each female performer in for a preliminary fitting, pinning and marking each costume item for necessary alteration(s);

**g.** Sending the costume(s) to the **Cutter/Fitter**(s) for alterations;

**h.** Calling each female performer in for a final fitting;

**i.** If no further alterations are required, cataloguing each costume, along with the costume accessories, by actor and/or character name and the scene number in which the costume is worn;

▼ **During the PRODUCTION Process:**

**j.** Seeing that all costume items are given into the custody of the **Key Wardrobe** person as soon as possible prior to the scheduled shooting of the scenes requiring those costume items;

**k.** Being present at all times during shooting to assure that costumes worn by female performers are correct, complete and not in need of repair or alteration;

**l.** Otherwise carrying out the duties normally required of this classification;

**m.** Providing the hand tools normally employed in this craft.

**3. Considerations:**

**a.** A **Key Women's Costumer** functions on any production requiring any sort of "character" or period costuming whether fabricated, purchased or rented.

**b.** The **Key Women's Costumer** is given a sufficient length of time to carry out pre-production, production and post-production duties.

## J. ASSISTANT COSTUMER

**1. Responsibilities:** The **Assistant Costumer** is directly responsible to the **Key Costumer** to whom assigned, assisting in the performance of Costuming Category duties.

**2. Duties—all during PRE-PRODUCTION and PRODUCTION:**

**a.** Assisting the **Key Costumer**s in the procurement, handling, maintenance and return of costume items;

**b.** Serving as a liaison between the **Key Costumer**s and the **Set Wardrobe** person in bringing costuming items to the set, or from the set to the **Key Costumer**s for sizing or special conditioning modification;

**c.** Assisting the **Key Costumer**s in the performance of Costuming Category duties;

**d.** Otherwise carrying out the duties normally required of this classification;

**e.** Providing the hand tools normally employed in this craft.

**3. Considerations:** An **Assistant Costumer** works under the supervision of a **Key Costumer**.

## K. CUTTER/FITTER

**1. Responsibilities:** The **Cutter/Fitter** is directly responsible to the **Key Men's Costumer** when altering male costuming and to the **Key Women's Costumer** when altering female costuming for accurately and efficiently marking, pinning and altering such attire to properly fit each performer and atmosphere person in order to achieve optimum cinematographic effect of such attire.

**2. Duties—all during PRE-PRODUCTION:**

**a.** During the fitting process on the particular performer, and under the supervision of the **Key Men's** or **Key Women's Costumer**, marking, cutting and pinning costume items to indicate the necessary alterations in those costume item(s) in order to ensure a proper fit;

**b.** Cutting the garment, as necessary, to conform to the fitting marks;

**c.** Pinning the trimmed elements together;

**d.** Taking the garment to the **Seamstress** for sewing the trimmed elements together in preparation for a final fitting;

**e.** Picking up the garment from the **Seamstress** and taking it to the final fitting;

**f.** At the final fitting, making any alterations required to ensure an appropriate fit;

**g.** Seeing that the **Key Men's** or **Key Women's Costumer** receives custody of the altered, properly fitting and approved costume;

**h.** Otherwise carrying out the duties normally required of these classifications;

**i.** Providing the hand tools normally employed in these crafts.

**3. Considerations: Dressers/Fitters** are employed on those productions on which the type, quantity and quality of costuming items require fabrication and/or alterations in order to maintain the costume items in optimum condition for cinematographic purposes.

## L. SEAMSTRESS

**1. Responsibilities:** The **Seamstress** is directly responsible to the **Key Men's Costumer** when assembling and sewing male costumes and to the **Key Women's Costumer** when assembling and sewing female costumes for accurately and efficiently finishing such attire so that it is properly put together and fits each performer in order to achieve optimum cinematographic effect of such attire.

**2. Duties—all during PRE-PRODUCTION:**

**a.** Sewing items of male or female costuming apparel in order to achieve a complete, functional and integrated costume which fits and holds together for the performer wearing it;

**b.** Separating and resewing items of costume which the **Cutter/Fitter** has marked and altered to achieve a better fit for the specific performer;

**c.** Using sewing techniques in line with the period the costume represents;

**d.** Delivering all costumes on which the alterations have been completed to the **Cutter/Fitter** for further fittings, or to return to the particular **Key Costumer**;

**e.** Otherwise carrying out the duties normally required of this classification;

**f.** Providing the hand tools normally employed in this craft.

**3. Considerations: Seamstress**es are employed on those productions which require costume fabrication and/or alterations in order to maintain the costume items in optimum condition for cinematographic purposes.

<u>**NOTES**</u>

# Wardrobe Category Organizational Chart

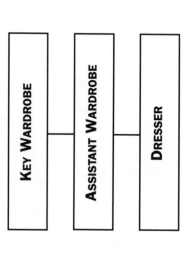

Key Wardrobe

Assistant Wardrobe

Dresser

# 14

# WARDROBE CATEGORY

**A. Category Classifications:** There are three (3) classifications in the Wardrobe Category:

**1. Key Wardrobe (Category Head)**

**2. Assistant Wardrobe**

**3. Dresser**

**B. Category Criteria:**

**1.** Employees holding classification within the Wardrobe Category perform all job functions pertaining to production wardrobe procedures which are utilized on interior or exterior production, on location and/or on the sound stage.

**2.** A **Key Wardrobe** person is used on a set or location site when items of wardrobe are supplied by the Company and also when supplied by the cast when such personal wardrobe items require custodial care and/or maintenance during production, and is in charge of all technical procedures directly pertaining to wardrobe during the production process.

**3.** A **Key Wardrobe** person needs to know and apply: Strict accountability procedures to the acquiring, organizing, use, placing, maintaining, inventorying and storing of wardrobe items entrusted to his or her care.

**4.** During production shooting, the **Key Wardrobe** person is physically present on the set at all times.

**5.** When a **Costume Supervisor** is used, the **Key Wardrobe** person is directly responsible to the **Costume Supervisor**.

**6.** When an **Art Director** and **Costume Supervisor** are not used, the **Key Wardrobe** person is directly responsible to the **Production Manager**.

**7.** When the **Key Wardrobe** person requires assistance in the procurement, handling, maintenance and return of items of wardrobe, an **Assistant Wardrobe** person is used.

**8.** When the **Key Wardrobe** person requires assistance in dressing performers into items of wardrobe and in making needed alternations in such wardrobe, a **Dresser** is used.

**9.** When the **Key Wardrobe** person requires assistance in fitting performers into items of wardrobe and in making needed alternations in such wardrobe, a **Fitter/Cutter** from the Costuming Category is used.

**10.** Wardrobe Category personnel are not required to tailor, clean, press or launder any clothing, but are directly responsible for having such work done, as needed, for the production, excepting in the event of emergency during shooting.

11. All Wardrobe personnel operating underwater with breathing apparatus must be SCUBA certified.

12. The **Key Wardrobe** person must ensure that wardrobe personnel do not attempt work under any unsafe condition(s), as specified by the Employer, OSHA, Building and Safety Code and fire laws, or in violation of any other safety regulation(s) and practice(s).

C. **Category Responsibilities:** It is the responsibility of each Employee in the Wardrobe Category to work cooperatively with the **Key Wardrobe** person in order to assist in achieving the optimum and most efficient operation of the various procedures within this category.

D. **Category Function**: The principal function of Wardrobe Category personnel involves custodial work during production shooting with items of wardrobe and the accompanying accessories worn by the performers and seeing that the performers are properly attired in the appropriate wardrobe and with the appropriate accessories for each scene to be photographed.

E. **Category Considerations:**

1. Wardrobe Category personnel are used on each production on which items of wardrobe, worn by performers, are photographed.

2. The classification(s) used depends upon the type and quantity of such wardrobe items.

F. **Category Requirements:** Employees in each Wardrobe Category classification must know and follow the chain-of-command and lines-of-communication and must be able to effectively and safely organize and manage all items of wardrobe selected for each job and associated with their respective craft classification.

G. **KEY WARDROBE**

1. **Responsibilities:** The **Key Wardrobe** person is directly responsible as specified in Category Criteria, above, and is directly responsible for the appropriate selection (when so directed), organization, maintenance and application of wardrobe items in order to achieve their optimum photographic realization.

2. **Duties:**

▼ **During PRE-PRODUCTION:**

a. Reading and annotating the script and analyzing it within the context of wardrobe considerations—type and number of costumes and accessories for each actor and atmosphere person for each scene;

b. Preparing a costume schedule (wardrobe plot) which includes, by scene number and character, the costume items and changes to be effected during the production by each performer;

c. Getting from the **Costume Supervisor** the physical measurements and clothes sizes of all actors in order to assure proper fit of all costume items;

▼ **During the PRODUCTION Process:**

d. Supervising the making of minor alternations in, and repairs of, items of costume;

e. Assigning dressing rooms and stocking them with towels and facial tissues;

f. Assembling each change for each actor on a separate hanger as a numbered unit—each change includes complete costume from head to foot including all visible accessories;

g. Maintaining all costume items in appropriate condition, ready for use on-camera;

h. Inventorying all costume items at the close of production, and returning those items of costume when authorized by the **Costume Supervisor** and **Production Manager**;

i. Otherwise carrying out the duties normally required of this classification;

j. Providing the hand tools normally employed in this craft.

3. **Considerations:**

a. A **Key Wardrobe** person functions on any production requiring any sort of "character" or period costuming, or requiring multiple changes and/or multiple conditioning of any type of clothing or costumes worn by cast or atmosphere members.

b. The **Key Wardrobe** person is given a sufficient length of time to carry out pre-production, production and post-production duties.

## H. ASSISTANT WARDROBE

1. **Responsibilities:** The **Assistant Wardrobe** person is directly responsible to the **Key Wardrobe** person, assisting in the performance of Wardrobe Category duties.

2. **Duties—all during the PRODUCTION Process:**

a. Arranging, identifying and tagging complete costume changes, including accessories, for each performer for each scene in the production;

b. Making minor repairs and alterations on items of wardrobe, as directed;

c. Picking up and returning wardrobe items from the **Assistant Costumer** or supply source during production, as directed;

d. Taking wardrobe to be cleaned and pressed and picking it up again, as directed;

e. Assisting the **Utility Sound Technician** (film) or **Audio Assistant** (video) in the placement of the RF microphone and transmitter on the person of each performer using such sound equipment;

    **f.** Assisting the **Key Wardrobe** person in the performance of Wardrobe duties;

    **g.** Otherwise carrying out the duties normally required of this classification;

    **h.** Providing the hand tools normally employed in this craft.

**3. Considerations:** An **Assistant Wardrobe** person works under the supervision of the **Key Wardrobe** person.

## I. DRESSER

**1. Responsibilities:** The **Dresser** is directly responsible to the **Key Wardrobe** person and assists in the performance of Wardrobe Category duties.

**2. Duties—all during the PRODUCTION Process:**

    **a.** Seeing that a full costume, complete with accessories, is delivered to each performer's dressing room at the start of a production day and any costume change is delivered prior to each planned scene which requires such costume change;

    **b.** Assisting a performer in donning a costume when requested to do so;

    **c.** Making sure that all required items of costume are in place on the person of the performer for the scene to be shot;

    **d.** Making sure that no personal effects are being worn by performers appearing on-camera;

    **e.** Spot cleaning and/or pressing costumes on the job;

    **f.** Taking out and picking up wardrobe for cleaning or laundering;

    **g.** Dying items of costume, as directed;

    **h.** Picking up and returning items of wardrobe, as directed;

    **i.** Otherwise carrying out the duties normally required of these classifications;

    **j.** Providing the hand tools normally employed in these crafts.

**3. Considerations: Dresser**s are employed on those productions on which the quantity and quality of the items of wardrobe require considerable and specific care and organization in order to keep in optimum condition and preparation for photographic purposes.

<u>**NOTES**</u>

# MAKEUP CATEGORY ORGANIZATIONAL CHART

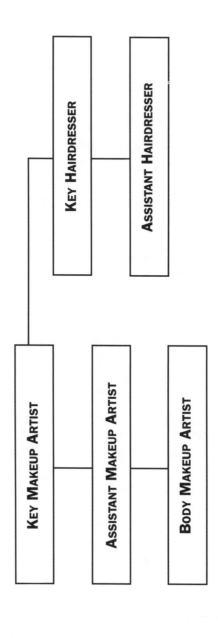

# 15

# MAKEUP CATEGORY

**A. Category Classifications:** There are five (5) classifications in the Makeup Category:

1. **Key Makeup Artist (Category Head)**

2. **Assistant Makeup Artist**

3. **Body Makeup Artist**

4. **Key Hairdresser [Hairstylist] (Category Sub-Head)**

5. **Assistant Hairdresser**

**B. Category Criteria:**

1. Employees holding classification within the Makeup Category perform all job functions pertaining to cinematographic makeup procedures which are utilized on interior or exterior production, on location and/or on the sound stage.

2. A **Key Makeup Artist** is used on a set or location when makeup is used on the performer(s) for cinematographic production purposes, and is in charge of all technical procedures directly pertaining to the production process.

3. A **Key Makeup Artist** needs to know and apply: The cosmetological techniques and matériel needed to accomplish cinematographic and special effects makeup as well as the measures to safely apply and remove all such makeup.

4. During production shooting, the **Key Makeup Artist** is physically present on the set at all times.

5. The **Key Makeup Artist** is directly responsible to:

   a. The **Art Director/Production Designer**, when used on a production, otherwise to the **Director**, for makeup styling;

   b. The **Director of Photography** for the photographic acceptance (color, shading and density) of the makeup.

6. **Production makeup** is divided into the following four (4) types:

   a. **Straight**, or "**street**," **makeup:** Cosmetic makeup—cream, liquid, pancake and/or powder—which is applied to the face, forehead, scalp (balding or thinning areas), ears, neck, arms and hands in order to better convey the effect of a natural look of the performer(s) for photographic purposes.

   b. **Character makeup:** Cosmetic and specialized makeup, using such material as rubber, cloth, latex stipple, plastic, prosthetics, bald caps, hair goods,

**173**

metals, foil, etc, which are applied to the person of the performer(s), including the eyes, mouth and teeth, and appropriately painted, in order to convey the effect of: Physical metamorphosis or physical change resulting from aging, injury, emotional strain, occult or scientific influence; weather or physical exertion; a particular racial origin or age; animal, robot or humanoid being, morphing processes, etc, for photographic purposes.

c. **Special effects makeup:** Specialized makeup by use of prosthetics, rubber, plastics, metals, foil, tubes, reservoir sacks, pumps, etc, in order to create the illusion of running sores or wounds, dismemberment, disembowelment, etc, or the illusion of a humanoid, robot or animal, or of a human becoming or morphing into any such, for photographic purposes.

d. **Body makeup:** Cosmetic makeup which is applied to all or part of the human body from the collar bone to the bottom of the feet, excluding the arms and hands, of the performer(s) for photographic purposes.

7. The **Key Makeup Artist** may work in conjunction with a **Propmaker** or **Key Special Effects Technician** in the preparation, execution and/or operation of special effects makeup.

8. All of the makeup, hairdressing supplies and equipment applicable thereto which is used on humans should be of standard quality and sterility thereby conforming to the State laws governing cosmetology and barbering.

9. **Makeup Artist**s do not cut hair, other than trimming or feathering the performer's hair or false hair, but do apply all false hair or hair pieces if there is not sufficient amount of this work to necessitate the use of a **Key Hairdresser**.

10. When the **Key Makeup Artist** requires assistance in the application of makeup to the performers, an **Assistant Makeup Artist** is used.

11. When the **Key Makeup Artist** requires assistance in the application of makeup to the bodies of performers, **Body Makeup Artist**s of the same gender as the performers worked on are used.

12. When the **Key Hairdresser** requires assistance in dressing the hair, an **Assistant Hairdresser** is used.

13. All Makeup personnel operating underwater with breathing apparatus must be SCUBA certified.

14. The **Key Makeup Artist** and the **Key Hairdresser** must ensure that makeup personnel under their supervision do not attempt work under any unsafe condition(s), as specified by the Employer, OSHA, Building and Safety Code and fire laws, or in violation of any other safety regulation(s) and practice(s).

C. **Category Responsibilities:** It is the responsibility of each Employee in the Makeup Category to work cooperatively with the **Key Makeup Artist**, or with the **Key Hairdresser**, to whom assigned, in order to assist in achieving the optimum and most efficient operation of the makeup and hairdressing procedures.

MAKEUP

**D. Category Function:** The principal function of Makeup Category personnel involves the application of photographically balanced makeup and/or styling and dressing the hair of the performer(s) in order to create and achieve optimum and consistent photographic realization thereof.

**E. Category Considerations:**

**1.** Makeup Category personnel are utilized on each production on which makeup is used on, or worn by, the performer(s), or on which the performer's hair requires dressing, styling, or augmenting.

**2.** The classification(s) used depends upon the type of makeup and the number of performers who require the application of makeup and/or hairdressing care.

**F. Category Requirements:** Employees in each Makeup Category classification must know and follow the chain-of-command and lines-of-communication and must be able to effectively and safely apply to, and/or remove appropriate cosmetic materials from, the persons of performers adjusting the makeup for interiors or exteriors, in the studio or on location, during day or evening scenes, whether weathered, emphasizing wear and tear, or for underwater scenes.

**G. KEY MAKEUP ARTIST**

**1. Responsibilities:** The **Key Makeup Artist** is directly responsible as specified in Category Criteria, above, and is responsible for the selection of proper makeup materials and applying them in a style best suited to help assure optimum aesthetic photographic realization thereof.

**2. Duties:**

▼ **During PRE-PRODUCTION:**

**a.** Reading and annotating the script within the context of makeup and hairdressing matériel requirements—type and amount, and number of performers and extras to be attended to;

**b.** Preparing a makeup schedule which includes the type of makeup styling called for, the makeup items employed (by manufacturer number) and a plot of the application of that makeup (if required) by character and scene number;

▼ **During the PRODUCTION Process:**

**c.** Briefing the **Assistant Makeup Artist**(s) and the **Hairdresser**(s) as to the type of makeup and/or hair styling required;

**d.** Scheduling and assigning Makeup Category personnel to certain actors and/or extras;

**e.** Applying to the actors' persons all makeup required, and removing it, if required;

**f.** Touching up actors' makeup between takes, as necessary;

**g.** Otherwise carrying out the duties normally required of this classification;

MAKEUP

    **h.** Providing a Makeup Kit along with the supplies and hand tools normally employed in this craft, and being duly compensated for the use thereof.

**3. Considerations:**

    **a.** A **Key Makeup Artist** is used for each unit utilizing makeup when such units are shooting concurrently.

    **b.** Only **Key Makeup Artist**s apply special effects makeup.

    **c.** There may be more than one (1) **Key Makeup Artist** used on a production unit when production makeup requires such staffing.

## H. ASSISTANT MAKEUP ARTIST

**1. Responsibilities and Duties—all during the PRODUCTION Process:** The **Assistant Makeup Artist** is directly responsible to the **Key Makeup Artist** and assists in the performance of makeup duties.

**2. Considerations:**

    **a.** An **Assistant Makeup Artist** is permitted to apply and touch up makeup as specified and supervised by the **Key Makeup Artist.**

    **b.** Each **Assistant Makeup Artist** provides a Makeup Kit along with the supplies and hand tools normally employed in this craft and is duly compensated for the use thereof.

## I. BODY MAKEUP ARTIST

**1. Responsibilities:** The **Body Makeup Artist** is directly responsible to the **Key Makeup Artist** for applying body makeup in a style best suited to help assure optimum photographic realization thereof.

**2. Duties—all during the PRODUCTION Process:**

    **a.** Applying to the actors' persons, from the base of the neck to, and including the feet, body makeup of the type and amount required by the production;

    **b.** Touching up the actors' body makeup between takes, as necessary;

    **c.** Removing the body makeup at the end of a shooting day, if required;

    **d.** Otherwise carrying out the duties normally required of this classification;

    **e.** Providing the supplies and hand tools normally employed in this craft, and being duly compensated therefor.

**3. Considerations: Body Makeup Artist**s will be of the same gender as the performers to which they apply or remove body makeup.

## J. KEY HAIRDRESSER [HAIRSTYLIST]

**1. Responsibilities:** The **Key Hairdresser [Hairstylist]** is directly responsible to the **Key Makeup Artist** for dressing and/or styling the hair of actors in a style best suited to help assure optimum aesthetic photographic realization thereof.

**2. Duties—all during the PRODUCTION Process:**

**a.** Reading and annotating the script within the context of hairstyling;

**b.** Shampooing, barbering and/or styling and setting the hair, for production purposes, of actors engaged in the production;

**c.** Selection of and "dressing" all wigs, toupees, switches, falls, etc, required for the production, and applying them to the actors;

**d.** Touching up, combing and/or spraying actors' hair between takes, as needed;

**e.** Drying hair, as directed, when actors have been immersed in water or performing in rain scenes;

**f.** Otherwise carrying out the duties normally required of this classification;

**g.** Providing the supplies and hand tools normally employed in this craft, and being duly compensated for the use thereof.

**3. Considerations:**

**a.** A **Key Hairdresser** is used for each production unit requiring hair dressing or hair styling work.

**b.** Only **Key Hairdressers** create hair styles for members of the cast.

**c.** There may be more than one (1) **Key Hairdresser** used on a production when production hairdressing or hairstyling requires such staffing.

**K. ASSISTANT HAIRDRESSER**

**1. Responsibilities and Duties—all during the PRODUCTION Process:** The **Assistant Hairdresser** is directly responsible to the **Key Hairdresser** and assists in the performance of hairdressing duties.

**2. Considerations:** An **Assistant Hairdresser** applies hairdressing materials and dresses hair as specified and supervised by the **Key Hairdresser**. Each **Assistant Hairdresser** provides the supplies, hair irons, a portable hair dryer and hand tools normally employed in this craft and is duly compensated for their use.

# TRANSPORTATION CATEGORY ORGANIZATIONAL CHART

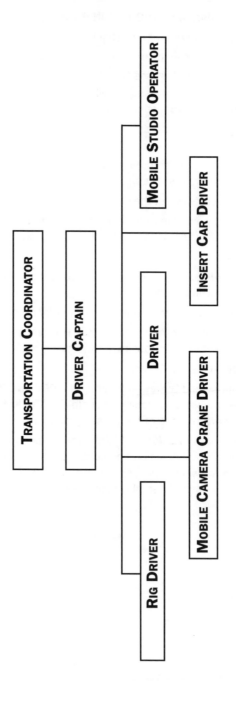

# 16

# TRANSPORTATION CATEGORY

**A. Category Classifications:** There are seven (7) classifications in the Transportation Category:

1. **Transportation Coordinator (Category Head)**
2. **Driver Captain (Category Co-Head)**
3. **Rig Driver**
4. **Driver**

▼ **Specialized Drivers—Mobile Camera Platform Operators:**

5. **Mobile Studio Operator (Category Sub-Head)**
6. **Insert Car Driver (Category Sub-Head)**
7. **Mobile Camera Crane Driver (Category Sub-Head)**

**B. Category Criteria:**

1. Employees holding classification within the Transportation Category perform all job functions pertaining to production transportation procedures which are utilized on interior or exterior production, on location and/or on the sound stage.

2. A **Transportation Coordinator** is used on productions which depend upon substantial logistical support and efficiency during the production process;

3. On productions not using a **Transportation Coordinator**, the **Driver Captain** is Category Head;

4. A **Driver Captain** is used when there are three (3) or more **Driver**s employed on a production. The **Driver Captain** may function as an operating **Driver**.

5. A **Driver Captain** needs to have and apply: A thorough knowledge of the capability and carrying capacity of various vehicles in his or her care; an ability to prepare transportation scheduling and make all **Driver** assignments.

6. The number and classification(s) of Transportation Category personnel to be employed are determined by the **Producer** or **Production Manager**, in accordance with Union and Guild bargaining agreements. Among the determining factors are:

   **a.** Quantity, weight and type of matériel to be transported;

   **b.** Number of staff, cast and crew to be transported;

   **c.** The distance to be traveled;

   **d.** The topography and roadway conditions existent en route;

   **e.** Predicted weather to be expected en route;

   **f.** The type of vehicle(s) to be used;

   **g.** The number of vehicles to be used.

**TRANSPOR-TATION**

7. A **Driver** of appropriate classification is assigned to each vehicle being used.

8. On non-stop long-distance and/or cross-country assignments, two (2) **Rig Driver**s are normally assigned to a heavy-duty rig.

9. A **Driver** shall be properly licensed, for the type of vehicle operated, by the State in which that **Driver** resides. For example, in **California**:

   a. The **Class 1 License** is for **Driver**s operating semi (tractor-trailer) rigs or for doubles (two trailers) exceeding 6,000 pounds in weight;

   b. The **Class 2 License** is for **Driver**s operating vehicles with three (3) or more axles, up to 6,000 pounds in weight, or for vehicles carrying more than ten (10) persons;

   c. The **Class 3 License** is for **Driver**s operating vehicles with two (2) axles, weighing less than 6,000 pounds, and for vehicles carrying not more than ten (10) persons.

10. A **Driver** may be directly assigned to a Category Head, in which event the **Driver** is directly responsible to that Category Head, otherwise to the **Production Manager**.

11. The **Driver Captain** and each Sub-Head must ensure that transportation personnel do not attempt work under any unsafe condition(s), as specified by the Employer, OSHA, Building and Safety Code and fire laws, or in violation of any other safety regulation(s) and practice(s).

C. **Category Responsibilities:** It is the responsibility of each Employee in the Transportation Category to work cooperatively with the Category Head, or Sub-Head, to whom assigned, in order to assist in achieving the optimum and most efficient logistical operation of the transportation process.

D. **Category Function:** The principal function of Transportation Category personnel involves the driving, positioning, loading, unloading and care of vehicles used in production logistics as well as for camera transport and shot movement.

E. **Category Considerations:**

   1. Transportation Category personnel are used on each production on which vehicles are used for logistical purposes and/or for camera insert cars and motorized camera cranes.

   2. The classification(s) used depends upon the type and quantity of vehicle(s) being used.

F. **Category Requirements:** Employees in each Transportation Category classification must know and follow the chain-of-command and lines-of-communication and must be able to effectively and safely operate the transportation equipment selected for each job and associated with their respective craft classification.

G. **TRANSPORTATION COORDINATOR**

   1. **Responsibilities**: The **Transportation Coordinator** is directly responsible to the **Production Manager** for properly and efficiently carrying out the logistical and transportation functions of a production.

**2. Duties—all during PRE-PRODUCTION and PRODUCTION:**

**a.** Reading and annotating the script within the context of transportation and logistics—number and type of vehicles and licensed **Drivers**;

**b.** Checking with each Category Head to determine transportation requirements concerning personnel and matériel for the production;

**c.** Preparing a breakdown list of transportation requirements for the - **Production Manager**;

**d.** Notifying the **Driver Captain** of the number and type of vehicles required for each production day and the production department to which each vehicle is assigned;

**e.** Otherwise carrying out the duties normally required of this classification;

**f.** Providing the hand tools normally employed in this craft.

**3. Considerations:** The **Transportation Coordinator** functions as the liaison between the various production departments and the Transportation department.

## H. DRIVER CAPTAIN

**1. Responsibilities**: The **Driver Captain** is directly responsible to the **Transportation Coordinator** for properly and efficiently carrying out the logistical and transportation functions of a production.

**2. Duties—all during the PRODUCTION Process:**

**a.** Reading and annotating the script within the context of transportation and logistics—number and type of vehicles and licensed **Drivers**;

**b.** Preparing a breakdown list of transportation requirements for the **Production Manager**;

**c.** Checking that each **Driver** is properly licensed to operate the type of vehicle to which assigned;

**d.** Making all **Driver** assignments and checking **Drivers** in and/out;

**e.** Supervising the process of parking, loading and unloading of all Company vehicles;

**f.** Seeing that each vehicle is parked as close as possible to the working area of specific category or department personnel whose equipment, material, supplies and/or tools it is carrying;

**g.** Assuring that all Company vehicles are within proper and safe load limits, operationally safe, fueled and ready to roll;

**h.** Driving an assigned Company vehicle;

**i.** Operating loading lifts or winches attached to the vehicle;

**j.** Observing proper and adequate safety and protective procedures for personnel and equipment being loaded and transported in his or her care under prevailing highway and weather conditions;

**k.** Insuring that transportation personnel do not attempt work under any unsafe condition(s), as specified by the Building and Safety Code and fire laws, or in violation of any other safety regulation(s) and practice(s);

**l.** Otherwise carrying out the duties normally required of this classification;

**m.** Providing the hand tools normally employed in this craft.

**3. Considerations:**

**a.** The **Driver Captain** may fill in by driving a vehicle when necessary.

**b.** When there are six (6) or more Company vehicles on a production, the **Driver Captain** may operate more efficiently by not being assigned a vehicle to drive.

**c.** The **Driver Captain** shall be properly licensed by the State of residence, holding not less than a **Class 2 Driver**'s **License**.

## I. RIG DRIVER

**1. Responsibilities:** The **Rig Driver** is directly responsible to the **Driver Captain**, or to the Category Head or Sub-Head to whom assigned, or if no **Driver Captain**, to the **Production Manager**, for safely and efficiently operating the assigned rig in a manner to insure the prime condition of the production cargo while helping expedite the production process.

**2. Duties—all during PRE-PRODUCTION and PRODUCTION:**

**a.** Operating the assigned tractor-trailer or doubles rig;

**b.** Attaching and detaching all coupling between the tractor and trailer(s);

**c.** Operating loading lifts or winches attached to the vehicular equipment;

**d.** Loading and unloading the assigned vehicle, tying off and otherwise securing such load as necessary;

**e.** Maintaining safe load limits for the vehicle;

**f.** Observing proper and adequate safety and protective procedures for personnel and equipment being transported in the assigned vehicle under existing highway and weather conditions;

**g.** Obtaining a cash advance for per diem allowance and for cash pay-outs for fueling and servicing the vehicle en route, retaining all cash receipts;

**h.** Otherwise carrying out the duties normally required of this classification;

**i.** Providing the hand tools normally employed in this craft.

**3. Considerations:**

**a.** A **Rig Driver** shall be properly licensed by the State of residence, holding not less than a **Class 1 Driver**'s **License**.

**b.** **Rig Driver**s are used when tractor-trailer or doubles rigs are utilized during a production.

## J. DRIVER

**1. Responsibilities:** The **Driver** is directly responsible to the **Driver Captain**, if employed, otherwise to the **Production Manager**, or as specified in Category Criteria, above, for maintaining the assigned vehicle in constant readiness, operating it in a manner to ensure the safety and comfort of personnel and matériel carried in the assigned vehicle, thereby helping expedite the production process.

**2. Duties—all during the PRODUCTION Process:**

**a.** Operating the assigned vehicle at all times required;

**b.** Maintaining the assigned vehicle fueled and in readiness, retaining cash pay-out receipts as a reimbursement record, and submitting them to the **Production Manager;**

**c.** Operating loading lifts or winches attached to the vehicle;

**d.** Loading and unloading the assigned vehicle, tying off and otherwise securing such load as necessary;

**e.** Maintaining safe load limits for the vehicle;

**f.** Observing proper and adequate safety and protective procedures for personnel and matériel being transported in the assigned vehicle under existing highway and weather conditions;

**g.** Otherwise carrying out the duties normally required of this classification;

**h.** Providing the hand tools normally employed in this craft.

**3. Considerations:**

**a.** A **Driver** shall be properly licensed by the State of residence, holding not less than a **Class 3 Driver**'s **License** or a **Class 2 Driver**'s **License**, as the assigned vehicle requires.

**b.** **Driver**s are used when Company vehicles requiring operators holding a **Class 3** or **Class 2 Driver**'s **License** are utilized.

▼ **SPECIALIZED DRIVERS—Mobile Camera Platform Operators** ▼

**K. MOBILE STUDIO OPERATOR**

**1. Responsibilities:** The **Mobile Studio Operator** is directly responsible to the **Driver Captain,** or to the **Production Manager** if a **Driver Captain** is not necessary, and as a **Driver** and **Equipment Maintenance Specialist**, is responsible for operating and maintaining the mobile studio vehicle, its accommodations and accessories, in constant readiness, operating it in a manner to best insure the safety and comfort of personnel and matériel being transported therein, thereby helping expedite the production process.

**2. Duties—all during the PRODUCTION Process:**

**a.** Placing all equipment and matériel ordered by the Company in the appropriate modular compartments aboard the mobile studio;

**b.** Maintaining and inventorying all equipment and material aboard the vehicle;

**c.** Driving the mobile studio vehicle at all times required;

**d.** Maintaining the mobile studio vehicle, its accommodations, accessories and equipment, in functional readiness;

**e.** Operating the master controls and all built-in and/or attached accessories aboard;

f.  Supervising the removal of matériel from the mobile studio for production use and its prompt and proper replacement;

g.  Maintaining safe load limits for the mobile studio at all times;

h.  Observing proper and adequate safety and protective procedures for personnel and matériel being transported in the mobile studio under prevailing highway and weather conditions;

i.  Otherwise carrying out the duties normally required of this classification;

j.  Providing the hand tools normally employed in this craft.

3.  **Considerations:** A **Mobile Studio Operator** shall be properly licensed by the State of residence as a **Driver** for the type of vehicle and cargo he or she may drive, holding not less than a **Class 2 Driver**'s **License**.

## L. INSERT CAR DRIVER

1.  **Responsibilities:** The **Insert Car Driver** is directly responsible to the **Driver Captain**, or to the **Production Manager** if a **Driver Captain** is not necessary, and as a specialized **Mobile Camera Platform Operator**, is responsible for operating and maintaining the insert camera car, its accommodations and accessories, in constant readiness, operating it in a manner to best ensure the safety of personnel and matériel being transported thereon, while thereby helping expedite the production process.

2.  **Duties—all during the PRODUCTION Process:**

    a.  Reading and annotating the script within the context of mobile camera placement, movement and logistics;

    b.  Maintaining the assigned vehicle fueled and in readiness, retaining cash pay-out receipts as a reimbursement record, and submitting the receipts to the **Production Manager**;

    c.  Observing proper and adequate safety and protective procedures for personnel and equipment being loaded and transported in his or her care under prevailing highway and weather conditions, and/or the planned camera car right-of-way;

    d.  Checking to make sure that the camera vehicle is mechanically sound, operational and safe;

    e.  Making sure that all attached equipment and systems are operational, secure and safe for personnel to be around and to operate;

    f.  Personally doing, or supervising, all coupling of towed platforms or vehicles;

    g.  Placing protective posts and cabling around the perimeter of towed platforms on which personnel will be riding while working;

    h.  Ensuring that all equipment on a towed platform is properly secured and that all personnel riding thereon are securely safetied to the platform;

    i.  Limiting the number of people riding on the camera vehicle during rehearsals and shooting;

    j.  Placing protective shielding and bars to protect camera personnel positioned in front and low when following and filming a vehicle losing parts or dumping cargo;

**k.** Otherwise carrying out the duties normally required of this classification;

**l.** Providing the hand tools normally employed in this craft.

**3. Considerations:** An **Insert Car Driver** shall be properly licensed by the State of residence as a **Driver** for the type of vehicle he or she may drive, holding not less than a **Class 2 Driver**'s **License.**

## M. MOBILE CAMERA CRANE DRIVER

**1. Responsibilities:** The **Mobile Crane Driver** is directly responsible to the **Driver Captain**, or to the **Production Manager** if a **Driver Captain** is not necessary, and as a specialized **Mobile Camera Platform Operator**, is responsible for operating and maintaining the mobile camera crane, its accommodations and accessories, in constant readiness, operating it in a manner to best ensure the safety and comfort of personnel and matériel being transported thereon, thereby helping expedite the production process.

**2. Duties—all during the PRODUCTION Process:**

**a.** Reading and annotating the script within the context of mobile camera placement, movement and logistics;

**b.** Maintaining the assigned vehicle fueled and in readiness, retaining cash pay-out receipts as a reimbursement record, and submitting the receipts to the **Production Manager**;

**c.** Observing proper and adequate safety and protective procedures for personnel and equipment being loaded and transported in his or her care under prevailing surface and weather conditions, and/or the planned camera crane right-of-way;

**d.** Checking to make sure that the mobile camera crane vehicle is mechanically sound, operational and safe;

**e.** Making sure that all attached equipment and systems are operational, secure and safe for personnel to be around, ride, and to operate;

**f.** Personally doing, or supervising, all coupling of towed platforms or vehicles;

**g.** Placing protective posts and cabling around the perimeter of towed platforms on which personnel will be riding while working;

**h.** Limiting the number of people riding on the mobile crane vehicle during rehearsals and shooting;

**i.** Otherwise carrying out the duties normally required of this classification;

**j.** Providing the hand tools normally employed in this craft.

**3. Considerations:** A **Mobile Camera Crane Driver** shall be properly licensed by the State of residence as a **Driver** for the type of vehicle he or she may drive, holding not less than a **Class 2 Driver**'s **License.**

# Special Services Categories

*[there is no category head, therefore no chain-of-command]*

| Publicist | First Aid Technician | Studio Teacher |
|---|---|---|
| Puppeteer | Crafts Service | Aircraft Pilot |
| Animal Specialist | Utility Person | Stunt Driver |
| Wrangler | | Office Workers |

# 17

# SPECIAL SERVICES CATEGORY

**A. Category Classifications:** There are eleven (11) classifications in the Special Services Category:

1. **Film Publicist (Category Sub-Head)**

2. **Puppeteer (Category Sub-Head)**

3. **Animal Specialist/Trainer (Category Sub-Head)**

4. **Wrangler (Category Sub-Head)**

5. **First Aid Technician (Category Sub-Head)**

6. **Crafts Service (Category Sub-Head)**

7. **Utility Person**

8. **Studio Teacher/Welfare Worker (Category Sub-Head)**

9. **Aircraft Pilot**

10. **Stunt Driver**

11. **Office Workers: Secretaries, Bookkeepers, Clerks**

**B. Category Criteria:**

1. Employees holding classification within the Special Services Category perform specialized job functions which are outside the purview of other job craft categories listed in this handbook, but which are utilized on interior or exterior production, on location and/or on the sound stage.

2. The Special Services Category has no Category Head because of the varied nature of the job classifications listed within this general category.

3. Where not otherwise specified or assigned, Special Services Category personnel are directly responsible to the **Production Manager** or **First Assistant Director**.

4. When operating on a set or production site during production shooting, **Animal Specialist**s, **Wranglers**, **First Aid Technician**s, **Studio Teacher**s and unassigned **Utility** personnel are directly responsible to the **First Assistant Director**.

5. When a **Production Assistant** requires assistance in pickup and delivery procedures, a **Utility** person may be used.

6. When an **Animal Specialist** requires assistance in the handling of wild, venomous, dangerous or delicate animals, another **Animal Specialist** is used.

7. When a **Wrangler** requires assistance in helping performers dismount from bucking horses or bulls, a **Pickup Wrangler** is used.

**8.** When Special Services personnel require assistance of a non-technical, non-skilled nature, such as preparatory or clean-up manual labor, pickup and delivery, or moving matériel, **Utility** personnel may be used.

**9.** Each Special Services Sub-Head must ensure that neither they nor production personnel under their supervision attempt work under any unsafe condition(s), as specified by the Employer, OSHA, Building and Safety Code and fire laws, or in violation of any other safety regulation(s) and practice(s).

**C. Category Responsibilities:** It is the responsibility of each Employee in the Special Services Category to work cooperatively with the Category Head, or Sub-Head, to whom assigned, in order to assist in achieving the optimum and most efficient operation of the particular specialty involved.

**D. Category Function:** The principal function of Special Services Category personnel involves the application to the production process of specialized talents and abilities which fall outside the purview of other more regularly functioning categories, in order to help achieve an efficient operation and/or a desired pictorial result on film or video tape.

**E. Category Considerations:**

**1.** Special Services Category personnel are used on each production on which particular specialized services are used.

**2.** The classification(s) used depends upon the type of production and upon the type(s) and amount of specialized service(s) needed to achieve the desired result(s).

**F. Category Requirements:** Employees in each Special Services Category classification must know and follow the chain-of-command and lines-of-communication in circumstances wherein these procedures apply and must be able to effectively and safely set up and operate the applicable equipment selected for each job and associated with their respective craft classification.

**G. FILM PUBLICIST**

**1. Responsibilities:** The **Film Publicist** is directly responsible to the **Marketing Director** or to the Employer for publicizing the Company name, product, and personnel, as authorized, in any and all media, to the benefit of the Company.

**2. Duties—during PRE-PRODUCTION, PRODUCTION and PRODUCTION:**

**a.** Reading and annotating the script within the context of publicity;

**b.** Preparing a publicity campaign for the specific picture, or for a desired result, on behalf of the Company;

**c.** Preparing and planting blurbs and feature stories regarding the production and its personnel in the appropriate media—print, radio, television, etc;

**d.** Operating in the best interests of the Company from a public relations standpoint;

**e.** Planning and executing the production press book;

f. Arranging media interviews with, and photographs of, cast members, staff and production personnel;

g. Otherwise carrying out the duties normally required of this classification;

h. Providing the hand tools normally employed in this craft.

3. **Considerations:**

a. A **Film Publicist** is used when the Company desires a publicity campaign.

b. The **Film Publicist** receives an adequate accountable expense allowance, if authorized and caused to engage in public relations activity on behalf of the company.

c. The **Film Publicist** is fully compensated for all Company-authorized expenses.

## H. PUPPETEER

1. **Responsibilities:** Each **Puppeteer** is directly responsible for operating the puppet, or specific functions thereof, under his or her control, and to the **Director** for the performance thereof.

2. **Duties:**

▼ **During PRE-PRODUCITON:**

a. Reading and annotating the script within the context of puppetry—the operation of a puppet or puppets for a cinematic production;

b. Determining, with input from the **Director**, the extent of movement, mobility and expression required of the puppet(s);

c. Seeing that the puppets are constructed with the necessary mechanical capability requested and expected by the **Director**;

d. Testing the mechanical capability of the puppets to determine functional expectations;

▼ **During the PRODUCTION Process:**

e. Operating a remote control board to activate mechanisms which will animate the puppets;

f. Otherwise carrying out the duties normally required of this classification;

g. Providing the hand tools necessary and normal to this function, being reimbursed for their use.

3. **Considerations: Puppeteer**s are used whenever puppets are to be fabricated for, and/or operated on, a cinematic production.

## I. ANIMAL SPECIALIST/TRAINER

1. **Responsibilities:** The **Animal Specialist/Trainer** is directly responsible to the **Director** and as specified in Category Criteria, above, for safely, efficiently and effectively handling and directing the animal(s) in his or her charge in a manner best suited to help assure the safety of personnel, no injury to the animals and optimum photographic utilization of the animals.

### 2. Duties—during the PRODUCTION Process:

**a.** Reading and annotating the script and analyzing sequences in which the particular animal(s) play a part;

**b.** Handling and care of specially trained animals, undomesticated, dangerous, venomous, delicate or wild creatures, and equipment pertaining thereto;

**c.** Handling animals requiring special care;

**d.** Directing and/or placing such animals as indicated by the **Director**;

**e.** Taking care that no rule of the SPCA is violated against any animal under his or her care used on that production;

**f.** Arranging for loading, transportation, care and feeding of animals in his or her charge, in transit and during production;

**g.** Otherwise carrying out the duties normally required of this classification;

**h.** Providing the hand tools normally employed in this craft.

### 3. Considerations:

**a.** An **Animal Specialist** is a **Trainer**, **Keeper** or **Handler** of small creatures, such as dogs, cats, fowl, reptiles or insects.

**b.** An **Animal Specialist** also may be considered a **Trainer** for purposes of classification.

**c.** Should a wild, poisonous or potentially vicious animal be required for the production, an **Animal Specialist** must be used.

**d.** It is considered prudent to have two (2) **Animal Specialist**s for each four (4) domesticated animals and two (2) **Animal Specialist**s for each large cat or carnivore or wild or undomesticated animal.

## J. WRANGLER

### 1. Responsibilities: The **Wrangler** is directly responsible as specified in Category Criteria, above, for safely, efficiently and effectively handling the assigned animal(s) in a manner best suited to help assure optimum photographic realization thereof.

### 2. Duties:

#### ▼ During PRE-PRODUCTION:

**a.** Reading the script and annotating the sequences in which livestock plays a part;

**b.** Selecting animals to be used in the production;

**c.** Making necessary arrangement for rental and/or purchase of animals with approval by the **Production Manager**;

#### ▼ During the PRODUCTION Process:

**d.** Arranging for loading, transportation, care and feeding of assigned animals in transit and during production;

**e.** Arranging for any necessary harness, equipment and/or rolling stock (wagons, etc) needed to work with the animals on the production;

**f.** Maintaining such equipment and rolling stock;

**g.** Applying such equipment and rolling stock to the animals, as needed, within the rules of the SPCA, making such preparations promptly to avoid delays;

**h.** Leading or riding all such animals onto the set and placing and tethering such animals, as directed by the **Director** or **Assistant Director**;

**i.** Assisting members of the cast in handling, mounting, riding and dismounting such animals;

**j.** Taking charge of such animals again between takes and at the end of each scene;

**k.** Taking care that no animal becomes a hazard to staff, cast or crew;

**l.** Taking care that no rule of the SPCA is violated against any animal used by the production;

**m.** Preparing orders for animals, feed and special equipment, and for transportating them;

**n.** Returning animals to their owners;

**o.** Otherwise carrying out the duties normally required of this classification;

**p.** Providing the hand tools normally employed in this craft.

**3. Considerations:**

**a.** When any horse, burro, mule, cow, goat, sheep, hog, or other animal classed as "livestock" is used in a production, a **Wrangler** is used.

**b.** Should more than six (6) such animals be used for any such scene, an additional **Wrangler** is used for each additional four (4) such animals, and/or when more than one (1) **Wrangler** is used, the first **Wrangler** hired is given the designation of **Ramrod Wrangler** and is in charge of all **Wrangler**s.

**c.** The **Wrangler** is not used to act as **Animal Specialist** (**Trainer**, **Keeper** or **Handler** of small creatures, such as dogs, cats, fowl, reptiles, insects, etc).

**d.** A **Wrangler** is not used to handle, or care for, wild, poisonous, or potentially vicious animals.

**e.** A person experienced and designated as **Pickup Wrangler** is used to assist performers in dismounting whenever any bucking horses or wild bulls are used.

**f.** At the request of the **Property Master**, the **Wrangler** assists in obtaining wagons or any rolling stock, or any unusual piece of equipment, relating to the animals being handled.

## K. FIRST AID TECHNICIAN

**1. Responsibilities:** The **First Aid Technician** is a **Medic** and is directly responsible to the **Company Doctor**, if any, or to the Employer or the designated representative, as specified in Category Criteria, above, for the health and well-being of all personnel associated with the production.

**2. Duties—all during the PRODUCTION Process:**

 **a.** Giving emergency first aid to Company personnel as needed;

 **b.** Dispensing medication for the aid and benefit of Company personnel;

 **c.** Registering all personnel who receive treatment or medication;

 **d.** Being available at the work site at all times;

 **e.** Arranging ready access to a medical doctor, an ambulance service and/or a hospital;

 **f.** Otherwise carrying out the duties normally required of this classification;

 **g.** Providing the hand tools and medication necessary and normal to this function, being reimbursed for their use.

**3. Considerations:**

 **a.** A licensed **First Aid Technician** is present on all location or hazardous job sites and/or a licensed physician, ambulance and hospital service shall be readily available in event of emergency medical need.

 **b.** The **First Aid Technician** will be compensated for use of the first aid kit and supplies provided by the **First Aid Technician**.

## L. CRAFTS SERVICE

**1. Responsibilities:** The **Crafts Service** person is directly responsible to the **Production Manager** for ordering a variety of food and beverage supplies and maintaining an adequate presentation thereof on the stage or location, during all working hours, for the convenience of cast, staff and crew.

**2. Duties:**

 **a.** Checking with the **Production Manager** as to the expected average number of people to be fed per day;

 **b.** Receiving a budgeted food and beverage allowance from the **Production Manager**;

 **c.** Determining, purchasing and picking up the appropriate quantity and quality of food and beverages permitted by the budgeted allowance;

 **d.** Preparing and setting out the food and beverages, both hot and cold, for the use and convenience of cast, staff and crew, whether on stage or on location;

 **e.** Putting out plates, cups, napkins and eating implements for use by consumers;

 **f.** Keeping the food surface areas clean at all times;

SPECIAL SERVICES

**g.** Seeing that the stage floor is clean and free of trash, refuse, sediment and liquid spills at all times;

**h.** Upon notice, immediately mopping up any spill occurring on the stage floor or in the shooting area;

**i.** Sweeping or cleaning the operational areas of the stage floor, as requested;

**j.** Otherwise carrying out the duties normally required of this classification;

**k.** Providing the hand tools normally employed in this craft.

**3. Considerations:**

**a.** When food is provided throughout the shooting day on an ongoing basis for production personnel, a **Crafts Service** person is employed to provide this service.

**b.** When the **Crafts Service** person needs assistance in the performance of duties, a **Utility** person may be used.

## M. UTILITY PERSON

**1. Responsibilities:** The **Utility Person** is directly responsible as specified in Category Criteria, above, or to the Category Head to whom assigned, for keeping the shooting area and environs clean, and free from refuse and extraneous material, in order to help expedite the production.

**2. Duties—during PRE-PRODUCTION, PRODUCTION and POST-PRODUCTION:**

**a.** General manual labor of an unskilled nature;

**b.** Guarding the premises, equipment and matériel;

**c.** Keeping onlookers outside the working perimeter;

**d.** Assisting **Construction Specialists** in their duties;

**e.** Running errands;

**f.** Replenishing comfort stations and dressing rooms with necessary supplies, as needed;

**g.** Keeping the set(s) and location site(s) clean and disposing of refuse;

**h.** Opening and closing the stage door(s) and vent(s) between setups, as required, unless a **Grip** has been specifically assigned these duties;

**i.** Digging, filling, stacking, removing or preparing anything not specifically or normally within the province of another category or classification, as directed;

**j.** Otherwise carrying out the duties normally required of this classification;

**k.** Utilizing the hand tools supplied by the Company, as required.

**3. Considerations:**

**a.** A **Utility Person** may be used on a production requiring general, unskilled labor.

 **b.** A **Utility Person** may be directly assigned to a Category Head, in which case the **Utility Person** is directly responsible to that Category Head.

 **c.** A **Utility Person** may not do work specifically or normally assigned to any of the other classifications, unless specifically assigned such work by the Category Head to whom assigned.

## N. STUDIO TEACHER/WELFARE WORKER

**1. Responsibilities:** The **Studio Teacher** is also a **Welfare Worker**, holding both elementary and secondary teaching credentials and certified by the California Labor Commissioner; is responsible for instructing all school-age minors employed by the production in the appropriate curricula for each respective minor for the proper amount of time, and generally supervising such minors during off time as required by **Title 8 of the California Code of Regulations, the applicable sections of both the Labor Code and the Education Code.**

**2. Duties—all during the PRODUCTION Process:**

 **a.** Verifying the Entertainment Work Permit and signing it when the minor reports for work, returning it to the minor before the working day ends;

 **b.** Ensuring that adequate facilities for school, rest and recreation have been provided for minors, including small children and/or infants employed by the production, and that the physical work surroundings provide no physical or health hazard;

 **c.** Teaching school-age minors at least three (3) hours during each school day, insuring that no schooling period is shorter than twenty (20) minutes, and noting such hours, as required in Teacher's Report forms;

 **d.** Keeping uninvited persons, parents and guardians out of the schoolroom area;

 **e.** Ensuring that the moral tone of the working environment—the language, behavior, attire and attitudes—offers a suitable atmosphere for the presence of a minor;

 **f.** Ensuring that rest and meal periods are provided, as specified by State Labor Law;

 **g.** Keeping parents, guardians and Employer apprised of the Rules and Regulations and of applicable State Labor Law, as appropriate and necessary;

 **h.** Ensuring that no minor is without the general supervision of a **Studio Teacher** when employed in any manner;

 **i.** Reporting in writing on appropriate form any irregularities, violation(s) of laws, rules and regulations, or lack of cooperation by Employer, Employees, parents, or minors to the State Division of Labor Law Enforcement;

 **j.** Preparing the official Teacher's Report, including attendance, place(s) of employment, hours, grade, etc, and at the conclusion of each work assignment, giving one (1) copy to the minor;

 **k.** Otherwise carrying out the duties normally required of this classification.

**3. Considerations:**

    **a.** California companies employing children in California, or employing California children outside of California, must hire a **Studio Teacher**.

    **b.** Each State in which minors will be employed in cinematic production may have its own set of requirements pertaining to the hiring, employment and supervision of such minors and should be consulted with regard to laws and regulations governing such employment.

## O. AIRCRAFT PILOT

**1. Responsibilities:** The **Aircraft Pilot** is directly responsible to the **Production Manager**, and to the **Stunt Coordinator** if taking part in a stunt, and as a specialized **Mobile Camera Platform Operator** if flying an aerial camera mission; is responsible for operating and maintaining the aircraft, its accommodations and accessories, in constant readiness, and operating it in a manner to best ensure the safety and comfort of personnel and matériel being transported therein, thereby helping expedite the production process.

**2. Duties—all during the PRODUCTION Process:**

▼ **When flying AERIAL CAMERA and/or STUNT Missions:**

    **a.** Reading and annotating the script within the context of aerial camera placement, movement and logistics;

    **b.** Observing proper and adequate safety and protective procedures for personnel and equipment being loaded and transported in his or her care under prevailing weather conditions, and for the planned camera move in relation to the subject matter on the ground and in the air;

    **c.** Checking to make sure that the aircraft is mechanically sound, operational and safe;

    **d.** Making sure that all attached equipment and systems are operational, secure and safe for personnel to be around, ride, and to operate;

    **e.** Personally doing, or supervising installation of all exterior camera housings on the aircraft;

    **f.** Limiting the number of people riding in the aircraft during rehearsals and shooting;

    **g.** Making certain that all camera equipment is securely mounted and that all personnel aboard are properly safetied in the aircraft;

    **h.** Participating in the careful planning of each shot with the **Director**, **Aerial Cinematographer**, **Stunt Coordinator**, if any, and **Pilot**s of subject or stunt aircraft;

    **i.** Following the flight plan and path precisely as agreed to for each take;

    **j.** Personally doing, or supervising, all coupling of towed banners or unpowered aircraft;

    **k.** Otherwise carrying out the duties normally required of this classification;

    **l.** Providing the hand tools normally employed in this craft.

**SPECIAL SERVICES**

3. **Considerations:** An **Aircraft Pilot** shall be properly licensed by the Federal Aviation Administration as a **Pilot** for the type of aircraft that he or she is to operate.

## P. STUNT DRIVER

1. **Responsibilities:** The **Stunt Driver** is directly responsible to the **Stunt Coordinator**, and as a specialized **Mobile Camera Platform Operator**, is responsible for operating the stunt vehicle in a manner to best ensure the safety of personnel and matériel being transported therein or, when being photographed, taking measures to ensure the safety and visual effectiveness of the stunt, thereby helping expedite the production process.

2. **Duties—all during the PRODUCTION Process:**

   ▼ **When driving STUNT CAMERA or STUNTS:**

   **a.** Reading and annotating the script within the context of camera placement, movement, stunt choreography and logistics;

   **b.** Making certain that the elements of the stunt are thoroughly understood by all personnel involved with the stunt—stunt, camera and support personnel;

   **c.** Making a dry run at reduced speed in order to allow all personnel involved to confirm the planned path and timing, to check surface conditions and/or weather conditions, to affirm camera placement and to refine the choreography of other stunt vehicles and stunt performers involved;

   **d.** Observing proper and adequate safety and protective procedures for personnel and equipment being transported in his or her care along the planned camera right-of-way under prevailing surface and/or weather conditions;

   **e.** Checking to make sure that the stunt vehicle is mechanically sound, operational and safe;

   **f.** Making sure that all attached equipment and systems are operational, secure and safe for personnel to be around, ride, and to operate;

   **g.** Participating in the careful planning of each shot with the **Director**, **Stunt Coordinator** and **Driver**s of subject vehicles;

   **h.** Following the stunt plan and path precisely as agreed to for each take;

   **i.** Personally doing, or supervising, all coupling of towed platforms and/or vehicles;

   **j.** Limiting the number of people riding in or on the stunt vehicle during rehearsals and shooting;

   **k.** Making sure that personnel riding in the stunt vehicles are properly safetied in place;

   **l.** Otherwise carrying out the duties normally required of this classification;

   **m.** Providing the hand tools normally employed in this craft.

3. **Considerations:** A **Stunt Driver** shall be properly licensed by the State of residence as a **Driver** for the type of vehicle he or she may drive, holding not less than a **Class 2 Driver's License.**

## Q. OFFICE WORKERS: SECRETARIES, BOOKKEEPERS, CLERKS

1. **Responsibilities: Office Worker**s are directly responsible to the Employer, or to the Category Head to whom assigned, for efficiently carrying out assigned office duties.

2. **Duties—during PRE-PRODUCTION, PRODUCTION and POST-PRODUCTION:**

   **a.** Receiving and screening all telephone calls, mail, deliveries, salesmen, solicitors and visitors;

   **b.** Preparing for and confirming meetings, and making reservations for travel, lodging, dining and entertainment, as requested;

   **c.** Taking dictation, transcribing notes, typing and formatting letters and memoranda on the word processor for signature;

   **d.** Producing, duplicating, collating, binding and distributing scripts, as requested;

   **e.** Addressing and mailing all required material;

   **f.** Setting up and maintaining all files, indexes and calendars;

   **g.** Ordering, inventorying and maintaining the stock of supplies and office matériel;

   **h.** Keeping books of daily financial account, and billing, as necessary;

   **i.** Setting up and maintaining all files and reference material for efficient use;

   **j.** Operating a computer terminal, as required;

   **k.** Otherwise carrying out the duties normally required of these respective **Office Worker** functions.

3. **Considerations: Office Worker**s are used to assist the production process by handling the various details pertaining to office administrative procedures.

# FILM LABORATORY CATEGORY ORGANIZATIONAL CHART

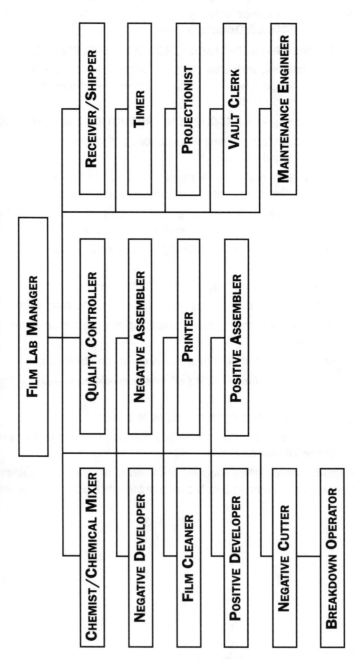

# 18

# FILM LABORATORY CATEGORY

**A. Category Classifications:** There are not less than sixteen (16) principal classifications in the Film Laboratory Category:

1. **Laboratory Manager (Category Head)**
2. **Receiver/Shipper**
3. **Chemist/Chemical Mixer**
4. **Quality Controller**
5. **Negative Developer**
6. **Negative Assembler**
7. **Timer**
8. **Film Cleaner**
9. **Printer**
10. **Positive Developer**
11. **Positive Assembler**
12. **Projectionist**
13. **Vault Clerk**
14. **Negative Cutter (Category Sub-Head)**
15. **Breakdown Operator**
16. **Maintenance Engineer**

▼ In large, full-service film laboratories, additional classifications to help handle specific duties related to the laboratory work processes might include one or more of the following six (6) classifications for a total of up to twenty-two (22) working classifications:

17. **Customer Service Rep**
18. **Negative Breakdown/Make-up Operator**
19. **Sensitometrist/Densitometrist**
20. **Release Inspector**
21. **Tape Puncher**
22. **Magnetic Sound Striper**

**B. Category Criteria:**

1. Employees holding classification within the Film Laboratory Category perform all job functions pertaining to film laboratory procedures.

2. A **Laboratory Manager** needs to know and evaluate: Each lab procedure so that a client's film is handled and reproduced safely and efficiently, and is returned to the client with all elements intact, undamaged and reproduced to client specifications.

3. Depending upon the size of the film laboratory and the volume of work it handles, there may be a **Foreman (Category Sub-Head)** in charge of each of the above film servicing departmental functions and who may have one or more assistants.

4. The **Laboratory Manager** and each Film Laboratory Category Sub-Head must ensure that laboratory personnel do not attempt work under any unsafe condition(s), as specified by the Employer, OSHA, Building and Safety Code and fire laws, or in violation of any other safety regulation(s) and practice(s).

C. **Category Responsibilities:** It is the responsibility of each Employee in the Film Laboratory Category to work cooperatively with the Category Head, or Sub-Head, to whom assigned, in order to assist in achieving the optimum and most efficient operation during film processing operations.

D. **Category Function:** The principal function of Film Laboratory personnel involves the care, development and handling of exposed camera original, duplicate and print materials.

E. **Category Considerations:** With heavy work volume, specified duties of each of the above listed classifications may be separated and given to other specific sub-classifications established to handle those work duties.

F. **Category Requirements:** Employees in each Film Laboratory Category classification must know and follow the chain-of-command and lines-of-communication and must be able to effectively and safely operate the film lab equipment utilized in each job and associated with their respective craft classification.

G. **LABORATORY MANAGER**

1. **Responsibilities:** The **Laboratory Manager** is directly responsible to the client for properly and efficiently overseeing the care, processing, printing, storage and handling of all negative and positive film materials, and their related records, placed with the film laboratory by the client, in order to ensure that the film entrusted to the expertise and care of the laboratory receives the optimum degree of quality control and is not damaged, and that all elements are returned to the client in pristine condition and in a timely manner.

2. **Duties—during PRODUCTION and POST-PRODUCTION:**

   a. Maintaining optimum processing, printing, handling and storage standards for all negative and positive film elements and records;

   b. Personalizing the laboratory services by being the contact person between the lab processes and the customer and/or the **Director of Photography** of the film;

   c. Keeping the customer fully informed, responding promptly to all questions, at all times regarding the progress of the film through lab and of any problems detected during the lab processes;

**d.** Arranging credit and running credit checks in setting up customer accounts;

**e.** Checking job orders to confirm status, completion and accuracy;

**f.** Hiring and firing personnel, as necessary;

**g.** Assigning personnel to specific job orders;

**h.** Scheduling the work flow;

**i.** Overseeing the routing of all film materials moving through the lab;

**j.** Prioritizing specific job orders, as necessary;

**k.** Otherwise carrying out the duties normally required of this classification.

## H. RECEIVER/SHIPPER

**1. Responsibilities:** The **Receiver/Shipper** is responsible to the **Laboratory Manager** for the proper receipt, logging and handling of all film elements received from the client, and for routing them to the **Negative Developer** or to the vault for temporary storage. Following the complete processing process, with the processed film elements in hand, the **Receiver/Shipper** is responsible for careful and proper packaging, labeling and addressing of the elements for delivery to, or pick up by, the client.

**2. Duties—during PRODUCTION and POST-PRODUCTION:**

▼ **The receiving process:**

**a.** Receiving, receipting and logging into the lab facilities computer all film elements delivered to the film laboratory by the production company;

**b.** Entering into the lab facilities computer system the client's name, the title of the production, the date and time of its arrival, the type of film, number of rolls, and camera roll number for each roll conforming with information on the camera report attached to each film can;

**c.** Making special notice to the **Negative Developer** of special processing required by the client, such as forced development, or reported camera damage to the film;

▼ **The shipping process:**

**d.** Receiving and checking in all processed print and negative elements against the completed work order to assure that all elements are present and accounted for;

**e.** Routing all negative which is to be retained by the lab for future use, to the vault for long-term storage;

**f.** Forwarding all paperwork to billing;

**g.** Organizing, shelving and preparing the film elements for pick-up, delivery, or shipping, as specified by the customer;

**h.** Delivering all elements to the customer by pick-up, local delivery, or distant shipping;

**i.** Otherwise carrying out the duties normally required of this classification.

## I. CHEMIST/CHEMICAL MIXER

**1. Responsibilities:** The **Chemist/Chemical Mixer** is directly responsible to the **Laboratory Manager** for mixing the various solutions used in the processing machines, for checking on and maintaining the potency and purity of the solutions, and for seeing that the temperature and flow of the film through the processing machine is stable and consistent.

**2. Duties—during PRODUCTION and POST-PRODUCTION:**

    **a.** Ordering the chemicals used in the negative and positive, black and white and color, developing processes;

    **b.** Selecting, mixing and testing the appropriate chemicals and solutions for the specific process and the type of film to be processed;

    **c.** Seeing that all depleted processing solutions are drained from the mixing tanks and that the tanks are clean and ready for fresh solutions;

    **d.** Placing proper amounts of the prepared solutions in the appropriate replenishing tanks which feed circulated and filtered solutions to and from the processing machine;

    **e.** Setting the specific temperature and film flow rate to be maintained for each solution in the developing and fixing processes;

    **f.** Periodically checking operating temperatures and modifying the temperature and/or film flow rate through the solutions;

    **g.** Sampling and testing the solutions from time to time to assure potency, and adding or changing chemicals, as necessary, to maintain quality control;

    **h.** Otherwise carrying out the duties normally required of this classification.

## J. QUALITY CONTROLLER

**1. Responsibilities:** The **Quality Controller** is directly responsible to the **Laboratory Manager** for maintaining reliable quality controls on all aspects of film processing in order to assure optimum results in negative and positive film processing and handling.

**2. Duties—during PRODUCTION and POST-PRODUCTION:**

    **a.** Handling all sensitometry and densitometry procedures;

    **b.** Regarding sensitometry: Preparing a test strip of film—a 21-step wedge to be run through the processing solutions periodically for every second double roll—to test the efficacy of the total processing procedure;

    **c.** Regarding densitometry: Examining the image density and color rendition of each developed test strip to determine the resultant quality of the film processing;

    **d.** Consulting with the **Chemist** when a change in the chemistry or temperature seems required;

    **e.** Ordering changes in the processing speed, as necessary;

    **f.** Examining all positive by viewing at high-speed projection rate all of it after it comes out of positive assembly;

g. Examining the negative or print when necessary in order to determine where the problem occurred;

h. Ordering reprocessing, reprinting, repair or replacement of film deemed incorrectly processed, timed, or handled;

i. Notifying the customer of any equipment malfunction which has apparently damaged the film or impaired the image;

j. Otherwise carrying out the duties normally required of this classification.

## K. NEGATIVE DEVELOPER

1. **Responsibilities:** The **Negative Developer** is directly responsible to the **Laboratory Manager** for receiving from the **Receiver/Shipper** all exposed, but undeveloped, negative elements and for the careful organizing, handling and processing thereof.

2. **Duties—during PRODUCTION and POST-PRODUCTION:**

▼ **Preparing the Negative:**

a. Carefully organizing, handling and processing all negative elements received from the lab receiving department;

b. Organizing all incoming negative in numerical order by company, shoot date and roll number, as indicated on the Camera Reports;

c. Placing leader in the processing machine, threading it over the rollers into and out of the solution tanks and on through the dryer;

d. Testing the rate of movement of the leader though the processor;

e. Checking for proper temperature of the solutions;

▼ **In the darkroom:**

f. Running a standard test strip through the processor in order to check processing consistency;

g. Removing each exposed negative roll from the can and affixing an identifying number on the tail end of each negative roll and placing the same number on the camera report attached to the film can from which the roll was removed;

h. Assembling, and splicing, each roll of negative, end to end, into larger 2,000´ rolls, while inspecting the film edges for possible damage;

i. Repairing any damage to the film detected during the assembly process;

j. Setting the computer interface for job number input in order to log the footage run and exit time through the processing machine;

k. Feeding the film into the film processing machine;

▼ **Out of the darkroom:**

l. Removing the film from the take-up end of the film processor;

m. If there is no computer interface, then physically measuring the length of the film and recording the time it comes off the processor;

n. Breaking down the large roll into the smaller rolls of negative as received by the lab and, matching identifying numbers, placing each developed roll in the can in which it came;

**o.** Routing the processed negative to negative assembly;

**p.** Otherwise carrying out the duties normally required of this classification.

## L. NEGATIVE ASSEMBLER

**1. Responsibilities:** The **Negative Assembler** is responsible to the **Laboratory Manager** for receiving the developed negative elements from the **Negative Developer** and then cleanly and carefully leadering, identifying and assembling the processed negative in preparation for the timing and printing processes.

**2. Duties—during PRODUCTION and POST-PRODUCTION:**

**a.** Leadering, measuring and placing an identifying designation on the head leader of each roll of negative received from negative developing;

**b.** Removing any repair tape and the residual backing from the base of the processed film;

**c.** Filling out a daily work order, specifying the client's instructions as to type of print—wet or dry, high or low contrast, or interpositive—on its purchase order and/or Camera Reports;

**d.** Routing the assembled negative directly to sonic cleaning, if destined for telecine transfer to 1″ video tape, or to color timing in preparation for printing;

**e.** Otherwise carrying out the duties normally required of this classification.

## M. TIMER

**1. Responsibilities:** The **Timer** is responsible to the **Laboratory Manager** for carefully handling and accurately timing the camera original, scene-by-scene, in order to achieve a print of consistent color balance, brightness and density, or, by client preference, a best-light, one-light work print.

**2. Duties—during PRODUCTION and POST-PRODUCTION:**

**a.** Placing each roll of negative into a color analyzer machine;

**b.** Referring to information written on the Camera Reports and special instructions from the **Director of Photography** accompanying the work order;

**c.** Determining and adjusting the intensity of the red, green and blue values for each scene, as displayed on a video monitor; or

**d.** Determining a best-light, one-light each for: All interiors, all day exteriors, all night exteriors, all day-for-night scenes, and all scenes to be composited with special optical or computer-generated effects;

**e.** Inputting the adjusted color balance settings to a computer for data storage of the exact footage and frames for each scene change on the roll;

**f.** Accessing the computer for readout of a punched tape for RGB and a second tape for footage and frame count for each scene change;

**g.** Routing the film to sonic cleaning;

**h.** Otherwise carrying out the duties normally required of this classification.

## N. FILM CLEANER

**1. Responsibilities:** The **Film Cleaner** is responsible to the **Laboratory Manager** for the careful and thorough cleaning of all negative and original elements in preparation for the printing or transfer process.

**2. Duties—during PRODUCTION and POST-PRODUCTION:**

**a.** Threading the film into the sonic cleaner, a conveyor-type machine which transports the film through a tank containing a sonically-induced vibrating solvent;

**b.** Checking the solvent level in the cleaning tank;

**c.** Starting the cleaning process as the film is transported through the ultrasound vibrating solvent causing surface dirt on the film to be removed;

**d.** Visually checking the film as it is wound heads out;

**e.** Routing the cleaned film to telecine, if it is to be transferred to video tape, or to the printing department, if it is to be printed;

**f.** Otherwise carrying out the duties normally required of this classification.

## O. PRINTER

**1. Responsibilities:** The **Printer** is responsible to the **Laboratory Manager** for the clean and careful handling of negative and positive elements and encoded printing tapes during the printing process.

**2. Duties—during PRODUCTION and POST-PRODUCTION:**

**a.** Loading the printing machine with the appropriate unexposed print stock;

**b.** Carefully placing the film, at its start mark, in the printing machine;

**c.** Inserting in the printer reader, in synchronization with the film, both the encoded tape with the color correction information and the tape with information regarding the footage and frame point of each change in color correction;

**d.** Placing the sound track, if any, in appropriate synchronous sound advance position with the picture element;

**e.** Activating the printing machine to start printing from the negative picture, and sound track elements, if any;

**f.** Routing the exposed print stock to positive developing;

**g.** Routing the negative picture and sound elements to the vault for safekeeping;

**h.** Otherwise carrying out the duties normally required of this classification.

## P. POSITIVE DEVELOPER

**1. Responsibilities:** The **Positive Developer** is responsible to the **Laboratory Manager** for cleanly and carefully handling the positive print material during the developing process.

## 2. Duties—during PRODUCTION and POST-PRODUCTION:

**Preparing the Positive:**

a. Carefully organizing, handling and processing all undeveloped positive elements received from printing;

b. Organizing all incoming undeveloped print stock in numerical order by company, shoot date and roll number, as indicated on the accompanying job order;

c. Placing leader in the processing machine, threading it over the rollers into and out of the solution tanks and on through the dryer;

d. Testing the rate of movement of the leader though the processor;

e. Checking for proper temperature of the solutions;

▼ **In the darkroom:**

f. Running a standard test strip through the processor in order to verify processing consistency;

g. Removing each exposed print roll from the can;

h. Assembling and splicing each roll of print, end to end, into larger rolls, while inspecting the film edges of material received from outside sources for possible damage;

i. Repairing any damage to the film detected during the assembly process;

j. Setting the computer interface for job number input in order to log the footage run and exit time through the processing machine;

k. Feeding the film into the film processing machine;

▼ **Out of the darkroom:**

l. Removing the film from the take-up end of the film processor;

m. Logging, from the digital interface, the length of the film, as well as recording the time it comes off the processor;

n. Breaking down the large roll into the smaller rolls of print stock as received from printing, and placing each developed roll in the can in which it came;

o. Routing the processed print to either projection for inspection or to positive assembly;

p. Otherwise carrying out the duties normally required of this classification.

## Q. POSITIVE ASSEMBLER

1. **Responsibilities:** The **Positive Assembler** is responsible to the **Laboratory Manager** for the clean and careful handling, leadering, identifying and assembly of positive print elements, and for their delivery to the **Laboratory Manager** or **Customer Service Representative** for high-speed projection inspection of the film.

2. **Duties—during PRODUCTION and POST-PRODUCTION:**

a. Leadering, measuring and placing an identifying designation on the head leader of each roll of print received from positive developing;

**b.** Removing any repair tape and the residual backing from the base of the processed film;

**c.** Inspecting the film for imperfections at high speed projection rate;

**d.** Ordering reprints of imperfect, correctable scenes;

**e** Mounting release print on reels for projection;

**f.** Routing the print film to projection for customer inspection, or to shipping;

**g.** Otherwise carrying out the duties normally required of this classification.

## R. PROJECTIONIST

**1. Responsibilities:** The **Projectionist** is directly responsible to the **Laboratory Manager** for optimizing the visual and audio aspects of film projection and for the careful handling of all film elements during projection.

**2. Duties—during PRODUCTION and POST-PRODUCTION:**

**a.** Scheduling projection time;

**b.** Receiving positive print film from positive development and/or positive assembly or from the customer for screening inspection;

**c.** Threading film into the proper projector—standard or high-speed, 16mm, 35mm or 70mm—maintaining proper emulsion position and loop size;

**d.** Placing the appropriate lens and aspect matte in the projector(s) used;

**e.** Positioning the projection screen aspect mattes, if any, to conform to the projected aspect ratio;

**f.** Setting and maintaining the projection lamp at proper brilliance and color temperature;

**g.** Setting and maintaining optimum focus of the image on the screen;

**h.** Setting and maintaining optimum sound level during projection;

**i.** Metering and adjusting the color temperature and luminance reading of the illuminated projection screen;

**j.** Informing whoever is in the screening room when the projector is loaded and ready to roll;

**k.** Rewinding the film and handing it to the viewing customer, or, if damaged during projection, sending it to positive assembly for repair;

**l.** Otherwise carrying out the duties normally required of this classification;

## S. VAULT CLERK

**1. Responsibilities:** The **Vault Clerk** is directly responsible to the **Laboratory Manager** for carefully and accurately storing and retrieving camera original, negative, dupe negative and intermediate film elements in a temperature- and humidity-controlled, fire-proofed storage facility.

**2. Duties—during PRODUCTION and POST-PRODUCTION:**

**a.** Receiving camera original, negative, dupe negative and intermediate film elements from shipping or negative assembly for custodial storage by the laboratory;

**b.** Logging in all film elements destined for storage in the vault;

**c.** Logging out all film elements requested by an authorized source;

**d.** Periodically checking, testing, adjusting and otherwise maintaining constant temperature and humidity settings for the vault;

**e.** Otherwise carrying out the duties normally required of this classification.

## T. NEGATIVE CUTTER

**1. Responsibilities: The Negative Cutter** is directly responsible to the **Laboratory Manager** for responsibly handling each assignment and to the **Producer** for accurately, efficiently and with extreme care, handling the negative, cutting it to conform to the **Picture Editor**'s specifications as reflected by the shot progression and optical markings in the work print.

**2. Duties—all during POST-PRODUCTION:**

**a.** Breaking down, cataloguing, filing and proper storage of original reversal and or negative picture (black and white or color) and/or fine grains, CRIs and optical or magnetic track;

**b.** Recording and cataloguing edge numbers of the final work print;

**c.** Writing orders for dupes, fine grains and CRIs;

**d.** Dispatching prepared negative to the laboratory for duping and/or fine grains and CRIs for optical duping and/or for additional prints, coding, cleaning or treatment;

**e.** Matching reversal original or negative picture (and optical track, if used) to conform to the edited work print;

**f.** Conforming, cutting, assembling and splicing the negative or reversal original;

**g.** Attaching academy head and tail leaders to each completed roll of cut original film, providing printer's head and tail sync marks and leader labels on reversal original or picture negative or CRI and track(s) ready for release printing;

**h.** Splicing negative picture and negative track(s), as necessary;

**i.** Cleaning and repairing the reversal original or negative or CRI, as necessary;

**j.** Otherwise carrying out the duties normally required of this classification;

**k.** Providing the hand tools normally employed in this craft.

**3. Considerations:**

**a.** A **Negative Cutter** is used to conform and cut camera original film (reversal or negative) and dupe negative, as used, to the finalized workprint.

**b.** In no event may the **Negative Cutter** modify picture or track(s) of a workprint, reversal original or camera negative without express consent of the **Picture Editor** and/or **Producer**.

## U. BREAKDOWN OPERATOR

**1. Responsibilities:** The **Breakdown Operator** is directly responsible to the **Negative Cutter** and assists in the performance of duties by accurately, efficiently and with extreme care, breaking down, cataloguing and splicing aligned camera original or negative film.

**2. Duties—all during POST-PRODUCTION:**

**a.** Cataloguing and breaking down camera original reversal and negative and dupe negative, as directed;

**b.** Labeling and storing the canned original film material;

**c.** Splicing the negative/original, as directed;

**d.** Delivering the conformed negative/original to the film laboratory for printing and processing;

**e.** Keeping the cutting room clean, orderly and adequately supplied with expendables;

**f.** Assisting the **Negative Cutter** in the performance of negative handling duties;

**g.** Otherwise carrying out the duties normally required of this craft;

**h.** Supplying the hand tools normally employed in this craft.

**3. Considerations:** A **Breakdown Operator** assists the **Negative Cutter** and does not cut camera original film (reversal or negative) to match the work print.

## V. MAINTENANCE ENGINEER

**1. Responsibilities:** The **Maintenance Engineer** is directly responsible to the **Laboratory Manager** for maintaining optimum operational performance of the components comprising the wet and dry laboratory processes.

**2. Duties—during PRODUCTION and POST-PRODUCTION:**

▼ **Wet maintenance:**

**a.** Repairing, replacing, adjusting and cleaning components in the wet processing chain, including the replenishing tanks, the film feed racks and rollers in the developing chain, and the solution holding tanks;

**b.** Draining and cleaning the processing tanks at the conclusion of the day's run;

**c.** Ordering components and cleaning solutions for the processing chain;

▼ **Dry maintenance:**

**d.** Repairing, replacing, adjusting and cleaning components of all other hardware associated with the dry handling of the film elements;

**e.** Otherwise carrying out the duties normally required of this classification.

# Editing Category Organizational Chart

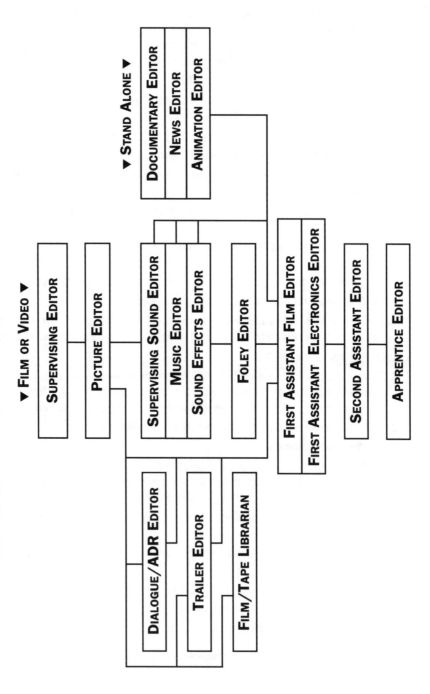

# 19

# EDITING CATEGORY

**A. Category Classifications:** There are sixteen (16) classifications in the Editing Category:

1. **Supervising Editor (Category Head)**

2. **Picture Editor (Category Head, when a Supervising Editor is not used)**

3. **Supervising Sound Editor (Category Sub-Head)**

4. **Music Editor**

5. **Sound Effects Editor**

6. **Dialogue/ADR Editor**

7. **Foley Editor**

8. **Trailer Editor (Category Head)**

9. **Documentary Editor (Category Head)**

10. **News Editor (Category Head)**

11. **Animation Editor (Category Head)**

12. **First Assistant Film Editor**

13. **First Assistant Electronics Editor**

14. **Second Assistant Editor**

15. **Apprentice Editor**

16. **Film/Tape Librarian (Category Sub-Head)**

**B. Category Criteria:**

1. Employees holding classification within the Editing Category perform all job functions pertaining to cinematic film and video tape editing and assembly of 16mm, 35mm and 70mm film stocks, video tape of any dimension and digital data on disk, tape or hard drive. (See **Video Tape Editor** in Chapter 21 Video Category.)

2. The number and classification(s) of Editing Category personnel to be used are determined by the **Producer** within the parameters of the collective bargaining agreement under which the aforementioned categories are covered, taking into consideration:

   **a.** The type of film/tape to be edited;

   **b.** The amount of uncut footage to edit;

   **c.** Estimated total length of the completed production;

   **d.** The number and types of optical and/or CGI effects required;

e. The number of voice, music and sound effects tracks and cues required;

f. Whether the voice track(s) is lip synchronous voice(s), wild narration or loop synchronous voice(s)—ADR dubbed or looped voice(s)—or a combination thereof;

g. Whether the music track(s) is to be from an original score or from canned music;

h. The number and type of sound effects to be built into the sound tracks— whether specially made by the Foley process, specially recorded, canned or a mix of both techniques;

i. The estimated time element from start to finish;

j. Whether there is an irrevocable deadline for delivery of the completed film/tape and/or release prints.

3. A film or video **Editor** of appropriate classification specialty is used on each type of specific film or tape show which requires picture editing, and is in charge of all technical procedures directly pertaining to film editing during all phases of that process.

4. An **Editor** must be knowledgeable in non-linear electronic digital editing techniques, using an Avid, Media Composer, Lightworks or similar system.

5. An **Editor** must also be fluent in linear film editing using a multi-head flatbed editing platform or similar system.

6. An **Editor** needs to know and apply: Cinematic structure; principles of dramaturgy, of flow, rhythm and pace; electronic and computer editing skills.

7. The **Supervising Editor** is a coordinator and expediter and is normally used in television programming production when more than one (1) production, or a series, are in the editing process concurrently. The **Supervising Editor** may function as a **Picture Editor**, if supervisorial responsibilities do not require full time.

8. The **Supervising Editor** is directly responsible to the **Producer**.

9. When the **Supervising Editor** requires assistance in editing the picture elements, a **Picture Editor** is used.

10. The **Picture Editor** is directly responsible to the **Supervising Editor** when a **Supervising Editor** is used.

11. In the event a **Supervising Editor** is not used, the **Picture Editor** is directly responsible to the **Director** so long as the **Director** is charged with the responsibility for the first, or final, cut of the picture. Thereafter, the **Picture Editor** is directly responsible to the **Producer**.

12. A **Picture Editor** edits or re-edits motion picture film of a feature, featurette, theatrical short, nature or film special, MOW, TV programming series or commercial for television exhibition (see appropriate definitions in the Glossary).

13. A **Supervising Sound Editor** supervises the design and building of all the sound tracks in preparation for the final mix.

14. A **Music Editor** prepares a breakdown bar sheet and click-tracks of music cues to 1/10th second for picture segments, for the **Composer** and Music Conductor to follow during the scoring sessions; is present during all scoring sessions; edits and places all music cues in the picture and, if digital tracking is required, uses the Pro Tools workstation system for such editing.

15. A **Sound Effects Editor** places the recorded sound effects in alignment with the picture in order to provide a realistic ambiance for the visuals and, if digital tracking is required, uses the Pro Tools workstation system for such editing.

16. A **Dialogue/ADR Editor** replaces unacceptable production dialogue with automated or looped dialogue that has been recorded in synchronization with the picture.

17. A **Foley Editor** places manufactured, specially recorded and canned sound effects in the picture where required.

18. A **Documentary Editor** edits documentary-type productions, as defined in the Glossary. For editing purposes, a documentary is further defined as:

    **a.** A production produced for non-theatrical use and not for commercial television; and/or

    **b.** A production without a professional cast; and/or

    **c.** A production assembled totally from stock reportorial-type footage; and/or

    **d.** A production shot on 35mm, 16mm or 8mm film, or on video tape.

19. A **News Editor** edits news-type productions, as defined in the Glossary. In addition, for editing consideration, a news production may be assembled from stock footage as well as from current coverage of a newsworthy event shot on motion picture film or video tape of any dimension.

20. An **Animation Editor** edits animation-type productions, as defined in the Glossary.

21. The **Trailer Editor** works with the **Picture Editor** in accessing scenes which the **Producer** wants to use in the trailer.

22. It is the responsibility of each **Editor** who edits/builds voice, music and/or sound effects tracks to prepare, or to supervise the **Assistant Editor** in preparing, detailed cue sheets, specifying start, stop and duration of each voice, music and sound effects cue, in order to facilitate an efficient sound mixing procedure.

23. A **First Assistant Editor** may be used to set up an Editing Room and to log, synchronize, deliver and pick up dailies following projection, to see that digitized tape data is imported into the computerized editing system, and to act as liaison between the assigned **Editor** and other Editing personnel, but may not perform any other editing function unless directly under the supervision of an **Editor**.

24. The **First Assistant Editor** assigned to the **Picture Editor** acts as liaison between the **Picture Editor** and the **Supervising Sound Editor, Dialogue Editor, Music Editor**, and **Sound Effects Editor**, keeping them advised and

updated about what is happening with the picture, and is also the go-between for Editing personnel and the vendors.

25. The **Film Librarian** may not edit or re-edit video tape or positive or negative film except as noted in **Film Librarian** duties. (See **T-2** of this **Section**, below.)

26. In the event a **Supervising Editor** or **Picture Editor** is not used, the **Film Librarian** is directly responsible to the Employer.

27. When the **Picture**, **Documentary**, **News** or **Animation Editor** requires assistance:

   **a.** In editing the music track(s), a **Music Editor** is used;

   **b.** In editing the sound effects track(s), a **Sound Effects Editor** is used;

   **c.** In logging, splicing, cleaning and repairing workprint, sound tracks and with other such editing detail and maintenance work, a **First Assistant Editor** is used;

   **d.** In logging, assembling, conforming, splicing and cleaning picture original or negative, a **Negative Cutter** is used.

28. A **First Assistant Film Editor** assists the **Picture Editor** by working on the workprint and other film-only tasks.

29. A **First Assistant Electronics Editor** assists the **Picture Editor** by digitizing and cataloguing film for input to the Avid, Media Composer or Lightworks system.

30. When a **First Assistant Editor** requires assistance, a **Second Assistant Editor** is used.

31. A **Second Assistant Editor** assists a **First Assistant Editor**.

32. An **Apprentice Editor** may only work under supervision of an **Assistant Editor**, and only on assigned tasks.

33. When a **Negative Cutter** requires assistance in the logging, breakdown, splicing and cleaning of original film material and with other such negative cutting detail and maintenance work, a **Breakdown Operator** is used.

34. When the **Film/Tape Librarian** requires assistance in the performance of duties, an **Assistant Editor** may be used.

35. Each Editing Category Head and Sub-Head must ensure that editing personnel do not attempt work under any unsafe condition(s), as specified by the Employer, OSHA, Building and Safety Code and fire laws, or in violation of any other safety regulation(s) and practice(s).

**C. Category Responsibilities:** It is the responsibility of each Employee in the Editing Category to work cooperatively with the Category Head, or with the Sub-Head to whom assigned, in order to assist in achieving the optimum and most efficient operation of the various procedures within this category.

**D. Category Function:** The principal function of Editing Category personnel involves the handling, physical cutting and arranging of the visual and audial elements which have been recorded on motion picture film—16mm, 35mm or 70mm—and magnetic tape, respectively, in order to provide a dramatically viable and satisfying viewing experience in accord with the **Director**'s vision.

**E. Category Considerations:**

**1.** Editing Category personnel are used on each production or project on which motion picture film/tape and/or recorded sound are to be physically arranged to form a composite and complete motion picture entity.

**2.** The classification(s) used depends upon the type of production or project, its time schedule, and upon the type(s) of editing service(s) to be applied thereto.

**F. Category Requirements:** Employees in each Editing Category classification must know and follow the chain-of-command and lines-of-communication and must know and be able to effectively and safely operate the equipment involved as well as be able to effectively apply the techniques associated with their respective craft classification.

**G. SUPERVISING EDITOR**

**1. Responsibilities and Duties:** The **Supervising Editor** is directly responsible as specified in Category Criteria, above. The **Supervising Editor** supervises and schedules the work of Editing Category personnel and is responsible for efficient coordination and for encouraging precise and creative craftsmanship by Editing Category personnel in order to help achieve optimum cinematic realization of the final film in accordance with the **Director**'s intent.

**2. Considerations:** The **Supervising Editor** has **Picture Editor** capability and is charged with the responsibility of checking the selection and synchronicity of sound elements by running each completed film with selected tracks in interlock prior to pre-dubbing, for quality control.

**H. PICTURE EDITOR**

**1. Responsibilities:** The **Picture Editor** is directly responsible as specified in Category Criteria, above, and is responsible for creatively editing the picture imagery, the production dialogue and all other elements within his or her province in order to achieve optimum cinematic realization of the film vehicle coincident with the **Director**'s intent.

**2. Duties:**

▼ **During the PRODUCTION Process:**

**a.** Reading, analyzing and referring to the shooting script as a guide to the overall editing pattern of the project at hand;

**b.** Being present on the set for consultation during shooting, if requested by the **Director**;

**c.** Viewing all screened dailies with the **Director** to determine if coverage has been adequate and intrascene cuts will match in action and visual quality;

▼ **During PRODUCTION and POST-PRODUCTION:**

**d.** When editing on film:

**(1)** Editing, using a flatbed or other editing machine, and physically selecting, cutting and arranging the visual elements, the shots, in the picture workprint;

**(2)** Marking the work print clearly, with all necessary information—sync start, cuts, fades, dissolves, inserts—for the **Assistant Editor** to assemble and splice;

**(3)** Seeing that the **Assistant Editor** has properly assembled and clearly marked the workprint for screenings and for the **Negative Cutter**;

**(4)** Editing—physically cutting and arranging voice cues in—the production track to conform to the workprint;

**(5)** Determining what scenes require voice replacement;

**(6)** Directing the **Assistant Editor** to prepare picture loops and/or voice guide track loops or digitized segments needed for voice dubbing or ADR sessions, if there is no **Dialogue/ADR Editor**;

**e.** When editing digitally:

**(1)** Editing, using an Avid or Lightworks system to select, cut and arrange the visual elements;

**(2)** Ensuring that all necessary information, such as, cuts, fades, dissolves, wipes and supeimposures have been inputted into the digital editing system;

**(3)** Editing—selecting, cutting and arranging the production dialogue elements in—the voice dialogue track(s);

**(4)** Determining picture/voice segments for voice dubbing or ADR sessions;

**(5)** Including in any run-through up to eight tracks of sound with production sound and additional representative voice-over, music and sound effects, for assisting the **Director** in assessing the potential of the edited material;

**f.** Viewing the processed intermediate film duplicating elements for quality control;

**g.** Viewing composite answer prints for quality control;

**h.** Otherwise carrying out the duties normally required of this classification;

**i.** Providing the hand tools normally employed in this craft.

**3. Considerations:**

**a.** The **Picture Editor** cuts the picture during production scene by scene when the complete coverage for each scene is received.

**b.** The **Picture Editor** is often expected to have a rough assembly of the picture completed a week following principal photography and, working with the **Director**, ten (10) weeks thereafter to a polished cut.

## I. SUPERVISING SOUND EDITOR

**1. Responsibilities:** The **Supervising Sound Editor** is directly responsible to the **Supervising Editor**, if any, otherwise, to the **Picture Editor**, and is responsible for developing the sound design of the production and for efficiently and creatively assembling the dialogue and the substitute music and sound effects tracks for the temp dub.

2. **Duties—all during POST-PRODUCTION:**

   **a.** Reading and annotating the shooting script from a total sound design viewpoint;

   **b.** Preparing cue sheets for representative sound elements gathered for the temp dub session from the **Music Editor** and the **Sound Effects Editor**;

   **c.** Scheduling a temp dub session with the **Picture Editor** and **Director** in attendance;

   **d.** Delivering the rolls of sound elements and picture reels to the **Lead Recordist** for the re-recording process;

   **e.** Running and checking quality of all production dialogue tracks;

   **f.** Scheduling ADR sessions to replace unsatisfactory production dialogue;

   **g.** Scheduling Foley sound effects sessions;

   **h.** Checking synchronization accuracy of all tracks—voice, music, and sound effects—with the picture and the accuracy of all logged cues on each cue sheet;

   **i.** Distributing cue sheets to the **Re-Recording Mixer**s;

   **j.** Supervising the temp dub session;

   **k.** Scheduling and attending the pre-dub sessions with the **Picture Editor**, **Director** and **Producer**;

   **l.** Making any repairs to, or adjustments in, the sound tracks during the pre-dub, as necessary;

   **m.** Otherwise carrying out the duties normally required of this classification;

   **n.** Providing the hand tools normally employed in this craft.

3. **Considerations:** A **Supervising Sound Editor** assembles the sound elements and checks or prepares the cue sheets for the various dubbing sessions.

## J. MUSIC EDITOR

1. **Responsibilities:** The **Music Editor** is directly responsible to the **Supervising Editor**, if any, otherwise, to the **Picture Editor** and **Supervising Sound Editor**, and is responsible for creatively selecting and/or editing the music track(s) in order to help achieve optimum cinematic realization thereof.

2. **Duties—all during POST-PRODUCTION:**

   **a.** Reading the script within the context of music augmentation;

   **b.** Preparing picture segments, click tracks and music cue, or bar, sheets for use by the **Composer** and **Music Conductor**, if original music is to be composed and performed to score the picture;

   **c.** Examining and analyzing the edited workprint, reel by reel, listing all needed music cues;

**d.** Selecting appropriate music cues, when canned music is required;

**e.** Selecting representative canned music and placing it in the picture for the temp dub, or playing or recording a piano sketch to be used;

**f.** Being present at the temp dubs to monitor the effect of the representative music with the dialogue and sound effects;

**g.** Being present at scoring sessions when live music is being recorded;

**h.** Preparing orders for transferral of music to the work track;

**i.** Building the music track(s) in conformance with the approved work print;

**j.** Checking synchronization of all completed music tracks with picture;

**k.** Preparing music cue sheets for dubbing purposes;

**l.** Otherwise carrying out the duties normally required of this classification;

**m.** Providing the hand tools normally employed in this craft.

### 3. Considerations:

**a.** A **Music Editor** is used when the **Picture Editor** requires assistance in selecting, transferring and editing music cues for a production.

**b.** A **Music Editor** should be able to read a music lead sheet and should be proficient with a musical instrument as well.

**c.** A **Music Editor** may not edit or modify the picture work print in any way without express approval of the **Picture Editor**.

## K. SOUND EFFECTS EDITOR

### 1. Responsibilities:
The **Sound Effects Editor** is directly responsible to the **Supervising Editor**, if any, otherwise to the **Picture Editor** and **Supervising Sound Editor**, and is responsible for creatively selecting sound effects and editing the sound effects track(s) in order to help achieve optimum cinematic realization thereof.

### 2. Duties—all during POST-PRODUCTION:

**a.** Reading and annotating the final shooting script within the context of sound placement and design;

**b.** Developing a plan of overall sound design for the cinematic product;

**c.** Examining and analyzing the edited workprint, reel by reel, listing all needed sound effects;

**d.** Selecting appropriate sound effects from available stock;

**e.** Creating and/or synthesizing sound effects from various sound elements:

**f.** Selecting representative canned sound effects and placing these elements in the picture for the temp dub;

**g.** Being present at the temp dubs to monitor the effect of the representative music with the dialogue and sound effects;

**h.** Preparing orders for recording and/or transferral of sound effects to the work track(s);

**i.** Building the sound effects track(s) in conformance with the approved work print;

**j.** Checking synchronization of all completed sound effects tracks with picture;

**k.** Preparing sound effects cue sheets for dubbing purposes;

**l.** Otherwise carrying out the duties normally required of this classification;

**m.** Providing the hand tools normally employed in this craft.

**3. Considerations:**

**a.** A **Sound Effects Editor** is used when a **Picture Editor** requires assistance in selecting, transferring and editing sound effects.

**b.** A **Sound Effects Editor** may not edit or modify the picture work print in any way without express approval of the **Picture Editor**.

## L. DIALOGUE/ADR EDITOR

**1. Responsibilities:** The **Dialogue/ADR Editor** is directly responsible to the **Picture Editor** for selecting and accurately placing the dialogue replacement segments in perfect synchronization with the picture.

**2. Duties—all during POST-PRODUCTION:**

**a.** Checking the shooting script and picture for those dialogue segments selected for replacement;

**b.** Extracting and preparing the picture segments for transfer to video tape along with the recorded dialogue track as an audible guide for the ADR process;

**c.** Scheduling ADR and group loop sessions with the approval of the **Director** and the **Production Manager** or **Producer**;

**d.** Delivering all prepared voice replacement video tape segments to the **ADR Mixer**;

**e.** Sitting in on the ADR and group loop sessions with the **Director** and **ADR Mixer**

**f.** Receiving the recorded takes of the sessions from the Transfer Studio and cutting the chosen takes into the picture, replacing the faulty production dialogue and placing group loop babble and voice cues where planned and appropriate;

**g.** Delivering the ADR material to the **Supervising Sound Editor** for inclusion in the picture along with canned and production recorded sound effects;

**h.** Otherwise carrying out the duties normally required of this classification;

**i.** Providing the hand tools normally employed in this craft.

**3. Considerations:** An **ADR Editor** is used on productions where production dialogue is to be replaced and background voices are to be added.

## M. FOLEY EDITOR

**1. Responsibilities:** The **Foley Editor** is directly responsible to the **Picture Editor** for selecting and accurately placing the Foley-made sound effects in perfect synchronization with the appropriate picture elements.

**2. Duties—all during POST-PRODUCTION:**

**a.** Checking the shooting script and picture for those portions of the picture requiring augmentative sound effects;

**b.** Listing the required sound effects for each shot, scene and sequence for each reel, throughout the entire picture;

**c.** Scheduling Foley sessions with the approval of the **Director** and the **Production Manager** or **Producer**;

**d.** Meeting with the **Foley Mixer** and **Foley Artist**s with respect to the required sound effects;

**e.** Sitting in on the Foley sessions with the **Director**, **Foley Mixer** and **Foley Artist**;

**f.** Receiving the recorded takes of the sessions from the Transfer Studio and cutting the chosen takes into the picture and placing the sound effects where planned and appropriate;

**g.** Delivering the recorded Foley effects material to the **Supervising Sound Editor** or **Sound Effects Editor** for inclusion in the picture along with canned and production recorded sound effects;

**h.** Otherwise carrying out the duties normally required of this classification;

**i.** Providing the hand tools normally employed in this craft.

**3. Considerations:** A **Foley Editor** is used on productions where sound effects are to be replaced and background voices are to be added.

## N. TRAILER EDITOR

**1. Responsibilities:** The **Trailer Editor** is directly responsible to the **Picture Editor** for the technical quality and to the **Producer** for the selected content of the trailer, and is responsible for selecting and/or organizing visuals and sound clips from the picture for inclusion in trailer, editing all elements which are included in the trailer piece.

**2. Duties—all during POST-PRODUCTION:**

**a.** Checking the **Producer**'s list of key scenes from which to excerpt action segments for the trailer;

**b.** Looking at the workprint and selecting clips from scenes to be utilized in building and editing the trailer for the picture;

**c.** Ordering dupes of the scenes to be included in the trailer;

**d.** Editing the picture workprint—physically cutting and arranging the visual elements, the shots;

**e.** Marking the work print clearly, with all necessary information, for the **Negative Cutter**;

**f.** Editing the voice dialogue track(s)—physically cutting and arranging the production dialogue elements;

**g.** Preparing voice track cue sheets for dubbing sessions;

**h.** Planning, scheduling and supervising dubbing sessions;

      **i.** Checking synchronization accuracy of all tracks—voice, music and sound effects—with the picture and the accuracy of all logged cues on each cue sheet;

      **j.** Preparing and/or approving orders for opticals, sound transfers, and other laboratory services, editing supplies and rentals, stock footage and titles;

      **k.** Viewing the fine grain or CRI for quality control;

      **l.** Viewing composite answer prints for quality control;

      **m.** Otherwise carrying out the duties normally required of this classification;

      **n.** Providing the hand tools normally employed in this craft.

   **3. Considerations:** When a trailer is to be prepared for a production, a **Trailer Editor** is used.

## O. DOCUMENTARY EDITOR

   **1. Responsibilities:** The **Documentary Editor** is directly responsible to the Employer for creatively editing the picture film and all other elements within this province in order to help achieve optimum cinematic realization of the film vehicle.

   **2. Duties:**

      ▼ **During the PRODUCTION Process:**

      **a.** Reading and analyzing the script or structural outline and/or developing a script from the assembled footage;

      **b.** Editing or re-editing motion picture film of a documentary nature, as defined in the Glossary;

      **c.** Preparing and viewing dailies;

      **d.** Logging and organizing the footage;

      ▼ **During POST-PRODUCTION:**

      **e.** Editing all tracks, as necessary;

      **f.** Preparing orders for laboratory work, sound transfer, editing supplies and rentals, stock footage and titles;

      **g.** Preparing cue sheets for the sound tracks;

      **h.** Scheduling and conducting sound mixing sessions;

      **i.** Viewing composite answer prints for quality control;

      **j.** Otherwise carrying out the duties normally required of this classification;

      **k.** Providing the hand tools normally employed in this craft.

   **3. Considerations:** The **Documentary Editor**, although normally doing all editing functions, is responsible for coordinating all work done by Editing Category staff required for a documentary film production.

## P. NEWS EDITOR

   **1. Responsibilities:** The **News Editor** is directly responsible to the Employer or **News Writer** for editing the newsreel film and all associated elements in the very limited time usually afforded in order to achieve optimum cinematic realization of the film vehicle.

**2. Duties—during PRODUCTION and POST-PRODUCTION:**

    **a.** Editing or re-editing motion picture film of news and/or sporting events in the form of a news event or news report, as defined in the Glossary;

    **b.** Preparing and viewing dailies;

    **c.** Arranging the footage in conformance with the news report, or with the direction of the **News Writer**;

    **d.** Editing sound track, whether of single system or double system and whether wild or synchronous voice and/or sound tracks;

    **e.** Preparing orders for laboratory work, editing supplies and rentals, stock footage, titles and captions;

    **f.** Preparing cue sheets;

    **g.** Scheduling and conducting dubbing sessions;

    **h.** Otherwise carrying out the duties normally required of this classification;

    **i.** Providing the hand tools normally employed in this craft.

**3. Considerations:** The **News Editor**, although normally performing all editing functions, is responsible for coordinating all work done by Editing Category personnel for a newsreel production.

## Q. ANIMATION EDITOR

    **1. Responsibilities:** The **Animation Editor** is directly responsible to the Employer for editing the animation film and all associated elements in order to help achieve optimum cinematic realization of the film vehicle.

    **2. Duties—during PRODUCTION and POST-PRODUCTION:**

        **a.** Using the final script as guide during the editing process;

        **b.** Editing or re-editing motion picture film of an animation nature, as defined in the Glossary;

        **c.** Reading sound tracks—voice, sound effects and/or music—and transposing to exposure, or bar, sheets;

        **d.** Preparing and viewing dailies;

        **e.** Editing the picture, sound and music tracks for animation material;

        **f.** Editing live action picture and track inserts for animation films;

        **g.** Preparing orders for laboratory work, editing supplies and rentals, stock footage and titles;

        **h.** Preparing cue sheets;

        **i.** Scheduling and conducting dubbing sessions;

        **j.** Viewing composite answer prints for quality control;

        **k.** Otherwise carrying out the duties normally required of this classification;

        **l.** Providing the hand tools normally employed in this craft.

3. **Considerations:** The **Animation Editor**, although normally performing all editing functions, is responsible for coordinating all work done by Editing Category personnel required for an animation production.

## R. FIRST ASSISTANT FILM EDITOR

1. **Responsibilities:** The **First Assistant Film Editor** is directly responsible to, and assists, the **Picture Editor**, and is responsible for accurately and efficiently carrying out the assigned duties in order to help assure optimum cinematic realization of the film vehicle.

The **First Assistant Film Editor** is in charge of the film workprint and magnetic sound tapes throughout the editing process—from the first day of syncing dailies ot the last day of wrapping the show and makes sure that the **Picture Editor** has everything needed in a film-only editing system in order to make selections and do the edits.

2. **Duties**:

▼ **During PRE-PRODUCTION:**

  a. Setting up the editing room;

  b. Ordering matériel—equipment and supplies;

  c. Setting up vendor accounts—lab processing, printing, optical effects, sound transfer, etc;

▼ **During the PRODUCTION Process:**

  d. In a film-only and/or digital editing process:

   **(1)** Synchronizing daily workprint with the transferred daily sound on mag track and otherwise preparing dailies for rush viewing;

   **(2)** Logging each take, noting the length of each take in feet and frames for each camera used;

   **(3)** Coding dailies (picture and voice track), as required;

   **(4)** Breaking down dailies after daily viewing, as authorized;

   **(5)** Numbering, cataloguing and filing each printed take for each scene (work print and corresponding voice track by its roll number and inclusive beginning and ending edge numbers, noting and logging each scene and take number which occurs on each roll;

   **(6)** Measuring and recording incoming and outgoing footage, picture and tracks, as required, and keeping record of same;

  e. In a digital editing process for features:

   **(1)** Synchronizing daily workprint with the daily sound that has been transferred to 35mm mag track, and otherwise preparing dailies for rush viewing;

   **(2)** Logging each take, noting the precise length of each take in feet and frames for each camera used;

   **(3)** Coding dailies (edge numbering workprint and magnetic voice track), as required;

**(4)** Sending the workprint and log sheet to a telecine house for transfer to 3/4" or Beta SP tape within given parameters which meet the specifications and requirements of either the Avid or Lightworks system which gives the machine a reference to each frame of film for the non-linear digital editing process;

**(5)** Breaking down each reel of dailies into a numbered roll for each printed take of picture and corresponding voice track, noting and logging the scene and take number which occurs on that take roll;

**(6)** After the digitizing process, retrieving the film and tape, putting the film in the film library and putting the tape in the tape library;

**(7)** Accessing the film and tape in the library to modify the workprint when the change list requires it;

**f.** Writing up and delivering orders for laboratory work, editing supplies and rentals, stock footage, opticals and titles, as required;

▼ **During POST-PRODUCTION:**

**g.** In a film-only process:

**(1)** Papering off scenes for reprints and opticals;

**(2)** Marking and ordering opticals and cutting in optical work print;

**(3)** Cleaning all film and track, as required;

**(4)** Blooping tracks and release prints as necessary;

**(5)** Cleaning, degaussing and maintaining editing equipment;

**(6)** Splicing picture workprint and mag tracks;

**(7)** Preparing workprint and voice track reels for periodic interlock screenings, as required;

**(8)** Preparing picture loops and/or voice guide track loops or segments needed for voice dubbing or ADR sessions;

**(9)** Keeping the editing room clean, orderly and adequately supplied with expendables;

**(10)** Assisting the assigned-to **Editor** in the performance of duties;

**(11)** Otherwise carrying out the duties normally required of this classification;

**(12)** Providing the hand tools normally employed in this craft.

**h.** In a digital editing process for television programming and/or feature film production:

**(1)** Assembling the picture from scenes selected and edited by the **Picture Editor** as per the cut lists outputted by the electronic editing system;

**(2)** Maintaining the change-list of scenes as the **Picture Editor** recuts the picture;

**(3)** Going to the film library and pulling the respective rolls and scenes from those rolls and placing them in the order spelled out by the editing system lists;

**(4)** Checking that all the lists and the info exiting the editing system are accurate;

**(5)** Maintaining the integrity of the digital system—of its input and output;

**(6)** Checking that all stations in the media share network are functioning properly;

**(7)** When the picture is locked, and all sound elements are conformed, taking the reels of film or video tape or video cassettes to the post-production sound mixing facility for the final dubbing session;

**(8)** After each film reel of the picture is mixed, it is turned over to the **Negative Cutter** to begin conforming the negative to the picture.

### 3. Considerations:

**a.** A **First Assistant Film Editor** does not perform functions specifically assigned to **Editor** classifications.

**b.** When a **First Assistant Film Editor** requires assistance, another **Assistant Editor** is used; this is normally the situation when more than one (1) **Editor** is working concurrently on the same project which may require an **Assistant** for each **Editor**.

## S. FIRST ASSISTANT ELECTRONICS EDITOR

**1. Responsibilities:** The **First Assistant Electronics Editor** is directly responsible to the **Editor** to whom assigned to assist and is responsible for accurately and efficiently carrying out the assigned duties in order to help assure optimum cinematic realization of the film vehicle. The **Electronics Assistant** must be knowledgeable and fluent with the Mac or PC platform and with the Avid Media Composer and Lightworks systems and is in charge of all computer-generated lists, keeping them current and accurate, and making sure that the **Picture Editor** has everything needed in the digital editing system in order to make selections and do the edits.

**2. Duties:**

▼ **During PRE-PRODUCTION:**

**a.** Setting up the digital editing system in the editing room;

**b.** Ordering matériel—equipment and supplies;

**c.** Setting up vendor accounts—supplies, services, etc;

▼ **During the PRODUCTION Process:**

**d.** In a digital editing process for television programming:

**(1)** Digitizing the tape coming from the telecine transfer of the negative imagery weekly for an entire sitcom show, or daily for an episodic show, a process which addresses each frame of film;

**(2)** Digitally logging each take, noting the precise length of each take in feet and frames for each camera used;

**(3)** Organizing the digital data and inputting it into an Avid, Media Composer or Lightworks system for use by the **Picture Editor**;

**(4)** Updating the digital data list with each edit change to keep it current and useful for the **Picture Editor**;

**e.** In a digital editing process for features:

**(1 )** Logging each take, noting the precise length of each take in feet and frames for each camera used;

**(2)** Sending the workprint and log sheet to a telecine house for transfer to 3/4" or Beta SP tape within given parameters which meet the specifications that meet the requirements of either the Avid or Lightworks system which gives the machine a reference to each frame of film;

**(3)** Inputting/digitizing the analog tape data from the transfer into the Avid or Lightworks system for use by the **Picture Editor**;

**(4)** Modifying and organizing the data when the change list requires it;

**f.** Writing up and delivering orders for laboratory work, editing supplies and rentals, stock footage, opticals and titles, as required;

**▼ During POST-PRODUCTION:**

**g.** In a digital editing process for television programming and/or feature film production:

**(1)** Maintaining the change-list of scenes as the **Picture Editor** recuts the picture;

**(2)** Checking that all the lists and the info exiting the editing system are accurate;

**(3)** Maintaining the integrity of the digital system—of its input and out-put;

**(4)** Checking that all stations in the media share network are functioning properly;

**(5)** When the picture is locked, and all sound elements are conformed, the reels of film or video tape or video cassettes, are taken to the post-production sound mixing facility for the final dubbing session;

**3. Considerations:**

**a.** A **First Assistant Electronics Editor** does not perform functions specifically assigned to **Editor** classifications.

**b.** When a **First Assistant Electronics Editor** requires assistance, another **Assistant Editor** is used; this is normally the situation when more than one (1) **Editor** is working concurrently on the same project which may require an **Assistant** for each **Editor**.

## T. SECOND ASSISTANT EDITOR

**1. Responsibilities:** The **Second Assistant Editor** is directly responsible to the **First Assistant Editor** to whom assigned, and is responsible for assisting that person in assigned duties in order to help maintain and efficient editing operation.

2. **Duties—all during Production and Post-Production.**

3. **Considerations:** A **Second Assistant Editor** is used when a **First Assistant Editor** requires assistance in the performance of film and/or digital editing duties.

## U. APPRENTICE EDITOR

1. **Responsibilities and Duties—all during POST-PRODUCTION:** The **Apprentice Editor** is directly responsible to the **Assistant Editor** to whom assigned for assisting in that person's duties.

2. **Considerations:** An **Apprentice Editor** is a person learning the editing craft and is used when an **Assistant Editor** has the time to supervise this person.

## V. FILM/TAPE LIBRARIAN

1. **Responsibilities:** The **Film/Tape Librarian** is directly responsible as specified in Category Criteria, above, and is responsible for establishing and maintaining all film and tape in the film/tape library in good condition, properly catalogued and labeled for efficient reference.

2. **Duties—all during PRODUCTION and POST-PRODUCTION:**

   **a.** Breaking down footage for cataloguing;

   **b.** Cataloguing film and tape footage—picture, track and negative—by production number, scene and take number, edge number(s), length of scene, scene description, and/or by existing library code or reference system, and cost per foot;

   **c.** Maintaining accurate record of incoming and outgoing film and tape;

   **d.** Preparing orders for fine grain, CRI and duplicate prints of library stock footage for the library, Editorial staff, or library clients;

   **e.** Notifying clients that orders are ready for pick up or delivery;

   **f.** Billing clients, as required;

   **g.** Splicing, repairing, cleaning and sending film to the laboratory for reconditioning, as necessary;

   **h.** Otherwise carrying out the duties normally required of this classification;

   **i.** Providing the hand tools normally employed in this craft.

3. **Considerations:**

   **a.** A **Film/Tape Librarian** is used when an inventory of stock shots, still photos, transparencies, and negatives requires organizing, cataloguing and maintaining.

   **b.** A **Film/Tape Librarian** may not edit film—print, track, negative or original reversal—or video tape.

# COMPUTER GRAPHICS CATEGORY ORGANIZATIONAL CHART

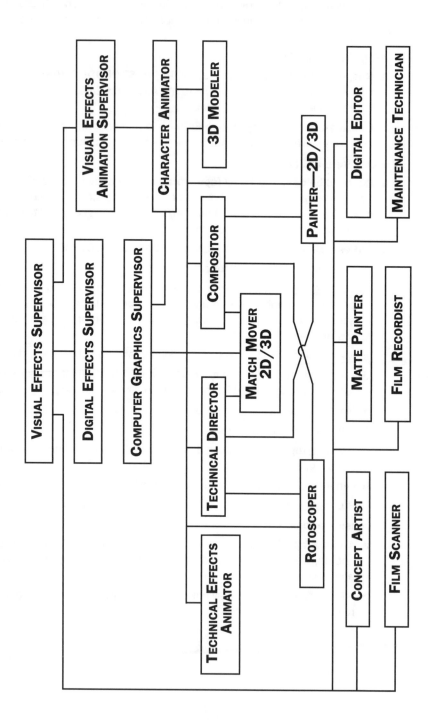

# 20

# CGI: COMPUTER GRAPHICS CATEGORY

**A. Category Classifications:** There are eighteen (18) classifications in the Computer Graphics (CG) Category:

**1. Visual Effects Supervisor (Category Head)**

**2. Digital Effects Supervisor (Category Sub-Head)**

**3. Visual Effects Animation Supervisor (Category Sub-Head)**

**4. Computer Graphics Supervisor (Category Sub-Head)**

**5. Character Animator**

**6. Technical Director**

**7. Technical Effects Animator**

**8. Compositor**

**9. 3D Modeler**

**10. Rotoscoper**

**11. Painter—2D/3D**

**12. Match Mover—2D/3D**

▼ **In the SCANNING and RECORDING Department:**

**13. Film Scanner**

**14. Film Recordist**

▼ **In the EDITING Department:**

**15. Digital Editor**

▼ **In the ART Department:**

**16. Concept Artist**

**17. Matte Painter**

▼ **In the TECHNICAL MAINTENANCE Department:**

**18. Maintenance Technician**

**B. Category Criteria:**

**1.** The **Visual Effects Supervisor** has full authority over, and responsibility for, the operation and output of all contributing departments including models, miniatures, puppets, art, construction, property, camera, optical and editorial.

2. The **Digital Effects Supervisor** has authority over, and responsibility for, the operation and output of the computer graphics operation.

3. It is the **Computer Graphics Supervisor**'s responsibility for coordinating the efforts of CG personnel and to see that the visual results are seamlessly integrated into the composited product.

4. The **Visual Effects Supervisor** and each Computer Graphics Category Sub-Head must ensure that CG personnel do not attempt work under any unsafe condition(s), as specified by the Employer, OSHA, Building and Safety Code and fire laws, or in violation of any other safety regulation(s) and practice(s).

C. **Category Responsibilities:** It is the responsibility of each Employee in the CG Category to work closely and cooperatively with the **Visual Effects Supervisor** and the **Digital Effects Supervisor** in order to assist in the optimum and most efficient visual realization of the production in process.

D. **Category Function:** The principal function of CG Category personnel involves electronically augmenting and manipulating visual imagery originating on film, tape and/or the 2D and 3D digital elements generated in the computer, and seamlessly compositing the modified imagery back onto film or tape.

E. **Category Considerations:**

1. CG Category personnel are used on each production which utilizes computer generated imagery.

2. The classifications used depend upon the type of motion picture being produced, its budget, the production elements to be composited with computer graphics, and its shooting schedule.

F. **Category Requirements:** Employees in each CG Category classification must know and be able to effectively operate the hardware and apply the software associated with their respective craft classification.

G. **VISUAL EFFECTS SUPERVISOR**

1. **Responsibilities:** The **Visual Effects Supervisor** is the creative and administrative head of all CG operations, is directly responsible to the **Producer**, and is responsible for coordinating the efforts of CG personnel as creatively, efficiently and effectively as possible in order to ensure that all CG animation and effects are integrated into the final production visuals as seamlessly and effectively as possible.

2. **Duties—during PRODUCTION and POST-PRODUCTION:**

a. Reading and annotating the script for meaning, emotion, action, continuity, plot and character development, as necessary;

b. Reviewing the storyboard to determine the type, placement and number of technical effects required;

c. Examining film or tape plates, clips and stills of the background and/or principal action, as available;

**d.** Determining the type of computer generated imagery and/or selected physical elements, and where and how extensively they might be applied to the production;

**e.** Determining the extent and nature of CG effects, modeling and animation required;

**f.** Working closely with the **Producer, Director, Director of Photography** and **Production Designer** (**Model Builder**s and **Puppeteer**s, where applicable) in planning, designing, executing and approving CG elements;

**g.** Informing the **Director of Photography** of elements needed, such as blue or green screen, special positioning of the camera, etc., well in advance when a scene of principal photography which will include computer graphic compositing is being set up for shooting;

**h.** Setting up a production schedule for CG effects, modeling, puppetry and animation;

**i.** Setting up a shooting schedule for process plates;

**j.** Reviewing and approving all CG elements at each stage of development;

**k.** Supervising all compositing of elements;

**l.** Otherwise carrying out the duties normally required of this classification.

**3. Considerations:** When one (1) or more of the above duties are required, a **Visual Effects Supervisor** is called for.

**4. Requirements:** The **Visual Effects Supervisor** must be experienced in compositing and must have a thorough working knowledge of the UNIX, PC and Mac platforms, the SGI and Sun workstations, and of the various proprietary software programs utilized in CG work—principally, the 2D/3D programs: Maya by Alias/Wavefront, Softimage, and Side Effects (Houdini and Prism); the 2D programs: Parallax and Discrete Logic (Flint, for paint and minor compositing; Flame, for video compositing; and Inferno, for film compositing); Adobe (Photoshop); and photographic and optical effects techniques. Managerial skills are also a must.

## H. DIGITAL EFFECTS SUPERVISOR

**1. Responsibilities:** The **Digital Effects Supervisor** is the technical head of CG operations, is creative consultant to and directly responsible to the **Visual Effects Supervisor**, and is responsible for all digital effects generated by CG personnel.

**2. Duties—during PRODUCTION and POST-PRODUCTION:**

**a.** Reading and annotating the script for meaning, emotion, action, continuity, plot and character development, as necessary;

**b.** Reviewing the storyboard to determine the type, placement and number of digital effects required;

**c.** Examining film or tape plates, clips and stills of the background and/or principal action, as available;

**COMPUTER GRAPHICS**

**d.** Determining the type of computer generated imagery, and where and how extensively it might be applied to the production;

**e.** Determining the extent of CG digital effects required;

**f.** Working closely with the **Visual Effects Supervisor** and the **Visual Effects Animation Supervisor**, in planning, designing, executing and approving digital CG elements;

**g.** Setting up a production schedule for CG effects, modeling and animation;

**h.** Assigning specific CG personnel to each production requiring CG;

**i.** Setting up a shooting schedule for process plates;

**j.** Reviewing and approving all CG elements at each stage of development;

**k.** Supervising all final compositing of elements;

**l.** Otherwise carrying out the duties normally required of this classification.

**3. Considerations:** When one (1) or more of the above duties are required, a **Digital Effects Supervisor** is called for.

**4. Requirements:** The **Digital Effects Supervisor** must be experienced in compositing and must have a thorough working knowledge of the UNIX, PC and Mac platforms, the SGI and Sun workstations, and of the various proprietary software programs utilized in CG work—principally, the 2D/3D programs: Maya by Alias/Wavefront, Softimage, and Side Effects (Houdini and Prism); the 2D programs: Parallax and Discrete Logic (Flint, Flame and Inferno); Adobe (Photoshop); and photographic and optical effects techniques. Managerial skills are also a must.

## I. VISUAL EFFECTS ANIMATION SUPERVISOR

**1. Responsibilities:** The **Visual Effects Animation Supervisor** is the creative and technical head of the CG animation and modeling operations, is directly responsible to the **Visual Effects Supervisor**, and is responsible for coordinating the efforts of CG animation and modeling personnel as creatively, effectively and efficiently as possible in order to assure the seamless integration of the work with the live action elements.

**2. Duties:**

**a.** Reading and annotating the script for meaning, emotion, action, continuity, plot and character development, as necessary;

**b.** Reviewing the storyboard to determine the type, placement and number of technical effects required;

**c.** Examining film or tape plates, clips and stills of the background and/or principal action, as available;

**d.** Determining the type of computer generated animated and modeled imagery, and where and how extensively these elements might be applied to the production;

**e.** Assigning specific animation and/or modeling operations to specific personnel;

**f.** Reviewing and approving all CG animation and modeling elements at each stage of development;

**g.** Conferring regularly with the **Visual Effects Supervisor** to apprise him or her of the progress of CG animation and modeling work;

**h.** Otherwise carrying out the duties normally required of this classification.

**3. Considerations:** When one (1) or more of the above duties are required, a **Visual Effects Animation Supervisor** is called for.

**4. Requirements:** The **Visual Effects Animation Supervisor** must be highly experienced in CG animation work and must have a thorough working knowledge of the UNIX, PC and Mac platforms, the SGI and Sun workstations, and of the various proprietary software programs utilized in CG work—principally, the 2D/3D packages by: Maya by Alias/Wavefront, Softimage, and Side Effects (Houdini and Prism); the 2D packages: Parallax and Discrete Logic (Flint, Flame and Inferno); and Adobe (Photoshop). Managerial skills are also important.

## J. COMPUTER GRAPHICS SUPERVISOR

**1. Responsibilities:** The **Computer Graphics Supervisor** is the creative and technical head of the CG visual effects operations, is directly responsible to the **Digital Effects Supervisor**, and is responsible for coordinating the efforts of CG personnel in creating virtual visual technical effects, rotoscoping, painting, match moving, modeling and compositing the imagery as creatively, effectively and efficiently as possible in order to assure the seamless integration of the work with the live action elements as well as lighting, shading, modeling and animation aspects.

**2. Duties:**

**a.** Reading and annotating the script for meaning, emotion, action, continuity, plot and character development, as necessary;

**b.** Reviewing the storyboard to determine the type, placement and number of technical effects required;

**c.** Examining film or tape plates, clips and stills of the background and/or principal action, as available;

**d.** Determining the type, and where and how extensively computer generated visual effects and modeled imagery might be applied to the production;

**e.** Assigning specific CG personnel to each production requiring CG;

**f.** Assigning specific visual effects and/or modeling operations to specific personnel;

**g.** Reviewing and approving all CG visual effects and modeling elements at each stage of development;

**h.** Conferring regularly with the **Digital Effects Supervisor** to apprise him or her of the progress of the visual effects and modeling work;

**i.** Otherwise carrying out the duties normally required of this classification.

3. **Considerations:** When one (1) or more of the above duties are required, a **Computer Graphics Supervisor** is called for.

4. **Requirements:** The **Computer Graphics Supervisor** must be highly experienced in CG animation work and must have a thorough working knowledge of the UNIX, PC and Mac platforms, the SGI and Sun workstations, and of the various proprietary software programs utilized in CG work—principally, the 2D/3D packages by: Maya by Alias/Wavefront, Softimage, and Side Effects (Houdini and Prism); the 2D packages: Parallax and Discrete Logic (Flint, Flame and Inferno); and Adobe (Photoshop). Managerial skills are also important.

## K. CHARACTER ANIMATOR

1. **Responsibilities:** The **Character Animator** is directly responsible to the **Visual Effects Animation Supervisor**, is responsive to the **Computer Graphics Supervisor**, and is responsible for creating and animating the character(s) developed for the production in order to assure seamless integration of the work with live action and other digital elements.

2. **Duties:**

   a. Reading and annotating the script for meaning, emotion, action, continuity, plot and character development, as necessary;

   b. Reviewing the storyboard to determine the type, placement and number of technical effects required;

   c. Examining film or tape plates, clips and stills of the background and/or principal action, as available;

   d. Suggesting the type, and where and how effectively computer generated animation and modeled imagery might be applied to the production;

   e. Preparing tests of proposed animation to show to the **Visual Effects Animation Supervisor**, the **Computer Graphics Supervisor** for approval;

   f. Getting approval from the **Visual Effects Animation Supervisor** of all CG character animation and modeling elements being developed at each stage of development;

   g. Conferring regularly with the **Visual Effects Animation Supervisor** and the **Computer Graphics Supervisor** to apprise them of the progress and synchronization of the character animation and modeling work;

   h. Otherwise carrying out the duties normally required of this classification.

3. **Considerations:** When one (1) or more of the above duties are required, a **Character Animator** is called for.

4. **Requirements:** The **Character Animator** must be experienced in traditional forms of animation and in CG animation work and must have a thorough working knowledge of the UNIX and Mac platforms, the SGI and Sun workstations, and of the various proprietary software programs utilized in CG work—principally, the 2D/3D packages by: Alias/Wavefront, Softimage, and

Side Effects (Houdini and Prism); the 2D packages: Parallax and Discrete Logic (Flint, Flame and Inferno); and Adobe (Photoshop).

## L. TECHNICAL DIRECTOR

1. **Responsibilities:** The **Technical Director** is directly responsible to the **Computer Graphics Supervisor**, and is responsible for the effect and conformity of technical effects such as direction and intensity of light and lighting patterns on form and color, and the resulting shading.

2. **Duties:**

   a. Reading and annotating the script for meaning, emotion, action, continuity, plot and character development, as necessary;

   b. Examining film or tape plates, clips and stills of the background and/or principal action, as available;

   c. Examining and evaluating the look of computer graphics—animation, 3D modeling and technical effects—for visual consistency and/or adding or modifying lighting and shading, as necessary;

   d. Preparing tests of proposed lighting and shading to show to the **Computer Graphics Supervisor** for approval;

   e. Conferring regularly with the **Computer Graphics Supervisor** to apprise him or her of the progress and synchronization of the technical effects work;

   f. Otherwise carrying out the duties normally required of this classification.

3. **Considerations:** When one (1) or more of the above duties are required, a **Technical Director** is called for.

4. **Requirements:** The **Technical Director** must have at least minimal compositing experience, must understand the photographic principles of light and shadow, must be highly experienced in CG technical effects work and must have a thorough working knowledge of the PC and Mac platforms, the SGI and Sun workstations, and of the various proprietary software programs utilized in CG work—principally, the 2D/3D packages by: Alias/Wavefront, Softimage, and Side Effects (Houdini and Prism); the 2D packages: Parallax and Discrete Logic (Flint, Flame and Inferno); and the 2D program Adobe Photoshop.

## M. TECHNICAL EFFECTS ANIMATOR

1. **Responsibilities:** The **Technical Effects Animator** is directly responsible to the **Computer Graphics Supervisor**, and is responsible for creating and adding weather effects—rain, snow, fog, wind, water, lightning, fire—and object modification—squashing, twisting or hurling vehicles, objects, people and/or animals, in order to seamlessly conform to the visual requirements of the scene.

2. **Duties:**

   a. Reading and annotating the script for meaning, emotion, action, continuity, plot and character development, as necessary;

**b.** Reviewing the storyboard to determine the type, placement and number of technical effects required;

**c.** Examining the film or tape plates, clips and stills of the background and/or principal action, as available;

**d.** Examining and evaluating the look of computer graphics—animation, 3D modeling and technical effects—for visual consistency and/or adding weather effects, object modification and/or laser effects;

**e.** Preparing tests of proposed technical effects to show to the **Graphics Supervisor** for approval;

**f.** Conferring regularly with the **Computer Graphics Supervisor** to apprise him or her of the progress and synchronization of the technical effects work;

**g.** Otherwise carrying out the duties normally required of this classification.

**3. Considerations:** When one (1) or more of the above duties are required, a **Technical Effects Animator** is called for.

**4. Requirements:** The **Technical Effects Animator** must be experienced in CG technical effects work and must have a thorough working knowledge of the UNIX, PC and Mac platforms, the SGI and Sun workstations, and of the various proprietary software programs utilized in CG work—principally, the 2D/3D packages by: Alias/Wavefront, Softimage, and Side Effects (Houdini and Prism); the 2D packages: Parallax and Discrete Logic (Flint, Flame and Inferno); and the 2D program Adobe Photoshop.

## N. COMPOSITOR

**1. Responsibilities:** The **Compositor** is directly responsible to the **Computer Graphics Supervisor**, and is responsible for layering the final refined elements received from all CG, scanning/recording, art and editing craftspeople in as consistent and seamless a result as possible.

**2. Duties:**

**a.** Reading and annotating the script for meaning, emotion, action, continuity, plot and character development, as necessary;

**b.** Reviewing the storyboard to determine the type, placement and number of visual layers required;

**c.** Examining the film or tape plates, clips and stills of the background and/or principal action, as available;

**d.** Examining and evaluating the look of computer graphics—animation, 3D modeling and technical effects—for visual consistency and/or determining the order of layering required;

**e.** Preparing tests of proposed layering to show to the **Computer Graphics Supervisor** for approval;

**f.** Conferring regularly with the **Computer Graphics Supervisor** to apprise him or her of the progress and synchronization of the compositing work;

**g.** Otherwise carrying out the duties normally required of this classification.

COMPUTER GRAPHICS

3. **Considerations:** When one (1) or more of the above duties are required, a **Compositor** is called for.

4. **Requirements:** The **Compositor** must be highly experienced in digital compositing systems and techniques, and must have a thorough working knowledge of the UNIX, PC and Mac platforms, the SGI and Sun workstations, and of the various proprietary software programs utilized in CG work—principally, the 2D/3D packages: Alias/Wavefront, Softimage, Composer and Side Effects (Houdini and Prism); the 2D packages: Parallax and Discrete Logic (Flint, Flame and Inferno); and Adobe Photoshop.

## O. 3D MODELER

1. **Responsibilities:** The **3D Modeler** is directly responsible to the **Computer Graphics Supervisor** for final approval of 3D modeling work and to the **Character Animator** for coordination with other elements of the overall look, and is responsible for developing the 3D armature of the model and adding virtual skin, hair and/or feathers or other appropriate covering, as required, in order to achieve a seamless reality to the model in keeping with the scene(s) in which the model appears.

2. **Duties:**

   a. Reading and annotating the script for meaning, emotion, action, continuity, plot and character development, as necessary;

   b. Reviewing the storyboard to determine the type, placement and number of models required;

   c. Examining the film or tape plates, clips and stills of the background and/or principal action the model will be composited with, as available;

   d. Examining and evaluating the look of 3D model graphics for visual consistency;

   e. Preparing tests of the proposed model(s) to show to the **Computer Graphics Supervisor** and **Character Animator** for their input and approval;

   f. Conferring regularly with the **Computer Graphics Supervisor** and **Character Animator** to apprise them of the progress of the 3D modeling work;

   g. Otherwise carrying out the duties normally required of this classification.

3. **Considerations:** When one (1) or more of the above duties are required, a **3D Modeler** is called for.

4. **Requirements:** The **3D Modeler** must be experienced in CG three-dimensional modeling and must have a thorough working knowledge of the UNIX and Mac platforms, the SGI and Sun workstations, and of the various proprietary software programs utilized in CG work—principally, the 2D/3D packages: Maya by Alias/Wavefront, Softimage, and Side Effects (Houdini and Prism).

## P. ROTOSCOPER

1. **Responsibilities:** The **Rotoscoper** is directly responsible to the **Computer Graphics Supervisor** for final approval of rotoscoping work, to the **Technical**

**Director** for technical conformity of the elements, and to the **Compositor** for coordination of the overall look, and is responsible for generating mattes to cover unwanted material or to cover certain areas of the frame in which to insert either optical or CG material as seamlessly as possible.

2. **Duties:**

   a. Reading and annotating the script for meaning, emotion, action, continuity, plot and character development, as necessary;

   b. Reviewing the storyboard to determine the type, placement and number of electronic mattes required;

   c. Examining the film or tape plates, clips and stills of the background and/or principal action the mattes will be composited with, as available;

   d. Examining and evaluating the look of matte graphics for visual consistency;

   e. Preparing tests of proposed mattes to show to the **Computer Graphics Supervisor** and **Technical Director** for their input and approval;

   f. Conferring regularly with the **Computer Graphics Supervisor** and **Technical Director** to apprise them of the progress of the electronic matte work;

   g. Otherwise carrying out the duties normally required of this classification.

3. **Considerations:** When one (1) or more of the above duties is required, a **Rotoscoper** is called for.

4. **Requirements:** The **Rotoscoper** must have a working knowledge of optical techniques, must be experienced in constructing CG running mattes and must have a thorough working knowledge of the UNIX and Mac platforms, the SGI and Sun workstations, and of the various proprietary software programs utilized in CG work—principally, the 2D Parallax package.

## Q. PAINTER—2D/3D

1. **Responsibilities:** The **Painter—2D/3D** is directly responsible to the **Computer Graphics Supervisor** for final approval of 2D and 3D painting, to the **Technical Director** for technical conformity of the elements, and to the **Compositor** for coordinating the overall look for layering purposes, and is responsible for painting character skin and surface and/or covering details and for removing anomalies in CG material set for compositing for optimum visual effect.

2. **Duties:**

   a. Reading and annotating the script for meaning, emotion, action, continuity, plot and character development, as necessary;

   b. Reviewing the storyboard to determine the type, placement and amount of 2D and 3D CG painting required;

   c. Examining the film or tape plates, clips and stills of the background and/or principal action with which the 2D and 3D painting will be composited, as available;

    **d.** Examining and evaluating the look of 2D and 3D painting for visual consistency;

    **e.** Preparing paint tests of proposed model to show to the **Computer Graphics Supervisor** and **Compositor** for their input and approval;

    **f.** Conferring regularly with the **Computer Graphics Supervisor** and **Compositor** to apprise them of the progress of the 2D and 3D matte design work;

    **g.** Otherwise carrying out the duties normally required of this classification.

**3. Considerations:** When one (1) or more of the above duties is required, a **Painter—2D/3D** is called for.

**4. Requirements:** The **Painter—2D/3D** must be experienced in traditional and CG painting techniques and must have a thorough working knowledge of the UNIX and Mac platforms, the SGI and Sun workstations, and of the various software programs utilized in CG work—principally, the 2D/3D packages: Maya by Alias/Wavefront and Softimage; and the 2D packages: Matador and Adobe Photoshop.

## R. MATCH MOVER—2D/3D

**1. Responsibilities:** The **Match Mover—2D/3D** is directly responsible to the **Computer Graphics Supervisor** for final approval of all match moving elements, to the **Technical Director** for conformity of the elements, and to the **Compositor** for coordination of the overall look, and is responsible for tracking elements and matching camera movement with object movement, thereby translating live camera movement into a 3D environment, in order to help achieve an optimum visual effect.

**2. Duties:**

    **a.** Reading and annotating the script for meaning, emotion, action, continuity, plot and character development, as necessary;

    **b.** Reviewing the storyboard to determine the type, placement and amount of 2D and 3D CG match moving required;

    **c.** Examining the film or tape plates, clips and stills of the background and/or principal action and camera moves which will need to be matched;

    **d.** Applying cinematic techniques in the use of the camera, lenses, film stocks and formats;

    **e.** Applying tracking and pin-blocking techniques;

    **f.** Examining and evaluating the look of 2D and 3D match moves for visual consistency and effect;

    **g.** Preparing tests of proposed 2D/3D match moves to show to the **Computer Graphics Supervisor** for input and approval;

    **h.** Conferring regularly with the **Computer Graphics Supervisor** to apprise him or her of the progress of the 2D and 3D match moving work;

    **i.** Otherwise carrying out the duties normally required of this classification.

3. **Considerations:** When one (1) or more of the above duties are required, a **Match Mover—2D/3D** is called for.

4. **Requirements:** The **Match Mover—2D/3D** must be experienced in CG match moving of objects in frame and must have a thorough working knowledge of the 2D and 3D tracking programs on the UNIX platform, the SGI and Sun workstations, and of the various proprietary software programs utilized in CG work—principally, the 2D/3D packages: Maya by Alias/Wavefront, Softimage and Side Effects (Houdini and Prism).

▼ **In the SCANNING & RECORDING Department** ▼

**S. FILM SCANNER**

1. **Responsibilities:** The **Film Scanner** is directly responsible to the **Visual Effects Supervisor**, and is responsible for carefully handling, scanning and digitizing film—negative, positive or print—to tape or computer disk at an appropriate rate of memory for use in the computer to generate and manipulate that imagery.

2. **Duties:**

   a. Setting up, tying in, adjusting, aligning, focusing, registering, color balancing and operating the flying spot scanner, laser scanner or similar device with input directly to computer memory;

   b. Cleaning the film material prior to the transferring process;

   c. Threading and unthreading film in the film scanner;

   d. Keeping accurate video tape transfer logs (film-to-tape);

   e. Returning film material to the client, or returning it to storage;

   f. Otherwise carrying out the duties normally required of this classification.

3. **Considerations:** When one (1) or more of the above duties are required, a **Film Scanner** is called for.

4. **Requirements:** The **Film Scanner** must be experienced in the UNIX platform and use of the Maya operating program, and in operating film scanning devices, and in the care and handling of original film material.

**T. FILM RECORDIST**

1. **Responsibilities:** The **Film Recordist** is directly responsible to the **Visual Effects Supervisor**, and is responsible for transferring the final digitally manipulated shots, scenes and sequences to film in a manner to optimize the visual quality on film.

2. **Duties:**

   a. Setting up, tying in, calibrating, adjusting, aligning, focusing, registering, color balancing and operating the film printer (tape-to-film) or the film projector and flying spot scanner, laser scanner or similar device, and the three-tube (three-color—RGB) prismatic image pick-up, in conjunction with the **Video Tape Operator**, under the supervision of a video **TD** (film-to-tape) or **Video Colorist**;

COMPUTER GRAPHICS

**b.** Setting the aspect ratio matte and cleaning the film gate and lens of the film printer;

**c.** Loading and unloading the film printer magazines;

**d.** Threading and unthreading film in the film printer;

**e.** Keeping accurate film printer reports;

**f.** Canning exposed film and unexposed short ends and marking proper identification on each can of exposed film prepared for shipment to the film lab for processing;

**g.** Otherwise carrying out the duties normally required of this classification.

**3. Considerations:** When one (1) or more of the above duties are required, a **Film Recordist** is called for.

**4. Requirements:** The **Film Recordist** must be experienced in the UNIX system and in operating devices which transfer CG elements to film.

### ▼ In the EDITING Department ▼

## U. DIGITAL EDITOR

**1. Responsibilities:** The **Digital Editor** is directly responsible to the **Visual Effects Supervisor,** and is responsible for carefully arranging the CG material in an order designed for optimum visual effect.

**2. Duties:**

**a.** Reading, analyzing and annotating the shooting script and referring to it for rhythm and flow;

**b.** Working with the produced material from a count sheet (done in hours: minutes:seconds:frames) supplied by the **Digital Effects Supervisor;**

**c.** Supervising all patching of the control system as accomplished by the **Maintenance Technician;**

**d.** Assembling and logging the production and CG elements for editing, using the electronic frame code if applicable and available;

**e.** Transferring production elements to video tape and/or video laser disc, and the film and CG insert elements to video tape, as necessary;

**f.** Applying electronic frame coding to those elements, as necessary;

**g.** Preparing a computerized punch tape from the elements log for use in automatic computerized on-line editing;

**h.** Doing manual on- or off-line editing—switching, fading, dissolving, wiping, irising, supers, etc—as necessary;

**i.** Rough editing 1/2″ or 1″ video tape off-line onto 2″ quad, video cassette, digital tape and/or laser disc or hard drive, as necessary;

**j.** Selecting, transferring, positioning, combining and recombining all video tape and CG production elements into a finalized product;

**k.** Physically splicing and/or repairing video tape;

**l.** Marking proper identification on the final edited work and returning it and all original elements to the **Producer**'s designee;

**m.** Otherwise carrying out the duties normally required of this classification.

**3. Considerations:**

    **a.** During off-line video tape editing, using reel-to-reel or video cassette 1″, 3/4″, 1/2″ or 1/4″ helical tape recorder(s) and/or laser discs or hard drives, the **Digital Editor** normally requires no assistance.

    **b.** During on-line editing or re-recording, using quad tape (2″) VTRs, the **Digital Editor** functions as a video **Technical Director** over other functioning technical operators, including the **Video Tape Operator**, the **Telecine Operator** and the **Chyron Operator**.

    **c.** A **Digital Editor** is used when video tape requires transfer editing, sweetening, or other electronic editing procedures.

**4. Requirements:** The **Digital Editor** must be able to operate the Avid system, and must be fluent with UNIX and the PC and Mac platforms.

### ▼ In the ART Department ▼

## V. CONCEPT ARTIST

**1. Responsibilities:** The **Concept Artist** is directly responsible to the **Visual Effects Supervisor** for conceptualizing sequences discussed and/or formulated between the **Director** and **Visual Effects Supervisor**, and is responsible for creating sketches and renderings which will be used in designing and constructing models, miniatures, puppets, technical effects, virtual elements and settings for optimum consistent overall visual effect.

**2. Duties:**

    **a.** Reading and annotating the script for meaning, emotion, action, continuity, plot and character development, as necessary;

    **b.** Determining the type, placement and number of models, miniatures, puppets, technical effects and virtual elements and settings which will be needed and implemented;

    **c.** Executing a story board with all elements represented;

    **d.** Reviewing the storyboard with the **Visual Effects Supervisor** to set the CG elements and to determine the type and amount of CG and complementary work and elements will be required;

    **e.** Examining film or tape plates, clips and stills of the background and/or principal action with which CG elements will be composited;

    **f.** Examining and evaluating the look of 2D and 3D painting for visual consistency;

    **g.** Preparing preliminary CG displays of proposed CG elements to show to the **Visual Effects Supervisor** for input and approval;

    **h.** Conferring regularly with the **Visual Effects Supervisor** as the concept art progresses;

i. Otherwise carrying out the duties normally required of this classification.

**3. Considerations:** When one (1) or more of the above duties are required, a **Concept Artist** is called for.

**4. Requirements:** The **Concept Artist** must be experienced in the UNIX system, and in operating the Mac platform using Adobe Photoshop.

## W. MATTE PAINTER

**1. Responsibilities:** The **Matte Painter** is directly responsible to the **Visual Effects Supervisor**, and is responsible for designing and painting scenic and/or background mattes in a style and manner best suited to combine seamlessly with the CG elements in frame.

**2. Duties:**

a. When executing artwork for a specific production, reading the script for an understanding of the scenic requirements;

b. Preparing orders for painting materials and any special equipment needed in the preparation and application of the materials to the backings, drops, flats, cycloramas and/or glass mattes;

c. Preparing and/or working from approved sketches of the planned matte rendering(s);

d. Supervising all **Artist**s assigned to assist in preparing matte art work;

e. Supervising film and/or video tests of matte art work;

f. Otherwise carrying out the duties normally required of this classification.

**3. Considerations:**

a. A **Matte Painter** is used when the design and execution of matte art is necessary.

b. The **Matte Painter** may be assisted by one (1) or more **Artist**s when necessary.

**4. Requirements:** The **Matte Painter** must be experienced in the UNIX system, and in operating the Mac platform using Adobe Photoshop.

▼ **In the TECHNICAL MAINTENANCE Department** ▼

## X. MAINTENANCE TECHNICIAN

**1. Responsibilities:** The **Maintenance Technician** is directly responsible to the **Visual Effects Supervisor**, and is responsible for maintaining all electronic and mechanical equipment associated with the computer and video chain (including audio) at optimum operating standards.

**2. Duties:**

a. Supervising the physical setting up, connecting and adjusting of all electronic CG, video and audio equipment used in CG operations;

b. Patching all CG, video and audio equipment into line, as required by operational necessity and optimum operation thereof;

**c.** Repairing, adjusting, aligning, modifying, cleaning, testing and maintaining all electronic and mechanical equipment, cameras, projectors, meters, recorders and other equipment associated with the CG, video and audio chain(s);

**d.** Checking and replacing circuit boards, tubes, resistors, transistors, transformers, condensers, diodes and the like, as necessary;

**e.** Preparing and repairing all cables, power cords and wiring used;

**f.** Inventorying the supply of spare parts and repair materials and preparing orders for parts, materials, tools and instruments;

**g.** Making periodic frequency checks of the electronic equipment and troubleshooting, as necessary;

**h.** Aligning all reproduction and recording heads on all recording equipment;

**i.** Otherwise carrying out the duties normally required of this classification.

**j.** Providing the hand tools normally employed in this craft.

**3. Considerations:**

**a.** A **Maintenance Technician** repairs and maintains all components related to the video chain (including audio) and provides a distortion meter and a volt/ohm/ammeter plus the hand tools normally employed in this craft, unless on staff, in which case the Company provides such test equipment and tools.

**b.** A **Maintenance Technician** is used during each CG operation in order to maintain optimum performance of the electronic CG, video and audio systems and the components thereof.

**4. Requirements:** The **Maintenance Technician** must be knowledgeable in the repair, replacement and maintenance of computer, film, video and audio components, particularly the UNIX, PC and Mac platforms and the SGI and Sun workstations.

[NOTE: Some of the computer graphics facilities divide their organizational hierarchy into two connected operations—2D functions and 3D functions—along with some modification of classification titles and duties compared with the chart which heads this chapter and with the responsibilities and duties described which follow it in the text. The chart on the facing page is an example of this particular alternate organizational setup. See Glossary for these alternate craft definitions.]

# ALTERNATE COMPUTER GRAPHICS CATEGORY ORGANIZATIONAL CHART

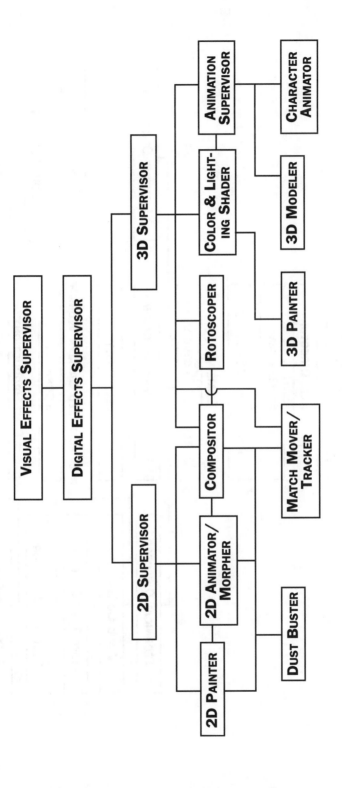

# Video Category Organizational Chart

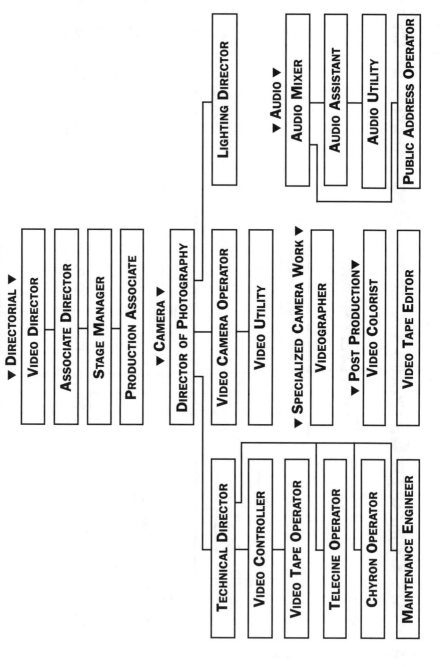

# 21

# VIDEO CATEGORY

**A. Category Classifications:** There are twenty-one (21) classifications in the Video Category:

▼ **For DIRECTORIAL Procedures:**

1. **Video Director (Category Head)**

2. **Associate Director**

3. **Stage Manager (Category Sub-Head)**

4. **Production Associate**

▼ **For CAMERA & LIGHTING Procedures:**

5. **Director of Photography—Video** (Category Head of technical production staff)

6. **Technical Director [Switcher]** (Category Head of electronic technical production staff)

7. **Lighting Director** (Category Sub-Head of electrical/lighting staff)

8. **Video Controller** (Category Sub-Head of technical production staff)

9. **Video Camera Operator**

10. **Video Tape Operator**

11. **Video Utility**

12. **Videographer (Category Sub-Head)**

▼ **For AUDIO Procedures:**

13. **Audio Mixer (Category Sub-Head)**

14. **Audio Assistant**

15. **Public Address Operator**

16. **Audio Utility**

▼ **For POST & EDITORIAL Procedures:**

17. **Video Colorist (Category Sub-Head)**

18. **Telecine Operator**

19. **Chyron Operator**

20. **Video Tape Editor (Category Head**, during post-production)

▼ **For MAINTENANCE Procedures:**

21. **Video Maintenance Engineer**

**B. Category Criteria:**

1. Employees holding classification within the Video Category perform all job functions pertaining to electronic video production procedures which are utilized on interior or exterior production, airborne or under water, on location and/or on the sound stage.

2. A **Technical Director** is used on a set or location where electronic video recording takes place, and is in charge of all technical procedures directly pertaining to video and audio recording during the production process.

3. A **Technical Director** needs to have and apply: A thorough knowledge of video electronics, the camera control system, patching lines into and out of the control console and a sure sense of timing during the on-line switching process.

4. All technical video and audio production personnel are directly responsible to the **Technical Director** during the production process, except, as noted, when a **Director of Photography** is used.

5. When the **Technical Director** requires assistance:

   a. In lighting a production, a **Lighting Director** is used;

   b. During warm-up, alignment, registering, balancing and adjusting the video cameras, video tape recorders, telecine and chyron units to the video control units and maintaining optimum video emission and pictorial quality during recording or transmission, a **Video Controller** is used;

   c. In the setting up, aligning, registering, balancing, adjusting and operating of video cameras, **Video Camera Operator**s are used;

   d. In the adjustment and operation of the video tape recorder, a **Video Tape Operator** is used;

   e. In the warm up, alignment, registering, balancing, adjustment and operation of the telecine chain, a **Telecine Operator** is used;

   f. In the setting up, balancing, adjustment and operation of audio recording equipment, an **Audio Mixer** is used;

   g. In the setting up, adjustment and operation of public address equipment, a **Public Address Operator** is used.

6. The **Technical Director** and **Video Controller** are directly responsible to the **Director of Photography** in matters concerning the illumination and registration of the photographic subject matter on mixed-media productions and also when a **DP** is used on video tape productions; the **DP** is subordinate to the **TD** in all matters concerning the technical requirements of the electronic systems.

7. On video tape production, only the **Technical Director** or his designee may issue instructions to production personnel during dress rehearsal and production recording, except that the **Video Director** issues such instructions during preliminary rehearsals as well as during the taping of unrehearsed productions.

VIDEO

8. **Video Utility** and **Audio Assistant** and **Audio Utility** personnel may be assigned to set up video and audio equipment, respectively, during preparation time without other video or audio personnel being present at the time so long as their work is done under the supervision of the **Technical Director**, **Video Controller**, or the **Video Maintenance Engineer**.

9. Prior to FAX (i.e., when all electronic facilities are ready) all setup personnel are directly responsible to the **Video Controller**, the **TD**'s designee, until FAX is completed.

10. On video production, the **Lighting Director** performs lighting functions of, and with responsibilities similar to, those of both the **Director of Photography** and **Gaffer** in film production, unless a **Director of Photography** is being used, in which event the **LD** is responsible to the **DP**.

11. The video crafts used in a production are augmented by other categories and classifications of film crafts when utilized on a video or mixed-media production.

12. When video personnel require assistance of a non-technical, non-skilled nature, such as preparatory, operational or breakdown manual labor, pickup and delivery or moving matériel, **Video Utility** personnel may be used.

13. During the process of video tape editing, the **Video Controller**, **Video Tape Operator**, **Telecine Operator**, **Video Colorist**, **Chyron Operator**, **Audio Mixer** and **Video Utility** personnel used are directly responsible to the **Video Tape Editor**.

14. All technical video post-production personnel are directly responsible to the **Video Tape Editor**.

15. All Video personnel operating underwater with breathing apparatus must be SCUBA certified.

16. Each Video Category Head and Sub-Head must ensure that video personnel do not attempt work under any unsafe condition(s), as specified by the Employer, OSHA, Building and Safety Code and fire laws, or in violation of any other safety regulation(s) and practice(s).

17. Video tape production is defined as a production technique using electronic cameras and a video control unit (VCU), including a camera control unit (CCU), to pick up, process and record visual images and audio signals on magnetic video tape or disc, and the finished product thereof is to be edited, if necessary, and exhibited in final form later.

18. Mixed-media production is defined as a production technique using motion picture cameras and **Camera Operator**s with film as the principal recording material, but utilizing a television transduction chain originating in or on the film camera(s), either single or (but principally) multi-camera coverage of production action, and recording such action on a video tape recorder (for instant playback purposes), as necessary.

**VIDEO**

C. **Category Responsibilities:** It is the responsibility of each Employee in the Video Category to work cooperatively with the **Technical Director** during production, with the **Video Controller** during pre-production FAX, or with the **Video Tape Editor** during post-production, in order to assist in achieving the optimum and most efficient operation of the various procedures within this category.

D. **Category Function:** The principal function of Video Category personnel involves the operation of electronic video and audio recording equipment in the video tape motion picture production process.

E. **Category Considerations:**

1. Video Category personnel are used on each production on which video equipment is used and/or on which video tape or disc is used to record the visual and audio elements.

2. The classification(s) used depends upon the type of production and upon the type and quantity of video equipment employed.

F. **Category Requirements:** Employees in each Video Category classification must know and follow the chain-of-command and lines-of-communication and must be able to effectively and safely set up and operate the video equipment selected for each job and associated with their respective craft classification.

▼ **Classifications Used for DIRECTORIAL Procedures** ▼

G. **VIDEO DIRECTOR**

1. **Responsibilities:** The **Video Director** is directly responsible to the **Producer**, and is responsible for directing the production activities of the staff, cast and crew as creatively and efficiently as possible in order to obtain optimum (dramatic) interpretation of the script, outline and/or storyboard, within the constraints of time and budget, while obtaining optimum photographic coverage thereof so that each shot, scene and sequence will cut together, flow and give life to the finally realized production, whether dramatic, comedic, promotional, documentary, sports, special event or news in nature.

2. **Duties:**

▼ **During PRE-PRODUCTION:**

a. Reading and annotating the script within the context of directing the action and intercutting the camera coverage during the scene takes;

b. Consulting with the **Art Director/Production Designer** regarding set design and the overall creative conceptual visualization for the production;

c. Determining the requirements of the set, set dressing, costumes, makeup, props, etc, for their proper dramatic perspective and functioning;

d. Surveying the locations and having a voice in selecting them;

e. Plotting the camera angles and movement for such scenes and shots;

f. Placing numbers on the shooting script indicating cut-points, where and when each camera will be on-line and the subject matter to be included in that shot angle;

**VIDEO**

▼ **During the PRODUCTION Process:**

**g.** Translating and transferring the written word to cinematic images—telling the written story visually/cinematically;

**h.** Planning and executing the work in such a way as to most efficiently utilize the talents of staff, cast and crew;

**i.** Blocking and directing the action of all actors, extras, vehicles, livestock, and the camera(s);

**j.** Working closely with the **Director of Photography** in communicating the desired "**look**" of the production, scene by scene and in its totality, and in setting angles and camera movement;

**k.** Rehearsing cast, extras, special effects and stunt personnel, and camera and sound prior to the take;

**l.** Advising the **Stage Manager** to cue actors and crew during rehearsals and takes;

**m.** Directing the dialogue;

**n.** Making script changes as deemed necessary in order to achieve appropriate transferal of the story—its action line and dialogue—to the recording medium;

**o.** Deciding on the use and placement of cueing equipment;

**p.** Signaling the **TD/Switcher** when to make each "on-air" cut of camera shots comprising the show;

▼ **During POST-PRODUCTION:**

**q.** Making pickup shots to correct production problems, as needed;

**r.** Reviewing the **Producer**'s or **Tape Editor**'s cut of the show and making adjustments, as necessary;

**s.** Otherwise carrying out the duties normally required of this classification;

**t.** Providing the hand tools normally employed in this craft.

**3. Considerations:**

    **a.** When one or more of the above duties are required, a **Video Director** is called for.

    **b.** The **Video Director** is employed for a sufficient period to satisfactorily carry out pre-production, production shooting (including conferences and viewing rushes) and post-production (through the first or final cut) responsibilities, as granted by agreement with the **Producer**.

## H. ASSOCIATE DIRECTOR

**1. Responsibilities:** The **Associate Director (AD)** is directly responsible to the **Video Director** for maintaining and modifying the shot cut-points on the **Director**'s shooting script, giving an accurate shot list (shot numbers and coverage) to each **Camera Operator**, and calling the shot numbers in a timely manner over the PL to the **Camera Operator**s during run-throughs and tapings.

VIDEO

**2. Duties:**

▼ **During PRE-PRODUCTION:**

**a.** Reading the script;

**b.** Copying the **Video Director**'s camera cut-point markings, coverage and sequential numbers from the **Video Director**'s script onto a duplicate script;

▼ **During the PRODUCTION Process:**

**c.** Giving on-air shot numbers and coverage, and off-air ISO (isolation) shots for each camera for the entire show to the **Camera Operator**s assembled prior to taking to the floor;

**d.** Calling shot numbers from the floor to the **Camera Operator**s who are following their individual shot list during the preview run-through by the cast for each sequence, prior to on-camera run-though and rehearsals;

**e.** Calling shot numbers from the control booth to the **Camera Operator**s during all on-camera run-throughs, rehearsals and tapings;

**f.** Seeing that each upcoming shot is properly composed, framed, in focus, and ready to go on-line with the **Video Director**'s take-cue to the **Switcher** (the **TD**);

**g.** Alerting any **Camera Operator** whose shot is not properly composed, framed, in focus and ready to be put on-line to correct the fault;

**h.** Noting and/or advising the **Script Supervisor** of any problem shot that goes on-line;

**i.** Otherwise carrying out the duties normally required of this classification;

**j.** Providing the hand tools normally employed in this craft.

**3. Considerations:** An **Associate Director** is used on all multi-camera video productions in order to assist the **Video Director** in utilizing the cameras to achieve the desired coverage in a maximally effective way.

**I. STAGE MANAGER**

**1. Responsibilities:** The **Stage Manager** operates on the stage floor and is directly responsible to the **Director**, and is the liaison between the **Director**, and/or the **Associate Director** and the cast and, when required, between the **Technical Director** and the technical personnel, in order to expedite communication from the control booth to both artists and technicians on stage.

**2. Duties:**

▼ **During PRE-PRODUCTION:**

**a.** Reading and annotating the script within the context of stage management;

**b.** Having a thorough knowledge and understanding of current union and guild working rules and wage rates and of the particular agreements which the **Producer** or Production Company may have with these labor organizations and with individuals employed on the production;

▼ **During the PRODUCTION Process**:

**c.** Wearing an intercom headset at all times while working in the shooting area;

**d.** Getting performers on stage, on time, on their marks;

**e.** Transmitting the **Director**'s instructions to the cast and the **Technical Director**'s instructions to the crew, as necessary;

**f.** Knowing all the standard hand-cueing signals and applying them, as directed and as necessary;

**g.** Checking that all props are properly placed;

**h.** Manipulating title and flip cards and/or credit crawl apparatus when a **Cuer** or **Prompter Operator** is not used;

**i.** Advising the **Associate Director** of all imminent meal, rest and overtime periods;

**j.** Releasing performers at the close of their particular scheduled shooting, and seeing that each day player has signed a voucher form;

**k.** Otherwise carrying out the duties normally required of this classification;

**l.** Providing the hand tools normally employed in this craft.

**3. Considerations:** A **Stage Manager** is used on video productions and may be used on those film productions employing a live TV technique with multiple film cameras.

## J. PRODUCTION ASSOCIATE

**1. Responsibilities:** The **Production Associate (PA)** is directly responsible to the **Producer** or **Production Manager**, and as the liaison between the **Director** and Production Management, is responsible for maintaining an efficient flow of communications between these entities and of handling scheduling matters, as requested.

**2. Duties—during PRE-PRODUCTION and PRODUCTION:**

**a. In assisting the Director and/or Associate Director:**

**(1)** Reading and annotating the script, as necessary;

**(2)** Taking assigned production notes during casting sessions, blocking, run-throughs and rehearsals;

**(3)** Taking production notes and timings from television commercial storyboards and conferences and transcribing them;

**(4)** Transcribing all assigned production notes for the convenience of Directorial and Production Management;

**(5)** Informing Production Management of any changes in scheduling—cast, special equipment, scene changes, etc—requested by Directorial;

**(6)** Keeping clients informed and making arrangements for meetings, luncheons, dinners and hotel, travel and transportation reservations, as necessary;

**(7)** Bringing refreshments, as needed;

**(8)** Running errands.

**b. In assisting the Production Manager:**

**(1)** Reading and annotating the script, as necessary;

**(2)** Keeping and transcribing production notes and reports;

**(3)** Typing, duplicating and distributing Call Sheets to staff, cast, crew;

**(4)** Arranging staff, cast and crew reservations for meals, lodging and travel;

**(5)** Attending/answering the stage telephones and taking messages for the staff, cast and crew;

**(6)** Collating/integrating revised script pages into current script copies;

**(7)** Running errands.

**c. In assisting the Producer, Director, Associate Director and/or Unit Production Manager** to whom assigned, in the performance of their duties;

**(1)** Reading and annotating the script, as necessary;

**(2)** Otherwise carrying out the duties normally required of this classification;

**(3)** Providing the hand tools normally employed in this craft.

**3. Considerations:**

**a.** A **Production Associate** is used to assist the Directorial unit during television pre-production and production phases and to provide liaison with Production Management.

**b.** The purpose of the **Production Associate** is to assist in the coordination and efficient operation of the Directorial and administrative production processes, but not to function in duty areas covered by any individual technical production classification.

**▼ Classifications Used for CAMERA & LIGHTING Procedures ▼**

**K. DIRECTOR OF PHOTOGRAPHY—VIDEO**

**1. Responsibilities:** The **Director of Photography (DP)** is responsible for the lighting and visual look of the production, supervises the technical production personnel, and is directly responsible to the **Director** and/or **Producer** for the efficient functioning of those categories and classifications under his or her technical direction and for assisting the **Director** in translating the teleplay into visual images, within the creative and budgetary latitude afforded, for optimum aesthetic visual effect.

**2. Duties:**

**▼ During PRE-PRODUCTION:**

**a.** Reading the script and annotating it regarding visual ideas, mood, lighting, special mechanical and/or optical/digital add-on effects and camera moves;

**b.** Scouting all locations and shooting sites;

**c.** Consulting with the **Director, Art Director/Production Designer** and **Producer** regarding production values, set and setting design, and matériel and time requirements;

**d.** Selecting the camera(s), its accessories and associated equipment to be used;

**e.** Selecting the video tape stock to be used;

**f.** Determining and/or approving the type, quality and quantity of lighting and grip equipment to be used;

**g.** Preparing comparative equipment and materials budgets in support of the type, quality and quantity of camera, lighting and grip equipment requested, if necessary;

▼ **During the PRODUCTION Process:**

**h.** Visually checking, and/or tape-testing, sets, settings, scenic art, set dressing, costumes, actors, hair, makeup, props, special effects and process components for photographic purposes;

**i.** Maintaining optimum photographic quality of the production;

**j.** Supervising (directly or indirectly) the personnel on each of the cameras in use on the production (first and second units);

**k.** Insuring that camera and production personnel do not attempt work under any unsafe condition(s), as specified by the Building and Safety Code and fire laws, or in violation of any other safety regulation(s) and practice(s);

**l.** Determining whether sound booms will work from the floor or from the greenbeds above;

**m.** Planning and supervising all production lighting—developing the light plot, determining the position of key, fill, back-cross and background lighting units, the lighting ratios (balance), the color and/or degree of diffused quality, if any, of the light, etc;

**n.** Setting the brightness, hue and contrast levels with the **TD** and **VC**;

**o.** Determining all exposures;

**p.** Selecting the lens for each show;

**q.** Selecting lenticular diffusion, if any, for each scene and sequence;

**r.** Viewing all video tape runs for quality control;

▼ **During POST-PRODUCTION:**

**s.** Supervising the colorizing during transfer to laser disc or video tape;

**t.** Otherwise carrying out the duties normally required of this classification;

**u.** Providing the exposure meters and hand tools normally employed in this craft.

**3. Considerations:**

   **a.** When one (1) or more of the above duties are required, use of a **Director of Photography—Video** is indicated.

   **b.** The **Director of Photography** is normally given adequate pre-production time to plan and prepare for the production work.

   **c.** The **Director of Photography** directs the technical work of the entire crew (first and second units) during the production process.

   **d.** It is highly recommended that the **Director of Photography** be included in pre-production consultation and in any location scouting trips in order to better insure optimum and efficient photographic utilization of the location site(s) and the set(s).

   **e.** It is also highly recommended that the **Director of Photography** be present at the tape-to-tape or tape-to-disk transfer sessions when image colorizing, resizing and/or repositioning is to take place.

## L. TECHNICAL DIRECTOR [SWITCHER]

   **1. Responsibilities:** The **Technical Director (TD) [aka: Switcher]** is in charge of the entire technical video production operation and the technical integrity thereof, is directly responsible to the **Director of Photography (DP)**, when used, for helping achieve the particular visual look desired by the **DP** during both rehearsal(s) and production taping, is directly responsible to the **Video Director** and follows the instructions of the **Video Director** regarding camera switching, fading, dissolving, wiping, chroma-keying, and other optical matte and applied visual effects which are applied during set-up, rehearsals and takes, is responsible for the production of a technically acceptable electronic picture image appearing on the production monitor(s) and on the video tape, and is in technical charge of the studio or location site, of the television chain, and of personnel operating such equipment during the production process.

   **2. Duties—all during the PRODUCTION Process:**

   **a.** Reading and annotating the script within the context of technical direction;

   **b.** Determining, ordering and supervising the assembly, warm-up, technical adjustment, operation and wrapping of the type and amount of video, audio and other technical equipment utilized;

   **c.** Issuing instructions to technical personnel during dress rehearsal and production recording;

   **d.** Switching, fading, dissolving and/or wiping from camera to camera, setting chroma-key and other visual matte and special effects during setup, rehearsals and takes;

   **e.** Supervising all panel controls, feeds, tie-ins and adjustments and supervising and being responsible for the technical performance of the entire assigned group of technicians engaged in setting up, aligning, registering, balancing, adjusting, operating and wrapping the video and audio components of the television chain, and supervising all other technical functions necessary in video production;

f. Determining and maintaining the quality standards for the television chain, both video and audio, in mood, special effects, perspective, etc;

g. During mixed-media production, working with the **Director of Photography** to help achieve optimum lighting standards for both the television chain and the resulting video tape recordings and for the simultaneously running motion picture camera film;

h. Utilizing the vector scope, wave form monitors and other instrumentation to assure optimum functioning of all components and an optimal visual result;

i. Otherwise carrying out the duties normally required of this classification;

j. Providing the hand tools normally employed in this craft.

3. **Considerations:** A **Technical Director** is used on all video productions and on those film productions utilizing a video chain in conjunction with motion picture camera equipment.

## M. LIGHTING DIRECTOR

1. **Responsibilities:** The **Lighting Director (LD)** is directly responsible to the **Technical Director**, and works in close cooperation with the **Video Controller**, except as noted in Category Criteria, above, for the placement, control and balance of that lighting in order to achieve an appropriate aesthetic effect on the foreground, midground, action and background areas of each scene as recorded on the electronic system.

2. **Duties:**

▼ **During PRE-PRODUCTION:**

a. Reading, analyzing and annotating the script within the context of the production lighting;

b. Preparing a lighting plot for the video production;

c. Determining the type and amount of lighting equipment, control accessories and electrical personnel required to handle the production;

d. Ordering such equipment;

▼ **During the PRODUCTION Process:**

e. Directing electrical lighting personnel in the setting up, rigging, placement, control, operation and wrapping of all lighting equipment;

f. Insuring that lighting personnel do not attempt work under any unsafe condition(s), as specified by the Building and Safety Code and fire laws, or in violation of any other safety regulation(s) and practice(s);

g. Supervising all exterior and interior lighting procedures;

h. Key-lighting interiors at appropriate foot-candle level and balancing with fill lighting of sufficient intensity to achieve optimum dramatic effect and electronic reproduction;

**i.** Balancing exterior light with applied fill light of sufficient intensity to bring the contrast ratio (especially the foreground-to-sky intensities) to an acceptable level for the electronic system;

**j.** Lighting interiors and exteriors to provide the system with a white reference area and a black reference area for optimum pictorial electronic adjustment;

**k.** Setting and operating the lighting control panel, if any, during rehearsal(s) and production taping;

**l.** Seeing that lamps are turned off when not required for photographic purposes and that all incandescent bulbs are periodically rotated in order to minimize burn-outs;

**m.** Otherwise carrying out the duties normally required of this classification;

**n.** Providing the exposure meter(s) and hand tools normally employed in this craft.

**3. Considerations:** A **Lighting Director** is used when lighting equipment is utilized on a video production.

## N. VIDEO CONTROLLER

**1. Responsibilities:** The **Video Controller (VC)** is directly responsible to the **Technical Director** for the preparation—warm-up, registering, balancing and adjustment—of the video control unit (VCU), consisting of the remote control panel (RCP) and the master control panel (MCP), the video camera(s), the video tape recorder(s) (VTR), the telecine chain and the character/image generator(s), and for the quality control of the video emission, maintaining optimum pictorial quality throughout the video chain during rehearsal(s) and production taping.

**2. Duties—during the PRODUCTION Process:**

**a.** Reading and annotating the script within the context of video control work;

**b.** Setting up, tying in, testing and adjusting the electronic feed of the video chain from each camera picture tube (cathode ray tube—CRT), if any, or charge-coupled device (CCD) to its monitor and to the video tape recorder and/or to the telecine chain and image generator, if any, for proper balance, registration, alignment and operation;

**c.** Supervising the setting up and wrapping of all video equipment;

**d.** Adjusting and maintaining optimum matching electronic alignment, registration, black and white level, contrast balance, color balance and mechanical and electronic focus of each camera CRT or CCD and its monitor in conjunction with the **Operator** of each camera;

**e.** Adjusting, balancing, registering and setting timing, pulse advance and flare compensation; maintaining optimum matching electronic contrast (pedestal control), brightness (iris control), quality and edge definition (image enhancement) of each camera picture tube or CCD and its monitor; and/or checking the functioning of automatic controls on equipment so fitted;

**f.** Adjusting and maintaining optimum matching electronic color balance (chroma—hue and saturation) of each camera CRT or CCD and its monitor, totally matching camera inputs to the VCU;

**g.** Monitoring and maintaining optimum technical quality of the electronic inputs and output during rehearsal(s) and taping by referring to the vector scopes and wave form monitors and monitoring and adjusting any of 32 immediate controls for color consistency (RGB), exposure (iris) and density (master black level), checking up to 18 points of registration per camera, also monitoring optical and electrical focus, encoder integrity and system timing, and making adjustments thereto, as required;

**h.** Checking the wave form monitor(s) and the vector scope(s) and advising the **Director of Photography**, if any, or the **Lighting Director** of the lighting values required for the optimum operation of the video production camera(s);

**i.** Supervising the breaking down and preparing of the television components for transportation, when necessary;

**j.** Otherwise carrying out the duties normally required of this classification;

**k.** Providing the hand tools normally employed in this craft.

**3. Considerations:** A **Video Controller** is used on those video productions where the **Technical Director** requires assistance in satisfactorily carrying out VCU setup and operating control duties.

## O. VIDEO CAMERA OPERATOR

**1. Responsibilities:** The **Video Camera Operator** is directly responsible to the **Technical Director**, or to the **Video Controller** during electronic setup and FAX, when the **TD** is not required, for maintaining the composition, focus and camera position and movement desired by the **Director**.

**2. Duties—all during the PRODUCTION Process:**

**a.** Reading and annotating the script within the context of camera operating;

**b.** Setting up the assigned camera on its mount and later wrapping it, or supervising these procedures, as required;

**c.** Plugging in co-axial cable to the camera and tying off such cable to the camera mount;

**d.** Placing the assigned lens on the assigned camera;

**e.** Placing the proper lens extender, filter(s) and/or diopter(s) in the optical system, as required;

**f.** Checking the optical system for cleanliness;

**g.** Checking and adjusting hydraulic pressure in the camera pedestal mount, when used;

**h.** Aligning and balancing the camera on the camera mount;

**i.** Verifying positive operation of pan, tilt, follow-focus and zoom lens movement mechanisms and adjusting the controls for appropriate positioning and sensitivity;

**j.** Verifying positive operation of the rolling, rising and falling movement(s) of the camera pedestal mount;

**k.** Operating—panning, tilting, focusing, setting lens position or zooming the variable focal length lens—and adjusting the camera and its pedestal at all times during FAX (facilities prep and check out time), camera rehearsals and production taping;

**l.** Wearing an intercom headset at all times that the assigned camera is required for FAX and for production operation;

**m.** Assisting the **Video Controller** in matching—registering and balancing—the assigned camera to the electronic system;

**n.** Framing and focusing the camera on registration and color chip charts under normal set or exterior lighting;

**o.** Mechanically and/or electronically adjusting back-focus of the camera picture tube;

**p.** Electronically adjusting coarse horizontal and vertical alignment of the camera viewfinding monitor and the brightness thereof, and adjusting the position of the monitor for convenient viewing;

**q.** Color balancing the camera by adjusting the primary color controls for the green, red and blue spectra on the assigned camera, under supervision of the **Video Controller**;

**r.** Assisting the **Prompter Operator** in installing electronic cueing apparatus on the video camera, and in removing it;

**s.** Preparing a shot reference card—noting camera location and lens height, the actor(s) or object(s) in frame, type of shot (LS, MS, CU), actor and camera position and movement—during technical and/or blocking rehearsal(s);

**t.** Having the camera focused and framed on the proper shot—actor(s) or object(s)—at the proper time;

**u.** Taking and conforming to all directions received from the **Director**, or the **Director**'s designee (normally the **Associate Director**), for lens size selection, framing, composition, camera floor position and movement and height, and zoom lens movement;

**v.** Handholding a light-weight, portable video camera, with or without special camera support mechanism, such as Steadicam¤, when such equipment and technique are used;

**w.** Otherwise carrying out the duties normally required of this classification;

**x.** Providing the hand tools normally employed in this craft.

**3. Considerations:** A **Video Camera Operator** is used to operate each video production camera which is utilized on a production.

## P. VIDEO TAPE OPERATOR

**1. Responsibilities:** The **Video Tape Operator (VTO)** is directly responsible to the **Technical Director**, during the production process, and to the **Video Tape Editor**, during the post-production on-line process, for properly and efficiently operating the video tape recorder (VTR) and/or the disc recorder (for slow-motion or stop-motion) in record or playback mode.

**2. Duties—all during the PRODUCTION Process:**

**a.** Setting up, tying in, adjusting, aligning, color balancing and operating the video tape recorder or video disc recorder (high speed for slow motion, or hold-frame for scanning) in conjunction with, and under the supervision of, the **Video Controller** or **TD**;

**b.** Cleaning the recording/playback head(s) of the assigned recorder(s);

**c.** Maintaining an adequate supply of raw stock—video tape and/or disc;

**d.** Threading the VTR and/or loading the video disc recorder;

**e.** Assisting the **Video Controller** in matching the assigned VTR or disc recorder to the electronic system;

**f.** Setting and adjusting the electronic frame/time/identification coding, as necessary;

**g.** Setting and adjusting the time counter read-out (hours:minutes:seconds:frames);

**h.** Setting timing devices used to activate the video recorders;

**i.** Logging the start and stop time read-out of each take and playing back any take requested by the **Technical Director** or **Video Tape Editor**, during production or post-production, respectively;

**j.** Performing tape-to-film, film-to-tape and tape-to-tape transfers in conjunction with the **Technical Director** and **Telecine Operator**;

**k.** Observing the off-the-tape VTR monitor for quality control of the recorded image during the recording process;

**l.** Reporting any observed reproduction imperfections (glitches) or equipment malfunctions to the **Technical Director**;

**m.** Informing the **Associate Director** of the amount of recording time remaining on the video tape roll or disc, as indicated by the electronic time-count read-out;

**n.** Identifying each recorded roll of video tape and/or each recorded video disc, as well as each container thereof, in conformance with the electronic frame coding information;

    **o.** Delivering the recorded video tape and/or video disc(s) to the Employer's representative at the end of each production or post-production session;

    **p.** Otherwise carrying out the duties normally required of this classification;

    **q.** Providing the hand tools normally employed in this craft.

**3. Considerations:** A **Video Tape Operator** is used on those video productions whereon the **Technical Director** requires assistance to satisfactorily operate a video tape or disc recorder on the video chain.

## Q. VIDEO UTILITY

**1. Responsibilities: Video Utility** personnel are directly responsible to the video technician to whom assigned by the **Technical Director** for the purpose of assisting that technician in the performance of his or her duties.

**2. Duties—all during the PRODUCTION Process:**

    **a.** Setting up, checking out (with the **Video Controller**) and striking assigned video equipment, including laying and wrapping video cable between the operations truck or control room and the cameras and monitors at the shooting site;

    **b.** Assisting in assigned operations during the FAX, rehearsal, production and post-production phases;

    **c.** Operating the assigned camera dolly or crane when a **Dolly**, **Crane** or **Boom Grip** is not used;

    **d.** Assisting the **Video Camera Operator** during complex pedestal moves;

    **e.** Pulling and dressing camera cable during rehearsals and takes, as assigned and as necessary;

    **f.** Assisting the **Video Camera Operator** during hand-held video camera shots;

    **g.** Bringing coffee, beverages or water to the various operating video technicians, as requested;

    **h.** Otherwise carrying out the duties normally required of this classification;

    **i.** Providing the hand tools normally employed in this craft.

**3. Considerations: Video Utility** personnel are used on video productions on which the video technicians require assistance in the performance of their duties.

## R. VIDEOGRAPHER

**1. Responsibilities:** The **Videographer** operates a video camera and sets minimal lighting, is directly responsible to the **Director**, or **Producer** for electronic news gathering (ENG) work, for effectively and efficiently operating the video camera and setting minimal lighting units, and is responsible for assisting the **Director** in capturing the visual images required, within the creative and budgetary latitude afforded, for optimum aesthetic visual effect.

**2. Duties:**

▼ **During PRE-PRODUCTION:**

a. Reading the script, storyboard or outline and annotating it regarding visual ideas, mood, lighting, special mechanical and/or optical/digital add-on effects and camera moves;

b. Scouting all locations and shooting sites, as required;

c. Consulting with the **Director, Art Director/Production Designer** and **Producer** regarding production values, and matériel and time requirements;

d. Selecting the camera, its accessories and associated equipment to be used;

e. Selecting the tape stock(s) to be used;

f. Determining the type, quality and quantity of lighting and grip equipment to be used;

g. Preparing comparative equipment and materials budgets, if requested;

h. Visually checking, and/or tape-testing, sets, settings, scenic art, set dressing, costumes, actors, hair, makeup, props, special effects and process components for photographic purposes;

▼ **During the PRODUCTION Process:**

i. Checking all functions on the camera for operational reliability—battery, cables, zoom lens and focusing functions, iris for automatic and manual modes, etc;

j. White-balancing the camera prior to shooting;

k. Working with the **Director** in the general lining up and matching of both action and screen direction, etc, of the shots;

l. Setting the camera positions, angles and moves with the **Director**;

m. Planning and supervising all production lighting—determining the position of key, fill, back and background lighting units, the lighting ratios, the color and/or degree of diffused quality, if any, of the light, etc;

n. Selecting the lens sizing for each shot;

o. Selecting lenticular diffusion, if any, for each shot;

p. Determining the composition during each shot— framing and following the action;

q. Determining all exposures;

r. Maintaining optimum photographic quality of the production;

s. Performing the functions and duties of a **Video Camera Operator** insofar as operating the particular camera and its various configurations are concerned [see **Section O**, above];

VIDEO

**▼ During POST-PRODUCTION:**

**t.** Viewing all shot footage for quality control;

**u.** Supervising the colorization, resizing and/or repositioning during the transfer to video tape or laser disk;

**v.** Otherwise carrying out the duties normally required of this classification;

**w.** Providing the exposure meters and hand tools normally employed in this craft.

**3. Considerations:**

**a.** When one (1) or more of the above duties are required, use of a **Videographer** is indicated.

**b.** The **Videographer** is normally given adequate pre-production time to plan and prepare for the production work.

**▼ Classifications Used for AUDIO Procedures ▼**

**S. AUDIO MIXER**

**1. Responsibilities:** The **Audio Mixer** is directly responsible to the **Technical Director**, during production, for picking up (and recording, when using double system sound) all production sound and special sound effects necessary, or to the **Video Tape Editor**, during post-production editing, for audio input re-recording, and maintaining such sound pick-up or input, respectively, at optimum level and quality at all times.

**2. Duties:**

**▼ During PRE-PRODUCTION:**

**a.** Reading, analyzing and annotating the script within the context of sound recording and pickup;

**b.** Selecting all audio mixing consoles, recorders, microphones, mounts, windscreens and related equipment to be used in the production, including the use of RF sound pick-up equipment;

**▼ During the PRODUCTION Process:**

**c.** Setting up, making pre-ops check and striking all audio equipment;

**d.** Operation of the mixing console (and of the recorder(s), when double system sound is being taken);

**e.** Loading and unloading tape in and from the double system audio recorder(s);

**f.** Patching the double system audio system and selecting appropriate sound filtering;

**g.** Riding sound input level(s) at all times for each microphone in use;

**h.** Switching/fading microphones in and out as necessary in order to avoid undesired sound pick-up or feedback;

**i.** Checking out each studio and location site for extraneous ambient noise and for characteristic sound quality prior to rehearsal and/or taping;

**j.** During rehearsal and production, riding gain and maintaining proper audio level and perspective for voice and sound effects;

**k.** Recording a presence track at each studio and location site used;

▼ **During PRODUCTION and POST-PRODUCTION:**

**l.** During post-production editing, doing simple re-recording, transferring and mixing of voice tracks while maintaining proper level and perspective;

**m.** Logging all takes during production and post-production;

**n.** Identifying (marking) and delivering to the **Producer** each recorded reel of audio tape;

**o.** Otherwise carrying out the duties normally required of this classification;

**p.** Providing the hand tools normally employed in this craft.

**3. Considerations:** An **Audio Mixer** is used on those video productions which utilize audio pick-up and recording thereof.

**T. AUDIO ASSISTANT**

**1. Responsibilities:** The **Audio Assistant** is directly responsible to the **Audio Mixer** for operating the microphone boom or fishpole or handling the shotgun or parabolic microphone, in order to pick up the desired voice, sound effects and/or music at the perspective desired by the **Audio Mixer**, giving special attention to the frame line limits given by the **Video Camera Operator**(s), thereby causing no microphone or boom or their shadows to appear within camera frame.

**2. Duties—all during the PRODUCTION Process:**

**a.** Reading the script and noting the performer(s) to be covered and their positions during each shot or scene;

**b.** Setting up, breaking down, and wrapping the microphone boom, fishpole and/or stand, the microphones, and associated equipment;

**c.** Assisting the **Audio Mixer** in attaching the proper microphone to the mic boom, fishpole or stand, or to the person of actors;

**d.** Assisting the **Costumer** in the placement of the RF microphone and its transmitter on the person of each performer using such equipment;

**e.** While operating the boom or fishpole, the shotgun or parabolic microphone, keeping the microphone placed and faced in the proper position at all times in order to achieve the acoustic results required for each sound take, and wearing earphones to facilitate this;

**f.** Working closely with the camera, lighting and grip crews to assure that the microphone will not appear in the shot or cast mic or boom shadows which will be photographed;

**g.** Assisting the **Audio Mixer** in setting up and testing RF transmitting equipment;

**h.** Voice slating wild sound takes;

**i.** Assisting the **Audio Mixer** in the performance of duties;

**j.** Otherwise carrying out the duties normally required of this classification;

**k.** Providing the hand tools normally employed in this craft.

3. **Considerations:** An **Audio Assistant** is used on any set or location where a fishpole or microphone boom is used, or when a shotgun or parabolic microphone is used, or when the **Audio Mixer** requires assistance in setting up, installing or affixing audio recording equipment to performers or mounts.

## U. PUBLIC ADDRESS OPERATOR

1. **Responsibilities:** The **Public Address Operator (PA)** is directly responsible to the **Audio Mixer** for setting and maintaining appropriate level(s) of the public address system when used in audience participation or other type productions requiring public address or playback facilities.

2. **Duties—all during the PRODUCTION Process:**

**a.** Reading and annotating the script or show outline within the context of public address operation;

**b.** Setting up, operating and striking all public address and playback equipment;

**c.** Opening and closing any microphone input to the PA console in order to control desired sound pick-up and to avoid feedback or undesired sound input;

**d.** From a position in, or in close proximity to, the audience area or to where playback or public address procedures are required, riding audio gain at optimum level for each microphone to achieve sound clarity and to avoid feedback;

**e.** When lip synchronous playback procedures are required, starting playback at proper start mark, at proper speed, and on **Director**'s signal, riding audio gain for optimum playback clarity and effect;

**f.** Otherwise carrying out the duties normally required of this classification;

**g.** Providing the hand tools normally employed in this craft.

3. **Considerations:** A **Public Address Operator** is used on those video productions which utilize public address and/or playback procedures and equipment.

## V. AUDIO UTILITY

1. **Responsibilities:** **Audio Utility** personnel are directly responsible to the audio technician to whom assigned by the **Technical Director** for assisting such technician in the performance of duties.

**2. Duties—all during the PRODUCTION Process:**

    **a.** Setting up, checking out (with the **Audio Mixer**) and striking assigned audio equipment, including running and wrapping audio cable between the operations truck or control room and the microphones at the shooting site;

    **b.** Assisting in assigned operations during the FAX, rehearsal, production and post-production phases;

    **c.** Moving the microphone boom perambulator, during and between shots, as necessary;

    **d.** Pulling and dressing audio cable during rehearsals and takes, as assigned and as necessary;

    **e.** Assisting the **Audio Assistant** by handing or attaching a microphone to each performer, as necessary, and collecting or removing it from each person when the performance has been completed;

    **f.** Making adjustments in the position of RF receiver-transmitter(s) at the direction of the **Audio Mixer**;

    **g.** Bringing coffee, beverages or water to the various operating audio technicians, as requested;

    **h.** Otherwise carrying out the duties normally required of this classification;

    **i.** Providing the hand tools normally employed in this craft.

**3. Considerations: Audio Utility** personnel are used on video productions on which the audio technicians require assistance in the performance of their duties.

▼ **Classifications Used for POST & EDITORIAL Procedures** ▼

**W. VIDEO COLORIST**

**1. Responsibilities:** The **Video Colorist** is a **Telecine Operator** who specializes in the transfer of film images to video tape and is directly responsible to the Supervisor of the post-production facility, is responsive to the client, and is responsible for efficiently and effectively analyzing and appraising the image quality of the material to be transferred in order to efficiently achieve maximum visual quality thereof.

**2. Duties—all during POST-PRODUCTION:**

    **a.** Seeing that the **Telecine Operator** has the film stock—negative or positive—ready to load in the telecine scanner for transfer to video tape and that a roll of video tape or tape cassette is in place to record the transfer;

    **b.** Referring to the camera reports and/or written instructions of the **Director of Photography** regarding desired image density, color rendition, special colorization, resizing and/or repositioning required, and how "problem shots" are to be handled during the telecine transfer;

    **c.** Checking that picture and sound track are put in timecode sync and interlocked;

    **d.** Running and examining the show take-by-take and scene-by-scene to determine whether problems exist which need attending to;

    **e.** Checking colorizing input to ensure optimum quality and consistency;

    **f.** Checking resizing and repositioning input to ensure optimum placement and consistency with other camera coverage;

    **g.** Entering all modifications, such as overall RGB corrections, or image resizing and/or repositioning, into the computer;

    **h.** Rerunning the take to check the modification inputs and effect on the images;

    **i.** If everything checks out, transferring the take to tape;

    **j.** Putting the next take in sync and continuing the process;

    **k.** Otherwise carrying out the duties normally required of this classification;

    **l.** Providing the hand tools normally employed in this craft;

**3. Considerations:** A **Video Colorist** is used when adjustments in color, density, resizing or repositioning of images are required during film-to-tape, tape-to-tape, or tape-to-film transfer.

## X. TELECINE OPERATOR

**1. Responsibility:** The **Telecine Operator (TO)** is directly responsible to the **Technical Director** during production, or to the **Video Colorist** during film-to-tape or tape-to-film transfer, for setting up the visual material in the proper order in the multiplex unit and/or film projector and/or flying-spot scanner or similar equipment for the operation thereof.

**2. Duties—during PRODUCTION or POST-PRODUCTION:**

    **a.** Cleaning and aligning the motion picture and slide projectors, slide drum, optical system and all slides, film and other display material placed in the multiplex unit or projector(s) for the production or post-production process;

    **b.** Tying in, adjusting, aligning and color balancing the video multiplex camera to the electronic video system, under supervision of the **Video Controller**;

    **c.** When operating the telecine during a taping, reading and annotating the script within the context of telecine operation;

    **d.** When operating the telecine during a transfer session, receiving and placing in order the required materials to be transferred;

    **e.** Placing required slide transparencies in the proper designated order in the slide drum;

    **f.** Placing required slide transparencies in the proper order in the multiplex unit;

    **g.** Threading the film projector(s) used, placing the film at the proper start mark;

VIDEO

**h.** Checking the projector(s) and multiplex unit for proper operation—projector picture lamp, sound track exciter lamp (if an optical track) or magnetic sound pickup head (if a magnetic track) and the movement of the slide drum, projector, etc—prior to on-line production or post-production use;

**i.** Running a time check of the visual material, if required;

**j.** Returning the visual display material after its use;

**k.** Performing film-to-tape and tape-to-film transfers in conjunction with the **Technical Director** and **Video Tape Operator**(s);

**l.** During tape-to-film or film-to-tape transfers:

**(1)** Setting up, tying in, adjusting, aligning, focusing, registering, color balancing and operating the film printer (tape-to-film) or the film projector and flying spot scanner, laser scanner or similar device, and the three-tube (three-color—RGB) prismatic image pick-up, in conjunction with the **Video Tape Operator**, under the supervision of the **TD** (film-to-tape) or **Video Colorist**;

**(2)** Setting the aspect ratio matte and cleaning the film gate and lens of the film printer (tape-to-film) and cleaning the film material prior to the copying process (film-to-tape);

**(3)** Loading and unloading the film printer magazines (tape-to-film);

**(4)** Threading and unthreading film in the film printer (tape-to-film) or in the film projector (film-to-tape);

**(5)** Keeping accurate film printer (tape-to-film) reports or video tape transfer logs (film-to-tape);

**(6)** Canning exposed film and unexposed short ends and marking proper identification on each can of exposed film prepared for shipment to the film lab for processing;

**m.** Otherwise carrying out the duties normally required of this classification;

**n.** Providing the hand tools normally employed in this craft.

**3. Considerations:** A **Telecine Operator** is used when multiplex equipment, or a slide and/or motion picture projector is utilized on a video production or post-production or when film-to-tape or tape-to-film transfer require telecine operation.

## Y. CHYRON OPERATOR

**1. Responsibilities:** The **Chyron Operator** is directly responsible to the **Technical Director** during production, and to the **Video Tape Editor** during on-line re-recording or transfer editing, otherwise to the Employer, for all character, animation or image generation utilizing computers and/or video synthesis technique and in so doing, maintaining optimum desired aesthetic quality of the specially electronically generated and/or enhanced characters, images and/or effects.

VIDEO

**2. Duties—during PRODUCTION or POST-PRODUCTION:**

a. Reading and annotating the script within the context of electronically generated matting and image input;

b. Receiving from the **Producer** or **Production Associate** instructions on what to prepare, position, and matte;

c. Informing the **TD** regarding position in frame of the matte content;

d. Having a thorough knowledge of fonts and font styles;

e. Being a fast and accurate typist and excellent in spelling and grammar;

f. Setting up, adjusting and operating all image input of computerized special effects and video synthesizer character, animation or image generating equipment;

g. On a special effects system, altering: The horizontal or vertical aspect ratio; the original shape of an object; the size and/or position of an object; the coloring, definition, perspective and/or movement of an imaged object/character—recorded, animated or live;

h. Creating special visual effects by operating and/or manipulating: A computer generated analog/digital recording system; a standard TV video control chain; a video character, graphics or animation generator; an instrument or chain which produces visual imagery of any type;

i. Otherwise carrying out the duties normally required of this classification;

j. Providing the hand tools normally employed in this craft.

**3. Considerations:** A **Chyron Operator** is used when character/image generating equipment of whatever type is utilized.

## Z. VIDEO TAPE EDITOR

**1. Responsibilities:** The **Video Tape Editor** is directly responsible to the **Director**, or to the assigned **Associate Director**, or to the **Producer** or the designee thereof, for efficiently achieving optimum selection, positioning and/or combination of the video and audio production elements through the process of transfer editing in order to achieve the final re-recorded visual and audial effect desired by the **Director**, or assigned supervisor.

**2. Duties—all during POST-PRODUCTION:**

a. Reading, analyzing and annotating the shooting script within an editorial context and referring to it for pace, rhythm and flow;

b. Working with the produced material from a count sheet (done in hours:minutes:seconds:frames) supplied by the **Director** or **Producer**;

c. Supervising all patching of the control system as accomplished by the **Video Maintenance Engineer**;

d. Assembling and logging the production elements for editing, using the electronic frame code if applicable and available;

VIDEO

**e.** Transferring production elements to video tape, video laser disc and/or other digital medium, and the film insert elements to video tape, as necessary;

**f.** Applying electronic frame coding to those elements, as necessary;

**g.** Preparing a computerized punch tape or software program from the elements log for use in automatic computerized on-line editing, using an Avid or comparable platform;

**h.** Doing manual on- or off-line editing—switching, fading, dissolving, wiping, irising, supers, etc—as necessary;

**i.** Rough editing 3/4″ or 1″ video tape off-line onto 2″ quad tape, video cassette and/or laser disc or other recording medium, as necessary;

**j.** Selecting, transferring, positioning, combining and recombining all video tape production elements into a finalized product;

**k.** Physically splicing and/or repairing video tape;

**l.** Marking proper identification on the final edited work and returning it and all original elements to the **Producer**'s designee;

**m.** Otherwise carrying out the duties normally required of this classification;

**n.** Providing the hand tools normally employed in this craft.

### 3. Considerations:

**a.** During off-line video tape editing, using reel-to-reel or video cassette 1″, 3/4″, 1/2″, 8mm or 1/4″ helical tape recorder(s), or such component composite tape formats as Beta SP, digital S, D1–D9 for video and DA88 for audio, and/or laser discs, the **Video Tape Editor** normally requires no assistance.

**b.** During on-line editing or re-recording, using the Avid system with VTRs and disc players, quad (2″) tape VTRs, the **Video Tape Editor** functions as a **Technical Director** over other functioning technical operators, including the **Video Tape Operator**, the **Telecine Operator** and the **Chyron Operator**.

**c.** A **Video Tape Editor** is used when video tape requires transfer editing, sweetening, or other electronic editing procedures.

#### ▼ Classification Used for MAINTENANCE Prodecures ▼

## AA. VIDEO MAINTENANCE ENGINEER

**1. Responsibilities:** The **Video Maintenance Engineer** is directly responsible to the Employer, and to the **Technical Director** during set-up, FAX and production phases of operations, for maintaining all electronic and mechanical equipment associated with the video chain (including audio) at optimum operating standards.

VIDEO

**2. Duties:—during PRE-PRODUCTION, PRODUCTION and POST-PRODUCTION:**

   **a.** Supervising the physical setting up, wrapping and transporting of all electronic video and audio equipment;

   **b.** Patching all video and audio equipment into line, as required by production necessity and optimum operation thereof;

   **c.** Repairing, adjusting, aligning, modifying, cleaning, testing and maintaining all electronic and mechanical equipment, cameras, projectors, meters, recorders and other equipment associated with the video and audio chain(s);

   **d.** Checking and replacing tubes, resistors, transistors, transformers, condensers, diodes and the like, as necessary;

   **e.** Preparing and repairing all cables, power cords and wiring used;

   **f.** Inventorying the supply of spare parts and repair materials and preparing orders for parts, materials, tools and instruments;

   **g.** Making periodic frequency checks of the electronic equipment and troubleshooting, as necessary;

   **h.** Aligning all reproduction and recording heads on all recording equipment;

   **i.** Otherwise carrying out the duties normally required of this classification;

   **j.** Providing the hand tools normally employed in this craft.

**3. Considerations:**

   **a.** A **Video Maintenance Engineer** repairs and maintains all components related to the video chain (including audio) and provides a volt/ohm/ammeter and distortion meter plus the hand tools normally employed in this craft, unless on staff, in which case the Company provides such test equipment and tools.

   **b.** A **Video Maintenance Engineer** is used on each video production in order to maintain optimum performance of the electronic video and audio systems and the components thereof.

## NOTES

# FAST FINDER FOR THE APPENDICES

## SUGGESTED CATEGORIES FOR SOME SKILLS IN THE CAREER GUIDE

**With this skill/interest** — try these categories:

**agility** — camera or construction
**architecture** — art
**business administration** — producing or production management
**camera handling** — camera or video
**camera maintenance** — camera or video
**carpentry** — grip
**carrying** — camera, construction or grip
**chemistry** — film lab
**climbing** — camera, grip or lighting
**computer skills** — computer graphics or editing
**construction** — construction or grip
**coordination** — camera, sound or video
**detailing** — art, construction or costuming
**drawing** — computer graphics
**electrical** — construction or lighting
**electronic engineering** — video
**film editing** — directing or editing
**firearms** — property or special effects
**history** — art or costuming
**installation** — construction, grip or lighting
**lifting** — camera, construction, grip or lighting
**lighting design** — camera, computer graphics or lighting
**manipulating things** — art, grip or lighting
**manipulating time & space** — directing or editing
**mechanical ability** — special effects
**model making** — computer graphics, construction or property
**organizational skills** — producing, production management, property, set decoration, special effects, transportation or wardrobe
**sewing** — costuming
**structural design** — computer graphics
**structural engineering** — grip
**timing** — directing or editing
**visual composition** — art, camera or computer graphics
**writing** — directing or editing

# A CAREER GUIDE TO THE CRAFTS

Each craft in the cinematic chain has its specialized details which must be learned before competence can be attained. This section will not deal with each craft individually, but will focus on the knowledge and skills required of each Category Head and, in some cases, essential assistants, followed by an appraisal of the needed elements—physicality, skills, knowledge, education/training and experience—which will best prepare one for each particular category of work covered in this handbook. In addition, the Union(s) representing personnel in each craft category involved in major studio, broadcast and independent production is noted.

First, one enters the craft as an apprentice to learn, as an assistant, from master craftspeople. As one practices and gains experience in the chosen craft, one also moves up the ladder of responsibility, which involves setting the example and leading the craft category personnel in their contribution to the collaborative effort with other crafts.

In each craft category, as a person moves to ever higher positions of responsibility, interpersonal relations become increasingly important and management skills become essential. Understanding and executing job responsibilities and duties are essential in the highly collaborative cinematic production procedures.

**CAREER GUIDE**

## ART

**Production Designer**, the top job in the Art Category, requires a thorough and practical knowledge of set design, construction and decoration, with an understanding of architectural principles and history. Managerial and liaison-type skills are necessary.

**Physical requirements:** minimal.

**Skills needed:** art, design, drawing, illustrating, structural detailing, composition.

**Knowledge needed:** art tools, terminology and techniques; art matériel; techniques for preparation and application; craft responsibilities and duties.

**Education/Training:** art major; architecture; history; performing arts.

**Experience:** sketching; illustrating; theatrical design; stagecraft; working for an in-house film/video production facility.

**Union representation:** IATSE.

---

## CAMERA

**Director of Photography**, the top job in the Camera Category, requires a thorough and practical knowledge of motion picture film and film processing, cameras, optics, lenses, filters, lighting and the equipment used while capturing the imagery on film or tape in accord with the Director's visual concept. As leader of the technical production crew, the DP's managerial skills are important. The **Camera Operator** needs the skill and hand-eye-body coordination to frame and follow the assigned subject matter. The **First Assistant Camera Operator** must know the equipment, get it assembled and checked, operate the several variable settings on the camera as necessary—mainly focus and sizing—carefully coordinating the setting adjustments with camera and subject matter movement.

**Physical requirements:** extensive—lifting, carrying, climbing, agility, coordination.

**Skills needed:** photography, optics, lighting, composition.

**Knowledge needed:** camera tools, terminology and techniques; photographic processes; optics; camera mechanics; craft responsibilities and duties.

**Education/Training:** film school; visual and performing arts.

**Experience:** camera maintenance; camera handling—film and/or video; film and/or video production; cinematography or videography; working for an in-house film/video production facility.

**Union representation:** IATSE.

---

## COMPUTER GRAPHICS

**Visual Effects Supervisor**, the top job in the Computer Graphics Category, requires a thorough and practical knowledge of computer graphics programs and the work platforms on which these programs are run, along with the animation, matting and morphing techniques used to create the visual effects. Managerial skills are important.

**Physical requirements:** minimal.

**Skills needed:** perceptual; computer literacy; computer graphics, modeling, art, animation; lighting, graphic and structural design; masking, matting and painting; compositing.

**Knowledge needed:** computer graphics tools, terminology and techniques; animation; graphics design; craft responsibilities and duties.

**Education/Training:** drawing; animation; computer science; digital image creation—still and in motion.

**Experience:** freehand and computer drawing and animation.

**Union representation:** IATSE.

## CONSTRUCTION

**Construction Coordinator**, the top job in the Construction Category, requires a thorough knowledge of all aspects of set, model, miniature, action prop and special effects preparation and construction. Managerial skills are important.

**Physical requirements:** extensive—lifting, moving, carrying, climbing, manipulating.

**Skills needed:** organizational; carpentry; wood and metal mill work; electrical; plumbing; construction; finishing; painting; installation of elements.

**Knowledge needed:** construction tools, terminology and techniques; craft responsibilities and duties.

**Education/Training:** tech/trade school; woodshop; handcrafts; model making; community or college theatre arts, film or video production.

**Experience:** handcrafts; building trades—construction, remodeling; community or college theatre arts, film or video production.

**Union representation:** IATSE.

## COSTUMING

Although **Costume Designer** is the top job in creating fabricated costuming for a production, the **Costume Supervisor** is the top job in the Costuming Category, seeing that the costuming—garments and accessories—accurately reflects the period and that all costuming is complete, camera-ready, and is properly fitted to each performer.

**Physical requirements:** minimal.

**Skills needed:** costume design and fabrication; working with fabrics, color, accessories, jewelry, footwear, headwear; detailing, aging and teching costume items.

**Knowledge needed:** costuming tools, terminology and techniques; history of dress, fashions and style; craft responsibilities and duties.

**Education/Training:** dressmaking; tailoring.

**Experience:** community or college theatre costuming and wardrobe; dressmaking; working for an in-house film/video production facility.

**Union representation:** IATSE.

## DIRECTING

**Director**, the top job in the motion picture production process, is the leader of the movie-making process from pre-production through the production and post-production phases—from the planning through the finalizing processes of editing and dubbing the sound tracks. Managerial skills are important. The **Assistant Director** is the Director's principal assistant and is the on-the-set expediter. The **Script Supervisor** is the Director's detail person, keeping the shooting script current in all respects.

**Physical requirements:** minimal.

**Skills needed:** dramaturgy; arranging and manipulating cinematic structure; cinematic production process; acting/performing; manipulating time and space; writing; film editing; lenses and perspective.

**Knowledge needed:** directorial terminology and techniques; broad and general; story development techniques; craft responsibilities and duties.

**Education/Training:** cinema major; drama; directing; writing; acting; film editing.

**Experience:** community or college theatre, film or television; working for an in-house film/video production facility.

**Union representation:** DGA.

## EDITING

**Picture Editor**, the top job in the Editing Category, is the person the **Director** works with to put the motion picture together shot-by-shot, scene-by-scene, sequence-by-sequence, after which the sound elements are developed and placed in synchronization with the picture to comprise the finished product.

**Physical requirements:** minimal.

**Skills needed:** linear film editing; computerized non-linear editing; dramaturgy; cinematic structure; rhythm, pacing and timing; manipulating time and space; understanding acting/performing techniques and movement; writing; film editing; lenses and perspective.

**Knowledge needed:** editing tools, terminology and techniques; linear and non-linear computerized editing; craft responsibilities and duties.

**Education/Training:** cinema major; drama; directing; writing; acting; film editing.

**Experience:** linear and non-linear editing; working for an in-house film/video production facility.

**Union representation:** IATSE.

## FILM LAB

**Laboratory Manager**, the lead job in the Film Laboratory Category, is the one responsible for seeing that laboratory processes run effectively and efficiently while protecting the condition of the precious camera original entrusted to the lab's care. Managerial skills are necessary.

**Physical requirements:** minimal.

**Skills needed:** film processing procedures—chemistry, time and temperature standards—operational procedures, film assembly, quality control.

**Knowledge needed:** film lab tools, terminology and techniques; craft responsibilities and duties.

**Education/Training:** cinema major; film preparation and processing.

**Experience:** still film preparation and processing; motion picture film preparation and processing.

**Union representation:** IATSE.

## GRIP

**Key Grip**, the key job in the Grip Category, is the classification that is responsible for controlling and shaping light coverage, laying and leveling dolly track, operating cranes, dollies and jib arms, constructing scaffolding and supports for cameras, lighting and special effects, and moving and placing set pieces.

**Physical requirements:** extensive—lifting, moving, carrying, climbing, manipulating.

**Skills needed:** construction; installation; knowledge of the grip equipment and nomenclature used.

**Knowledge needed:** grip tools, terminology and techniques; craft responsibilities and duties.

**Education/Training:** carpentry; structural engineering.

**Experience:** carpentry; structural engineering; film or video production; working for an in-house film/video production facility.

**Union representation:** IATSE.

## LIGHTING

**Gaffer**, the key job in the Lighting Category, is the classification responsible for seeing that lighting units are put in place to light the areas and objects in those areas as specified by the **Director of Photography**.

**Physical requirements:** extensive—lifting, moving, carrying, climbing, manipulating.

CAREER GUIDE

**Skills needed:** electrical; installation; knowledge of the capability of production lighting units and the nomenclature used.

**Knowledge needed:** lighting tools, terminology and techniques; electricity and lighting; craft responsibilities and duties.

**Education/Training:** cinema or drama major; working for an in-house film/video production facility.

**Experience:** film or video production; community or college theatre; working for an in-house film/video production facility.

**Union representation:** IATSE and IBEW (Generator Operator only).

## MAKEUP

**Key Makeup Artist**, the lead job in the Makeup Category, sees that all performers are properly made up for photographic purposes.

**Physical requirements:** minimal.

**Skills needed:** skillful use of matériel in applying makeup appropriately, safely and seamlessly.

**Knowledge needed:** makeup tools, terminology and techniques; knowing the matériel used and how to apply it properly; craft responsibilities and duties.

**Education/Training:** cinema or drama major; cosmetology; makeup in theater and performing arts.

**Experience:** working in small theatre, amateur film or video productions; working for an in-house film/video production facility.

**Union representation:** IATSE.

## PRODUCING

**Producer**, the essential position, is the person who gathers all the ingredients and gets the project started, progressing, finished and presented to the public.

**Physical requirements:** minimal.

**Skills needed:** Managerial, business administrative and organizational.

**Knowledge needed:** producing terminology and techniques; craft responsibilities and duties; a thorough understanding of each phase of filmmaking from concept through marketing.

**Education/Training:** film/video major; business administration minor; working for or as an independent producer.

**Experience:** film/video production management.

**Union representation:** none.

## PRODUCTION MANAGEMENT

**Production Manager**, the head job in dealing with the nitty-gritty, day-to-day details of running a production and keeping it on schedule and under budget.

**Physical requirements:** minimal.

**Skills needed:** managerial and business administration.

**Knowledge needed:** production management terminology and techniques; craft responsibilities and duties.

**Education/Training:** film/video major; business administration minor; working for or as an independent producer.

**Experience:** film/video production management.

**Union representation:** DGA.

## PROPERTY

**Property Master**, the head job in the Property Department, is responsible for all company property used in a production, including the sets and settings, and the items of dressing and props which decorate those performing areas.

**Physical requirements:** moderate.

**Skills needed:** being highly organized; knowing where to find any requested item—fast.

**Knowledge needed:** property terminology and techniques; care of props, firearms and ammunition.

**Education/Training:** working in a prop rental facility.

**Experience:** community or college theatre, film or video production; working for an in-house film/video production facility.

**Union representation:** IATSE.

## SET DECORATING

**Set Decorator**, the lead job in the Set Decorating Category, is responsible for acquiring items of set dressing and seeing that each set and setting is dressed with an appropriate type and number of set dressing items.

**Physical requirements:** moderate.

**Skills needed:** knowing where to find needed items of set dressing.

**Knowledge needed:** set decorating terminology and techniques; craft responsibilities and duties.

**Education/Training:** working on community or college theatre arts, film or video productions or for an in-house film/video production facility.

**Experience:** community or college theatre, film or video production; working for an in-house film/video production facility.

**Union representation:** IATSE.

---

## SOUND—Post-Production

**Key Re-recording Mixer**, the lead job in the Post-Production Section of the Sound Category, is responsible for seeing that all sound elements are present and in place for each dubbing session.

**Physical requirements:** minimal.

**Skills needed:** an understanding of audio principles and techniques used to balance, boost, clarify, combine and perspectively place the various sound elements.

**Knowledge needed:** sound re-recording tools, terminology and techniques; craft responsibilities and duties; principles of sound re-recording—mixing and combining same type and diverse types of sound tracks.

**Education/Training:** film or video major; sound engineering; college film/video production.

**Experience:** sound transfer; sound recording; sound re-recording.

**Union representation:** IATSE.

---

## SOUND—Production

**Production Mixer**, the head job in the Production Sound Section of the Sound Category, is responsible for seeing that all production dialogue is captured with the highest quality possible. The **Boom Operator** is the Production Mixer's principal assistant whose job it is to operate fishpoles and mic booms, accurately placing and facing the attached microphone in order to obtain the clearest and cleanest dialogue sound possible from the performers.

**Physical requirements:** moderate.

**Skills needed:** an understanding of audio principles and techniques used to capture, balance, boost and clarify or minimize or eliminate selected production sound elements; a good memory for lines delivered by each performer; good hand-eye-body coordination.

**Knowledge needed:** production sound tools, terminology and techniques; craft responsibilities and duties; capabilities of various types of microphones; principles of sound reproduction—mixing and recording techniques.

**Education/Training:** film or video major; sound engineering; college film/video production.

**Experience:** working for an in-house film/video production facility.

**Union representation:** IATSE, IBEW and NABET.

## SPECIAL EFFECTS

**Special Effects Coordinator**, the lead job in the Special Effects Category, sees that all special effects elements are scheduled and prepared on schedule.

**Physical requirements:** varies—moderate to extensive.

**Skills needed:** organizational; handling explosives, pyrotechnics, fire; mechanical ability to construct and operate mechanical and wire gags; enhanced sense of timing.

**Knowledge needed:** special effects tools, terminology and techniques; craft responsibilities and duties.

**Education/Training:** apprenticeship to a licensed powder expert.

**Experience:** work in a propmaking shop.

**Union representation:** IATSE.

## TRANSPORTATION

**Transportation Coordinator**, the lead job in the Transportation Category, sees that appropriate vehicles and Drivers are ordered and assigned to production categories requiring logistical support.

**Physical requirements:** moderate.

**Skills needed:** organizational; driving passengers and rigs.

**Knowledge needed:** transportation tools, terminology and techniques; logistics; craft responsibilities and duties.

**Education/Training:** driving various type vehicles—autos, trucks, rigs.

**Experience:** driving various type vehicles—autos, trucks, rigs, insert cars, cranes.

**Union representation:** IBT.

## VIDEO

**Video Director**, head job in the creative aspect of the Video Category, **Director of Photography—Video**, lead job in the camera and lighting aspect, and **Technical Director**, key job in the electronic aspects, are principally responsible for the making the technical aspects of a video production viable. The **Video Camera Operator** needs the skill and hand-eye-body coordination to frame, focus, size, ped in out left right up or down while following the assigned subject matter.

**Physical requirements:** minimal to moderate.

**Skills needed:** electronic engineering; hand-eye-body coordination.

**Knowledge needed:** video tools, terminology and techniques; craft responsibilities and duties.

**Education/Training:** video major in tech school or college.

**Experience:** camera maintenance; camera handling—film and/or video; film and/or video production; cinematography or videography; working for an in-house film/video production facility.

**Union representation:** IATSE, IBEW and NABET.

---

# WARDROBE

**Key Wardrobe,** the lead job in the Wardrobe Category, sees that all items of wardrobe are on set, labeled and ready for the performers to wear.

**Physical requirements:** minimal.

**Skills needed:** organizational; attention to details.

**Knowledge needed:** wardrobe tools, terminology and techniques; craft responsibilities and duties.

**Education/Training:** working in a wardrobe rental facility.

**Experience:** college or community theatre; working for an in-house film/video production facility.

**Union representation:** IATSE.

APPENDIX 2

# ANIMATION CATEGORY CLASSIFICATIONS

The importance of animation to the art and craft of cinematic processes cannot be minimized. Its terminology and techniques are being applied in the digital realm of computer graphics work.

The craft of animation requires many skills to bring line drawing and rendering of two-dimensional figures to life. There can be as many as fifty specialized craftspeople working on various aspects of an animated production. The thirty classifications listed below are the principal crafts involved in the animation process.

It was felt that the principal animation classifications should be listed for convenient referral by the reader. Because of space limitations, the responsibilities and duties of the animation classifications will not be detailed in this edition of the handbook.

**A. Category Classifictions:** There are thirty (30) classifications in the Animation Category:

[NOTE: There can be as many as fifty-two (52) classifications under four (4) general headings:
1. CREATIVE = Layout & Design
2. RENDERING = Animation & Background
3. TECHNICIANS & CHECKERS
4. PAINT & XEROX = Digital Manipulation]

| | |
|---|---|
| 1. Animator | 16. Ink Checker |
| 2. Assistant Animator | 17. Special Effects |
| 3. Background Artist | 18. Color Modelist |
| 4. Layout Artist | 19. Painter/Opaquer |
| 5. Model Designer | 20. Xerox Processor |
| 6. Animation Story Person | 21. Xerox Checker |
| 7. Breakdown | 22. Animation Stock Librarian |
| 8. Inbetweener | 23. Production Final Checker/Mark-Up |
| 9. Blue Sketch Artist | 24. Paint Checker |
| 10. Story Sketch Artist | 25. Picture Set-Up |
| 11. Assistant Director | 26. Scan Checker |
| 12. Sheet Timer | 27. Cel Service |
| 13. Scene Planner | 28. Mix and Match |
| 14. Animation Checker | 29. Paint Technician |
| 15. Inker | 30. Letter Artist |

# PROFESSIONAL SOCIETIES & ASSOCIATIONS

Academy of Motion Picture Arts and Sciences (AMPAS)

Academy of Television Arts and Sciences (ATAS)

American Cinema Editors (ACE)

American Society of Cinematographers (ASC)

American Society of Lighting Designers (ASLD)

Association of Austrian Cinematographers (AAC)

Association of French Cinematographers (AFC)

Association of Independent Commercial Producerss (AICP)

Association of Italian Cinematographers (AIC)

Association of Motion Picture and Television Producers (AMPTP)

Australian Cinematographers Society (ACS)

Belgian Society of Cinematographers (SBS)

British Society of Cinematographers (BSC)

Canadian Society of Cinematographers (CSC)

Casting Society of America (CSA)

Danish Society of Cinematographers (DFF)

Dutch Society of Cinematographers (DSC)

German Society of Cinematographers (Bundesverband Kamera e.V. —BVK)

Hong Kong Society of Cinematographers (HKSC)

Hungarian Society of Cinematographers (HSC)

IMAGO

Russian Society of Cinematographers (RSC)

Slovenian Society of Cinematographers (SLO)

Swiss Cinematographers Society (SCS)

Society of Cinematographers in Estonia (EST)

Society of Cinematographers in Finland (FST)

Society of Cinematographers in Iceland (ICE)

Society of Cinematographers in Norway (SCN)

Society of Motion Picture and Television Engineers (SMPTE)

Society of Motion Picture Still Photographers (SMPSP)

Society of Operating Cameramen (SOC)

South African Society of Cinematographers (SASC)

Swedish Society of Cinematographers (FSF)

# Appendix 4

# GUILDS & UNIONS

American Federation of Television and Radio Actors (AFTRA)

American Federation of Labor (AFL)

American Guild of Variety Artists (AGVA)

Communication Workers of America (CWA)

Congress of Industrial Organizations (CIO)

Canadian Labour Congress (CLC)

Directors Guild of America (DGA)

International Alliance of Theatrical Stage Employees (IATSE)

International Cinematographers Guild (ICG)

International Brotherhood of Electrical Workers (IBEW)

International Brotherhood of Teamsters (IBT)

National Association of Broadcast Employees and Technicians (NABET)

Producers Guild of America (PGA)

Screen Actors Guild (SAG)

Writers Guild of America (WGA)

# GLOSSARY

This is a working glossary, one designed to be optimally useful to those wanting quick access to the meaning of common terms used by craftspeople in each of the various craft categories covered by this handbook.

## FAST FINDER FOR THE GLOSSARY

For the sake of convenience, the glossary has been divided into three parts. In **Part 1—Category Definitions**, each of the twenty-one craft categories in the book has been given its own section devoted to terms generic to, and commonly used by personnel in, that craft. **Part 2—General Definitions** contains those terms in general usage by more than one craft. **Part 3—Operational Definitions** deals with the various types of production and cinematography as well as set dressing and props, all of which are defined in greater detail.

## 1. CATEGORY DEFINITIONS

### ART

**Art Director**—one who is responsible for and coordinates the artistic consistency and integrity of a cinematic product

**board**—(See storyboard)

**Costume Designer**—one who designs the costumes and accessories within the parameters set by the Art Director/ Production Designer

**design elements**—sets, settings, scenic backings and drops, set dressing, costumes, makeup, hairdressing

**Draftsperson**—one who draws plan and elevation schematics for set construc-

GLOSSARY

tion based on data supplied by the Set Designer

**forced perspective**—where normal perspective is distorted by placing elements in the scene which are sized and positioned to give the visual impression of being farther removed by being larger or smaller in frame and/or by being positioned closer or farther from the camera viewpoint

**illustrations**—a picture, painting or sketch designed to elucidate a product or process

**Illustrator**—one who prepares illustrations for a storyboard

**Matte Painter**—one who prepares and paints photographic mattes

**matte painting**—the process of painting mattes which, when applied to optical work or glass shots, will effectively bar imagery from being recorded in specific portions of the shot, thereby permitting the compositing of other imagery in its place during the optical compositing process

**Production Designer**—one who conceives, coordinates and is responsible for the overall look and consistency of all design elements in a production

**renderings**—finalized representations or depictions of people, places or things

**Scenic Artist**—one who paints scenic background views on cycloramas, backings, drops and glass for photographic rendering

**Set Designer**—one who designs the sets and settings within the parameters set by the Art Director/Production Designer

**sketch**—a drawing, representing a person, place or thing, which emphasizes its chief features

**Sketch Artist**—one who makes line drawings of the essential aspects of

sets, settings, set dressing, props, costumes, makeup and hairdressing within parameters set by the Production, Set or Costume Designer

**storyboard**—the illustrative device by which a story or sequence is presented shot by shot in order to encourage and clarify visual thinking and production planning

**Stylist**—one who conforms the dressed look of a commercial to its product and setting

## CAMERA

**Aerial Cinematographer**—one who shoots motion pictures while airborne

**aerial photography**—photography done while airborne air-to-air and/or air-to-ground

**ambiance**—the light which exists in the production environment

**anamorphic**—an extremely wide viewing aspect ratio, often 2:1 to 2.5:1

**Animation Camera Operator**—one who sets up and operates an optical camera

**Animation Checker**—one who checks the cel, camera, stand and table positions and records this data in the Camera Log

**aperture**—camera: the opening in the front plate of the camera body which allows light to enter the camera; lens: the size of the internal circumference, including the diaphragmatic setting, which will allow light to pass

**ASA rating**—an American Standards Association (now ANSI) rating of the sensitivity of a given film emulsion to light

**ASC**—American Society of Cinematographers

**aspect ratio**—the outer dimensions within which captured imagery is composed and framed [expressed as the relationship of width to height, i.e., 1.33 to 1, 1.33:1, or simply 1.33]

**aspect ratio matte** [also **aspect matte**]—the solid frame which sets the shape of the camera aperture through which light reflected from the imagery passes

**Assistant Still Photographer**—one who assists the Still Photographer

**background**—that part of a shot occupied by imagery which is farthest from the camera lens

**bar sheet**—a logged record of the sound track of an animated film which shows the frame placement of each syllable of each word occurring in the sound track

**barney**—a fitted padded covering placed over the camera magazine in order to dampen the sound of the running camera

**bi-packing**—placing two film stocks, one the unexposed negative, the other the developed negative or print, emulsion to emulsion in the optical printer

**blimp**—a camera housing which dampens and confines sound emissions from a running camera

**BSC**—British Society of Cinematographers

**buckle switch**—the internal leaf plate which turns the camera off when film fails to feed into the film magazine and buckles into the film chamber pressing against the buckle plate

**burn-ins**—titles, captions or superimposures which are well overexposed and placed over neutral, still or action backgrounds

**cam**—a shaped metallic template designed for each taking lens used in cameras with parallax viewfinders in order

for the cam follower to direct the finder to the focus points for the particular taking lens while following focus

**camera**—a light-tight chamber through the lens of which a controlled amount of light is introduced to record an image on a light-sensitive medium—a film emulsion, CRT, or CCD

**camera angle**—a viewing perspective consisting of the position of the camera and the choice of taking lens in relation to the subject matter

**camera components**—the essential, constituent parts of the camera; the camera body, the film drive and transport mechanism, the film gate, the lens port

**camera control head**—the mechanism which allows the camera to be panned, tilted and/or canted

**Camera Log**—an animation camera record of takes made during the animation filming process

**Camera Operator**—the one responsible for framing and following the blocked action as monitored through the viewfinder

**camera platform**—any surface, static or mobile, upon which a camera can be positioned and from which the camera can be operated

**Camera Report**—contains a listing of footage exposed for each take along with indication of printed takes and special instructions on processing, filtration and special frame rates used and identifies the production, production company, date, and emulsion used

**camera support**—any device on which a camera and its control head can be mounted and operated

**cant**—to slant or tip a camera sideways on its lenticular axis; also called "dutching"

**cels**—plastic or celluloid sheets on which animation is drawn and painted

**ciné camera**—a motion picture film camera

**Cinematographer**—one who is in charge of directing the photographic aspects of a cinematic production

**cinex**—a small strip of film of ten frames or so taken from each scene of dailies and showing the exposure range of a black and white film

**color absorption**—the capability of certain media to absorb certain colors of the light spectrum, i.e., water: the deeper and denser the more the red range is absorbed and the blue range predominates

**color compensation**—use of colored filters to conform to the color temperature of the film emulsion being used

**color correction**—use of colored filters in the camera or optical printer to modify the overall tint or hue of a given scene or segment

**color chart**—a chart, displaying the red, green, blue, yellow, magenta, and cyan color chips along with the greyscale chips, which is shot at the head end of each fresh film roll prior to filming principal action; used by the Timer or Colorist to set exposure and color values during printing or transfer to video tape

**color temperature**—measure of the color quality of a light source having a continuous spectrum expressed in degrees Kelvin

**color temperature meter**—an instrument sensitive to the color transmission of light rays

**composition**—the arranging of subject matter in frame, or the selection of the frame size and position around existing subject matter

**composing**—arranging the subject matter in frame by positioning the subject matter and/or the camera

**contrast ratio**—computed as the combined intensity of the key light plus the fill light to the fill light only; the greater this ratio, the higher the contrast

**crystal control**—a crystal-based component which precisely maintains a camera's frame rate

**CSC**—Canadian Society of Cinematographers

**dailies**—work print of accepted takes made the previous working day

**dampen, drag**—to check or restrain movement in a camera control head

**depth of field**—the area between the nearest and farthest objects from the lens which are in acceptable focus

**depth of focus**—the extremely finite area between the surface of the rear element of the taking lens and the film focal plane where light rays converge to form points on the surface of the film emulsion; the degree at which the points of convergence are on the film plane determines the sharpness of the imagery; if the point of convergence occurs either before or after the light rays reach the film plane, the imagery will be less sharp and well-defined

**diaphragm**—the adjustable mechanism in the lens which controls the intensity of light reaching the film plane

**diffusion**—any material which diffuses or softens light rays directly or reflectively

**diopter**—an auxiliary lens which, when placed in the lenticular system, modifies the characteristics of the taking lens; also a setting on the eyepiece to provide the viewer registered visual conformity of the displayed image

**Director of Photography**—the one in charge of the technical production crew—camera, lighting and grip

**Documentary Cinematographer**—one who directs photography of a documentary nature

**double exposure**—a procedure during which a length of film is exposed twice in the camera in order to combine imagery which cannot otherwise be photographed together during a single take

**doubler**—a lens accessory added to the mounting end of a lens, which effectively doubles the focal length of the lens

**downloading**—removing exposed and unexposed film from a camera magazine, canning and identifying each roll

**DP**—Director of Photography

**dry run**—a run-through rehearsal in real time with the cast or with stand-ins

**"dutching"**—slanting or tipping a camera sideways on its lenticular axis

**ease-in/ease-out**—a progressive acceleration and deceleration of movement at the beginning and end of a pan, tilt, dutch, zoom, dolly, crane, or a combination of moves

**EI**—exposure index

**emulsion**—the light-sensitive material which coats a surface of the film base and upon which latent imagery is captured

**exposure**—the amount of light which will be allowed to reach the light-sensitive surface of film, CRT or CCD

**exposure sheet**— a chart on which are listed all the cels, backgrounds, zoom and pantograph moves computed pans and number of frames required for each element thereof in preparation for animation photography

**exposure/count sheets**—a listing of the optical subject matter to be filmed, the length of each shot and the passes to be made for each shot

**extension tubes**—a lens accessory added to the mounting end of a lens which extends the focal length of a lens and which requires additional exposure

**film gate**—the component of the camera through which the film passes and which holds the film flat behind the camera aperture during the exposure interval

**film test**—exposing film to determine its exposure range, color rendition, grain and resolution; to test makeup or wardrobe reproduction on film; or to film actors being considered for roles

**filter**—a lenticular device which absorbs or modifies color, intensity, quality and/or direction of light

**First Assistant Camera Operator**—the one responsible for setting up and checking out the camera and for following focus and handling zoom lens sizing and other adjustments and applications during operating procedures

**focusing**—the process of keeping the captured imagery in acceptably sharp or defined resolution

**follow focus**—the process of changing the focal settings on the lens to maintain sharp focus as the camera and subject matter move in relation to each other

**following**—moving the camera control head and/or the camera platform in order to maintain the moving subject matter in frame at all times

**footage counter**—a mechanical or digital readout which indicates the number of feet of film which have run through the camera

**foreground**—that part of a shot occupied by imagery which is nearest the camera lens

**foreshortening**—the process of placing a subject close to a wide angle camera lens in order to render its near parts greatly exaggerated compared with its farther removed parts and with other background elements in frame

**fps**—frames per second

**frame**—a single complete photograph on motion picture film or video tape (tape has two fields composing each frame); the basic linear visual element in cinematic structure

**frame counter**—a mechanism mounted on an animation camera which indicates how many frames of film have been exposed

**frame rate**—the rapidity with which the film passes through the camera or projector; the number of frames per second which are being exposed in the camera

**framing**—the process of manipulating the camera in a way that will carry and hold specific imagery in frame as seen through the viewfinder

**friction head**—a camera control head on which control surfaces interface and rub against one another when being activated

**f-stop**—a standard calculation and setting representing the ratio of the opening in the diaphragm to the focal length of a particular lens

**garbage mattes**—photographic mattes which remove unwanted clutter from a shot

**geared head**—a camera control head which uses gears and gear ratios to control pan and tilt modes of movement

**gimbal head**—a camera control head which maintains plumb while the sup-

port is freely tipped or inclined in any direction

**glass shots**—shots made in-camera through a glass plate which has been painted to exclude certain areas of the background while adding pictorial detail to the shot

**grain**—the moving particles sometimes seen in projected film images

**greyscale**—the chart, holding the six chip values from pure white through 20% increments to pure black, used to help the Timer or Colorist determine exposure and density values

**ground glass**—positioned in the viewfinding ocular in alignment with the film plane, the image from the taking lens is formed on the optically ground surface of the glass, on which is etched the aspect ratio, within which the imagery is framed

**headset**—a device, hard wired or RF, worn on the person for sending and receiving verbal communications; worn by the Camera Operator and Dolly Grip during multi-camera sitcom productions; worn by the Director, Dialogue Director and Script Supervisor during sound takes to hear the dialogue

**housing**—the protective enclosure for a crash or underwater camera

**incident light**—light emanating from a source

**incident light meter**—a light-sensitive device which measures light rays emanating from a source

**increment**—a unit of measurement (100 to an inch) for moves to be made on an animation stand

**intermittent**—the movement of motion picture film as it is transported through the film gate at the camera aperture with each frame held stationary in place during the exposure interval before being moved ahead for the next frame to be exposed

**iris**—an adjustable diaphragm with a central opening which controls the amount of light passing through a lens

**key light**—the principal modeling light, often the light on which exposure is based

**lead** [leed] **framing**—allowing more frame space in the direction of the look or movement of subject matter

**lead space**—same as lead framing

**lenticular**—all optical devices and elements through which light passes to reach the light-sensitive surface

**lenticular diffusion**—filtration placed in the optical system

**Line-Up Technician**—one who prepares the Exposure or Count Sheet for use by the Optical Printer Operator in the lining up and compositing of dupe negative picture elements

**liquid gate**—a liquid-filled film gate chamber in an optical printer through which original film is rephotographed (printed) in order to diminish the effect of mars and scratches

**Loader**—one who loads and downloads film into and out of camera magazines

**loading**—the process of putting unexposed film in a camera magazine

**master**—the widest, most inclusive camera angle of an action and/or setting

**matte**—any opaque painted or placed material positioned to stop light from reaching certain areas in frame

**matted supers**—superimposures which have been matted/composited into a shot

**matte passes**—each optical pass using a hold-out matte

**midground**—that area before the lens which lies between the foreground and background

**mm**—millimeter

**monitor**—the electronic display device which shows the output of the video tap from of each of the film cameras

**motion control**—the process of computer logging of each axis of camera, dolly and subject movement with the ability to exactly repeat that movement any number of times

**Motion Control Cinematographer**—one who sets up, programs and shoots motion control scenes

**multiple exposure**—a technique during which a length of film is exposed more than once in the camera in order to combine imagery which cannot be photographed together at the same time

**News Cinematographer**—one who films news events

**ocular**—the eyepiece; the viewfinding system of a camera

**one-light print**— where one printing light setting is used for printing dailies; for color film, this means one setting each for R, G and B: for interiors, for day exteriors, for night exteriors

**on-the-air**—a camera move or angle which will be used in the final cut

**optical cuts**—cuts done in an optical printer rather than a spliced cut

**optical effects**—visual effects done optically, bi-packing hold-out mattes and original material, and composited during multiple passes in the optical printer; optical effects include: burn-ins, diffusion, distortions, fades, filtration, flips, flow-ups, hold frame(s), irising, matted and double-matted supers, oil dissolves, pop-ons and pop-offs, reductions, reframing, registrations, repositioning, resizing, rotoscoping, scratch-offs, shot pushes, skip frame, slit-scans, smears, soft effects, spins, split screen, squeezing and unsqueezing anamorphic material, streaks and smears, superimposures, traveling mattes, wipes, etc

**optical printer**—a film printing machine, consisting of a synchronized projector and printer, which projects a negative image into the lens of the printer thereby exposing unexposed film stock a frame at a time

**Optical Printer Operator**—one who operates an optical printer

**pan**—to rotate the camera view horizontally

**parallax**—the angular deviation of the line of sight through the externally mounted viewfinder from the axis line of the taking lens when both lines are centered (focused) on the same object

**pellicle**—a prism through which light from the lens passes and is then split and directed to the film plane (major portion) and to the ocular (smaller portion)

**platen**—a glass plate and frame that holds cels, photos, sketches or illustrations flat on an animation or copy stand

**playback**—pre-recorded sound played back while performers are recorded performing and lip syncing to the sound

**pressure plate**—a recessed metal plate placed in the film gate of a camera or projector in order to hold the film flat in the gate as the film is being exposed when in alignment with the camera aperture

**principal cinematography**—shooting scenes in which the principal cast members perform

**principal photography**—same as principal cinematography

**process photography**—cinematography combining live action with front or rear projected screened imagery

**Process Projectionist**—one who sets up the process screen, loads film print in the projector and operates and adjusts the projector, as necessary

**ramp control**—interlocked and synchronized control of the frame rate and T-stop or shutter angle in order to maintain precise exposure during a change in frame rate

**raw stock**—fresh and unexposed film

**reflected light**—light which is returned/reflected from a surface

**reflected light meter**—a light-sensitive device which measures light reflected from subject matter in the scene

**reflex viewing**—seeing the imagery through the lens as it is being captured

**refractive light**—light which is deflected at the point it leaves one medium and enters another, such as light entering a prism, or sunlight entering water

**registration shooting**—where an outgoing shot must be set up in perfect registration with an incoming shot and where, at the joining point, all elements of each shot must match in all respects

**resolution**—clarity of detail

**rotoscoping**—the process of removing unwanted background material with a traveling matte in order to cleanly insert the desired imagery

**traveling matte**—a matte which travels with the material to be included in frame

**rushes**—specially processed film which may be prepared for screening later the same day on which it was shot

**screen direction**—the direction in which performers are facing or moving during a take

**SCUBA**—Self-Contained Underwater Breathing Apparatus

**SCUBA certified**—one who has been tested and certified in the use of SCUBA gear and underwater procedures

**Second Assistant Camera Operator**—one who assists the First Assistant Camera Operator

**second unit photography**—cinematography involving the shooting of doubles, establishing shots, scenics, process plates, stunt action and special effects, all without principal performers involved

**setup**—a camera angle for which lighting, set dressing and sound are arranged in order to accommodate that angle

**short-end**—the remainder of unexposed film in a film magazine after the exposed footage has been separated and removed

**shot**—consists of a sequential series of frames and is the continuous recording of an action from a given camera angle

**shutter**—the camera shutter controls the duration of exposure of a frame

**shutter angle**—the open angle of the camera shutter which will allow light to pass on to the film

**sizing**—the process of manipulating the zoom lens in order to place subjects at an appropriate size in frame

**slate**—the device on which the scene and take numbers are noted and presented to the camera at the start of each take to properly identify the take on film

**SOC**—Society of Operating Cameramen

**spot meter**—a reflected light meter with a limited angle of acceptance of from 1° to 20°, depending upon make

**Still Photographer**—one who shoots still photos

**step printer**—a contact or optical printer in which each frame printed is stopped and held in the printer aperture during exposure

**stop or freeze frame**—holding on and continuing to print a final frame in an action shot

**superimposures**—composited visual images from various sources, overlaying one another

**supers**—short for superimposures

**take**—the process of recording an action on film or tape

**taking lens**—the lens through which a take is made

**tilt**—to rotate the camera view vertically

**time code**—a system which addresses each frame of film for electronic editing purposes

**time lapse**—allowing a given amount of time to pass between each single-frame exposure

**tear sheet**—a form on which is listed all references in each scene of the script relating to items pertaining to camera procedures

**T-stop**—a standard calculation and setting based on actual transmission of light through a calibrated lens

**turn-over dupes**—dupes shot to optically change the orientation of the imagery

**Underwater Cinematographer**—one who shoots and is in charge of underwater cinematography

**underwater photography**—photography done while submerged underwater

**U.P.**—Under Protest; entered on the camera slate and Camera Report to indicate a shot that was taken against the advice of the DP

**video assist**—the feed to floor monitors from a video tap placed in the viewfinding system of a reflex camera

**voice slating**—identifying the scene and take number vocally

**wild motor**—a non-synchronous motor which can be run at various speeds resulting in varied frame rates

**zoom**—the process of moving continuously through a given range of the variable focal lengths of the zoom lens during a rehearsal or take

**zoom control**—the mechanism by which the First Assistant varies the framing size of the captured imagery

**zoom lens**—a variable focal length lens

## COMPUTER GRAPHICS

**2D Animator/Morpher**—one who animates and/or morphs (merges) one two-dimensional image into another, often quite different from one another

**2D Painter**—one who uses a computer to paint two-dimensional elements

**2D Supervisor**—one who oversees all aspects of the two-dimensional CG process

**3D Modeler**—one who develops and completes 3D CG models

**3D Painter**—one who paints 3D CG models and characters

**3D Supervisor**—one who oversees all aspects of the three-dimensional CG process

**animatronics**—use of digitized models and puppets in the preliminary CG animation process

**background**—the setting over which the foreground elements are layered

**CG**—computer graphics

**CGI**—computer generated imagery; the process of adding to, modifying and/or manipulating the imagery of digitized pictorial or graphic material

**CGI effects**—digital CG effects created on computer by software tools

**Character Animator**—one who creates and animates the CG characters

**Color & Lighting Shader**—one who adds color and lighting to computer graphics

**compositing**—the combining or layering of CG elements resulting in a completed composition or scene

**Compositor**—the one who composites or layers together the work of other CG artists

**Computer Graphics Supervisor**—one in charge of all computer graphics developmental work

**Concept Artist**—the one who develops and sketches ideas for model, miniature, puppet, character, technical effects, and virtual elements and settings

**Digital Editor**—one who edits/arranges the digital CG elements

**Digital Effects Supervisor**—one who is technical head of CG digital operations

**digitizing**—the process of converting analog imagery to digital signals

**Dust Buster**—one who digitally removes extraneous matter from a frame or scene

**dust busting**—removing extraneous matter from a frame or scene

**extremes**—drawings made by the Animator depicting the beginning and ending positions of an animated subject

**Film Recordist**—one who records from a digital medium to film

**Film Scanner**—one who scans the film images onto a digital medium

**inbetween**—drawings done by an Inbetweener which fill in and complete the extreme movements drawn by the Animator

**Maintenance Technician**—one who installs, repairs and maintains the digital computer systems used in the CG operation

**Match Mover 2D/3D**—tracks elements and matches camera movement with object movement on all 2D and/or 3D axes

**match moving**—tracking elements and matching camera movement precisely with the action of object movement

**Matte Painter**—one who prepares and paints mattes for CG compositing

**matte passes**—each computer graphics pass using hold-out mattes

**morphing**—the process of transforming an image in virtual time into something quite different

**Painter 2D/3D**—one who digitally paints the surfaces of digital imagery

**plates**—process plates; shots over which CG elements will be layered and composited

**platform**—the computer hardware upon which the software programs run

**practical effects**—filmed visual effects of models, miniatures, material objects, puppets and/or people

**pre-viz**—pre-visualized data which should be incorporated into the multiple-pass design

**puppetry**—the fabrication, use and/or manipulation of puppets

**rendering**—the stage during which all CG elements in a scene are being composited into finalized imagery

**Rotoscoper**—one who generates mattes to cover unwanted material by placing desired imagery in its stead

**rotoscoping**—the process of removing unwanted background material with a traveling matte in order to cleanly layer in the desired imagery

**scanning**—the process of scanning film images onto a digital medium

**software**—the computer programming used in computer graphics work

**Technical Director**—one responsible for the effect and conformity of technical effects such as direction, uniformity and consistency of the intensity of light, its shading and color

**Technical Effects Animator**—one who creates digital technical effects

**tracking**—accurately following and duplicating moves

**virtual (sets/locations/costuming/action/etc)**—accurately represented and apparently real

**Visual Effects Animation Supervisor**—the one in charge of visual effects animation

**Visual Effects Supervisor**—the one in charge of the Computer Graphics operation

**workstation**—the work area for the CG artist for the use of proprietary hardware and software

## CONSTRUCTION

**beading**—a beaded molding

**Construction Coordinator**—one who coordinates all aspects of production construction from sets and settings to set, action, breakaway and trick props in the studio and on location

**Construction Specialists**—ones who are skilled in specialized crafts as well as those skilled in operating heavy equipment

**dado**—the lower decorated part of a wall on the set

**Draper**—one who measures, makes and hangs drapes, swags, festoons and the like appropriately about a set

**fascia**—a flat band under eaves and cornices

**Finisher**—one who adds the decorative and built-in elements to a set

**Floor Coverer**—a craftsperson who fits and places floor covering—linoleum, tiles or carpeting on set floors

**header**—the two to four feet added to the top of a standard eight foot set wall

**Key Painter**—the craftsperson responsible for painting the sets and settings

**Key Set Builder**—the one in charge of set and site construction

**Model Builder**—a Prop Shop craftsperson who constructs models and miniatures

**Ornamental Plasterer**—an artisan who prepares and applies ornamental plastering to a set or setting

**Painter**—one who assists the Key Painter in painting the sets and settings

**Paperhanger**—one who applies paper, cloth or other covering to set walls

**Propmaker Builder**—a construction specialist who assists the Key Set Builder

**Prop Shop**—the work place that creates and makes action and special effects props

**Prop Shop Propmaker**—a Prop Shop craftsperson who designs and constructs action and special effects props

**Sculptor**—an artisan who sculpts objects from different materials for addition to and decoration of sets and settings

**set/setting**—the construction or environment which will be used by the production company to stage the action

**Staff Shop**—the Company work place whose personnel paint, repair, renovate and maintain company facilities and fabricate and install furniture and built-ins

**Stand-By Painter**—one who is skilled at rapidly and accurately matching and blending paint on repaired or added surfaces to be photographed

**Tiler**—one who cuts and lays tile on surfaces of the set

**Upholsterer**—one who covers, repairs or recovers furniture used as set dressing

**valance**—a decorative drapery or covering across a window top

## COSTUMING

**Assistant Costumer**—one who assists the Key Costumers

**character costume**—apparel and accessories specially selected, fabricated and/or conditioned for the character played by a cast member

**costume**—the apparel, with accessories, worn by each member of the cast

**costume schedule**—a listing of items of apparel and accessories worn in each scene by each performer

**Costume Supervisor**—one who supervises the selection, fitting and/or fabrication of apparel and accessories for cast members within parameters set by the Costume Designer

**Cutter/Fitter**—one who measures, cuts, fits and pins costume garments to each player in preparation for sending the costume for sewing together and finishing

**fitting**—the process of assuring proper fit for each player of each item of apparel

**Key Men's Costumer**—one who sees that all items of each costume are complete, together, fit properly, are appropriate and that no personal accessories are worn by a performer

**Key Women's Costumer**—one who sees that all items of each costume are complete, together, fit properly, are appropriate and that no personal accessories are worn by a performer

**period costume**—wearing apparel and accessories common to a given period of time in the past

**Seamstress**—one who sews the fitted and pinned costume garments together

**street costume**—items of apparel commonly in fashion today

**teching**—aging, shading, weathering or otherwise modifying the look of items of costuming

**tear sheet**—a form on which is listed all references in each scene of the script pertaining to items of costuming

## DIRECTORIAL

**action**—the movements of performers, objects and camera which comprise the cinematic events

**action line**—the imaginary line connecting interacting players; during the interchange, the camera should maintain all coverage position(s) on one side of the line or the other

**AD**—Assistant Director

**atmosphere**—the extras (people in addition to the cast) used to populate the settings

**blocking**—the process by which the Director moves and positions both performers and the camera in preparation for taking the shot

**cast**—the starring actors and supporting players

**Casting Director**—one who interviews and selects potential acting personnel and then arranges and directs casting sessions, with the Producer and Director present to make final selections

**coverage**—varied shots of people, props and set dressing, of their placement and movement, to afford cutaways during the editing process

**CU**—closeup

**Cuer**—one who prepares text for presentation and operates the cueing apparatus

**cutaways**—shots of other staging elements, such as reaction shots of others and/or other things in the scene, which can be used in editing to break up, shorten or lengthen a scene

**Dialogue Director**—one who monitors and assists performers in the delivery of dialogue

**Director**—the one in charge of directing the production activities of the staff, cast and crew

**double**—a close look-alike who takes the place of a principal performer in risky and second unit staging

**dramaturgically**—art of composing dramatically and representing theatrically

**ECU**—extreme closeup

**extras**—people, in addition to the cast, used to provide human presence or atmosphere during rehearsals and takes

**First Assistant Director**—the on-the-set expediter and principal assistant to the Director

**first team**—the principal performers in a scene

**LS**—long shot

**MS**—medium shot

**pickup shot**—a take which covers only that portion of a shot which was not adequately covered or that had an audial or visual glitch that needs correcting

**ppd**—pages per day; the average number of pages which need to be shot each production day to conform to the shooting schedule

**principals**—the cast; the stars and lead supporting players

**rehearsal**—a run-through in real time without recording the event

**run-bys**—where vehicles, boats or animals are photographed as they pass rapidly by the camera position

**scene**—a complete action, which may consist of one or more shots

**screen direction**—the direction in which performers are facing or moving during a take

**Script Supervisor**—one who is in charge of keeping the shooting script current and accurate, with all coverage and modifications noted as they occur

**Second Assistant Director**—one who assists the First AD

**second team—stand-in**s used to replace performers during lighting and camera blocking procedures

**Second Unit Director**—the one who directs second unit production—sequences involving stunts, special effects, inserts and process plates

**sequence**—a complete series of actions, which may consist of one or more scenes

**shot**—consists of a sequential series of frames and is the continuous recording of an action from a given camera angle

**shot list**—the list of scenes to be covered and shots to be made each shooting day

**stand-in**—a person who takes the place and positioning of a cast member during lighting and blocking procedures

**Stunt Coordinator**—one who plans, choreographs and directs the execution of stunts; often is the Second Unit Director

**take**—the completed process of recording an action on film or tape

**TC**—Technical Coordinator

**Technical Coordinator**—the one who coordinates camera dolly movement and positioning on a multi-camera film sitcom

**wild sound takes**—sound which is taken without synchronization to a camera

## EDITING

**ACE**—American Cinema Editors

**ADR**—automatic dialogue replacement

**Animation Editor**—one who edits animation footage

**answer print**—the first print of picture and sound combined

**Apprentice Editor**—one who is in a learning capacity and serves under the tutelage of an Assistant Editor

**Avid**—a computerized/digital editing system

**background effects**—ambient on- or off-camera sound effects selected for scenes by the Sound Effects Editor and mixed in during the dubbing process

**blooping**—the act of removing extraneous sound from spliced magnetic track

**change list**—list of scene changes made by the Picture Editor which is printed out from the computerized editing system by the Assistant Editor and distributed to the Supervising Sound Editor, Dialogue Editor, Music Editor and Sound Effects Editor

**clip bin/clip sheet**—location where the visual and audio shots are stored for non-linear editing; analagous to film bin

**coding**—edge numbering the synchronized workprint and magnetic sound dialogue track

**core**—a rewind-compatible plastic or

metal cylinder around which film or magnetic film is wound

**coverage**—varied shots of people, props and set dressing, of their placement and movement, to afford cutaways during the editing process in order to expand or compress linear time

**cue sheets**—sheets prepared by the Dialogue, Music and Sound Effects Editors which indicate on which track and when a sound element begins and ends

**cut list**—a list of cuts or edits which is printed out from the computerized editing system and given to the First Assistant Film Editor to conform the workprint to

**Cutter**—term for Picture Editor

**cutting in**—inserting opticals and cutaway shots into the work print

**degaussing**—magnetically removing all sound patterns from magnetic tape; or demagnetizing metallic cutting and splicing instruments

**Dialogue/ADR Editor**—one who edits dialogue and ADR tracks

**dialogue dailies**—dailies with synchronized dialogue tracks

**dissolve**—where the images from the outgoing and incoming scene overlap with the outgoing scene fading out while the incoming scene fades in

**Documentary Editor**—one who edits documentary footage

**editing**—physically assembling, selecting, cutting and arranging the visual and audio elements of a production

**fades**—a fade-in is where the image at the beginning of a scene emerges from black; a fade-out is where the image at the end of a scene progresses to black

**Film/Tape Librarian**—the one in charge of a film and tape production library

**First Assistant Electronics Editor**—one who attends to all matters regarding keeping the digital input updated and in order

**First Assistant Film Editor**—one who attends to all matters regarding keeping the edited workprint updated and in order

**Foley**—designed sound effects, performed live in sync with picture

**Foley Editor**—one who edits Foley sound effects

**foot**—**a unit** of measurement of film length; 16mm has 40 frames per foot; 35mm has 16 frames per foot

**hard effects**—specific stock or specially recorded sound effects which are laid in and synchronized with specific action

**intercut**—shots, or pieces of shots, which are juxtaposed with other shots placed in linear continuity

**interlock**—a mechanical system whereby picture and one or more sound tracks are put in place and run in sync to review cuts during spotting sessions

**Lightworks**—a computerized/digital editing system

**linear**—the process of editing material sequentially in its final form, copying to make edits

**logging**—listing each take by scene and take number and its beginning and ending edge numbers

**loop**—picture print and/or dialogue tape, each spliced end-to-end to form an endless loop

**media share**—a digital editing system on which several Editors and/or Assistant Editors can access the data concurrently

**magnetic film**—perforated motion picture film coated with a magnetic recording medium

**montage**—a sequence comprising a linear series of short scenes, containing related subject matter which, in effect, either compresses or expands time and/or space

**Moviola**—an editing machine on which picture and optical or magnetic sound film can be run simultaneously in sync

**Music Editor**—one who selects and/or edits music tracks for a production

**News Editor**—one who edits news films

**non-linear**—the process of editing any part of a visual production in any sequence desired without having to recopy material which follows that edit; all preliminary editing is done non-linear

**opticals**—composite shots from production footage which are combined in the optical printer for insertion into the finalized product

**papering off**—pieces of paper are placed in a roll of negative at the beginning and end of shots or scenes to be printed or for optical processing

**Picture Editor**—one who edits the visual and dialogue elements of a production

**production track**—the voice or dialogue which has been recorded in sync with the camera during production shooting and then transferred to 35mm mag film

**Pro Tools**—a random access, direct-to-disc, digital workstation system used by the Music Editor and Sound Effects Editor in digitally building their tracks

**pull list**—a digital printout listing in feet and frames the footage to be pulled from specific scenes which will be used in the workprint

**repositioning**—moving the imagery in

frame up or down, left or right, during the optical or electronic transfer

**resizing**—enlarging or diminishing the imagery in frame during the optical or electronic transfer

**scene**—a complete action, which may consist of one or more shots

**Second Assistant Editor**—one who assists Editors in non-creative technical functions

**sequence**—a complete series of actions, which may consist of one or more scenes

**shot**—consists of a sequential series of frames and is the continuous recording of an action from a given camera angle

**Sound Effects Editor**—one who assembles, selects and edits sound effects elements for a production

**splicing**—joining and cementing, or taping, two pieces of film or tape together

**spotting sessions**—screening runs of the edited workprint with the Director, Picture Editor and Sound Effects Editor to determine whether cuts work and where sound effects and music can be placed

**stock footage**—film from various sources which is reproduced and used in productions of various types

**Supervising Editor**—the one in charge of editing procedures for a complex project or for a number of projects occurring concurrently

**Supervising Sound Editor**—one who is in charge of gathering sound—dialogue and representative music and sound effects—for a temp dub

**synchronizer**—a mechanical measuring device with sprocketted multi-channel drums which maintain frame-by-frame registration of picture and sound tracks as the elements are fed through the device

**sync sound**—synchronous sound; when dialogue is recorded or played back in synchronization with picture

**take**—the completed process of recording an action on film or tape

**TDM**—time division multiplexing, the operating principle of Pro Tools

**time code**—a system which addresses each frame of film or tape for electronic editing purposes

**trailer**—a presentation of excerpts from scenes in a feature film coming attraction which is designed to evoke viewer interest in seeing the production

**Trailer Editor**—one who edits trailers

**work print**—the un-color-corrected assembly of elements of printed takes which the Picture Editor has put together in conformance with the shooting script and the wishes of the Director, Producer and/or assigned Supervising Producer

## FILM LABORATORY

**academy leaders**—standard, SMPTE-approved standard head & tail leaders

**ACE**—adjustable contrast enhancement, a chemical process

**answer prints**—the first print from the cut negative to show the expected results

**best-light**—when one printing light setting, as determined by the Timer, is used for printing dailies; for color film, this means one RGB setting each for interiors, for day exteriors, and for night exteriors

**Breakdown Operator**—one who assists the Negative Cutter by breaking down, cataloguing and splicing aligned camera original or negative film

**CCE**—color contrast enhancement, a chemical process

**Chemist/Chemical Mixer**—the one who mixes the chemicals for film development

**contact printer**—a film printing machine which exposes print stock that has been bi-packed, emulsion to emulsion, with exposed camera negative and run past a controlled light source

**control strips**—used by the Timer to check printing results

**CRI**—color rendering index

**Customer Service Rep**—a liaison between the customer and the film lab

**dailies**—work print of accepted takes made the previous working day

**densitometer**—a device for measuring the image density of a shot by transmitted light

**density**—the relative opacity of a developed photographic emulsion

**developer**—a chemical solution in which the development of an exposed film emulsion takes place

**dupe**—a copy or duplicate of a negative or positive film

**Film Cleaner**—one who cleans all negative and original elements prior to the printing process

**film printer**—a machine which duplicates film imagery on unexposed print, negative or fine grain stock

**film processor**—the machine through which exposed film is developed as it passes through several chemical baths

**fine grain**—black & white intermediate stock used for striking dupes in order to reduce contrast buildup

**fixing**—the process of removing any residual silver halide crystals from a developed film in order to ensure the permanence of its imagery

**flashing**—the process of exposing undeveloped film, either before or after image exposure, to a minimal even amount of light

**foot**—the base of the characteristic gamma curve

**gamma**—a sensitometric measure of the characteristic curve of a photographic emulsion indicating the contrast reproduced in the negative image

**intensification**—process of chemically enhancing a weak photographic image

**internegative**—a dupe negative from which release prints are struck

**interpositive**—copied from the original negative; the intermediate step to a dupe negative

**Laboratory Manager**—the one who is in charge of operations in a film laboratory

**liquid gate printer**—an optical printer which runs the exposed negative through a liquid bath to reduce the effect of surface scratches while exposing each frame on a duplicating stock

**Magnetic Sound Striper**—one who applies magnetic sound striping to release prints

**Maintenance Engineer**—one who installs, repairs and maintains laboratory equipment and machinery

**negative**—motion picture film which reproduces the light areas of subject matter as dark areas and the dark areas as light areas and in complementary colors to those photographed

**Negative Assembler**—one who assembles the exposed negative in rolls in preparation for developing

**Negative Breakdown/Make-up Operator**—one who breaks down and makes up a roll of negative for duplication or printing

**Negative Cutter**—one who selects and cuts the production negative in conformance with the final approved work print

**Negative Developer**—one who feeds the negative into and from the film processor

**one-light**—where one printing light setting, as determined by the DP, is used for printing dailies; for color film, this means one setting each for R, G and B: for interiors, for day exteriors, for night exteriors

**positive**—motion picture film which reproduces the light and dark areas of subject matter as well as color as they would appear when photographed

**Positive Assembler**—one who assembles the positive on cores or reels for projection or shipping

**Positive Developer**—one who feeds the print positive into and removes it from the film processor

**Printer**—the one who prints from the developed negative

**printer reader**—the device interfaced with the film printer which reads the punched tape prepared by the Timer and automatically adjusts the RGB within the footage and frame specifications during the printing process

**Projectionist**—one who projects positive material normally or at high speed

**proof**—a strip of film showing a few printed frames from the beginning, middle and end of each scene of the answer print or timed dailies

**punched tape**—a computer readout on which the Timer has entered the RGB values for each shot and another tape with the footage and frame count for each scene

**Quality Controller**—one who checks

and maintains quality controls on all aspects of film processing

**Receiver/Shipper**—one who receives and ships film in its various stages

**Release Inspector**—one who views at high speed each roll of release print for quality control

**RGB**—red, green, blue—the three primary colors for light

**sensitometer**—a device for measuring and comparing the degree of sensitivity of a film emulsion to the various colors of the spectrum

**sensitometrist/densitometrist**—one who operates the sensitometer and/or densitometer

**shoulder**—the top of the characteristic gamma curve

**Tape Puncher**—one who punches the timing tapes during the timing process

**temperature**—important element in the development phase of film processing

**test strip**—a length of exposed negative run through the processor to check the efficacy of the chemical solutions

**time**—an important element in the development phase of film processing

**Timer**—one who adjusts and sets the color and density values of a film shot-by-shot in preparation for the printing process

**timing**—the process of assigning printer lights to each shot printed in dailies; and to each shot used in a conformed negative

**Vault Clerk**—one who is in charge of the storage and maintenance of film material in the film vault

**wedge**—film-based strip of calibrated variable density from clear to opaque, used for sensitometric tests of film emulsions

# GRIP

**"banana-ing"**—banana-shaped movement of performers or the mobile camera platform

**Best Boy Grip**—the principal assistant to the Key Grip

**Best Boy Rigging Grip**—the principal assistant to the Key Rigging Grip

**block-and-tackle**—a pulley with a hook and rope attached for hoisting or hauling heavy and/or bulky matériel

**boom** (as a noun)—a lengthy mechanical counterbalanced beam connected to a support post, which is swung and manipulated to position the camera and/or personnel aboard during a shot

**boom** (as a verb)—to swing the boom arm up, down, left or right

**catwalk**—a wooden walkway suspended above the stage floor

**cherry-picker**—a mobile platform with extendible boom arm for hoisting manned camera or lights

**"chinese-ing"**—a movement of the mobile camera platform directly across approaching movement or across the facing position of a performer

**crabbing**—when the camera dolly wheels are positioned to move the platform in a relatively lateral or sideways direction without changing the alignment of the chassis

**crane**—a mobile camera platform on which the camera can be mounted and positioned—raised or lowered, or swung to either side—at varied heights

**C-stand**—a versatile-use stand for setting flags, nets, leafy branches, glass for glass shots, bead board, reflectors and mirrors, etc

**cucaloris, cuke, cookie**—a light control pattern made from translucent, scrim or solid material to resemble leaves, venetian blinds or other entity when placed in front of a light

**cutter**—an opaque flat, usually a metal frame covered in duvetyn, used to control light output by stopping and absorbing light

**cyc, cyclorama**—a huge and expansive backing of plain color or of scenic view—clouds, mountains, trees, etc

**dance floor**—several pieces of 4´x8´ 3/4″ plyboard laid to provide a smooth and level surface upon which to move a camera dolly

**dolly**—a compact mobile camera platform with multiple directional tracking modes

**Dolly/Crane/Boom Grip**—technicians who operate camera dollies, cranes, booms and jib arms

**dollying**—to move the camera on a camera dolly while blocking, rehearsing or making a take

**dot**—a small and circular flag, net, silk or gel, placed to modify only a part of a light beam

**duvetyn**—a heavy black cloth material used to dampen light reflection and to cover frames for various sized flags, cutters and gobos

**finger**—a small and rectangular flag, net, silk or gel, placed to modify only a part of a light beam

**flag**—a small cutter

**gobo**—a large, black, solid light control device sometimes used to produce a large shadow in frame to cover a camera shadow or other unwanted shadows

**greenbeds**—temporary wooden catwalks, installed above and in alignment with set walls, on which lighting instruments are mounted

**Grip**—a technician who moves sets, camera dollies and cranes, constructing tracks therefor, and who controls lighting patterns

**Grip Box**—a lock-up cabinet containing grip matériel

**grip stand**—a stand for mounting cutters, flags, nets, silks, and foamcore, etc

**fishtailing**—a dolly move where the rear wheels are set to rotate the dolly back and forth using the front wheels as a pivot point

**gel**—colored sheet of gelatin placed in a beam of light to color that light

**jib arm**—a lengthy tubular device on which a remotely controlled camera can be mounted and which can be attached to a dolly or crane in order to extend the effective camera angle

**Key Grip**—one who is in charge of all grip production procedures

**Key Rigging Grip**—one who is in charge of all grip related rigging procedures

**net**—a black netting covering a metal frame used to reduce the intensity of a beam of light

**parallels**—a relatively small four-sided platform of limited height assembled from joined components

**patterns**—cutouts placed in front of a light source to create patterned shadows

**perms**—permanent walkways and supports installed high above the floor near the stage ceilings

**pipe grids**—suspended pipes arranged in a horizontal grid pattern to which lighting instruments are attached

**reflector boards**—mounted on a reflector stand, a reflector is used on exteriors to catch and direct the rays of sunlight or lighting units onto the assigned subject matter

**Rigging Grip**—a technician who installs and strikes grip related rigging

**safetied**—secured by a tie wire or strap to a solid mounting to prevent falling freely when a person, object or piece of equipment becomes detached or separated from a secured position

**scaffolding**—a temporary, elevated structure supporting a platform

**scissor-lift**—a mobile battery-powered lift

**shelf**—a flag placed horizontally to cut illumination from the lower portion of a light beam

**sider**—a flag placed vertically to cut illumination on one side of a light beam

**silk**—a silk-like fabric used to soften and reduce the light intensity on subject matter

**solid**—a completely opaque flag or cutter

**tear sheet**—a form on which is listed all references in each scene of the script pertaining to grip items

**topper**—a flag placed horizontally to cut illumination from the top portion of a light beam

**track**—rails laid and leveled on which a camera dolly will be mounted and moved

**tracking**—a mobile camera platform move which runs on laid tracks or dance floor

**translights**—backings which will pass light from behind as well as take lighting from the front

**trucking**—a mobile camera platform move made from an insert car or mobile exterior crane; a shot of a towed vehicle

**trusses**—a strong, lengthy bracket-like structure used to support overhead lighting units

**wild walls**—walls of the set which can be removed and/or replaced, as necessary, for photographic purposes

# LIGHTING

**ampere**—a unit of electrical current intensity; rate of flow of electricity

**AC**—alternating current

**arc light**—a lighting unit that makes light by means of an electrical arc

**back-cross**—direction of a light coming from behind, above and to the left or right of a subject

**background light**—light illuminating the background

**bail**—the yoke, or Y-shaped part of a lighting unit that attaches the unit to a mount

**barn doors**—hinged metal shields attached to a rotating ring that fits in the frontal mounting section of a lighting unit

**Best Boy**—the principal assistant to the Gaffer

**current**—flow rate of electricity

**DC**—direct current

**diffusion**—material placed in the light beam which scatters the light rays

**dimmer board**—the control console regulating power to several circuits and lighting units

**Dimmer Board Operator**—the technician who identifies and, on cue, activates all circuitry which feeds through the dimmer board

**effect light**—a light used to accentuate an object or defined area

**fill lighting**—the light which adds luminance to the shadows made by the key light

**foot-candle**—the amount of light given out by one candle one foot away from the subject; a basic unit of measurement of the intensity of light

**Fresnel**—a specially designed, heat-resistant lens of concentric stepped rings in a convex design, used principally in spot light units

**Gaffer**—the Chief Lighting Technician who is in charge of technical electrical lighting procedures

**gel**— a sheet of colored gelatin placed in a beam of light to color that light

**generator**—the power plant which creates and supplies electrical power, particularly on location

**Generator Operator**—the technician who operates and services the generator

**genny**—term for generator

**HMI**—halogen mercury iodide lighting unit

**impedance**—opposition to AC current flow

**incident light**—light which emanates from a source

**incident light meter**—a light-sensitive device which measures light rays emanating from a source

**key light**—the principal modeling light, often the light on which exposure is based

**Lighting Technician**—a technician who sets and installs lighting units and light control devices placed on or in those units

**luminance**—the presence of light

**luminaries**—lighting instruments/units/fixtures

**ohm**—a unit of electrical resistance

**reflected light**—light which is returned/reflected from a surface

**reflected light meter**—a light-sensitive light which measures light reflected from subject matter in the scene

**Repair Technician**—a technician who keeps all lighting equipment in operating order

**resistance**—opposition to DC current flow

**Rigging Best Boy**—the principal assistant to the Rigging Gaffer

**Rigging Gaffer**—one who is in charge of all electrical lighting related rigging procedures

**Rigging Technician**—a technician who installs and strikes electrical lighting related rigging

**safetied**—secured by a tie wire or strap to a solid mounting to prevent falling freely when a person, object or piece of equipment becomes detached or separated from an assigned position

**scrim**—a circular wire mesh placed in the frontal mounting section of a lighting unit to reduce the amount of light reaching its target area

**shutters**—used on arc lights to variably control the amount of light emanating from the unit

**snoot assembly**—a front end control device which limits the beam spread of a lighting unit

**Special Operator**—a technician who operates specialized lighting units, such as arcs, follow spots, handheld lights, and the like

**spiders**—bus bar boxes used to connect lug-ended feeder cables

**tear sheet**—a form on which is listed all references in each scene of the script pertaining to items of lighting

**volt**—a unit of electromotive force

**watt**—a unit of electrical power or activity equal to one volt-ampere

## MAKEUP

**Assistant Hairdresser**—one who assists the Key Hairdresser

**Assistant Makeup Artist**—one who assists the Key Makeup Artist

**body makeup**—makeup applied to all parts of the body not covered by a costume from the base of the neck down

**Body Makeup Artist**—one who applies body makeup to performers of the same gender—i.e., male technician to male performer

**character makeup**—makeup applied to a performer to alter his or her normal appearance and to conform to the character being played

**Key Hairdresser**—one who is responsible for the hair styling and its application for cast members

**Key Makeup Artist**—one who is responsible for the makeup design and its application for cast members

**makeup kit**—the kit containing items of makeup, the tools and materials used to apply makeup to the skin of performers to alter or enhance their normal appearance

**makeup schedule**—a listing of makeup items and procedures used on each player for each scene

**prosthetics**—artificial body parts added to the human body and made of such elements as rubber, plastic, metal, foil or cloth, using tubes, reservoir sacks and pumps to activate the makeup

**special effects makeup**—makeup applied to performers to alter or distort their normal appearance or to produce a morphing effect or an open and bleeding wound

**straight makeup**—often used to maintain a consistency of skin tone for each player during the production schedule for photographic purposes

**street makeup**—normal, everyday makeup

**tear sheet**—a form on which is listed all references in each scene of the script pertaining to special makeup and hairdressing requirements

## PRODUCING

**AMPTP**—Association of Motion Picture and Television Producers

**Associate Producer**—one who performs assigned duties by the Producer

**casting committee**—consists of the Producer and Director who interview and appraise performers brought in by the Casting Director

**Co-Producer**—one who shares Producer responsibilities and duties

**decision group**—a committee, consisting of the Producer, Art Director/Production Designer, Director, Director of Photography and Production Manager, which decides the locations for the production and approves the design of settings

**development**—the first phase of the producing process

**Executive Producer**—one who is responsible for approving and scheduling all production for a major studio or independent production company

**financing**—acquiring the funding for the project; part of first phase of producing

**focus-group**—a group of up to sixteen people chosen from a test screening audience to get comment regarding the screened product

**Line Producer**—oversees and handles details of actual production process

**marketing**—the fifth and final phase of the producing process—publicizing, releasing, distributing and exhibiting the finished product

**PGA**—Producers Guild of America

**post-production**—the fourth phase of producing during which the captured imagery and sound are edited, augmented, refined and finalized

**pre-production**—preparation for production; the second phase of producing

**Producer**—the person responsible for producing the picture or programming; the one everyone on the production is working for

**production**—the third phase of the producing process during which the script is transferred to captured imagery and sound

**scouting group**—a committee, consisting of the Director, Art Director/Production Designer, Director of Photography and Location Manager, which surveys and recommends location shooting sites

**Supervising Producer**—one who is involved with television programming production by overseeing certain aspects of the post-production process

## PRODUCTION MANAGEMENT

**Assistant Unit Production Manager**—one who assists the Unit Production Manager

**box rental**—an invoiced fee charged by technical personnel for the use of their personal tools and matériel

**call sheet**—the schedule prepared by the UPM on which is noted the call for each member of the crew and cast, the scenes to be shot, the time to report for makeup, etc

**clearances**—executed forms which allow the production company to shoot on and/or photograph public and private property

**deal memo**—[see General Section, which starts on page 319]

**location**—the geographic area away from the studio where the production will take place in part or in its entirety

**Location Manager**—one who locates, secures and manages location production sites

**logistics**—the transport, lodging and feeding of personnel and the movement of personnel and matériel during production

**PA**—Production Assistant (film); Production Associate (video)

**PM**—Production Manager

**Production Assistant**—one who assists Production Management personnel in attending to detail work

**Production Associate**—[See Video section below]

**Production Coordinator**—one who assists the Production Manager in coordinating certain aspects of the production process, handling communications with the staff, cast and crew

**Production Manager**—the off-the-set expediter in charge of administrative business and production details for a large budget production having several units simultaneously at work

**reimbursement**—repayment for receipted funds expended on Company-related business

**releases**—forms signed by individuals and property owners permitting their likeness or property to be photographed

**shooting schedule**—the breakdown listing specific scenes to be shot during the allotted time frame, whether studio or location, day or night, interior or exterior

**tear sheet**—a form on which is listed all items in each scene of the script pertaining to scheduling—cast, extras, technical personnel, major prop items

**Unit Production Manager**—the one who manages and expedites the administrative business production-related details of a single production unit

**UPM**—Unit Production Manager

## PROPERTY

**hand props**—items that are handled by cast members

**Home Economist**—one who is responsible for all food items prepared and displayed for photographic purposes

**Prop Box**—a lock-up cabinet containing myriad items for Company use

**Property Assistant**—one who assists the Property Master

**Property Master**—one who is in charge of all Company property and who is responsible for the security and condition of each set and setting once it is up and dressed and during the actual shooting process

**props**—all items belonging to or in the custody of the Company which have been constructed, manufactured, owned, leased, rented or borrowed

**Prop Wagon**—the vehicle containing prop items which is used on westerns and other locations

**set props**—items placed about the set or setting

**tear sheet**—a form on which is listed all references in each scene of the script pertaining to items of property

**working props**—devices that are operated by Special Effects personnel

## SET DECORATING

**greens**—live and artificial plants used to decorate a set or setting

**Greens Handler**—one who cares for and places greenery on the sets and settings

**Set Decorator**—the one who plans the decoration of the sets and settings

**Set Dresser**—the one who places set dressing on the sets and settings

**set dressing**—objects, fixtures and furnishings attached to, or hung from, the walls and ceilings of settings and/or placed on the floor or about the production site for cinematographic purposes

**tear sheet**—a form on which is listed all references in each scene of the script pertaining to items of set dressing

## SOUND

**ADR**—automatic dialogue replacement, used in a process called voice dubbing or looping

**AES**—Audio Engineering Society

**ADR Mixer**—the one who mixes and records sound bits during ADR sessions

**ambiance**—the sound which exists in the production environment

**audio**—all that pertains to sound, sound recording, sound transfer, or sound re-recording

**background sounds**—traffic, air, wind, rain, thunder, birds, crickets, and the like

**battens**—sound-absorbing material either suspended or laid on the floor

**boom**—the extendible arm to which the mic is attached and from which it is manipulated—swung, extended and faced

**Boom Operator**—one who operates and positions the mic boom or fishpole while facing the mic for dialogue pickup during production

**canned**—music or sound effects which are taken from a stock library of prerecorded material

**click-track**—a magnetic sound track on which the Music Editor has placed regularly spaced sound clicks as a guide to the musical tempo required during scoring and recording for a given shot, scene or sequence

**Comtek**—an RF headset communication system to feed production dialogue to the Director, Dialogue Director, Script Supervisor, Boom Operator and others with a need to hear clearly

**DA88**—digital eight-track audio tape

**DAT tape**—digital audio tape

**db level**—decibel level; unit of loudness

**degaussing**—magnetically removing all sound patterns from the magnetic tape

**dubbing session**—a sound re-recording session

**Dummy Loader**—the one who loads, threads, aligns and rewinds elements tracks in the sound dummies

**ear phones**—used to hear the voice pickup of actors during sync sound takes

**elements log**—a listing of all dialogue, music and sound effects cues and the placing and duration of each cue

**fishpole**—a lightweight, often lengthy, handheld extension rod on which a microphone can be mounted and faced

**Foley**—production of live sound effects done in synchronization with picture

**Foley Artist**—the one who designs, performs and produces sound effects

**Foley Mixer**—the one who mixes and records Foley sound effects

**Foley sounds**—footstep sounds, and prop sounds, such as utensil and dinnerware noise, doors opening and closing, glass breaking, swords clashing, water running, and the like

**group loop babble**—when a group of ADR actors gather to add voice presence to a scene depicting vocal interchange by multiple extras populating the scene

**hard effects**—specific on-camera effects such as a car starting, stopping and skidding; collisions; crashes; plane flybys; explosions; gunshots, and the like

**head tones**—sound tone placed at the head of each roll of audio tape

**interlock**—when all sound elements are synchronized and run in sync with the projector

**"jamming-the-slate"**—checking and setting the electronic slate every four (4) hours

**lavaliere**—a small microphone which can be clipped onto a tie, collar or jacket

**Lead Recordist**—the one who records recorded sound during a re-recording session

**Lead Re-Recording Mixer**—the head Re-Recording Mixer who combines multiple dialogue and/or music tracks during pre-dub and dubbing sessions

**M&E track**—music and sound effects only—without dialogue; a minus-voice track

**mag**—short for magnetic

**Maintenance Engineer**—the one who repairs, replaces, installs and maintains technical equipment at a sound facility

**mic**—a microphone

**mixing**—mixing, also called dubbing, is a process whereby various prearranged sound elements are refined and combined to conform to the perspective provided by the picture imagery

**mixing console**—the expansive control board housing the switchers and faders, used by post-production Mixers and Re-Recording Mixers

**MOS**—mit out sound; without synchronous sound

**Music Re-Recording Mixer**—the one who mixes the music tracks during a pre-dub and dubbing session

**Nagra**—a popular brand of 1/4" professional audio tape recorder

**News Sound Mixer**—the one who mixes and records sound during news events and interviews

**PA**—public address system

**parabolic mic**—a microphone which can be focused in such a way as to be able to pick up sound of a relatively distant event

**patching**—the process of connecting, by hard wire or digitally via patch bays, the control consoles with the sound dummies and sound recorders

**PB**—playback

**perambulator**—a three-wheeled mobile stand on which a microphone boom is mounted

**perspective**—the apparent physical distance a sound carries from its point of origin

**PL**—phone line

**Playback Operator**—the one who operates the playback system during a production

**pre-dub**—preliminary dub

**presence**—the acoustic quality of sound at a given location

**Production Mixer**—the one who mixes and records production dialogue and ambient sound

**Projectionist**—one who operates the projector and projects the picture

**projector**—a motion picture machine with a powerful light source which projects the images recorded on each frame of the print passing through the film gate past the lens aperture onto the reflective surface of a display screen

**raw stock**—fresh and unrecorded audio tape

**Recordist**—one who records production sound when the Production Mixer requires such assistance

**RF**—radio frequency signal

**riding gain**—maintaining sound volume at a desired level

**riding the control**—hands-on monitoring, control and adjustment of any variable setting device

**Scoring Mixer**—one who mixes live orchestral and instrumental ensembles during a scoring session for a production

**Scoring Recordist**—one who records live music during a scoring session for a production

**shotgun mic**—a microphone with a narrow cone of acceptance

**sound dummies**—the playback machines on which magnetic sound tracks are mounted for post-production mixing sessions

**sound effects**—there are four categories of sound: background/ambient, Foley feet, Foley props, and hard effects

**Sound Effects Re-Recording Mixer**—the one who mixes the sound effects tracks during a pre-dub and dubbing session

**Sound Effects Specialist**—one who designs, performs and produces sound effects in synchronization with picture; called a Foley Artist

**Sound Report**—a listing kept by the Production Mixer of each sound take made on a reel of 1/4" magnetic tape along with any directions or descriptive remarks for the Transfer Recordist

**sound track exciter lamp**—the lamp which reads the emissions from an optical sound track

**static mics**—mics that are mounted in a stationary position

**sub-dub**—process of selecting and combining elements to reduce tracks in preparation for the final mix

**synchronous sound**—sound which is in perfect match to the picture imagery, particularly the dialogue

**temp dub**—a trial or test dub done with substitute sound elements to convey a feeling of the final product

**Transfer Recordist**—one who transfers production dialogue and sound to tape or disc

**U.P.**—Under Protest; entered on the Sound Report to indicate a shot that was taken against the advice of the Production Mixer

**Utility Sound Technician**—one who assists Production Sound personnel

**voice slate**—a scene and take identified by voice only when recording wild sound pickups

**VU meter**—sound volume (intensity) unit meter

**wild sound**—sound which is non-synchronous; sound takes which are not taken in synchronization with a camera

## SPECIAL EFFECTS

**Armorer**—one who is in charge of firearms and other weaponry

**Assistant Special Effects Technician**—one who assists other Special Effects Technicians in their specialties

**atmospheric**—special effects dealing with wind, water, rain, snow, fog, smoke and fire

**Atmospheric Technician**—one who prepares the set or setting by adding atmospheric elements such as wind, water, rain, snow, fog, smoke or fire

**breakaways**—hand props made of glass, wood or plastic and scored to break into pieces upon moderate impact

**explosives**—material composed of gunpowder, nitroglycerin, or chemicals in powder, plastic, gel or liquid form

**gag**— a special effects device and or procedure designed to deliver a desired visual result

**Key Special Effects Technician**—one who is in charge of all special effects operations taking place on the set or location site

**Powder Technician**—one whose specialty is the preparing, shaping, placing and activation of explosives

**pyrotechnics**—fire, flame and fireworks

**Special Effects Coordinator**—one who coordinates the design of the special effect with input from Directorial, Camera, Computer Graphics, Editing and Production Management departments

**squibs**—wired explosive caps remotely detonated electrically; used to simulate bullet hits

**tear sheet**—a form on which is listed all references in each scene of the script pertaining to special effects

**weaponry**—instruments of combat, offensive and defensive

**Wire and Mechanical Gag Technician**—one who designs and constructs special effects gags which incorporate wire and mechanical elements, such as flying arrows, spears or knives to target, an actor in harness being knocked backward by a blast, or being flown above or about the set

**working props**—devices which can be manually or remotely activated

## SPECIAL SERVICES

**Aircraft Pilot**—one who is licensed to fly an aircraft

**Animal Specialist**—a Trainer, Keeper or Handler who has special training and ability to handle and/or train animals

**blurb**—a short publicity piece of 50 to 100 words

**Crafts Service**—the one who provides a supply and display of food and beverages for consumption by cast, staff and crew during production

**first aid kit**—contains medicines, materials and tools for administering first aid to staff, cast and crew

**First Aid Technician**—a medic who is licensed to dispense first aid assistance and medication

**Office Workers**—those secretaries, bookkeepers and clerks who work in staff support of the producing process

**press book**—the book which contains photos, text and art work detailing the high points about the production, including the stars and picture highlights

**Pickup Wrangler**—one who helps performers dismount from bucking horses or bulls

**Publicist**—one who publicizes the efforts and products of others

**publicity campaign**—a concerted effort to bring public attention to a production by advertising, personal appearances and news releases, etc

**Puppeteer**—one who designs, makes and operates puppets

**puppetry**—the fabrication, operation and manipulation of a puppet, or puppets, for purposes of cinematic image capture

**Ramrod Wrangler**—the head Wrangler of two or more Wranglers

**SPCA**—Society for the Prevention of Cruelty to Animals

**Studio Teacher**—a Welfare Worker who teaches and supervises all school-age minors employed on a production during off-camera time

**Stunt Driver**—one who drives vehicles engaged in stunt activities

**Teacher's Report**—a report including attendance, place(s) of employment, hours, grades, deportment, etc, of each school-age minor under supervision

**Utility Person**—one who provides general labor and assistance

**Wrangler**—one who is in charge of horses and other livestock

## TRANSPORTATION

**Driver**—one who is properly licensed to drive an assigned vehicle

**Driver Captain**—one who is in charge of all production transportation—Drivers and vehicles

**insert car**—a specially outfitted vehicle designed to carry mounted and manned cameras when shooting running shots—either following, side by side, or towing the subject vehicle; also called a camera car

**logistics**—the process of transporting personnel and matériel from location to location

**mobile camera crane**—a gasoline-powered camera crane capable of making moving shots at relatively high speeds

**mobile studio**—a self-contained mobile studio facility comprising compartmentalized storage for camera, lighting, grip, props, wardrobe, dressing rooms, lavatories, office space, communications and generator

**Mobile Studio Operator**—one who drives and manages the mobile studio

**Rig Driver**—one licensed to drive a tractor-trailer rig—an eighteen-wheeler

**Transportation Coordinator**—one who coordinates the transportation needs of the various production departments

## VIDEO

**AD**—Associate Director

**ADC**—analog to digital conversion

**aliasing**—image distortion in a video picture resulting in moiré or herringbone patterns, wavy lines and/or varied colors

**alignment**—the process of adjusting the R, G and B signals into registration

**analog**—any electronic signal that varies continuously

**Associate Director**—one who assists the Director by preparing and cueing the Camera Operators for their shots by calling out the number over the headsets for each upcoming shot

**ATTICS**—Advanced Television Systems Committee

**AT**—advanced television, includes standard, enhanced and high-def systems

**back-focus**—the mechanical and/or electronic adjustment of the camera lens to achieve optimum image focus on the tube or CCD black surface

**balancing**—adjusting all cameras to output uniform and matching imagery

**beating**—pulsating variation in image brightness

**black balance**—on a video camera, the black levels of red, green and blue are adjusted so black has no color

**black level**—the absolute black level of a video signal is set at 7.5 IRE

**black reference**—a black area in frame

**BRR**—bit rate reduction

**CCD**—charge-coupled device for video image pickup

**CCU**—camera control unit for video

**chroma-keying**—the process of shooting subject matter in front of a blue or green background, on which an imaged background will be electronically composited

**chyron** (ky-ron)—the interface that adds titles, captions and symbols to screen content

**Chyron Operator**—one who operates the Chyron equipment

**co-axial**—the cable connecting the camera to the CCU

**color bars**—a test signal of 30 to 60 seconds run at the head of each roll of video tape and used to check chrominance functions in the video signal

**Colorist**—adjusts the color, density, position, and size of images during film-to-tape, tape-to-tape or tape-to-film transfer

**compression**—the process of reducing data file size by removing image redundancies or other non-critical visual information

**CRT**—cathode ray tube for video image pickup

**cut-points**—places on the shooting script where the Director has indicated a change of camera angle during taping; usually at changes in dialogue delivery and/or when cast movement begins and ends

**DAC**—digital-to-analog converter

**DDR**—digital disk recorder

**digital**—circuitry carrying high or low level electronic signals triggering an on or off state in the system

**Director of Photography: Video**—one who is in charge of lighting and photography on video productions

**dressing camera cable**—keeping video cable out of the path of the video camera

**DTV**—digital television

**DVD**—digital versatile disk; digital video display

**DVE**—digital video effects

**EBU**—European Broadcasting Union

**ENG**—electronic news gathering

**FAX**—acronym for facilities preparation

**HDTV**—high definition television

**head tone**—a constant sound tone run for 30 to 60 seconds at the head of each roll of video tape and used to check sound response of the video tape

**helical**—one type of scanning pattern recorded on video tape

**IEEE**—Institute of Electrical & Electronic Engineers

**image enhancement**—electronic defining or sharpening of details in captured imagery

**interlace**—process of video scanning during which odd-numbered lines of frame imagery are transmitted followed by even-numbered lines resulting in two fields composing each video frame

**I/O**—input/output; refers to data transmission between devices

**IRE**—Institute of Radio Engineers, now called the Institute of Electrical & Electronic Engineers (IEEE); also the scale on a waveform monitor that defines the video signal—the scale begins at minus 40 units and ends at plus 100 units, a total of 140 units

**iris**—the electronic or manual adjustment which controls the amount of light entering and activating the electronic system

**iso**—isolated recording—one camera to a dedicated tape machine, as opposed to a switched feed of multiple cameras to one tape machine; also an isolation shot, a shot which has not been assigned to a camera, but can be used if needed

**LD**—Lighting Director

**Lighting Director**—one who supervises the electrical set lighting procedures

**Maintenance Engineer**—one who installs, repairs and maintains the electronic and mechanical equipment associated with the video chain, including audio

**monitor**—the electronic device which displays the output from each of the video cameras; also used as a viewfinder for each video camera

**MPEG**—Motion Pictures Expert Group, set up to create and promote standards for compressed moving pictures and audio

**multiplex unit**—a component of the telecine chain

**NTSC**—National Technical Standards Committee; set US standard of 525 scanning lines per raster

**off-line**—refers to a rough cut, or cuts-only, machine-to-machine editing system, when elements are being individually prepared for on-line combining

**on-air**—when the video signal is being broadcast live or when a feed from the camera is selected for the Director's cut to go on tape for later broadcast

**on-line**—the process of combining and refining all elements with opticals, DVE, computer graphics, dissolves, fades, wipes, supers along with dialogue, music and sound effects

**PA**—Production Associate

**PAL**—phase alternate line; standard of 625 scanning lines per raster and 50 fps, used in the UK, Europe and elsewhere in the world

**pan-and-scan**—procedure used to selectively crop scenes in a widescreen production to a 1.33 TV aspect ratio

**pedestal**—the mobile mount for a video camera

**ped level**—adjustable black level of a video signal is set at 7.5 to 10 IRE units

**pixel**—picture element

**Production Associate**—one who assists Production Management personnel in attending to detail work

**progressive**—process of video scanning during which lines of frame imagery are transmitted consecutively from the first through final line forming each frame

**quad split**—a device which divides a monitor into four equal quadrants, each quadrant with a feed from another camera

**quad tape**—2-inch video tape

**registration**—the process of aligning the R and B signals with the G signal

**repositioning**—reframing the imagery up or down, left or right, during the electronic transfer

**resizing**—enlarging or diminishing the imagery in frame during the electronic transfer

**SECAM**—sequential camera scan at standard of 625 lines per raster and 50 fps, used in Russia and being phased out in France

**server**—a digital disc storage system for audio and visual data accessible to clients

**shot card**—the reference card(s) on which a Video Camera Operator lists assigned numbered shots

**slide drum**—a device used in the telecine chain to hold slides for scanning into the presentation

**Stage Manager**—one who is in charge of stage operations during shooting—seeing that the sets are dressed, lit and ready; the cameras are checked out and ready; the performers are made up, costumed, on their marks and ready; cueing performers during rehearsals, taping and or broadcast

**striping**—putting 30 to 60 seconds of color bars and tone on head end of video tape

**Switcher**—term for Technical Director

**tally light**—the red light on the video camera, and in its monitor, which indicates to talent and the Camera Operator when the camera is on-line

**tape formats**—SONY Beta SP, D-1 through D-9, DA-88, including 8mm, 1/4″, 1/2″, 3/4″, 1″ and 2″

**TD**—Technical Director

**Technical Director**—one who is in charge of the technical electronic aspects of the production

**telecine** (tele-sin-ee)—the technical interface where film can be transferred to tape and tape to film

**Telecine Operator**—one who operates the telecine system

**time code**—a system which addresses each frame of tape for electronic editing purposes

**tone**—head tone of minus 20 db for digital recording

**VC**—Video Controller

**VCU**—video control unit

**vector scope**—used to determine chroma—color intensity and balance

**video camera**—an electronic camera

**Video Camera Operator**—one who operates a video camera

**Video Colorist**—one who transfers film images to video tape or other digital recording medium, while adjusting color, sizing and position

**Video Controller**—one who sets up and controls electronic settings on the video control unit

**Video Director**—the one in charge of putting the intercut version of the production on tape or on-air

**Video Tape Editor**—one who edits the video tape takes, arranging them into final form

**Video Tape Operator**—one who operates a video tape recorder

**Video Utility**—one who assists Video Camera Operators and the Video Controller, as necessary

**VTO**—Video Tape Operator

**VTR**—video tape recorder

**wave form monitors**—a specialized oscilloscope that plots voltage, presenting a view of different components of a video signal; a four-color display to determine iris level

**white balance**—adjusting the white level of the RGB channels so that a white object in the color temperature light being shot in will be white, which equates to 100 IRE on the wave form monitor

**white reference**—a pure white area in the frame

### WARDROBE

**Assistant Wardrobe**—one who assists the Key Wardrobe person

**Dresser**—the person who helps cast members into their costumes and checks to be sure each costume is complete and that no personal effects are being worn

**Key Wardrobe**—one who is in custodial charge of all items of wardrobe—costumes and accessories—received from the Costume Supervisor

**wardrobe plot**—a listing of all items of wardrobe for each scene and for each player appearing in that scene

## 2. GENERAL DEFINITIONS

**above-the-line**—production costs related to the so-called creative team—the Producer, Writer, Director and principal performers

**animation**—the process of giving the appearance of life to otherwise inanimate objects; illustrative representations of human, animal or insect life

**anomaly**—any deviation from planned procedure; an undesirable sound or visual quality

**ANSI**—American National Standards Institute

**axis**—a line through a body around which that body rotates

**below-the-line**—production costs related to the technical aspects—staff, crew, extras, matériel, logistics and operations

**block-and-shoot**—the process of blocking the camera moves for a shot, after which immediately taking the shot on film or tape

**blurb**—an brief item of publicity appearing in trade publications

**call**—the time and place to report for work

**call sheet**—the schedule prepared by the UPM on which is noted the call for each member of the crew and cast, the scenes to be shot, the time to report for makeup, etc

**cast**—the stars and principal supporting players

**collaborative**—the process of working together synergistically

**crew**—the technical craft production personnel

**dailies, rushes**—a screening of the printed takes from the previous day's work

**deal memo**—the agreement made between a craftsperson and production management which deals with areas not specifically covered in the Union contract, such as special above-scale rates, guaranteed working hours, carried days or weeks, stand-by pay, hazard pay, box rental, screen credit, etc

**decision group**—the creative group, often consisting of the Producer, Art Director/Production Designer, Director, Director of Photography and the Production Manager, which lays down the parameters and makes the final decision regarding location selection

**episodics**—series one-hour television programming, using single-camera technique

**executing**—carrying out and completing art work

**fabrication**—process of making costumes, drapery, upholstery, backings, props, sets, etc

**feature**—a long-form theatrical presentation, 90 minutes or more in length

**featurette**—a short subject three to four reels—30 to 45 minutes—in length

**financing**—the process of acquiring funds to produce a movie

**gimbals**—a device for allowing a body to incline freely in any direction

**hard-wired**—connected by an electric, or electronic, cable

**interface**—working directly with another category or craft

**locus**—the center of all possible positions

**marketing**—the process of publicizing, selling, distributing and exhibiting a finished production for public display and profit

**matériel**—equipment and material—hardware and expendables

**MOW**—movie-of-the-week, a long form of TV programming

**OSHA**—Occupational Safety and Health Agency

**packaging**—the process of acquiring a script, along with commitments to do the picture from a leading Director and top performers

**pass**—every time that shot or frame is run through an optical printer or digital compositing process

**per diem**—a monetary allowance given employees for living expenses on location

**persistence of vision**—a characteristic of human vision during which the retina retains viewed imagery for an extremely short interval after that imagery has been removed from view

**planting**—placing items of publicity in trade publications; also planting story points in screenplays

**polar orientation**—facing north, south, east or west

**pre-ops**—preliminary operations prior to shooting

**rendering**—representing or depicting by illustrative or scenic art

**safety, safetied, safetying**—securing personnel and/or equipment and material in order to restrain unwanted movement

**sitcom**—half-hour situation comedy format for television, using a multiple camera film or video technique

**SMPTE**—Society of Motion Picture and Television Engineers

**staff**—production and administrative personnel affiliated with Producing and Production Management

**striking the set**—breaking down and wrapping sets, set dressing, production setups, etc

**tear sheet**—an itemized breakdown sheet, torn from a pad of forms, used by each department to list items required in each scene and sequence in the script, noting their availability and cost

**theatrical short**—a short subject presented on a reel or two—10 to 20 minutes in length

**trailer**—a short presentation showing bits of selected scenes from an upcoming production designed to encourage viewers to come see the picture

**traveling mattes**—painted or placed and moved during each frame to stop light from reaching certain areas

**turnaround**—the elapsed time between finishing work on one shift, session or day's work and the call time for beginning the next work session

**TV**—television

**wrap, wrapping**—to gather, disassemble and store equipment and materials

# 3. OPERATIONAL DEFINITIONS

**A. PRODUCTION:** Production is defined as any possible, but viable, process of cinematically recording the desired matter on motion picture film, video tape, digital or laser disc, or other material.

**B. MOTION PICTURE FILM PRODUCTION:** It is production of a motion picture film nature when the people and/or objects are cinematically photographed with a production ciné camera, augmented by the recording of voices and other production sound, as necessary.

**C. FEATURE PRODUCTION:** It is production of a feature nature when the staged action of performers and other subject matter is cinematically photographed in accordance with a prepared dramatic or comedic scenario for the purpose of theatrical and/or commercial television exhibition.

**D. DOCUMENTARY PRODUCTION:** It is production of a documentary nature when the subject or work is presented in a factual, objective and representational manner. A documentary is also defined as a dramatically structured film of an actual event, or of a legitimate play, giving the impression of an actual event.

**E. NEWS PRODUCTION:** It is production of a news nature when the occurrence, event, personality or personalities to be filmed are available to the general public for viewing and/or filming, operating on its, his or their own schedule and where portable and/or handheld camera(s), light(s) and sound recording equipment may be employed.

**F. TELEVISION COMMERCIAL PRODUCTION:** It is production of a television commercial nature when the purpose thereof is to present cinematically a commercial product or service in the context of a sales message for test purposes or for television broadcast exhibition.

**G. ANIMATION PRODUCTION:** It is production of an animation nature when animation techniques are utilized cinematically to animate art work, objects, animals, puppets, cartoon characters, or people.

**H. VIDEO PRODUCTION:** It is production of a video tape nature when the people and/or objects are cinematically photographed by analog or digital electronic cameras, recording the images and sound on video tape or other digital medium which is to be edited, possibly transferred to laser disc, digital tape or film, and exhibited in final form later.

**I. MIXED MEDIA PRODUCTION:** It is production of a mixed media nature when video monitoring equipment is attached to, or made a part of, motion picture film cameras, with film being the principal recording medium.

**J. PRINCIPAL CINEMATOGRAPHY:** Principal cinematography is defined as the process of setting up, lighting and cinematically photographing the principal performers and essential action during the production process.

**K. SECOND UNIT CINEMATOGRAPHY:** Second unit cinematography is defined as the process of setting up, lighting and cinematically photographing ancillary material such as inserts, stock footage, run-bys, special effects, stunts, doubles and process plate backgrounds, which are to be included with the principal cinematography in the final cinematic product.

**L. SPECIAL EFFECTS CINEMATOGRAPHY:** Special effects cinematography is defined as the process of setting up, lighting and cinematically photographing by means of any such special technique as: Composite cinematography—rear or front process; blue backing; blue, green or red screen; chroma-key; glass, mirror or camera matte work; registration; time lapse and single frame; model or miniature; etc.

**M. MOTION CONTROL CINEMATOGRAPHY:** Motion control cinematography is defined as the process of setting up, lighting and cinematically photographing subject matter computer programmed so that multiple passes can be made with each pass precisely replicating the movement of camera and subject matter on each of their multiple axes of motion.

**N. OPTICAL PRINTING:** Optical printing is defined as the process of cinematically preparing and/or re-photographing optical units, combined with the original photography, in order to achieve a desired visual composite effect of these elements.

**O. COMPUTER GENERATED IMAGERY:** Computer generated imagery is the process of capturing and combining images on film or tape, digitizing them, and then digitally modifying those images before transferring them back to film or tape.

**P. AERIAL CINEMATOGRAPHY:** It is cinematography of an aerial nature when such cinematography is accomplished from camera(s) positioned in or on an airborne aircraft—airplane, helicopter, glider, blimp, balloon or kite—shooting either air-to-air or air-to-ground; this includes sky-diving cinematography.

**Q. UNDERWATER CINEMATOGRAPHY:** It is cinematography of an underwater nature when such cinematography is accomplished from camera(s) submerged and operating under water, with or without augmentative lighting units, set dressing and/or props, etc.

**R. SET DRESSING:** Set dressing is defined as those objects, fixtures and furnishings attached to, or hung on, the walls and ceilings of settings and/or placed on the floor or about the production site for cinematographic purposes.

**1. For interiors:** furniture, drapes, curtains, blinds and shutters; lighting fixtures; major standing appliances; all hardware, household appliances; potted plants; pictures, cabinets and other appurtenances affixed to the ground or positioned in or under water or made to be an integral part of such settings.

**2. For exteriors:** houses, shacks and out-buildings; fences; trees, shrubs, flower and grass; rocks, bricks and boards; rolling, floating and airborne stock of all types; animals and insects of all kinds; other appurtenances affixed to the ground or positioned in or under water or made to be an integral part of such settings.

**S. SET PROPS:** Set props are defined as those items of set dressing which are used and/or manipulated by the performers and which may be affixed to the set walls or ceiling and/or placed on the floor thereof, or are of such size or type as generally to be considered fixed, such as: Pictures and lighting fixtures; floor lamps, furniture and statuary; large appliances; large greenery—trees, shrubs, potted plants; rolling, floating and flying stock; large television commercial product(s); etc.

**T. HAND PROPS:** Hand props are defined as those items of property carried on or by the actor and used, carried, handled or manipulated by the performer(s), such as: Portable appliances; containers of all types; weapons and the ammunition therefor; tools; utensils; portable devices; eyeglasses; comb; money, money clip and wallet; watch; pocket planner; purse and its contents; pen and pencil; toys; games; sporting equipment; food and drink; portable mechanized props; TV commercial product(s); office and household supplies; etc.

**U. SOUND EFFECTS:** Sound effects are defined as all those sounds, exclusive of live voice or live music, which are used to help create and support the visual illusion required in a film or tape production.

# INDEX TO GLOSSARY

Job titles are in the book index.
Other glossary entries are listed here.

# BIBLIOGRAPHY

The following books are recommended as follow-up reading for learning more about the technical processes involved in selected craft categories:

## ART

Affron, Charles, and Mirella J Affron. *Sets In Motion*. New Brunswick, NJ: Rutgers Univ Press, 1995.

Bennett, Richard S. *Setting the Scene*. New York: Henry N Abrams, 1994.

Collins, John. *The Art of Scenic Painting*. London: Harrap, 1985.

Preston, Ward. *What An Art Director Does: An Introduction to Motion Picture Production Design*. Los Angeles: Silman-James Press, 1994.

Simon, Mark. *Storyboards: Motion In Art*. Orlando. FL: Nomis Creations, 1994.

Warre, Michael. *Designing and Making Stage Scenery*. London: Studio Vista Ltd, 1966.

## CAMERA

Alton, John. *Painting with Light*. Berkeley, CA: Univ of California Press, 1994.

Carlson, Sylvia and Verne Carlson. *Professional Cameraman's Handbook, 4th Ed*. Boston: Focal Press, 1994.

Edge, Martin. *The Underwater Photographer*. Boston: Focal Press, 1996.

Elkins, David E. *The Camera Assistant's Manual*. Boston: Focal Press, 1991.

Elkins, David E. *Camera Terms and Concepts*. Boston: Focal Press, 1993.

Fielding, Raymond. *Special Effects Cinematography, 4th Ed*. Boston: Focal Press, 1985.

Hart, Douglas C. *The Camera Assistant: A Complete Professional Handbook*. Boston: Focal Press, 1996.

Hines, William E. *Operating Cinematography for Film and Video: A Professional and Practical Guide*. Los Angeles: Ed-Venture Films/Books, 1998.

Lowell, Ross. *Matters of Light & Depth: Creating memorable images for video, film & stills through lighting*. Philadelphia, PA: Broad Street Books Publishing, 1992.

Mascelli, Joseph V. *The Five C's of Cinematography: Motion Picture Filming Techniques*. Los Angeles: Silman-James Press, 1998.

Perisic, Zoran. *Special Optical Effects*. Boston: Focal Press, 1980.

Purves, Frederick, ed. *The Focal Encyclopedia of Photography, Desk Ed*. New York: The Macmillan Co, 1960.

Ryan, Dr Rod, ed. *American Cinematographer Manual, 7th Ed*. Hollywood, CA: The ASC Press, 1993.

Samuelson, David W. *'Hands-on' Manual for Cinematographers, 2nd Ed*. Boston: Focal Press, 1998.

Samuelson, David W. *Motion Picture Camera Techniques, 2nd Ed*. Boston: Focal Press, 1984.

Samuelson, David W. *Panaflex Users Manual, 2nd Ed*. Boston: Focal Press, 1996.

Ward, Peter. *Multi-Camera Camerawork*. Boston: Focal Press, 1997.

## COMPUTER GRAPHICS

Baker, Christopher. *How Did They Do It?: Computer Illusion in Film & TV*. Indianapolis, IN: Alpha Books, 1994.

de Leeuw, Ben. *Digital Cinematography*. Boston: Academic Press, 1997.

Ebert, David S, F Fenton Mergrave, Darwyn Peachey, Ken Perlin, Steven Worley. *Texturing & Modeling: A Procedural Approach, 2nd Ed*. Boston: Academic Press, 1998.

Hayward, Stan. *Computers for Animation*. Boston: Focal Press, 1984.

Latham, Roy. *Dictionary of Computer Graphics Technology & Application, 2nd Ed*. New York: Spr Verlag, 1995.

Madsen, Roy. *Animated Film: Concepts, Methods, Uses*. New York: Interland Publishing Inc, 1969.

Rossano, Anthony. *Inside Softimage 3D*. Indianapolis, IN: New Riders Publishing, 1998.

Vince, John. *Dictionary of Computer Graphics*. White Plains, NY: Knowledge Industry Publications, 1984.

## CONSTRUCTION

Carter, Paul. *Backstage Handbook: An Illustrated Almanac of Technical Information, 3rd Ed*. Louisville, KY: Broadway Press, 1994.

Ionazzi, Daniel A. *The Stagecraft Hand Book: A Complete Guide to all aspects of constructing a stage set*. Cincinnati, OH: Betterway Books, 1996.

James, Thurston. *The Prop Builder's Molding & Casting Handbook*. Cincinnati, OH: Betterway Books, 1989.

Lord, William H. *Stagecraft One: Your introduction to backstage work*. London: Indianapolis, IN: William H Lord, 1978.

Warre, Michael. *Designing and Making Stage Scenery*. London: Studio Vista Ltd, 1966.

## COSTUMING

Baclawski, Karen. *The Guide to Historic Costume*. New York: Drama Books, 1995.

Ingham, Rosemary and Liz Covey. *The Costume Technician's Handbook*. Portsmouth, NH: Heinemann Educational Books, 1992.

## DIRECTING

Crisp, Mike. *Directing Single Camera Drama*. Boston: Focal Press, 1998.

Harmon, Renée. *Film Directing: Killer Style & Cutting Edge Technique*. Los Angeles: Lone Eagle Publishing Co, 1998.

Katz, Steven D. *Film Directing Shot By Shot*. Studio City, CA: Michael Wiese Prods, 1991.

Lumet, Sidney. *Making Movies*. NY: Vintage Books, 1996.

Rabiger, Michael. *Directing: Film Techniques and Aesthetics, 2nd Ed*. Boston: Focal Press, 1997.

Richards, Ron. *A Director's Method for Film and Television*. Boston: Focal Press, 1992.

Silver, Alan, and Elizabeth Ward. *The Film Director's Team: A Practical Guide for Organizing and Managing*

*Film and Television Production.* New York: Arco Publishing Inc, 1983.

## EDITING

Bayes, Steve. *The Avid Handbook*. Boston: Focal Press, 1995.

Browne, Steven E. *Nonlinear Editing Basics: Electronic Film and Video Editing*. Boston: Focal Press, 1998.

Dancyger, Ken. *The Technique of Film and Video Editing Theory and Practice. 2nd Ed*. Boston: Focal Press, 1997.

Murch, Walter. *In the Blink of An Eye: A Perspective on Film Editing*. Los Angeles: Silman-James Press, 1995.

Reisz, Karel, and Gavin Millar. *The Technique of Film Editing, 2nd Ed*. Boston: Focal Press, 1968

Rubin, Michael. *Nonlinear: A Guide to Digital Film and Video Editing*. Gainesville, FL: Triad Publishing Co, 1995

## FILM LAB

Case, Dominic. *Film Technology in Post Production*. Boston: Focal Press, 1997.

Case, Dominic. *Motion Picture Film Processing*. New York: Focal Press, 1985.

Happe, Bernard L. *Your Film and the Lab*. New York: Communication Arts Books, 1983.

## GRIP

Uva, Michael G, and Sabrina Uva. *The Cranes, Jibs, and Arms Book*. Boston: Focal Press, 1998.

Uva, Michael G, and Sabrina Uva. *The Grip Book*. Boston: Focal Press, 1997.

## LIGHTING

Box, Harry C. *Set Lighting Technician's Handbook: Film Lighting Equipment, Practice, and Electrical Distribution, 2nd Ed*. Boston: Focal Press, 1997.

Brown, Blain. *Motion Picture and Video Lighting*. Boston: Focal Press, 1990.

Carlson, Verne and Sylvia Carlson. *Professional Lighting Handbook, 2nd Ed*. Boston: Focal Press, 1991.

## MAKEUP

Kehoe, Vincent J-R. *Technique of Film and Television Makeup*. Boston: Focal Press, 1969.

## MARKETING

Goldberg, Fred. *Motion Picture Marketing and Distribution*. Boston: Focal Press, 1991.

Lukk, Tiiu. *Movie Marketing: Opening the Picture and Giving It Legs*. Los Angeles: Silman-James Press, 1997.

Wiese, Michael. *Film & Video Marketing*. Studio City, CA: Michael Wiese Productions, 1989.

## MUSIC SCORING

Bell, David. *Getting the Best Score for Your Film: A Filmmaker's Guide to Music Scoring*. Los Angeles: Silman-James Press, 1994.

Karlin, Fred and Rayburn Wright. *On the Track: A Guide to Contemporary Film Scoring*. New York: Schirmer Books, 1990.

## PRODUCING

Cones, John W. *Film Finance & Distribution: A Dictionary of Terms*. Los Angeles: Silman-James Press, 1992.

Houghton, Buck. *What A Producer Does: The Art of Moviemaking (Not the Business)*. Los Angeles: Silman-James Press, 1991.

Lazarus, Paul N, III. *The Film Producer*. New York: St Martin's Griffin, 1992.

Levison, Louise. *Filmmakers and Financing: Business Plans for Independents*. Boston: Focal Press, 1998.

Litwak, Mark. *Dealmaking in the Film & Television Industry from Negotiations to Final Contracts*. Los Angeles: Silman-James Press, 1994.

Seger, Linda and Edward Jan Whetmore. *From Script to Screen: The Collaborative Art of Filmmaking*. New York: Henry Holt and Co, 1994.

## PRODUCTION MANAGEMENT

Chamness, Danford. *The Hollywood Guide to Film Budgeting and Script Breakdown for Low-Budget Features*. Los Angeles: Stanley J Brooks Co, 1995.

Gates, Richard. *Production Management for Film and Video, 2nd Ed*. Boston: Focal Press, 1996

Koster, Robert J. *The On Production Budget Book*. Boston: Focal Press, 1997.

Silver, Alan, and Elizabeth Ward. *The Film Director's Team: A Practical Guide for Production Managers, Assistant Directors, and All Filmmakers*. Hollywood, CA: Silman-James Press, 1992.

Singleton, Ralph S. *Film Scheduling: The complete step-by-step guide to professional motion picture scheduling*. Beverly Hills, CA: Lone Eagle Publishing Co, 1984.

Wiese, Michael and Deke Simon. *Film & Video Budgets, 2nd Ed*. Studio City, CA: Michael Wiese Productions, 1995.

## PROPERTY

James, Thurston. *The What, Where, When of Theater Props*. Cincinnati, OH: Betterway Books, 1992.

## SET DECORATION

[See Property above.]

## SOUND—Post Production

Bumsey, Francis and Tim McCormick. *Sound and Recording, 3rd Ed*. Boston: Focal Press, 1997.

Mott, Robert L. *Sound Effects: Radio, TV and Film*. Boston: Focal Press, 1990.

## SOUND—Production

Bartlett, Bruce and Jenny. *Practical Recording Techniques: The Step-By-Step Approach to Professional Audio Recording, 2nd Ed*. Boston: Focal Press, 1998.

Zaza, Tony. *Mechanics of Sound Recording*. Englewood Cliffs, NJ: Prentice-Hall, 1992.

## SPECIAL EFFECTS

Abbott, L B. *Special Effects: Wire, Tape and Rubber Band Style*. Hollywood, CA: The ASC Press, 1984.

McCarthy, Robert E. *Secrets of Hollywood Special Effects*. Boston: Focal Press, 1992.

Wilkie, Bernard. *Creating Special Effects for TV & Films, 3rd Ed*. Boston: Focal Press, 1996.

Wilkie, Bernard. *Special Effects in Television, 3rd Ed*. Boston: Focal Press, 1995.

## VIDEO

Beacham, Frank. *American Cinematographer Video Manual*. Hollywood, CA: The ASC Press, 1994.

Caruso, James R, and Mavis E Arthur. *Video Editing and Post Production*. Englewood Cliffs, NJ: Prentice-Hall, 1992.

Kenney, Richard E. *Television Camera Operations According to Ritch*. Los Angeles: Silman-James Press, 1988.

Millerson, Gerald. *The Technique of Television Production, 12th Ed*. Boston: Focal Press, 1990.

Schneider, Arthur. *Electronic Post-Production and Video Tape Editing*. Stoneham, MA: Butterworth Publishers, 1989.

Wurtzel, Alan. *Television Production, 2nd Ed*. New York: McGraw-Hill book Co, 1983.

## WARDROBE

[See Costuming above.]

## WRITING

Seger, Linda. *Making a Good Script Great: A Guide for Writing and Rewriting, 2nd Ed*. Hollywood, CA: Samuel French Trade, 1994.

Trottier, David. *The Screenwriter's Bible: A Complete Guide to Writing, Formatting, and Selling Your Script, 3rd Ed*. Los Angeles: Silman-James Press, 1998.

## GENERAL

Arijon, Daniel. *Grammar of the Film Language*. Los Angeles: Silman-James Press, 1991.

Boorstin, Jon. *Making Movies Work: Thinking Like a Filmmaker* .Los Angeles: Silman-James Press, 1995.

Eisenstein, Sergei. *Film Form*. New York: Harcourt Brace Co, 1977.

Kawin, Bruce. *How Movies Work*. Berkeley, CA: Univ of California Press, 1992.

Konigsberg, Ira. *The Complete Film Dictionary*. White Plains, NY: Viking Penguin Books, 1997.

Lindgren, Ernest. *The Art of the Film*. London: George Allen & Unwin, Ltd, 1948.

Miller, Pat P. *Script Supervising & Film Continuity, 2nd Ed.* Boston: Focal Press, 1990.

Taub, Eric. *Gaffers, Grips and Best Boys: From Producer/Director to Gaffer and Best Boy, A Behind-the-Scenes Look at Who Does What in Filmmaking*. New York: St Martin's Press, 1987.

# Index

This index is coded as follows for ease of use. Numbers in **bold** are for the job description of each profession. Numbers in *italic* mean the entry is in the glossary. Numbers in ***bold italic*** locate the glossary definition for the term. Some job titles exist in more than one category, so they may have two job descriptions and two main entries in the glossary.

---

**Bold** = Job description    *Italic* = in Glossary    ***Bold Italic*** = Main entry in Glossary

---

---